THE GROWTH
OF
PRESIDENTIAL
POWER

THE GROWTH
OF
PRESIDENTIAL
POWER

A DOCUMENTED HISTORY

★★★★★★★★★★★★★★★★★★★★★★★★

by
WILLIAM M. GOLDSMITH
Brandeis University

with an Introductory Essay by
Arthur M. Schlesinger, jr.

Volume I
The Formative Years

CHELSEA HOUSE
NEW YORK 1983

To Margaret O'Rourke Goldsmith and Marianne Lovink Goldsmith—
Their love and faith made the difference.

Project Editor: Deborah Weiss
Managing Editor: Roberta Morgan
Assistant Editor: Kathryn Hammell
Editorial Consultant: Leon Freidman

This edition is an edited reprint of the 1974 edition
by Chelsea House Publishers

Library of Congress Cataloging in Publication Data

Goldsmith, William M.
    The growth of Presidential power.
    Includes bibliographies.
    CONTENTS: v. 1. The formative years.—v. 2. Decline and resurgence.—
v. 3. Triumph and reappraisal.
    1. Executive power—United States—History.
2. Presidents—United States—History. I. Title.
JK511.G64   353.03'2   74-9623
ISBN 0-87754-125-6

THE GROWTH
OF
PRESIDENTIAL POWER

Volume I
The Formative Years
Volume II
Decline and Resurgence
Volume III
Triumph and Reappraisal

FOREWORD

by Arthur M. Schlesinger, jr.

The growth of presidential power is hardly a new subject. But recent events in the life of the republic have placed it in a new perspective, thereby reminding the historian once again how effectively the present recreates the past. Until a decade ago scholars, and laymen too, tended to see the expansion of executive authority as inevitable and, on the whole, as benign. The presidency was celebrated as a wonderful American contribution to the art of democratic government. Today that expansion is perceived as profoundly ambiguous. "Power," as Henry Adams said, "is poison"—an aphorism that, we belatedly understand, holds as true for Presidents as for lesser mortals. We no longer rush by the thought, hidden away so long in the Supreme Court's decision in the case of *ex parte* Milligan, that the republic had no right to expect it would always have wise and humane rulers, sincerely attached to the principles of the Constitution. "Wicked men, ambitious of power, with hatred of liberty and contempt of law, may fill the place once occupied by Washington and Lincoln." In the earlier period Professor Goldsmith's book would have been invaluable. After Vietnam and Watergate it is indispensable.

We have had a series of learned and penetrating works on the presidency. But these have been mostly concerned with powers rather than with limitations; and they have mostly taken the form of analysis rather than of documentation. The vital sources are typically presented in bits, as they make the writer's point, rather than *in extenso*. But one capital lesson of the Vietnam-Watergate experience is the way old texts yield new insights. It is better therefore to print the key documents, as Professor Goldsmith does, at length. One never knows which old paragraphs may be brought to life by new circumstance. Vietnam sent a whole generation back to the Constitution, the debates at the Convention and the Federalist Papers in order to ponder the meaning of the war-making power, a question treated all too lightly in most standard works on the presidency. Impeachment had been a dead issue in the standard works for a century, until Watergate made it a problem of the highest moment. Passages in the history of presidential power may lie dormant for years until unforeseen events give them unexpected relevance.

Not every one will agree with Professor Goldsmith's choice of documents or of episodes, nor with his accounts of men and events. I do not myself. But at every point his case is carefully and lucidly argued. And his work does more than rescue scores of texts long buried in obscure places. If it did only this, it would be a labor of great value. But it also sets the documents in, so to speak, their working context. What is particularly impressive, I think, is Professor Goldsmith's sense of *milieu*, of the way, as Taine put it, "the external acts on the internal." Professor Goldsmith never forgets what he himself calls "the reality of concrete interests and institutions" and always endeavors to see the growth of presidential power in the "matrix of events." Events for him include not alone the tactical requirements of particular political situations, but the very texture of the political culture itself. This instinct for the subtle and complex interplay—the "creative dialectic"—between doctrine and social experience is especially helpful in the contemplation of a country where abstractions have so often been reshaped by evolving values, not to say by practical sagacity, expediency and opportunism. Nor has Professor Goldsmith been stampeded by the contemporary backlash against the strong presidency into an indiscriminate attack on an office that, for all its latter-day excesses, has on balance served the republic well and has sometimes served it nobly. Readers will no doubt dissent in detail, but I believe they will recognize this work as a remarkable *tour-de-force* of historical scholarship.

I

The Growth of Presidential Power raises the most basic questions about the past and future of American government. At the end of *Little Caesar* Edward G. Robinson, the gang leader, falls mortally wounded, and cries, "Mother of Mercy, is this the end of Rico?" A similar question arises after the epoch of little Caesarism in the White House. With Vietnam and Watergate behind us, one wonders whether the overweening presidency has really been brought under control—"Mother of Mercy, is this the end of the Imperial Presidency?"—or whether, as in the underworld, when Rico falls, another chieftain rises to take his place.

The answer depends on whether the United States can find some means of making its public decisions without excessive concentration of power in a single man or institution. Plainly the power of public decision must rest somewhere. In a democracy that power surely ought to rest in institutions directly accountable to the electorate. The United States has two such institutions: the presidency and the Congress. The Supreme Court, as Mr. Dooley pointed out long ago, has its own form of indirect accountability; but, though the Court has tried from time to time to assume legislative and even executive functions, this is not its genius nor its purpose; it is not a serious candidate for the continuing control of public policy.

The presidency and the Congress: potential partners, potential rivals. The uncertainty in their relationship is the consequence, of course, of one of the basic ideas of the Constitution—the idea of the separation of powers, an idea hardly understood at all abroad and understood imperfectly in the United States. One of the fundamental decisions taken after long argument in the Constitutional Convention was to give not Congress but the electorate the power to choose the Chief Executive. This represented a sharp break from the Articles of Confederation, which made no provision for a separate Executive at all and established, in effect, parliamentary government without a Prime Minister; likewise, it represented a sharp break from the parliamentary institutions evolving in Great Britain. Foreigners ever since have been baffled by the American polity. Even so astute a political observer as Bagehot concluded in a famous remark that the republic had endured not because of but in spite of the Constitution; "the men of Massachusetts could, I believe, work *any* Constitution."

Even the men of Massachusetts would have been hard put to work the American Constitution had the decision to make the President answerable to the electorate rather than to the Congress resulted in a high wall of separation between the executive and legislative branches. Actually the Constitution did not embody the doctrine of the separation of powers in any very dogmatic way. Hamilton took care to point out in Federalist No. 66 that "a partial intermixture of those departments for special purposes" was "not only proper but necessary to the mutual defence of the several members of the government against each other." Madison said in Federalist No. 47 that the doctrine "goes no farther than to prohibit any one of the entire departments from exercising the powers of another department." The Constitution, as Richard Neustadt has summed it up, created not a government of separated powers but "a government of separated institutions *sharing* powers." When Justice Black offered a more rigid version of separation in his opinion in the steel seizure case, Justice Jackson rightly responded that, while the Constitution had divided power in order to secure liberty, it had also supposed that practice would unite the divided powers into a workable government. It had therefore enjoined upon the branches of government "separateness but interdependence, autonomy but reciprocity."

But the Founding Fathers had not provided the means to assure interdependence and reciprocity; and the Constitution could hardly have worked had it not been for a mechanism unanticipated by many of the Fathers and feared by most of the few who did anticipate it: the party system. Party, an extra-constitutional instrumentality, arose, among other reasons, to supply, in Henry Jones Ford's phrase, the "administrative union" denied by the Constitution but required by a working government. "In England party elicits the expression of the will of the nation," as Ford was among the first to note:

> in this country it must also provide for its execution, so that it is virtually a part of the apparatus of government itself, connecting the executive and legislative departments, and occupying the place which in the parliamentary type of government is filled by the ministry.

Yet party was after all a fluid medium within which control might float to one end or the other of Pennsylvania Avenue; it alleviated but did not resolve the separation of powers. Interdependence and reciprocity remained matters of will more than of mechanism. When the will did not exist, the result was competition and the prospect guerrilla warfare.

II

Washington, through his moral command of the country, and Jefferson, through his masterful domination of Congress, succeeded in giving the presidency a certain head start. After Jefferson the presidency, still inhibited in its self-conception, became passive, and Congress made its first bid for supremacy. Historians have disagreed about the extent of its success. The pioneering work of Ralph V. Harlow (*The History of Legislative Methods in the Period Before 1825,*

1917) claimed a very considerable measure of efficiency and discipline for congressional self-organization and emphasized especially the authority of the caucus—an interpretation largely followed by Leonard D. White (*The Jeffersonians*, 1951). Mary P. Follett even described Henry Clay, the Speaker of the House, as "the most powerful man in the nation from 1811 to 1825" (*The Speaker of the House of Representatives*, 1896). Theodore J. Lowi, in a succinct modern formulation of the thesis of congressional supremacy (in *The American Party Systems*, W. N. Chambers and W. D. Burnham, ed., 1967), argues that the post-Jefferson Presidents had no base of power independent of Congress—they were chosen by the congressional caucus, their cabinet choices were cleared with and sometimes dictated by the congressional leaders, and the cabinet itself was increasingly seen as a group of administrators more accountable to Congress than to the Presidents. "All the evidence," Lowi writes, "points toward the emergence of a 'fusion of powers' in the United States during the first decades of political development despite the letter and spirit of the Constitution."

However, the more detailed research of James Sterling Young (*The Washington Community, 1800-1828*, 1966) effectively challenges the notion of the omnipotence of the congressional caucus. As for Clay, Young contends that he was popular rather than powerful; he had "no choice but to forsake strong party leadership if he wanted to retain the speakership." From Young's interesting work there emerges not congressional supremacy but a persuasive picture of Congress and the presidency on parallel, downward courses of confusion and decay.

The shouting crowd on the day of Jackson's inauguration, as Daniel Webster sourly observed, really seemed to think "the country is rescued from some dreadful danger." Historians have never doubted the shout but still argue about the danger. Still, whether the country turned to Jackson to rescue the national government from Congress (Lowi) or to rescue it from disintegration (Young), Jackson found an effective response to the evident popular frustration when he moved to reinvigorate the presidency. By appealing over the heads of Congress to the people and by using the party to organize his popular support, he succeeded both in giving the presidency, in Lowi's phrase, "a base of power independent of Congress," and in giving the people a sense of participation, partly but not altogether symbolic, in the affairs of government.

It is said that Jackson revolutionized the office of the presidency, and this is true. Yet the precedents he created were not systematically employed by any successor in time of peace for nearly three quarters of a century. Even his hand-picked heir, the architect of the party system that had confirmed his success—Martin Van Buren—failed to act on the Jacksonian model. Polk was perhaps his truer heir, but would Polk have been Polk without the Mexican War? The other Presidents between Jackson and the Civil War were ineffectual. Once again, the decline in the presidency was matched by the decline in Congress.

Fortunately the Jacksonian example was still within easy memory in 1861. Lincoln, though himself a Whig in the age of Jackson, lost no time in uncovering extraordinary resources of presidential power. The greatest crisis in American history brought public support to his conviction that "measures otherwise unconstitutional might become lawful by becoming indispensable to the preservation of the Constitution through the preservation of the nation."

III

Jackson's dramatic expansion of presidential power provoked the Whig reaction—that is, an attack on executive usurpation and a reassertion of the congressional prerogative. Though one of Jackson's precedents had been to secure the presidential right to remove cabinet ministers at his own pleasure, Congress, after his retirement, began to peck away at the presidential control of appointment and removal. Lincoln's revival of Jacksonianism in the next generation produced another Whig reaction, and this too concentrated on the appointment and removal questions. It reached its climax with the passage of the Tenure of Office Act in 1867 and the subsequent impeachment of Andrew Johnson for his alleged violation of that act.

It is fascinating to speculate what might have happened to the American political system had the impeachment of Johnson by the House been followed by his conviction and removal by the Senate. I suggested in *The Imperial Presidency* that the presidential system might have become a quasi-parliamentary regime, in which Congress would try to nominate and dominate the executive branch and the impeachment process might have served as the American equivalent of the British vote of confidence. It seems quite possible that a political order of the sort discerned by Lowi in the years between Jefferson and Jackson would have emerged; indeed, something close to that emerged anyway.

For, even though the President survived in 1868, the presidency went on the defensive. Seventeen years later, the young political scientist Woodrow Wilson, groping for a name to describe the post-Civil War political system, entitled his "study in American politics" *Congressional Government*. "We are really living," he wrote, "under a constitution essentially different from that which we have been so long worshipping." The separation of powers, the essence of the Constitution of 1787, now existed in name only. "The actual form of our present government is simply a scheme of congressional supremacy . . . a government by the Standing Committees of Congress." Wilson had already called the Speaker of the House "the most powerful man in the government of the United States in time of peace." Congress, he now said, had "entered more and more into the details of administration, until it has virtually taken into its own hands all the substantial powers of government."

This formulation suggested that the vacuum in the presidency was effectively filled in these years by the Congress. But *Congressional Government* had a covert polemical purpose. Wilson's private answer to government by the standing committees of Congress—to (as he had written in 1879) "the absorption of all power by a legislature which is practically irresponsible for its acts"—was "cabinet government," by which he meant that the President would choose his cabinet from among the members of Congress. Wilson did not argue this thesis in *Congressional Government*, but it remained a repressed major premise. He therefore tended to portray Congress as efficient but irresponsible in order to imply the advantages of cabinet government, which would be efficient and responsible.

One thus sees for the period 1866-1901 much the same perplexity as we have already seen in the period 1809-29: was congressional government a realistic alternative to presidential government? No doubt the absence of politically imperative issues in this period, aside from Reconstruction, made it matter little whether or not congressional government was efficient; and Reconstruction was shoved aside by general agreement. But there is reason to suppose, as Young contended for the earlier period, that decline in one branch was probably paralleled by decline in the other. This was certainly the impression of Henry Adams. "The government does not govern," Adams said; "Congress is inefficient, and shows itself more and more incompetent, as at present constituted, to wield the enormous powers that are forced upon it, while the Executive, in its full enjoyment of theoretical independence, is practically deprived of its necessary strength by the jealousy of the Legislature."

Congressional government was, in fact, an illusion—a point effectively made in 1898 by Henry Jones Ford, a perspicacious newspaper editor, in his original and neglected work *The Rise and Growth of American Politics*. "It is the rule of our politics," he wrote after a comprehensive historical review, "that no vexed question is settled except by executive policy." The intention of Presidents, he said, did not account for the rise of presidential authority; this seemed rather the product of political conditions that dominated all the branches of government:

> Congress itself shows an unconscious disposition to aggrandize the presidential office. The existence of a separate responsible authority to which questions of public policy may be resigned opens to Congress an easy way out of difficulty when the exercise of its own jurisdiction would be troublesome.

This passage forecast the comeback of the presidency with great prescience. The return to Jackson, Ford thought, was inherent in the evolution of American politics; and in the Jacksonian model "American democracy has revived the oldest political institution of the race, the elective kingship." Nor was Ford much dismayed by all this. The extension of executive authority, he believed, was "the only practical method of advancing popular rule," since it offered the only means "for the extrication of public authority from the control of particular interests." If one is less certain now that an elective king will be free from the control of particular interests, one can have no greater certainty that the congressional alternative would provide a more reliable method of advancing popular rule.

The Rise and Growth of American Politics was published a few months after the outbreak of the Spanish-American War. Ford had worked out his argument before the war, but the war now verified and consolidated his contentions about the functional necessity of presidential primacy. Indeed, as he contemplated the war, Wilson himself capitulated. In a preface, written in 1900, to the 15th edition of *Congressional Government*, he supplemented the Ford point with a brilliant emendation of his own:

> When foreign affairs play a prominent part in the politics and policy of a nation, its Executive must of necessity be its guide: must utter every initial judgment, take every first step of action, supply the information upon which it is to act and in large measure control its conduct. The President of the United States is now, as of course, at the front of affairs, as no

president, except Lincoln, has been since the first quarter of the nineteenth century, when the foreign relations of the new nation had first to be adjusted. . . . Upon his choice, his character, his experience hang some of the most weighty issues of the future. . . . Interesting things may come out of the singular change.

The last sentence was a great throwaway line. Wilson added, prudently, that the new developments might well "put this whole volume hopelessly out of date"—a condition he himself acknowledged more fully eight years later when he set forth a most expansionist view of the presidency in the eloquent pages of *Constitutional Government in the United States.* (That same year he prevailed upon Henry Jones Ford to become professor of politics at Princeton.)

IV

The insights of Wilson and Ford are about all that is required to explain the rise of the Imperial Presidency. Theodore Roosevelt emerged at once as the fulfillment of their joint prophecy. Professor Goldsmith is rarely more cogent than in the pages in which he displays TR as the inventor of the contemporary presidency. Wilson himself, once in the White House, was constrained by his prime ministerial conception of the office to see Congress as the necessary partner in presidential endeavor. The first Roosevelt, on the other hand, believed fervently in inherent presidential power and loosed that tricky doctrine upon the twentieth century.

The second Roosevelt tended more to follow the President he had served than the President to whom he was related. "In the event that the national emergency is still critical," as he said in his first inaugural address, ". . . I shall ask the Congress for the one remaining instrument to meet the crisis—broad Executive power." This was his characteristic disposition, even into the Second World War. The frequency of his cabinet meetings and press conferences, his accessibility to members of Congress, his habitual resort to legislation rather than to executive fiat—all expressed his instinctive understanding that an effective presidency rested on the capacity to elicit consent. Nor perhaps was this deference to Congress (a limited deference, but still real enough) altogether his own choice. For, if the presidency and the Congress fall together, as in 1809-29 and 1865-1901, they may also rise together. Even the first Roosevelt had to contend with an assertive congressional leadership, and Congress in the 1930s appears, looking back, a body of ability and force.

This was disguised at the time by newspaper talk of 'rubberstamp' Congresses. By definition a 'strong' presidency implies a President who dominates Congress; but this may only mean that Congress is somewhat weaker than the presidency, not necessarily that it is weak; the judgment is relative, not absolute. By later standards the Congress of FDR's day was exceptionally strong. One has only to recall the great names of the Senate: Norris, Glass, Wagner, Black, Byrnes, La Follette, Johnson, Borah, Taft, Barkley, Wheeler, Vandenberg, Long, Cutting, Robinson, Nye, Truman, Lodge, Pepper, McNary, McAdoo. . . . They were proud, independent and self-reliant men, like barons in the days before the king had broken the feudal system and created the modern state. They imposed legislative ideas on the President—the Wagner Labor Relations Act and the Federal Deposit Insurance Act, for example—defeated cherished ideas of his own, like the Court plan, and placed the most vital area of foreign policy out of presidential reach through the neutrality legislation. FDR worried about them, consulted them, propitiated them and took them very seriously indeed.

In retrospect, the New Deal was Congress's last hurrah. The flight from responsibility that Ford had detected 40 years earlier was beginning to show itself when Congress was under pressure, even in domestic affairs. The second Lodge, recalling his own senatorial days, later wrote: "Congress was looking desperately for some way to rid itself of its responsibility." The flow to the presidency "was not due to Roosevelt's lust for power but to the unwillingness and inability of Congress to grasp the nettle." When the Second World War made foreign affairs the absorbing national concern, Congress, for a long generation, went into a disorderly retreat halted only by Watergate. Professor Goldsmith's extension of Lawrence Chamberlain's classic study of executive influence on the legislative process shows how much more decisive a role presidential initiative played in the period 1945-64 than in 1880-1940. Even Watergate, it seemed, marked rather the end of the presidential offensive than the beginning of a congressional counterattack aimed at recovering lost ground. Hubert Humphrey, in a poignant outburst on the floor of the Senate, summed up the congressional condition in the second year of Watergate:

> I have served in the Executive Branch, and I want to tell you, it is easy to roll this body [Congress] because the Executive Branch comes in with power, comes in with information, is able to mobilize public opinion. . . . The Congress, lacking staff, expertise, information, and will, has been overwhelmed by the Executive juggernaut.

V

"Mother of Mercy, is this the end of the Imperial Presidency?" The Imperial Presidency may be defined as the condition resulting when the balance between presidential power and presidential accountability is destroyed. Such a condition invites remedy in one or another direction—either by cutting down power or by building up accountability.

Thus some would drive the nail in the heart of the Imperial Presidency by structural changes designed to enfeeble the presidential office forever. These, Professor Goldsmith says (in my view, rightly), are "altogether too simple solutions." They ignore the fact, so effectively illustrated in these pages, that the growth of presidential power has not been, except most marginally and lately, the consequence of the rapacity of Presidents. Rather it has been rooted in deep national necessities—above all, in the need, both moral and functional, for action bold and enlightened enough to enable a great nation to keep abreast of the problem of its age.

The Johnson and Nixon experiences have given currency to the thesis that, the greater a leader's power, the more distant he will be from reality. But it can hardly be said that Washington, Jefferson, Jackson, Lincoln, the two Roosevelts, Wilson, Truman or Kennedy were notably lacking in a sense of reality. Indeed, their reputations rest on the impression that they had in vital respects a *stronger* sense of reality than most of their contemporaries and called on the republic to face problems their fellow countrymen would have preferred to ignore. History makes it clear that power isolates Presidents only to the extent that they wish to be isolated. If they want to know what is going on, they have better facilities than anyone else for finding out.

The answer is not to emasculate the presidency. This would only result in crippling government in general at a time when a high quality of national leadership is required to meet the problems created by systemic inflation, by energy shortage, by environmental decay, by racial injustice and by the other afflictions of our epoch. The answer surely lies in the other direction—in strengthening the system of accountability.

Nor should this answer be dismissed as an exercise in wish-fulfillment. Presidential power is in considerable measure an optical illusion created by the retirement of other forces from the field. Presidents themselves never feel all that powerful. Lincoln, said Franklin Roosevelt, "was a sad man because he couldn't get it all at once. And nobody can." "Every President," Kennedy wrote, "must endure a gap between what he would like and what is possible." For Presidents, too, are at the mercy of the great forces of history. "I claim not to have controlled events," said Lincoln, "but confess plainly that events have controlled me." "The farmer," wrote Emerson:

> imagines power and place are fine things. But the President has paid dear for his White House. It has commonly cost him all his peace, and the best of his manly attributes. To preserve for a short time so conspicuous an appearance before the world, he is content to eat dust before the real masters who stand erect behind the throne.

I have suggested elsewhere that, in spite of the affectation of popular impotence in recent times, these have been in fact the years when public indignation prevented one Imperial President from seeking reelection and forced another to resign his office and power. The historical generalization to be derived from this period will certainly be, not that citizens are impotent and Presidents invincible, but that Presidents who abuse their power will suffer retribution.

The presidency is all-powerful only when the country permits it to be. The balance between power and accountability can be restored if that is what Americans really want. Congress, of course, has an essential role in the system of accountability. The answer to Little Caesar's question therefore depends in great part on the *will* of Congress: on whether Congress is morally prepared to resume its two constitutional roles—intrepid resistance to the misuse of executive power and responsible partnership in the use of that power. For under the Constitution either the executive branch governs on its own, which leads to abuse, or the legislative branch governs on its own, which leads nowhere, or they govern together, which is the idea of the Constitution.

The constitutional idea is not obsolete. The relationship between Congress and the presidency is not a zero-sum game, in which whatever one side wins the other loses. A bad season for the presidency has generally been a bad season for Congress; and, apart from wars, hot and cold, a good season for the presidency tends to be a good season for Congress. The national government belongs neither to the presidency nor to the Congress; it is rather a matter, in the phrases Hamilton used so long ago, of "joint possession," of "concurrent authority."

It is up to Congress to rise to its responsibilities if the age of the Imperial Presidency is to be brought to an end. This does not mean the harassment of Presidents; that would only swing the pendulum back toward presidential power. It means a genuine partnership. Still, given its own compulsion to minimize political risk, Congress will assert itself only fitfully unless it feels a steady demand for such assertion from the electorate. As Professor Goldsmith wisely observes, "In the broadest sense the key to the acquisition of political power in the American political system is the struggle for the support of the majority of the people." It is in the will of the voter, not on the desk of the President, where the buck finally stops.

New York City
November 1974

INTRODUCTION

by William M. Goldsmith

On the surface, at least, there is a certain arrogance about anyone attempting to write still another book or books on the American presidency. The Library of Congress lists 1433 volumes in a separate bibliography in this field. That was in 1963. By now the list has increased by at least another 100 or more titles and the production seems to be endless. Of course there are presidential biographies without number, special studies of various aspects of presidential responsibilities (e.g. foreign policy, administration, etc.), memoirs not only of Presidents, but of Presidents' wives, Presidents' children, cabinet members, press secretaries, cooks, butlers, newspaper correspondents, even the President's private physician. There are books about the White House, Presidents at war, Presidents and religion and Presidents and civil rights. These categories could be expanded almost endlessly. Any author venturing into this well-trodden field owes the reader an explanation as to why still another book on the American presidency should see the light of day.

Despite all of this, I believe I can present a good explanation, a rationale if you will, why these three volumes called *The Growth of Presidential Power* are a necessary and essential contribution to the field of presidential literature. The American presidency is an institution which very clearly was not handed down by the political oracles of either the seventeenth or eighteenth centuries, by John Locke or Charles de Secondat, Baron de Montesquieu; nor was it conceived in its present state by the Founding Fathers at the Constitutional Convention in Philadelphia in 1787. All of these creative individuals made their contributions to the shaping of the powers and responsibilities of the American Chief Executive, but their work along with other influential forces, such as the writers of the various state constitutions, produced the mere embryo of the American presidency in 1787. Its full physiology, its nerves, muscles, tendons, bones and fatty tissue developed over the course of the succeeding 180-plus years. They took shape in the roughly hewn crucible of historical experience.

Of course there was an original design, contained for the most part in Article II of the Constitution, but many of its clauses were very general, some extremely ambiguous, and all were characterized by a wise economy of words and limited definitions. This was due in part to the fact that a Constitution, like any public document prepared by a number of men representing still a greater number of constituents, is bound to be a compromise with respect to varied interests and principles. But in addition to this, there is every indication that the Founding Fathers had a very healthy respect for experience, and their extremely significant involvement in colonial government convinced them that no formal constitutional instrument could satisfactorily create an Executive office which could give immediate leadership and direction to a new nation of 3,000,000 citizens, or to a population which promised to increase ten fold, or several times that multiple, in the years to come.

There was real wisdom in their caution, but there was also an admission of their inability to design fully in theory and in the give and take of political compromise, an office which was to serve future history as a model of democracy's dynamic energy and resilience. They tried to settle some of the most important questions and establish guidelines for many others, but the product which emerged demanded equally as much, perhaps a great deal more, from the men who ultimately discharged presidential duties and the events to which they were forced to respond. In order to trace the growth of the American presidency, to see this institution take form and shape, one has to look at it in the context of its historical development.

The discussions at the Constitutional Convention and the forces and influences which shaped them are very much a part of that history, but so too are President Washington's formal defiance of the attempt by the House of Representatives to extract the secret correspondence and instructions which preceded the Jay Treaty; Jackson's defense of his removal of Secretary of the Treasury Duane; Lincoln's explanation to Congress of his so-called "unconstitutional" actions to preserve the Union; Theodore Roosevelt's corollary to the Monroe Doctrine; Wilson's use of the press conference to appeal to the people over the heads of Congress for support of tariff reform; Franklin Roosevelt's executive actions to salvage freedom and democratic institutions at home and abroad in the 1930s and early 40s; and John F. Kennedy's new definition of the government's responsibilities in the regulation and protection of the national economy. All of these are instances when presidential decisions and presidential actions further defined the structure of presidential power and responsibility. This leads me to the first explanation of why I put together these volumes.

Santayana has taught us that those who ignore history are condemned to relive it. I know of no other way to study a political or social institution than to begin to understand it first in the context of its historical development. This historical perspective is particularly valuable in the case of the American presidency. The presidency cannot be understood or appreciated without reflecting upon the struggles and problems that lie behind its present accumulation of power and responsibilities.

I became especially aware of this when I began to teach a course on this subject at Brandeis University ten years ago. I discovered that in the rich literature describing, explaining, analyzing and criticizing the development of the American presidency, there was no satisfactory book or set of books which presented the growth of presidential power in its historical context. One could find bits of it here and other parts of it there, but there was nothing dealing in a comprehensive fashion with these amazing two centuries of institutional growth. Edward S. Corwin's *The President: Office and Powers, 1787 - 1957* comes closest to filling this description, but despite its superb scholarship, from which all students of the presidency have profited, its rather skeletal, analytical treatment leaves out the rich narrative detail which makes history interesting and exciting. It also does not contain the documents upon which this narrative of incredible power and responsibility have been built.

Another book which approaches what I have done is the American Heritage volume on the *History of the Presidency*. It is a beautiful book and very ably edited, but again it does not accomplish what I have done or what I believe the study of the presidency requires. It is a long, rambling, insightful essay, punctuated by beautiful pictures, striking cartoons and extracts from presidential statements and documents. Its fragmentary presentation of the documents negates its use as a documentary source and its very general descriptive treatment of men and events prevents it from being used as a serious analytical study of critical presidential decisions.

My own three volumes are not simply books about the presidency or even histories of its development. They deal with the nurturing of presidential power and attempt to describe this development analytically from the early constitutional discussions up through the unfinished term of John Fitzgerald Kennedy and into the Johnson and Nixon administrations. This does not negate the significance of other books, such as the ones described above, but it does argue for the usefulness of these volumes, which present an analytical perspective and an historical narrative which is not available in the plethora of presidential literature.

After several years of chasing my students back and forth to the library to read dozens of narrative excerpts and documents from assorted texts in order to try to piece together this historical development, I decided to put it together so that both the narrative detail and the actual documents involved would be available in one source. Of course the project mushroomed as all projects do, and was interrupted from time to time because of the academic and other commitments which distracted any member of the university community with a strong social and political conscience during the turbulent 1960s. But the job is finally completed, the one volume intended has grown to three and the books have taken on a more formidable aspect than at first I had envisioned.

I have insisted upon the particular format I am using for all three volumes because I believe so strongly that both the narrative context and the documents are necessary to gain a full appreciation and understanding of the circumstances surrounding the decisions and actions which have taken place. If I had presented the narrative description only, the reader would still have had to repair to the library if he were curious about the documents involved or if he wished to challenge my account or evaluation of it. However, I also wanted this to be a source book. There is great historical continuity in these documents. Lincoln relied on Jackson's powerful arguments and Livingston's eloquence in preparing his own presidential defense of the Union, and Chief Justice Taft grounded his decision on the question of the removal power on Madison's speeches on this subject in the First Congress. And yet nowhere in the literature of political science or history can one readily obtain all of these significant documents collected to show the historical development of the critical institution of the presidency. Under these circumstances, it seemed to me mandatory to combine the narrative and documentary sources and provide the reader with a selected bibliography in each case, so he could go beyond the limits of my descriptions if he so desired.

There was a second reason why I wanted to present the book in the detailed form which I have selected. In more than ten years of teaching American undergraduates, I have discovered that most of them (brilliant and uninspired alike) have very little knowledge of American history. There are, of course, many angles from which to approach the subject and many levels of depth and scope in which this history can be studied. The historical analysis of the growth of presidential power is, however, one of the more interesting and useful ways of looking at American history. If a student approaches the study of the presidency from this perspective, he is liable to gain something more than an understanding of a particular political institution. In the course of his study, he may learn a little of the history of his own country, and, perhaps in the process, reflect a bit upon the presumptuous rejection by so many of so much that they only superficially comprehend.[1]

There is finally a very timely reason for reflecting upon the growth of presidential power. The degree and thrust of this power has frequently become the battleground of American politics, for there have been times in our history when groups, parties, even sections of the country have come to fear and oppose the power and responsibility that is identified with the American presidency; there have also been periods in our history when individuals and groups have argued persuasively that the Chief Executive has lacked the power to discharge the responsibilities which his position demanded of him. It is my hope that the following pages will throw some light on this continuing debate.

The problem is not simply a theoretical one, or a question emerging out of the complexities of a single event or a particular presidential action or inaction, as the case may be. It is a question which goes to the heart of our political process. If the President lacks adequate power to discharge his constitutional responsibilities, or if he possesses more power than he needs, in fact so much that he represents a challenge not only to the doctrine of the separation of powers but to the most effective operation of the American political system, then this is the kind of problem that needs, indeed demands, careful examination and analysis. An imbalance of power at the center can easily make the entire political system dysfunctional, or even worse, authoritarian and dangerous. A viable society can afford no less than the most vigilant and probing examination of such a problem.

In recent times this problem has become a topic for considerable discussion and in some cases rather critical and apprehensive concern. The powerful Senate Foreign Relations Committee, after examining the role of President Lyndon B. Johnson and his administration in the Vietnam situation, came to this unanimous and highly charged conclusion:

> Already possessing vast power over the country's foreign relations, the executive, by acquiring the authority to commit the country to war, now exercises something approaching absolute power over the life or death of every living American—to say nothing of millions of other people all over the world. There is no human being or group of human beings alive wise and competent enough to be entrusted with such vast power. Plenary powers in the hands of any man or group threatens all other men with tyranny or disaster. Recognizing the impossibility of assuring the wise exercise of power by any one man or institution, the American

Constitution divided that power among many men and several institutions and, in doing so, limited the ability of any one to impose tyranny or disaster on the country. The concentration in the hands of the President of virtually unlimited authority over matters of war and peace has all but removed the limits to executive power in the most important single area of our national life. Until they are restored the American people will be threatened with tyranny or disaster.[2]

The attack from academia was equally strong. Testifying before the Senate Foreign Relations Committee in the summer of 1967, Professor Ruhl J. Bartlett of Tufts University's Fletcher School of Law and Diplomacy argued:

Perhaps in conclusion I may be allowed a judgment to the basis of my study of human affairs and of American history. It is that the greatest danger of democracy in the United States and to the freedom of its people and to their welfare—as far as foreign affairs are concerned—is the erosion of legislative authority and oversight and the growth of a vast pyramid of centralized power in the Executive branch of the Government. The fear of the framers of the Constitution that executive power unless properly curbed could develop along monarchical lines was fully justified, but they provided curbs. There is no constitutional basis for the assumption that substantive powers were conferred on the President as the Executive. As one Supreme Court Justice remarked, if this were true no human intelligence could "define the fields of the President's permissible activities. A masked battery of constructual powers would complete the destruction of liberty." The same kind of comment applies to the idea that the President has authority as commander in chief to replace the authority of the Congress to declare war or to determine the use of the armed forces, or that he has the authority to define and execute treaties in any way he desires. The arguments of immediacy, expertness, superior information, and greater wisdom are equally fallacious as bases for enlarged Presidential authority. The framers of the Constitution bequeathed to the American people a great heritage, that of a constitutional, federal, representative government, with its powers limited in scope and divided among its three separate branches, and this system was devised not because it would produce efficiency or world dominion, but because it offered the greatest hope of preventing tyranny.[3]

In my opinion the present critics of presidential power are wrong, not in identifying a problem in the present imbalance between the legislative and the executive branches, but rather in their diagnosis that the root of the problem lies in the historical accumulation of tremendous power in the hands of the President. There is no doubt that the power is there. The growth of presidential power over the past 185 years has been extraordinary, persistent, and in my opinion, inevitable— responding dynamically to the expanding contours and development of the American nation and the political system which the Founding Fathers devised to govern it. The sheer size and complexity of the country, its growth in population and in economic and technological development, have created problems demanding solutions which could only come from strong executive leadership. This fantastic internal growth has also fostered America's expanding role and influence in foreign affairs, where the nature of the American constitutional system and the complexity and frequent urgency of international developments have dictated that these additional burdens and responsibilities be primarily assumed by the President. In war as well as in peace, whether acting with respect to routine administrative problems or extraordinary crises, the American presidency, particularly in this century, and even more particularly in mid-century, has developed into the most powerful political position in the world. No other political office of executive leadership can compare in scope and responsibility with it.

And it is time that we give this extraordinary accumulation of power adequate study and analysis. One must go beyond the immediate events at hand and consider the question in the light of the role of the presidency in history. We must look at the total political process, not simply one aspect of it, and inquire as to its functional suitability to the task at hand. The role of the Congress in particular must be examined and evaluated in its relationship to the growth of presidential power. An historical analysis of the problem may not provide the relevant answers as to precisely what must be done at this moment in history to cope with the current problems and those of the future, but it will certainly illuminate the questions and perhaps suggest the direction which the solutions must take.

Ultimately the question of limits must also be considered. To argue that the present state of presidential power has come about through the legitimate process of institutional growth in response to the realities of its historical, social, political and economic environment is not to state that this present imbalance of power in relation to the functions of the other elements of the system is proper or even desirable. This is clearly not the case. The presidency has assumed a status and role in the American political system which frequently dwarfs and even paralyzes the other elements of the system, not because Presidents or the institution of the presidency have seized new levels of power by stealth or design, but rather because the legislative branch of government and the people at large have not developed a concept of their own functional roles or their competence to perform them at a comparable rate of growth.

My conclusion is not that we strip the presidency of what I would argue is its necessary and essential power, but rather we must enhance or redefine both the functions and the objectives of the Congress and the American people so that they may carry out their appropriate roles in the future of a dynamic and democratic society. The presidency has borne the major burdens which the tremendous social and political changes have imposed upon this country for almost two centuries. The strain has been too great, and the imbalance at the center destructive to the quality of American life. But that is what *The Growth of Presidential Power* is all about. It deals not only with the study of the dramatic accumulation of presidential power, but also with the analysis of the ebb and flow of countervailing power in the hands of Congress and the people. This first volume begins the story of the creation of the presidency prior to the Constitutional Convention and sweeps through the exciting period of early American history when our first great Presidents engaged in the important task of defining and creating presidential power in its most fundamental roles. The second volume deals primarily with the humiliating decline of presidential power during the second half of the nineteenth century, when many Presidents struggled, frequently unsuccessfully, to maintain basic executive and administrative prerogatives and integrity against the increasing arrogance and intervention by both houses of Congress. The final volume records the triumph of the presidency in the twentieth century, and introduces the complex problems which accompany this triumph, and which have created the imbalance described above. It is in the spirit of tackling these major themes and raising these fundamental questions that this undertaking is justified.

The previous paragraphs were written long before Watergate, the episode that has disgraced the presidency and hung like a dark cloud over our lives and political institutions during the past two agonizing years. These events do not, however, render the foregoing remarks irrelevant. Quite to the contrary, I think they give the problem of the growth of presidential power new and commanding urgency. If the earlier events of the 1960s gave one cause for concern that the accumulation of power by the President had swept beyond the limits proper to the elected Executive of a democratic and representative republic, then America's recent tragedy has more than reemphasized these fears. These times cry out not simply for students of the presidency, but for all Americans who are serious about the future of their polity and the manner in which it affects and shapes their lives, to give substantial thought and consideration to this problem.

On the other hand, so much abuse was heaped upon the President (Nixon) in recent months, that it is difficult to think objectively about the presidency and to analyze the problem of the growth of presidential power in its true historical perspective. Yet we have to try to avoid what Daniel Boorstin has referred to as wandering "out of history." Perhaps this examination of the evolution of the office and its powers will help us to regain that perspective. To shape its future role in the political process, to be able to separate what is essential to its responsibilities in our complex and sensitive political system from what is destructive both to the office and to the operation of the body politic, is clearly one of the urgent demands of our society at this moment in history. Hopefully, my extensive and, I admit, loving assessment will contribute to that undertaking.

NOTES

1. A good example can be drawn from the writings of the prince of the new order—Abbie Hoffman: "America lost its balls in the frontier and since then there have been no mighty myths and now we hunt them in lonely balconies, watching Bonnie and Clyde." *Revolution for the Hell of It* (New York, 1968), 85.
2. U.S., Congress, Senate, Committee on Foreign Relations, *National Commitment,* S. Rept. 797, 90th Cong., 1st sess., 1967, 26-27.
3. U.S., Congress, Senate, Committee on Foreign Relations, Hearings, *United States Commitment to Foreign Powers,* 90th Cong., 1st sess., 1967, 21.

I. The Origins of
Presidential Power

THE ORIGINS OF
PRESIDENTIAL POWER

Early Controversy over the Question
of Executive Power in the Colonies

The written Constitution of the United States provides only the barest outline of the duties and responsibilities of the President of the United States. By stating that "The Executive Power shall be vested in a President of the United States," and that "he shall take care that the Laws be faithfully executed," without, in most cases, detailing what those executive and administrative responsibilities should be, the Constitution has provoked almost two centuries of furious debate and struggle to hammer out in the crucible of crises and events just what those words mean, and what the thrust and perimeters of presidential power are. If one understands the political process as a never-ending effort to organize men's collective strengths and adjust to their weaknesses in order to achieve common and individual ends, then one must also understand the constitutional process as a perpetual commitment to establish, define, modify, and sometimes even reverse the rules and precedents by which government is conducted. In 1787 too little was known about the nature of executive leadership in a democratic republic to spell out in any greater detail what the precise powers and limits of the presidential office should be.

The period in American history immediately prior to both the Revolutionary War and the Constitutional Convention in Philadelphia, however, was an extremely creative and significant era, particularly with respect to political thinking and experimentation. As the breach widened between the colonists and the mother country, a great deal was written and spoken in criticism of British practices and policies, and as Bernard Bailyn and others have pointed out, this highly charged, frequently abrasive atmosphere produced some of the best and most imaginative political theory that western man has yet developed. The colonists found themselves in a unique situation. They were at least virtual citizens of the most highly developed and sophisticated political system in the world, and at the same time increasingly plaintive colonial subjects of a constitutional monarchy which they found to be more and more oppressive to their real interests. This created the setting for dramatically new and dynamic arguments, all directed towards the protection of those interests and their increased representation in the councils of state where policies were determined affecting their lives.

In describing the content of their thought and expression during this period, Bailyn has written that these early Americans were doing nothing less than reconceiving "the fundamentals of government and of society's relationship to government."[1] They dealt with such questions as representation and consent, the nature of constitutions and of individual rights and the meaning of sovereignty—all of which went to the heart of the political question then emerging in the western world—how can free men best govern themselves?

There were a number of reasons why their situation was ideal for nurturing such an inquiry. Most early Americans had migrated to this continent from the British Isles and the political culture they had inherited and brought with them had already gone through several historical crises which established and reaffirmed basic concepts of human and civil rights. Their physical separation from Great Britain, however, and their obvious material interests in the new society 3,500 miles away, made them extremely conscious of these rights and privileges already fought for and won as Englishmen. In addition the complexity of implementing those rights and privileges as members of colonial communities far removed from the central seat of political power was a matter of early concern in the "new world." Several hundred years of constitutional political experience and progress clearly indicated that they could not turn backward but must push ahead with new answers to old problems. The openness of the new society, socially as well as geographically, suggested that these answers would be rooted in the values of the past, but adapted to the challenges and greater freedom of the new world.

The key to the transformation in thinking and ultimately in practice which took place during this period was the significant advance from the traditional concepts of government and divisions of society to the reality of concrete interests and institutions:

> The essential units participating in the constitution were no longer abstract categories, formal orders of society derived from the assumptions of classical antiquity; they were interests, which organized for political action, became factions and parties. Their constitutional role was not to manipulate independently a separate institution of government but to join in conflict within a single institution and "blend" themselves together in a general consensus. "Balance" was still involved, but with the repudiation of monarchy and nobility and confinement of society to "the democracy," the notion of what the social powers were that must be balanced and controlled was changing. What were now seen, though still only vaguely, were the shifting, transitory competitive groupings into which men of the eighteenth century actually organized themselves in the search for wealth, prestige, and power. And the concern with balance in government was shifting to a concern with social orders to that of functioning branches of government.
>
> This shift in ways of thinking about the social basis of politics was part of a more general turn towards realism in political and constitutional thought. By the time the debates on the first state constitutions had been concluded, the sense that public affairs were basically struggles among formal orders of society had begun to fade and with it the whole elaborate paradigm that lay at the heart of eighteenth century political thought.[2]

When the Founding Fathers came together to draw up the Constitution of the United States at Philadelphia in 1787, experience and representative self-interest served as more reliable guides to their work than the writings of political philosophers. John Roche has called the Philadelphia Convention a "Reform Caucus," and has argued very persuasively that questions of political self-interest, of the delegates' concern for the affairs and opinions of their constituents, were the basic motivating forces which produced the compromises that made the Constitution possible. He views the majority of the delegates as being revolutionary democrats, and, on the whole, favoring a strong central government, but nonetheless acting as representatives of local interests and opinions, tempering that enthusiasm for centralization with the sensitive awareness that their constituents would *not* ratify a Constitution which emasculated their local rights and interests as states.[3] Clinton Rossiter identifies them "as members of an elite adjusting the tensions of principle and interest within its own membership, and at the same time interacting with the publics to which it was ultimately accountable."[4]

But the delegates also underwent an enlightening experience at the Convention, and in the careful examination of the full implications of each proposal, they advanced their own knowledge of the problems. There was a clear development and a sharpening of issues as the weeks progressed, and this was particularly true with regard to the discussions of the method of selecting an executive and deciding what powers he should possess. What happened then in Philadelphia is what always happens at any genuinely political gathering: necessary accommodations were proposed and essential compromises skillfully negotiated, resulting in a document which finally won the approval of not only the overwhelming majority of the delegates, but which also was later approved by the required number of states.

To argue that practical concerns governed the basic decisions of the Constitutional Convention is not, however, to rule out the influence of political theorists, political models and political experience, all of which were influential in shaping the specific structure and provisions of the new Constitution. Since we are particularly concerned with the influences which went into defining the powers of the presidency rather than the Constitution as a whole, it is quite proper to start with the latter two—political models and political experience—both of which had direct impact upon Article II of the Constitution.

It can never be stressed too emphatically that the 55 delegates to the Constitutional Convention were men of such substantial political experience that it would have been difficult, if not impossible, to find their counterparts on such a broad scale in any other country in the world at that time. American independence may have been officially declared in Philadelphia in 1776, but for over 100 years prior to that the colonists had been waging a political battle with the institutions of colonialism. From almost the very beginning anti-colonial tendencies were reflected in the resistance to the authority of the King's representatives in the colonies, and through the years a considerable degree of political power had actually been won by the colonists. The focal point of the struggle was in the representative assemblies where the colonists could give voice to their views, but at issue was usually the power of the governor vis-à-vis the representative assemblies of the people:

This fact, that the governor was an English officer supported by the English government, and representing English power, soon placed him in great discredit among the body of the colonists. The colonists were opposed to a strong central government of any character whatever. They were especially hostile toward one whose source lay outside the colony, and very soon began their attempt to reduce it.[5]

. . . There is evidence that the colonists recognized in the governors the representatives, direct or indirect, of that absolute personal rule which they had known in England; that they claimed the right to limit that rule by means of popular assemblies "after the manner of Parliament;" and that in this way they continued on this side of the Atlantic the contest for popular government which was being waged on the other side of the sea.[6]

This early assertion of legislative influence over the executive produced tangible results for the colonists. They were able to make significant inroads into the colonial power complex by such efforts, not only weakening the colonial governor but also developing their own power and experience in a wide range of functional activities. This experience was extremely useful in a later period when they asserted their independence and desire for self-rule. Jack P. Greene has very succinctly summed up the impact of these efforts:

Colonial lower houses made their most important innovations in the area of legislative handling of executive affairs. Pushing their authority well beyond that of the British House of Commons, they demanded and in many cases obtained a significant share of the traditional powers of the executive. As a corollary to their extensive control over finance, they claimed the right to nominate and appoint all public officials concerned in collecting, handling, and disbursing local revenues. Quite logically, they stretched that claim to include the selection of most public officers, including supervisors of all public works and services, public printers, and colonial agents in London. Their financial authority also enabled them to play a significant part in military and Indian affairs. In return for money to finance those affairs, the lower houses insisted upon a share in determining policy and in some instances upon appointing officials to implement that policy. Finally, the lower houses sought to usurp executive power in church appointments by shifting the patronage from the governors to the local vestries and in judicial matters by establishing their right to erect courts and to settle judicial tenure. In the southern royal colonies, they were remarkably successful in attaining these powers and by the late colonial period were playing an important role in the conduct of executive affairs.[7]

The Cromwellian revolution in England strengthened the position of the assemblies as they fought to curtail the power of the colonial governor, just as Parliament was struggling against the King. In Virginia the assembly actually gained the upper hand for awhile:

The executive which before had been independent and supreme, was made entirely subordinate to, and dependent on the Assembly. The right and power of electing and removing all executive officers, including governor and council, was transferred to the legislative body. By this simple act the Assembly became the paramount organ of the government and remained so during the Commonwealth period.[8]

But with the Restoration in England such overt instances of total legislative ascendancy were stamped out, and the struggle between colonists and Crown went on for the next 130 years. Another student of the period has pointed out that although the opposition of the colonial assemblies to the prerogatives of the colonial governor "accomplished the end which it had in view, namely, the weakening of the governor," it resulted in the "very general distrust of the executive" expressed in the early state constitutions and encouraged "the tendency to make the governor as far as possible dependent upon and subordinate to the legislature."[9] Allan Nevins provides evidence of this tendency:

> The Americans of 1776 thought it was easy to keep the legislature a truly popular agency, but they knew no way of holding a powerful governor responsive to their will. . . . Each Constitution except New York made the Governor elective by the legislature. Maryland spoke for most of her sisters when she asserted that "a long continuance, in the first executive departments of power or trust, is dangerous to liberty." Hence in all the States the Governor or President was given a one-year term, save in New York and Delaware, where he had three years, and in South Carolina where he had two. In most States a marked check upon the Governor was provided in the shape of an executive council, varying in number from four to thirteen. In no State did the Governor have the final veto upon legislation, and in only three did he have a partial veto power. No State allowed him to adjourn the legislature, and the few which permitted prorogation, like New York, placed limitations upon the right. None of the States gave him any patronage for independent distribution. South Carolina, in a quaintly timid clause, specially forbade him to make war or peace or to enter into any treaties.[10]

The early constitutions clearly advanced the doctrine of legislative supremacy and relegated executive power to the will of the legislature. For example, the Virginia constitution, in describing the powers of the chief executive, declared that:

> He shall, with the advice of a Council of State, exercise the executive powers of government, *according to the laws of this commonwealth*; and shall not, under any pretence, exercise any power or prerogative, by virtue of any law, statute or custom of England.[11]

This kind of language, as Charles Thach has pointed out, invited legislative interference and strongly suggested "that all matters concerning the executive were subject to legislative determination."[12]

Before long, however, in North Carolina, Pennsylvania and Virginia, strong complaints were registered against the legislature. They were charged with using their broad grants of power to encroach further upon the defenseless executive and judiciary and to ignore constitutional limitations on their own powers. They appeared to be all but omnipotent, and, by their aggressive tactics, to render an already weak executive even weaker. Thomas Jefferson, certainly no enemy of a strong legislature, complained of the state of affairs in Virginia:

> All the powers of government, legislative, executive and judiciary, result to the legislative body. . . . The convention, which passed the ordinance of government, laid its foundations on this basis, that the legislative, executive and judiciary departments should be separate and distinct, so that no person should exercise the powers of more than one of them at the same time. But no barrier was provided between these several powers. The judiciary and executive members were left dependent on the legislature for their subsistence in office, and some of them for their continuance in it. If therefore the legislature assumes executive and judiciary powers, no opposition is likely to be made; nor, if made, can it be effectual; because in that case they may put their proceedings in the form of an act of assembly, which will render them obligatory on the other branches. They have accordingly in many instances, decided rights which have been left to the judiciary controversy; and the direction of the executive, during the whole time of the session, is becoming habitual and familiar.[13]

If this trend had continued up to the Constitutional Convention, the results of that meeting would certainly have been very different than they turned out to be. Fortunately, there were outstanding models of other state constitutions which provided the executive office with sufficient power and scope to demonstrate the advantages of a real division of "shared powers." The New York state constitution was the outstanding example, but in Massachusetts and also New Hampshire, good beginnings were made in establishing an executive office which was able to defend its independence and perform its regular executive functions.

The Strong Executive in State Constitutions

New York was forced to delay its drafting of a state constitution because General Howe's army carried the Revolutionary War to New York in the summer of 1776 and the Provincial Congress, which had been working on a constitution, was driven from town to town as the redcoats advanced. It was not until the spring of 1777 that a committee draft of the New York constitution was presented to a state constitutional convention. The draft was prepared by John Jay with the assistance of Robert Livingston and Gouverneur Morris. They had been scheduled to introduce the document the previous year, but Jay's deep involvement in paramilitary operations in support of the Revolutionary forces delayed them and made it impossible for them to present it before the following spring.

The New York charter was widely regarded as the best of the new state constitutions, and it overcame many of the deficiencies in the other charters. First of all, it provided for the election of the chief executive by popular ballot for a term of three years. The governor was vested with "the supreme power and authority of the State." He was to serve as commander in chief of the armed forces and was given the power to convene and prorogue the legislature for limited periods of time. In addition to this he was empowered to correspond with the Congress and the other states, and to recommend legislation. No privy council was created to surround him and restrict his actions, but he was required to sit on two councils—the Councils of Appointments and of Revisions; only with respect to these functions were his executive powers limited. The Council of Appointments was made up of the governor and four members of the upper house (the senate) appointed annually. It was the intention of the framers to have the governor propose appointments to the council, and restrict it to a veto power; but in effect this provision backfired, and the legislature was virtually able, through this structure, to control appointments. The Council of Revision was made up of the governor, the chancellor and three judges of the state supreme court. The presence of the governor and any two of the others was considered a quorum. The council was required to review all laws passed by the legislature, and if a majority considered a statute improper, would return it to the legislature, which could only then enact the measure by a two-thirds vote. The two councils proved to be cumbersome and to restrict the chief executive in matters of appointments and legislative influence to a greater extent than was intended, but on the whole the New York state constitution defined the role of its chief executive very wisely, and the office proved to be extremely effective in operation. George Clinton, New York's first governor, was an extremely capable and strong leader, and he was able to demonstrate the value of these constitutional provisions which provided him with the power to act, to lead, to defend his position against the encroachments of the legislature, and to provide New York with strong and efficient government.

New York State Constitution
Sections Dealing with the Executive
1777

Francis Newton Thorpe, ed., *The Federal and State Constitutions of the United States* (Washington, D.C., 1909) V, 2628; 2632-34.

III.   And whereas laws inconsistent with the spirit of this constitution, or with the public good, may be hastily and unadvisedly passed: Be it ordained, that the governor for the time being, the chancellor, and the judges of the supreme court, or any two of them, together with the governor, shall be, and hereby are, constituted a council to revise all bills about to be passed into laws by the legislature; and for that purpose shall assemble themselves from time to time, when the legislature shall be convened; for which, nevertheless, they shall not receive any salary or consideration, under any pretence whatever. And that all bills which have passed the senate and assembly shall, before they become laws, be presented to the said council for their revisal and consideration; and if, upon such revision and consideration, it should appear improper to the said council, or a majority of them, that the said bill should become a law of this State, that they return the same, together with their objections thereto in writing, to the senate or house of assembly (in which soever the same shall have originated) who shall enter the objection sent down by the council at large in their minutes, and proceed to reconsider the said bill. But if, after such reconsideration, two-thirds of the said senate or house of assembly shall, notwithstanding the said objections, agree to pass the same, it shall, together with the objections, be sent to the other branch of the legislature, where it shall also be reconsidered, and, if approved by two-thirds of the members present, shall be a law, within ten days after it shall have been presented, the same shall be a law, unless the legislature shall, by their adjournment, render a return of the said bill within ten days impracticable; in which case the bill shall be returned on the first day of the meeting of the legislature after the expiration of the said ten days. . . .

XVII. And this convention doth further, in the name and by the authority of the good people of this State, ordain, determine, and declare that the supreme executive power and authority of this State shall be vested in a governor; and that statedly, once in every three years, and as often as the seat of government shall become vacant, a wise and descreet freeholder of this State shall be, by ballot, elected governor, by the freeholders of this State, qualified, as before described, to elect senators; which elections shall be always held at the times and places of choosing representatives in assembly for each respective county; and that the person who hath the greatest number of votes within the said State shall be governor thereof.

XVIII. That the governor shall continue in office three years, and shall, by virtue of his office, be general and commander-in-chief of all the militia, and admiral of the navy of this State; that he shall have power to convene the assembly and senate on extraordinary occasions; to prorogue them from time to time, provided such prorogations shall not exceed sixty days in the space of any one year; and, at his discretion, to grant reprieves and pardons to persons convicted of crimes, other than treason or murder, in which he may suspend the execution of the sentence, until it shall be reported to the legislature at their subsequent meeting; and they shall either pardon or direct the execution of the criminal, or grant a further reprieve.

XIX. That it shall be the duty of the governor to inform the legislature, at every session, of the condition of the State, so far as may respect his department; to recommend such matters to their consideration as shall appear to him to concern its good government, welfare, and prosperity; to correspond with the Continental Congress, and other States; to transact all necessary business with the officers of government, civil and military; to take care that the laws are faithfully executed to the best of his ability; and to expedite all such measures as may be resolved upon by legislature. . . .

XXIII. That all officers, other than those who, by this constitution, are directed to be otherwise appointed, shall be appointed in the manner following, to wit: The assembly shall, once in every year, openly nominate and appoint one of the senators from each great district, which senators shall form a council for the appointment of the said officers, of which the governor for the time being, or the lieutenant-governor, or the president of the senate, when they shall respectively administer the government, shall be president and have a casting voice, but no other vote; and with the advice and consent of the said council, shall appoint all the said officers; and that a majority of the said council be a quorum. And further, the said senators shall not be eligible to the said council for two years successively.

XXIV. That all military officers be appointed during pleasure; that all commissioned officers, civil and military, be commissioned by the governor; and that the chancellor, the judges of the supreme court, and first judge of the county court in every county, hold their offices during good behavior or until they shall have respectively attained the age of sixty years.

The Massachusetts constitution came considerably later (1780), and was adopted by the people of the state after careful and laborious analysis and discussion. At the outset of the Revolution, Massachusetts decided to continue, at least temporarily, with the existing structure of its revoked charter, which placed the executive power in the hands of a council of 28. In 1778 a special constitutional convention was proposed by the Town Meeting of Concord and many towns demanded a general referendum of any proposed constitution. The legislature, however, wanted to short-circuit the method of first calling a special convention and then submitting its work to the people for ratification. It finally proposed that the voters consider the twofold purpose of constitution-making and legislation when they voted for their representatives in the upcoming election, and this plan was followed, although it met with widespread criticism. A committee of legislators drew up what was considered to be a very poor constitution, and one which proposed a pitifully weak executive. The chaplain of the house considered it so bad that he speculated that it had been drawn up with the express purpose of being rejected so that the old charter would remain in effect. Although the governor was to be elected by the people, all his actions were to be dependent upon the approval of the upper house in which he was to serve, and he was given no veto power over the acts of the legislature.

When this proposed constitution was submitted to the people, it was overwhelmingly defeated by a vote of 9,972 to 2,083, or better than four to one. Following this ballot, a number of prominent conservatives from Essex County met in Ipswich and issued a manifesto which they titled the "Essex Result," setting forth what they considered to be the desirable elements of a sound constitution. They attacked the lack of a bill of rights in the first proposed constitution, argued for greater independence of the three departments of government, and called for a fair system of apportionment and a better method of electing the upper house. The conservative emphasis of the group was explicit in its strong defense of property and their advocacy of arrangements for its proper protection in the voting qualifications of the upper house, but the document was most influential in its insistence upon a strong and independent executive, armed with a veto power.

In 1779 a special constitutional convention was held in Cambridge with delegates elected from every town in the state. John Adams performed the burden of the work of preparing the first draft of the second proposed constitution. The convention, meeting over a period of seven months, carefully considered each clause of the draft and finally submitted the results of their labors to the towns for full discussion and a vote in the spring of 1780. The people were instructed to vote on the constitution, clause by clause, and when all the towns had been heard from, the convention would meet again and fully tabulate the results. Fourteen full days were set aside for consideration and discussion of the proposed charter. A two-thirds vote in favor of each clause was required for adoption, and when specific changes were approved by a similar margin, they too were to be adopted by the convention.

The executive emerged almost as powerful in this Massachusetts constitution as in the New York charter, although he was held in check by annual elections. The governor was to be independent of the legislature and the judiciary but was to have a "privy council" which he was required to consult with and win approval from with regard to appointments, legislative vetoes and pardons. As in New York, he was given command of the militia, and he could adjourn or prorogue the legislature. In short, an executive office with power, dignity and independence had been created, and although it had come after New York and was, to a great extent, patterned after this strong example, its adoption in the leading New England state considerably reinforced the later attitudes for strong executive powers at the national Constitutional Convention.

Massachusetts State Constitution
Sections Dealing with the Executive
1780

Thorpe, III, 1899-1905.

CHAPTER II
EXECUTIVE POWER

Section I—Governor

I.

There shall be a supreme executive magistrate, who shall be styled—The Governor of the Commonwealth of Massachusetts; and whose title shall be—His Excellency.

II.

The governor shall be chosen annually; and no person shall be eligible to this office, unless, at the time of his election, he shall have been an inhabitant of this commonwealth for seven years next preceding; [and unless he shall at the same time be seised, in his own right, of a freehold, within the commonwealth, of the value of one thousand pounds;] [and unless he shall declare himself to be of the Christian religion.]

III.

Those persons who shall be qualified to vote for senators and representatives within the several towns of this commonwealth shall, at a meeting to be called for that purpose, on the [first Monday of April] annually, give in their votes for a governor, to the selectmen, who shall preside at such meetings; and the town clerk, in the presence and with the assistance of the selectmen, shall, in open town meeting, sort and count the votes, and form a list of the persons voted for, with the number of votes for each person against his name; and shall make a fair record of the same in the town books, and a public declaration thereof in the said meeting; and shall, in the presence of the inhabitants, seal up copies of the said list, attested by him and the selectmen, and transmit the same to the sheriff of the county, thirty days at least before the [last Wednesday in May]; and the sheriff shall transmit the same to the secretary's office, seventeen days at least before the said [last Wednesday in May]; or the selectmen may cause returns of the same to be made to the office of the secretary of the commonwealth, seventeen days at least before the said day; and the secretary shall lay the same before the senate and the house of representatives on the [last Wednesday in May], to be by them examined; and [in case of an election by a majority of all the votes returned], the choice shall be by them declared and published; [but if no person shall have a majority of votes, the house of representatives shall, by ballot, elect two out of four persons who had the highest number of votes, if so many shall have been voted for; but, if otherwise, out of the number voted for; and make return to the senate of the two persons so elected; on which the senate shall proceed, by ballot, to elect one, who shall be declared governor.]

IV.

The governor shall have authority, from time to time, at his discretion, to assemble and call together the councillors of this commonwealth for the time being; and the governor with the said councillors, or five of them at least, shall, and may, from time to time, hold and keep a council, for the ordering and directing the affairs of the commonwealth, agreeably to the constitution and the laws of the land.

V.

The governor, with advice of council, shall have full power and authority, during the session of the general court, to adjourn or prorogue the same to any time the two houses shall desire; [and to dissolve the same on the day next preceding the last Wednesday in May; and, in the recess of the said court, to prorogue the same from time to time, not exceeding ninety days in any one recess;] and to call it together sooner than the time to which it may be adjourned or prorogued, if the welfare of the commonwealth shall require the same; and in case of any infections distemper prevailing in the place where the said court is next at any time to convene, or any other cause happening, whereby danger may arise to the health of lives of the members from their attendance, he may direct the session to be held at some other, the most convenient place within the state.

[And the governor shall dissolve the said general court on the day next preceding the last Wednesday in May.]

VI.

In cases of disagreement between the two houses, with regard to the necessity, expediency, or time of adjournment or prorogation, the governor, with advice of the council, shall have a right to adjourn or prorogue the general court, not exceeding ninety days, as he shall determine the public good shall require.

VII.

The governor of this commonwealth, for the time being, shall be the commander-in-chief of the army and navy, and of all the military forces of the state, by sea and land; and shall have full power, by himself, or by any commander, or other officer or officers, from time to time, to train, instruct, exercise, and govern the militia and navy; and, for the special defence and safety of the commonwealth, to assemble in martial array, and put in warlike posture, the inhabitants thereof, and to lead and conduct them, and with them to encounter, repel, resist, expel, and pursue, by force of arms, as well by sea as by land, within or without the limits of this commonwealth, and also to kill, slay, and destroy, if necessary, and conquer, by all fitting ways, enterprises, and means whatsoever, all and every such person and persons as shall, at any time hereafter, in a hostile manner, attempt or enterprise the destruction, invasion, detriment, or annoyance of this commonwealth; and to use and exercise, over the army and navy, and over the militia in actual service, the law-martial, in time of war or invasion, and also in time of rebellion, declared by the legislature to exist, as occasion shall necessarily require; and to take and surprise, by all ways and means whatsoever, all and every such person or persons, with their ships, arms, ammunition, and other goods, as shall, in a hostile manner, invade, or attempt the invading, conquering, or annoying this commonwealth; and that the governor be intrusted with all these and other powers, incident to the offices of captain-general and commander-in-chief, and admiral, to be exercised agreeably to the rules and regulations of the constitution, and the laws of the land, and not otherwise.

Provided, that the said governor shall not, at any time hereafter, by virtue of any power by this constitution granted, or hereafter to be granted to him by the legislature, transport any of the inhabitants of this commonwealth, or oblige them to march out of the limits of the same, without their free and voluntary consent, or the consent of the general court; except so far as may be necessary to march or transport them by land or water, for the defence of such part of the state to which they cannot otherwise conveniently have access.

VIII.

The power of pardoning offences, except such as persons may be convicted of before the senate by an impeachment of the house, shall be in the governor, by and with the advice of council; but no charter of pardon, granted by the governor, with advice of the council before conviction, shall avail the party pleading the same, notwithstanding any general or particular expressions contained therein, descriptive of the offence or offences intended to be pardoned.

IX.

All judicial officers, [the attorney-general,] the solicitor-general, [all sheriffs,] coroners, [and registers of probate,] shall be nominated and appointed by the governor, by and with the advice and consent of the council; and every such nomination shall be made by the governor, and made at least seven days prior to such appointment.

X.

The captains and subalterns of the militia shall be elected by the written votes of the train-band and alarm list of their respective companies, [of twenty-one years of age and upwards;] the field officers of regiments shall be elected by the written votes of the captains and subalterns of their respective regiments; the brigadiers shall be elected, in like manner, by the field officers of their respective brigades; and such officers, so elected, shall be commissioned by the governor, who shall determine their rank.

The legislature shall, by standing laws, direct the time and manner of convening the electors, and of collecting votes, and of certifying to the governor, the officers elected.

The major-generals shall be appointed by the senate and house of representatives, each having a negative upon the other; and be commissioned by the governor.

And if the electors of brigadiers, field officers, captains or subalterns, shall neglect or refuse to make such elections, after being duly notified, according to the laws for the time being, then the governor, with the advice of council, shall appoint suitable persons to fill such offices.

[And no officer, duly commissioned to command in the militia, shall be removed from his office, but by the address of both houses to the governor, or by fair trial in court-martial, pursuant to the laws of the commonwealth for the time being.]

The commanding officers of regiments shall appoint their adjutants and quartermasters; the brigadiers their brigade-majors; and the major-generals their aids; and the governor shall appoint the adjutant-general.

The governor, with advice of council, shall appoint all officers of the continental army, whom by the confederation of the United States it is provided that this commonwealth shall appoint, as also all officers of forts and garrisons.

The divisions of the militia into brigades, regiments, and companies, made in pursuance of the militia laws now in force, shall be considered as the proper divisions of the militia of this commonwealth, until the same shall be altered in pursuance of some future law.

XI.

No moneys shall be issued out of the treasury of this commonwealth, and disposed of (except such sums as may be appropriated for the redemption of bills of credit or treasurer's notes, or for the payment of interest arising thereon) but by warrant under the hand of the governor for the time being, with the advice and consent of the council, for the necessary defence and support of the commonwealth; and for the protection and preservation of the inhabitants thereof, agreeably to the acts and resolves of the general court.

XII.

All public boards, the commissary-general, all superintending officers of public magazines and stores, belonging to this commonwealth, and all commanding officers of forts and garrisons within the same, shall once in every three months, officially, and without requisition, and at other times, when required by the governor, deliver to him an account of all goods, stores, provisions, ammunition, cannon with their appendages, and small arms with their accoutrements, and of all other public property whatever under their care respectively; distinguishing the quantity, number, quality and kind of each, as particularly as may be; together with the condition of such forts and garrisons; and the said commanding officer shall exhibit to the governor, when required by him, true and exact plans of such forts, and of the land and sea or harbor or harbors, adjacent.

And the said boards, and all public officers, shall communicate to the governor, as soon as may be after receiving the same, all letters, despatches, and intelligences of a public nature, which shall be directed to them respectively.

XIII.

As the public good requires that the governor should not be under the undue influence of any of the members of the general court by a dependence on them for his support, that he should in all cases act with freedom for the benefit of the public, that he should not have his attention necessarily diverted from that object to his private concerns, and that he should maintain the dignity of the commonwealth in the character of its chief magistrate, it is necessary that he should have an honorable stated salary, of a fixed and permanent value, amply sufficient for those purposes, and established by standing laws; and it shall be among the first acts of the general court, after the commencement of this constitution, to establish such salary by law accordingly.

Permanent and honorable salaries shall also be established by law for the justices of the supreme judicial court.

And if it shall be found that any of the salaries aforesaid, so established, are insufficient, they shall, from time to time, be enlarged, as the general court shall judge proper.

CHAPTER II

Section II—Lieutenant Governor

II.

The governor, and in his absence the lieutenant-governor, shall be president of the council, but shall have no vote in council; and the lieutenant-governor shall always be a member of the council, except when the chair of the governor shall be vacant.

III.

Whenever the chair of the governor shall be vacant, by reason of his death, or absence from the commonwealth, or otherwise, the lieutenant-governor, for the time being, shall, during such vacancy, perform all the duties incumbent upon the governor, and shall have and exercise all the powers and authorities, which by this constitution the governor is vested with, when personally present.

CHAPTER II

Section III—Council, and the Manner of Settling Elections by the Legislature

Article I.

There shall be a council for advising the governor in the executive part of the government, to consist of [nine] persons besides the lieutenant-governor, whom the governor, for the time being, shall have full power and authority, from time to time, at his discretion, to assemble and call together; and the governor, with the said councillors, or five of them at least, shall and may, from time to time, hold and keep a council, for the ordering and directing the affairs of the commonwealth, according to the laws of the land.

II.

[Nine councillors shall be annually chosen from among the persons returned for councillors and senators, on the last Wednesday in May, by the joint ballot of the senators and representatives assembled in one room; and in case there shall not be found upon the first choice, the whole number of nine persons who will accept a seat in the council, the deficiency shall be made up by the electors aforesaid from among the people at large; and the number of senators left shall constitute the senate for the year. The seats of the persons thus elected from the senate, and accepting the trust, shall be vacated in the senate.]

III.

The councillors, in the civil arrangements of the commonwealth, shall have rank next after the lieutenant-governor.

IV.

[Not more than two councillors shall be chosen out of any one district of this commonwealth.]

V.

The resolutions and advice of the council shall be recorded in a register, and signed by the members present; and this record may be called for at any time by either house of the legislature; and any member of the council may insert his opinion, contrary to the resolution of the majority.

VI.

Whenever the office of the governor and lieutenant-governor shall be vacant, by reason of death, absence, or otherwise, then the council, or the major part of them, shall, during such vacancy, have full power and authority to do, and execute, all and every such acts, matters, and things, as the governor or the lieutenant-governor might or could, by virtue of this constitution, do or execute, if they, or either of them, were personally present.

VII.

[And whereas the elections appointed to be made, by this constitution, on the last Wednesday in May annually, by the two houses of the legislature, may not be completed on that day, the said elections may be adjourned from day to day until the same shall be completed. And the order of elections shall be as follows: the vacancies in the senate, if any, shall first be filled up; the governor and lieutenant-governor shall then be elected, provided there should be no choice of them by the people; and afterwards the two houses shall proceed to the election of the council.]

CHAPTER III
JUDICIARY POWER

II.

Each branch of the legislature, as well as the governor and council, shall have authority to require the opinions of the justices of the supreme judicial court, upon important questions of law, and upon solemn occasions.

CHAPTER IV
INCOMPATABILITY OF AND EXCLUSION FROM OFFICE

II.

No governor, lieutenant-governor, or judge of the supreme judicial court, shall hold any other office or place, under the authority of this commonwealth, except such as by this constitution they are admitted to hold, saving that the judges of the said court may hold the offices of justices of the peace through the state; nor shall they hold any other place or office, or receive any pension or salary from any other state or government or power whatever.

No person shall be capable of holding or exercising at the same time, within this state, more than one of the following offices, viz.: judge of probate—sheriff—register of probate—or register of deeds; and never more than any two offices, which are to be held by appointment of the governor, or the governor and council, or the senate, or the house of representatives, or by the election of the people of the state at large, or of the people of any county, military offices, and the offices of justices of the peace excepted, shall be held by one person.

The immediate impact of the Massachusetts constitution was felt in New Hampshire. This state had jumped the gun and adopted a constitution six months before the Declaration of Independence was published, but it was a roughly-hewn, ill-considered charter with characteristic legislative supremacy. In 1778 a constitutional convention was called and a draft of a revised constitution was submitted to the towns, but "they made short work of it," not without cause, because it was, as Nevins had described it, "of a rather sorry kind."[14] A second attempt at revision was made in 1781, and this time the Massachusetts constitution was used as a model, but the voters of the state also rejected this effort on the basis that it was too conservative. A third try was defeated the following year, but by then the leaders had become somewhat apprehensive, for the original constitution was no longer valid after peace had been made with Great Britain. The fourth revision was presented to the people in the summer of 1783 and ratified that fall. It went into effect the following year. The new constitution incorporated many of the Massachusetts provisions, particularly with respect to the executive power (the title of president was used in New Hampshire), but with one major exception—the lack of a presidential veto of legislative measures.

New Hampshire State Constitution
Sections Dealing with the Executive
1784

Thorpe, IV, 2462-65.

There shall be a supreme executive magistrate, who shall be stiled, The President of the State of New-Hampshire; and whose title shall be His Excellency.

The President shall be chosen annually; and no person shall be eligible to this office, unless at the time of his election, he shall have been an inhabitant of this state for seven years next preceding, and unless he shall be of the age of thirty years; and unless he shall, at the same time, have an estate of the value of *five hundred pounds*, one half of which shall consist of a freehold, in his own right, within the state; and unless he shall be of the Protestant religion.

Those persons qualified to vote for senators and representatives, shall within the several towns, parishes or places, where they dwell, at a meeting to be called for that purpose, some day in the month of March annually, give in their votes for a president to the selectmen, who shall preside at such meeting, and the clerk in the presence and with the assistance of the selectmen, shall in open meeting sort and count the votes, and form a list of the persons voted for, with the number of votes for each person against his name, and shall make a fair record of the same in the town books, and a public declaration thereof in the said meeting; and shall in the presence of said inhabitants, seal up a copy of said list attested by him and the selectmen, and transmit the same to the sheriff of the county, thirty days at least before the first Wednesday of June, or shall cause returns of the same to be made to the office of the secretary of the state, seventeen days at least, before said day, who shall lay the same before the senate and house of representatives on the first Wednesday of June, to be by them examined; and in case of an election by a majority of votes through the state, the choice shall be by them declared, and published; but if no person shall have a majority of votes, the house of representatives shall by ballot elect two out of the four persons who had the highest number of votes, if so many shall have been voted for; but if otherwise, out of the number voted for; and make return to the senate of the two persons so elected, on which the senate shall proceed by ballot to elect one of them who shall be declared president.

The president of the state shall preside in the senate, shall have a vote equal with any other member; and shall also have a casting vote in case of a tie.

The president with advice of council, shall have full power and authority in the recess of the general court, to prorogue the same from time to time, not exceeding ninety days in any one recess of said court; and during the session of said court, to adjourn or prorogue it to any time the two houses may desire, and to call it together sooner than the time to which it may be adjourned, or prorogued, if the welfare of the state should require the same.

In cases of disagreement between the two houses, with regard to the time of adjournment, or prorogation, the president, with advice of council, shall have a right to adjourn or prorogue the general court, not exceeding ninety days, at any one time, as he may determine the public good may require. And he shall dissolve the same seven days before the said first Wednesday of June. And in case of any infections distemper prevailing in the place where the said court at any time is to convene, or any other cause whereby dangers may arise to the healths or lives of the members from their attendance, the president may direct the session to be holden at some other the most convenient place within the State.

The president of this state for the time being, shall be commander in chief of the army and navy, and all the military forces of the state, by sea and land; and shall have full power by himself, or by any chief commander, or other officer, or officers, from time to time, to train, instruct, exercise and govern the militia and navy; and for the special defence and safety of this state to assemble in martial array, and put in warlike posture, the inhabitants thereof, and to lead and conduct them, and with them to encounter, expulse, repel, resist and pursue by force of arms, as well by sea as by land, within and without the limits of this state; and also to kill slay, destroy, if necessary, and conquer by all fitting ways, enterprize and means, all and every such person and persons as shall, at any time hereafter, in a hostile manner, attempt or enterprize the destruction, invasion, detriment, or annoyance of this state; and to use and exercise over the army and navy, and over the militia in actual service, the law-martial in time of war, invasion, and also in rebellion, declared by the legislature to exist, as occasion shall necessarily require: and surprize by all ways and means whatsoever, all and every such person or persons, with their ships, arms, ammunition, and other goods, as shall in a hostile manner invade or attempt the invading, conquering, or annoying this state: and in fine, the president hereby is entrusted with all other powers incident to the office of captain-general and commander in chief, and admiral, to be exercised agreeably to the rules and regulations of the constitution, and the laws of the land; provided that the president shall not at any time hereafter, by virtue of any power by this constitution granted, or hereafter to be granted to him by the legislature, transport any of the inhabitants of this state, or oblige them to march out of the limits of the same, without their free and voluntary consent, or the consent of the general court, nor grant commissions for exercising the law-martial in any case, without the advice and consent of the council.

The power of pardoning offences, except such as persons may be convicted of before the senate by impeachment of the house, shall be in the president by and with the advice of the council: but no charter of pardon granted by the president with advice of council, before conviction, shall avail, the party pleading the same, notwithstanding any general or particular expressions contained therein, descriptive of the offence or offences intended to be pardoned.

All judicial officers, the attorney-general, solicitor-general, all sheriffs, coroners, registers of probate, and all officers of the navy, and general and field-officers of the militia, shall be nominated and appointed by the president and council; and every such nomination shall be made at least seven days prior to such appointment, and no appointment shall take place, unless three of the council agree thereto. The captains and subalterns in the respective regiments shall be nominated and recommended by the field-officers to the president, who is to issue their commissions immediately on receipt of such recommendation.

No officer duly commissioned to command in the militia, shall be removed from his office, but by the address of both houses to the president, or by fair trial in court-martial, pursuant to the laws of the state for the time being.

The commanding officers of the regiments shall appoint their adjutants and quarter-masters; the brigadiers their brigade-majors, the major generals their aids; the captains and subalterns their non-commissioned officers.

The president and council, shall appoint all officers of the continental army, whom by the confederation of the United States it is provided that this state shall appoint, as also all officers of forts and garrisons.

The division of the militia into brigades, regiments and companies, made in pursuance of the militia laws now in force, shall be considered as the proper division of the militia of this state, until the same shall be altered by some future law.

No monies shall be issued out of the treasury of this state, and disposed of (except such sums as may be appropriated for the redemption of bills of credit or treasurers' notes, or for the payment of interest arising thereon) but by warrant under the hand of the president for the time being, by and with the advice and consent of the council, for the necessary support and defence of this state, and for the necessary protection and preservation of the inhabitants thereof, agreeably to the acts and resolves of the general court.

All public boards, the commissary-general, all superintending officers of public magazines and stores, belonging to this state, and all commanding officers of forts and garrisons within the same, shall once in every three months, officially, and without requisition, and at other times, when required by the president, deliver to him an account of all goods, stores, provisions, ammunition, cannon, with their appendages, and small arms, with their accoutrements, and of all other public property under their care respectively; distinguishing the quantity, and kind of each, as particularly as may be; together with the condition of such forts and garrisons: and the commanding officer shall exhibit to the president, when required by him, true and exact plans of such forts, and of the land and sea, or harbour or harbours adjacent.

The president and council shall be compensated for their services from time to time by such grants as the general court shall think reasonable.

Permanent and honorable salaries shall be established by law for the justices of the superior court.

Whenever the chair of the president shall be vacant, by reason of his death, absence from the state, or otherwise, the senior senator for the time being, shall, during such vacancy, have and exercise all the powers and authorities which by this constitution the president is vested with when personally present.

The Articles of Confederation

Although the major political experience of the delegates to the Constitutional Convention had been their active participation in the representative assemblies of the colonial governments and later positions they held in the state governments which replaced them, 39 of the 55 delegates at Philadelphia had also served in the Continental Congresses or in their successor, the Congress of the United States, under the Articles of Confederation. These had not always been exhilarating experiences, but had provided very useful background for anyone who had to draw up a workable constitution for the whole nation. By the mid-1780s it was crystal-clear that the charter for the "federation" of the 13 states was woefully inadequate. The states were bound together by the loosest of bonds, and their compact did not provide them with the essential tools to govern.

The Articles of Confederation directed the Congress to provide for the common defense, to maintain the security of its members' liberty, to guarantee the rights and privileges of citizens of each state with respect to every other state, to provide for their mutual and general welfare and finally to recognize the laws and legal decisions of other states. They prohibited the states from conducting their own foreign policy, from entering into a treaty or alliance with any other state, and from engaging in war, unless provoked. But the means provided by the Articles for carrying out these ends did not go beyond a firm request; the requisition of taxes and the raising of an army and a navy could be undertaken only by appealing for state allocations. The Congress could legislate, but it could not enforce its legislation; it could levy taxes, but it could not collect them.

For all intents and purposes, the Articles provided for no real Executive. The Congress elected a presiding officer who had no administrative or executive responsibilities. While the Congress was in session, the body itself acted as supreme Executive, working through inadequately staffed administrative departments to implement its decisions. When the Congress was not in session, an executive committee made up of one delegate from each state presided over the government, but this committee magnified all the weaknesses of the Congress. Authority was divided among its members, and it had no more power than the Congress to impose its decisions on the member states. Merrill Jensen has argued persuasively that this weak federation was the form of government desired by men like Samuel Adams,

Patrick Henry, George Clinton and George Mason because they had come to the conclusion that the interests of their states would best be served by such a highly decentralized federation:

> Some of them had programs of political and social reform; others had none at all. Some had a vision of democracy; others had no desire except to control their states for whatever satisfactions such control might offer. Some were, in fact, as narrow and provincial as their opponents said they were. However, the best of them agreed that the central government needed more power, but they wanted that power given so as not to alter the basic character of the Articles of Confederation.[15]

Jensen refers to this group as "Federalists" (although all of them later opposed the Federalist party), and he identifies as "Nationalist" men like John Jay, Gouverneur Morris, Alexander Hamilton, James Wilson, James Madison and George Washington, whom he says were believers "in executive and judicial rather than legislative control of the state and local governments, in the rigorous collection of taxes, and, as creditors, in strict payment of public and private debts."[16]

> They declared that national honor and prestige could be maintained only by a powerful central government. . . . They deplored the fact that there was no check upon the actions of the majorities in State legislatures; that there was no central government to which minorities could appeal from the decisions of such majorities, as they had done before the Revolution. . . .
> While the Federalist leaders gradually moved to a position where they were willing to add specific powers to the Articles of Confederation, the nationalist leaders campaigned steadily for the kind of government they wanted. During the war they argued that it could not be won without creating a powerful central government. After the war they insisted that such government was necessary to do justice to public creditors, solve the problem of post-war trade, bring about recovery from depression, and win the respect of the world for the new nation. Meanwhile their experience with majorities in State legislatures merely intensified their desire.[17]

Hamilton had perceived most of the flaws in the old system as early as 1780, and in a brilliant letter to James Duane he analyzed the various weaknesses of the Congress and its administrative shortcomings. With regard to the Executive, he pointed out that:

> Another defect in our system is want of method and energy in the administration. This has partly resulted from the other defect [the weakness of Congress]; but in a great degree from prejudice, and the want of a proper executive. Congress have (sic) kept the power too much in their own hands, and have meddled too much with details of every sort. Congress is properly a deliberative corps and it forgets itself when it attempts to play the executive. It is impossible such a body, numerous as it is, constantly fluctuating, can ever act with sufficient decision, or with system.[18]

These negative reactions to the weaknesses of the government under the Articles of Confederation, particularly with its inadequate provisions for executive leadership and independence, had a significant effect upon the members of the Philadelphia Convention. They had experienced weak central leadership from the very beginning, and by 1787 most of the delegates were determined to strengthen the powers of the central government, and provide it with an Executive who could govern. Because it stands as an historic example of a constitution which fails to come to grips with the basic functions of government and almost totally ignores the executive responsibility of implementing legislation and policy, and Articles of Confederation is included as an instructive example of a constitutional structure inadequate to cope with the necessary concentration of power so essential to the ability to govern effectively.

The Articles of Confederation
1777

Merrill Jensen, *The Articles of Confederation* (Madison, Wisconsin, 1948), 263-70.

Between the States of New Hampshire, Massachusetts Bay, Rhode Island and Providence Plantations, Connecticut, New York, New Jersey, Pennsylvania, Delaware, Maryland, Virginia, North Carolina, South Carolina, Georgia.

Article 1

The stile of this confederacy shall be "The United States of America."

Article 2

Each State retains its sovereignty, freedom and independence, and every power, jurisdiction, and right, which is not by this confederation expressly delegated to the United States, in Congress assembled.

Article 3

The said states hereby severally enter into a firm league of friendship with each other for their common defence, the security of their liberties and their mutual and general welfare; binding themselves to assist each other against all force offered to, or attacks made upon them, or any of them, on account of religion, sovereignty, trade or any other pretence whatever.

Article 4

The better to secure and perpetuate mutual friendship and intercourse among the people of the different states in this union, the free inhabitants of each of these states, paupers, vagabonds, and fugitives from justice excepted, shall be entitled to all privileges and immunities of free citizens in the several states; and the people of each State shall have free ingress and regress to and from any other State, and shall enjoy therein all the privileges of trade and commerce, subject to the same duties, impositions, and restrictions, as the inhabitants thereof respectively; provided, that such restrictions shall not extend so far as to prevent the removal of property, imported into any State, to any other State of which the owner is an inhabitant; provided also, that no imposition, duties, or restriction, shall be laid by any State on the property of the United States, or either of them.

If any person guilty of, or charged with treason, felony, or other high misdemeanor in any State, shall flee from justice and be found in any of the United States, he shall, upon demand of the governor or executive power of the State from which he fled, be delivered up and removed to the State having jurisdiction of his offence.

Full faith and credit shall be given in each of these states to the records, acts, and judicial proceedings of the courts and magistrates of every other State.

Article 5

For the more convenient management of the general interests of the United States, delegates shall be annually appointed, in such manner as the legislature of each State shall direct, to meet in Congress, on the 1st Monday in November in every year, with a power reserved to each State to recall its delegates, or any of them, at any time within the year, and to send others in their stead for the remainder of the year.

No State shall be represented in Congress by less than two, nor by more than seven members; and no person shall be capable of being a delegate for more than three years in any term of six years; nor shall any person, being a delegate, be capable of holding any office under the United States, for which he, or any other for his benefit, receives any salary, fees, or emolument of any kind.

Each State shall maintain its own delegates in a meeting of the states, and while they act as members of the committee of the states.

In determining questions in the United States, in Congress assembled, each State shall have one vote.

Freedom of speech and debate in Congress shall not be impeached or questioned in any court or place out of Congress: and the members of Congress shall be protected in their persons from arrests and imprisonments, during the time of their going to and from, and attendance on Congress, *except for treason*, felony, or breach of peace.

Article 6

No State, without the consent of the United States, in Congress assembled, shall send any embassy to, or receive any embassy from, or enter into any conference, agreement, alliance, or treaty with any king, prince, or state; nor shall any person, holding any office of profit or trust under the United States, or any of them, accept of any present, emolument, office or title, of any kind whatever, from any king, prince, or foreign state; nor shall the United States, in Congress assembled, or any of them, grant any title of nobility.

No two or more states shall enter into any treaty, confederation, or alliance, whatever, between them, without the consent of the United States, in Congress assembled, specifying accurately the purposes for which the same is to be entered into, and how long it shall continue.

No state shall lay any imposts or duties which may interfere with any stipulations in treaties entered into by the United States, in Congress assembled, with any king, prince, or state, in pursuance of any treaties already proposed by Congress to the courts of France and Spain.

No vessels of war shall be kept up in time of peace by any State, except such number only as shall be deemed necessary by the United States, in Congress assembled, for the defence of such State or its trade; nor shall any body of forces be kept up by any State, in time of peace, except such number only as, in the judgment of the United States, in Congress assembled, shall be deemed requisite to garrison the forts necessary for the defence of such State; but every State shall always keep up a well regulated and disciplined militia, sufficiently armed and accoutred, and shall provide, and constantly have ready for use, in public stores, a due number of field pieces and tents, and a proper quantity of arms, ammunition and camp equipage.

No State shall engage in any war without the consent of the United States, in Congress assembled, unless such State be actually invaded by enemies, or shall have received certain advice of a resolution being formed by some nation of Indians to invade such State, and the danger is so imminent as not to admit of a delay till the United States, in Congress assembled, can be consulted; nor shall any State grant commissions to any ships or vessels of war, nor letters of marque or reprisal, except it be after a declaration of war by the United States, in Congress assembled, and then only against the kingdom or state, and the subjects thereof, against which war has been so declared, and under such regulations as shall be established by the United States, in Congress assembled, unless such State be infested by pirates, in which case vessels of war may be fitted out for that occasion, and kept so long as the danger shall continue, or until the United States, in Congress assembled, shall determine otherwise.

Article 7

When land forces are raised by any State for the common defence, all officers of or under the rank of colonel, shall be appointed by the legislature of each State respectively, by whom such forces shall be raised, or in such manner as such State shall direct; and all vacancies shall be filled up by the State which first made the appointment.

Article 8

All charges of war and all other expenses, that shall be incurred for the common defence or general welfare, and allowed by the United States, in Congress assembled, shall be defrayed out of a common treasury, which shall be supplied by the several states, in proportion to the value of all land within each State, granted to or surveyed for any person, as such land and the buildings and improvements thereon shall be estimated according to such mode as the United States, in Congress assembled, shall, from time to time, direct and appoint.

The taxes for paying that proportion shall be laid and levied by the authority and direction of the legislatures of the several states, within the time agreed upon by the United States, in Congress assembled.

Article 9

The United States, in Congress assembled, shall have the sole and exclusive right and power of determining on peace and war, except in the cases mentioned in the 6th article; of sending and receiving ambassadors; entering into treaties and alliances, provided that no treaty of commerce shall be made, whereby the legislative power of the respective states shall be restrained from imposing such imposts and duties on foreigners as their own people are subjected to, or from prohibiting the exportation or importation of any species of goods or commodities whatsoever; of establishing rules for deciding, in all cases, what captures on land or water shall be legal, and in what manner prizes, taken by land or naval forces in the service of the United States, shall be divided or appropriated; of granting letters of marque and reprisal in times of peace; appointing courts for the trial of piracies and felonies committed on the high seas, and establishing courts for receiving and determining, finally, appeals in all cases of captures; provided, that no member of Congress shall be appointed a judge of any of the said courts.

The United States, in Congress assembled, shall also be the last resort on appeal in all disputes and differences now subsisting, or that hereafter may arise between two or more states concerning boundary, jurisdiction or any other cause whatever; which authority shall always be exercised in the manner following: whenever the legislative or executive authority, or lawful agent of any State, in controversy with another, shall present a petition to Congress, stating the matter in question, and praying for a hearing, notice thereof shall be given, by order of Congress, to the legislative or executive authority of the other State in controversy, and a day assigned for the appearance of the parties by their lawful agents, who shall then be directed to appoint, by joint consent, commissioners or judges to constitute a court for hearing and determining the matter in question; but, if they cannot agree, Congress shall name three persons out of each of the United States, and from the list of such persons each party shall alternately strike out one, the petitioners beginning, until the number shall be reduced to thirteen; and from that number not less than seven, nor more than nine names, as Congress shall direct, shall, in the presence of Congress, be drawn out by lot; and the persons whose names shall be so drawn, or any five of them, shall be commissioners or judges to hear and finally determine the controversy, so always as a major part of the judges who shall hear the cause shall agree in the determination; and if either party shall neglect to attend at the day appointed, without shewing reasons which Congress shall judge sufficient, or, being present, shall refuse to strike, the Congress shall proceed to nominate three persons out of each State, and the secretary of Congress shall strike in behalf of such party absent or refusing; and the judgment and sentence of the court to be appointed, in the manner before prescribed, shall be final and conclusive; and if any of the parties shall refuse to submit to the authority of such court, or to appear or defend their claim or cause, the court shall nevertheless proceed to pronounce sentence or judgment, which shall, in like manner, be final and decisive, the judgment or sentence and other proceedings being, in either case, transmitted to Congress, and lodged among the acts of Congress for the security of the parties concerned: provided, that every commissioner, before he sits in judgment, shall take an oath, to be administered by one of the judges of the supreme or superior court of the State where the cause shall be tried, "well and truly to hear and determine the matter in question, according to the best of his judgment, without favour, affection, or hope of reward:" provided, also, that no State shall be deprived of territory for the benefit of the United States.

All controversies concerning the private right of soil, claimed under different grants of two or more states, whose jurisdictions, as they may respect such lands and the states which passed such grants, are adjusted, the said grants, or either of them, being at the same time claimed to have originated antecedent to such settlement of jurisdiction, shall, on the petition of either party to the Congress of the United States, be finally determined, as near as may be, in the same manner as is before prescribed for deciding disputes respecting territorial jurisdiction between different states.

The United States, in Congress assembled, shall also have the sole and exclusive right and power of regulating the alloy and value of coin struck by their own authority, or by that of the respective states; fixing the standard of weights and measures throughout the United States; regulating the trade and managing all affairs with the Indians not members of any of the states; provided that the legislative right of any State within its own limits be not infringed or violated; establishing and regulating post offices from one State to another throughout all the United States, and exacting such postage on the papers passing through the same as may be requisite to defray the expences of the said office; appointing all officers of the land forces in the service of the United States, excepting regimental officers; appointing all the officers of the naval forces, and commissioning all officers whatever in the service of the United States; making rules for the government and regulation of the said land and naval forces, and directing their operations.

The United States, in Congress assembled, shall have authority to appoint a committee to sit in the recess of Congress, to be denominated "a Committee of the States," and to consist of one delegate from each State, and to appoint such other committees and civil officers as may be necessary for managing the general affairs of the United States, under their direction; to appoint one of their number to preside; provided that no person be allowed to serve in the office of president more than one year in any term of three years; to ascertain the necessary sums of money to be raised for the service of the United States, and to appropriate and apply the same for defraying the public expenses; to borrow money or emit bills on the credit of the United States, transmitting, every half year, to the respective states, an account of the sums of money so borrowed or emitted; to build and equip a navy; to agree upon the number of land forces, and to make requisitions from each State for its quota, in proportion to the number of white inhabitants in such State; which requisitions shall be binding; and, thereupon, the legislature of each State shall appoint the regimental officers, raise the men, and cloathe, arm, and equip them in a soldier-like manner, at the expense of the United States; and the officers and men so cloathed, armed, and equipped, shall march to the place appointed and within the time agreed on by the United States, in Congress assembled; but if the United States, in Congress assembled, shall, on consideration of circumstances, judge proper that any State should not raise men, or should raise a smaller number than its quota, and that any other State should raise a greater number of men than the quota thereof, such extra number shall be raised, officered, cloathed, armed, and equipped in the same manner as the quota of such State, unless the legislature of such State shall judge that such extra number cannot be safely spared out of the same, in which case they shall raise, officer, cloathe, arm, and equip as many of such extra number as they judge can be safely spared. And the officers and men so cloathed, armed, and equipped, shall march to the place appointed and within the time agreed on by the United States, in Congress assembled.

The United States, in Congress assembled, shall never engage in a war, nor grant letters of marque and reprisal in time of peace, nor enter into any treaties or alliances, nor coin money, nor regulate the value thereof, nor ascertain the sums and expenses necessary for the defence and welfare of the United States, or any of them: nor emit bills, nor borrow money on the credit of the United States, nor appropriate money, nor agree upon the number of vessels of war to be built or purchased, or the number of land or sea forces to be raised, nor appoint a commander in chief of the army or navy, unless nine states assent to the same; nor shall a question on any other point, except for adjourning from day to day, be determined, unless by the votes of a majority of the United States, in Congress assembled.

The Congress of the United States shall have power to adjourn to any time within the year, and to any place within the United States, so that no period of adjournment be for a longer duration than the space of six months, and shall publish the journal of their proceedings monthly, except such parts thereof, relating to treaties, alliances or military operations, as, in their judgment, require secrecy; and the yeas and nays of the delegates of each State on any question shall be entered on the journal, when it is desired by any delegate; and the delegates of a State, or any of them, at his, or their request, shall be furnished with a transcript of the said journal, except such parts as are above excepted, to lay before the legislatures of the several states.

Article 10

The committee of the states, or any nine of them, shall be authorized to execute, in the recess of Congress, such of the powers of Congress as the United States, in Congress assembled, by the consent of nine states, shall, from time to time, think expedient to vest them with; provided, that no power be delegated to the said committee, for the exercise of which, by the articles of confederation, the voice of nine states, in the Congress of the United States assembled, is requisite.

Article 11

Canada acceding to this confederation, and joining in the measures of the United States, shall be admitted into and entitled to all the advantages of this union; but no other colony shall be admitted into the same, unless such admission be agreed to by nine states.

Article 12

All bills of credit emitted, monies borrowed and debts contracted by, or under the authority of Congress before the assembling of the United States, in pursuance of the present confederation, shall be deemed and considered as a charge against the United States, for payment and satisfaction whereof the said United States and the public faith are hereby solemnly pledged.

Article 13

Every State shall abide by the determinations of the United States, in Congress assembled, on all questions which, by this confederation, are submitted to them. And the articles of this confederation shall be inviolably observed by every State, and the union shall be perpetual; nor shall any alteration at any time hereafter be made in any of them, unless such alteration be agreed to in a Congress of the United States, and be afterwards confirmed by the legislatures of every State.

These articles shall be proposed to the legislatures of all the United States, to be considered, and if approved of by them, they are advised to authorize their delegates to ratify the same in the Congress of the United States; which being done, the same shall become conclusive.

European Influences on American Views of Executive Power

John Locke

Although political theory played a far less important role than practical experience in the formulation of the powers of the Executive at the Constitutional Convention, most of the delegates had learned a good deal from John Locke and Montesquieu which they did not fail to utilize. In fact, Locke's influence can be traced back to much earlier battles for popular sovereignty and legislative power during the colonial period, and to efforts to determine the relationship of the executive to the legislature in the early state constitutions. Locke maintained that the legislature was the senior partner in this relationship, and he insisted that the executive and federative power remain part of and responsible to the legislature. This is, in fact, the essence of parliamentary government and while our Constitution provides for something very different, much that Locke had to say about the actual powers vested in an Executive was obviously reflected in the Convention discussions and the charter they produced.

Locke argued that when the legislature is in session, its power is supreme, limited only by the sovereign people who can reject it or overthrow it when its actions are thoroughly destructive to their interests. The Executive assumes real power when the legislature is not in session in order for the laws to "have a constant and lasting force." There must be an existing power to "see to the execution of the laws that are made, and remain in force; and thus the legislature and the executive power come often to be separated."[19] The Lockian Executive is given the power of "assembling and dismissing" the legislature, but he pointed out that this does not raise the executive power above the legislative because this power is a "fiduciary trust," and along with other responsibilities, is to be held accountable to the legislature and ultimately to the people.

Two other aspects of Locke's treatment of the executive power are important and should be emphasized. He introduced the term federative power to cover the whole range of actions involved in the relations of the State with other countries, and although he carefully distinguished federative from executive responsibilities, he pointed out that they are "hardly to be separated and placed at the same time in the hands of distinct persons. . . . For both . . . require the force of the society for their exercise. . . ."[20] Locke also asserted the necessity of granting the Executive the "power to act according to discretion for the public good, without the prescription of the law, and sometimes even against it. . . ."[21] This is what he means by the term "prerogative." It is, of course, not an absolute power, unlimited by law, nor even an open invitation to defy the law. Its justification is based upon the need to act in defense of the public interest when laws are not on hand to ordain such action, or when existing laws, drawn up in an earlier period under different circumstances actually impede such action. There is no formal or legal limitation placed upon this power, but again, it is held in check by the ultimate veto power of public opinion. As Locke put it:

> But if there comes to be a question between the executive power and the people about a thing claimed as a prerogative, the tendency of the exercise of such prerogative to the good or hurt of the people will easily decide that question.[22]

The Constitution only suggests the vast reservoir of power inherent in the President's responsibilities in the area of foreign relations and with respect to executive prerogative; the history of this great office has seen this power develop to extraordinary levels. It would be foolish to trace such growth to the writings of John Locke, for in truth these developments came about essentially because men of strength and character in the presidential office were able to respond to the challenges with which history confronted them. Political theory had very little to do with this dynamic process. However, it is significant that this influential British philosopher, so widely read in America, possessed such rare insight into the nature of executive power that he could perceive some of the developments which were to evolve in the growth of the American presidency over the next 284 years. His writings had great initial influence upon all of the early political thought in this country, and his analysis helped delineate the fundamental principles upon which its political institutions were built.

John Locke
On the Executive
1690

John Locke, "Concerning Civil Government, Second Essay," in *Great Books of the Western World* (Chicago, 1952) XXXV, 58-64.

CHAP. XII. THE LEGISLATIVE, EXECUTIVE, AND FEDERATIVE POWER OF THE COMMONWEALTH

144. But because the laws that are at once, and in a short time made, have a constant and lasting force, and need a perpetual execution, or an attendance thereunto, therefore it is necessary there should be a power always in being which should see to the execution of the laws that are made, and remain in force. And thus the legislative and executive power come often to be separated.

145. There is another power in every commonwealth which one may call natural, because it is that which answers to the power every man naturally had before he entered into society. For though in a commonwealth the members of it are distinct persons, still, in reference to one another, and, as such, are governed by the laws of the society, yet, in reference to the rest of mankind, they make one body, which is, as every member of it before was, still in the state of Nature with the rest of mankind, so that the controversies that happen between any man of the society with those that are out of it are managed by the public, and an injury done to a member of their body engages the whole in the reparation of it. So that under this consideration the whole community is one body in the state of Nature in respect of all other states or persons out of its community.

146. This, therefore, contains the power of war and peace, leagues and alliances, and all the transactions with all persons and communities without the commonwealth, and may be called federative if any one pleases. So the thing be understood, I am indifferent as to the name.

147. These two powers, executive and federative, though they be really distinct in themselves, yet one comprehending the execution of the municipal laws of the society within itself upon all that are parts of it, the other the management of the security and interest of the public without with all those that it may receive benefit or damage from, yet they are always almost united. And though this federative power in the well or ill management of it be of great moment to the commonwealth, yet it is much less capable to be directed by antecedent, standing,

positive laws than the executive, and so must necessarily be left to the prudence and wisdom of those whose hands it is in, to be managed for the public good. For the laws that concern subjects one amongst another, being to direct their actions, may well enough precede them. But what is to be done in reference to foreigners depending much upon their actions, and the variation of designs and interests, must be left in great part to the prudence of those who have this power committed to them, to be managed by the best of their skill for the advantage of the commonwealth.

148. Though, as I said, the executive and federative power of every community be really distinct in themselves, yet they are hardly to be separated and placed at the same time in the hands of distinct persons. For both of them requiring the force of the society for their exercise, it is almost impracticable to place the force of the commonwealth in distinct and not subordinate hands, or that the executive and federative power should be placed in persons that might act separately, whereby the force of the public would be under different commands, which would be apt some time or other to cause disorder and ruin.

CHAP. XIII. OF THE SUBORDINATION OF THE POWERS OF THE COMMONWEALTH

149. Though in a constituted commonwealth standing upon its own basis and acting according to its own nature—that is, acting for the preservation of the community, there can be but one supreme power, which is the legislative, to which all the rest are and must be subordinate, yet the legislative being only a fiduciary power to act for certain ends, there remains still in the people a supreme power to remove or alter the legislative, when they find the legislative act contrary to the trust reposed in them. For all power given with trust for the attaining an end being limited by that end, whenever that end is manifestly neglected or opposed, the trust must necessarily be forefeited, and the power devolve into the hands of those that gave it, who may place it anew where they shall think best for their safety and security. And thus the community perpetually retains a supreme power of saving themselves from the attempts and designs of anybody, even of their legislators, whenever they shall be so foolish or so wicked as to lay and carry on designs against the liberties and properties of the subject. For no man or society of men having a power to deliver up their preservation, or consequently the means of it, to the absolute will and arbitrary dominion of another, whenever any one shall go about to bring them into such a slavish condition, they will always have a right to preserve what they have not a power to part with, and to rid themselves of those who invade this fundamental, sacred, and unalterable law of self-preservation for which they entered into society. And thus the community may be said in this respect to be always the supreme power, but not as considered under any form of government, because this power of the people can never take place till the government be dissolved.

150. In all cases whilst the government subsists, the legislative is the supreme

power. For what can give laws to another must needs be superior to him, and since the legislative is no otherwise legislative of the society but by the right it has to make laws for all the parts, and every member of the society prescribing rules to their actions, and giving power of execution where they are transgressed, the legislative must needs be the supreme, and all other powers in any members or parts of the society derived from and subordinate to it.

151. In some commonwealths where the legislative is not always in being, and the executive is vested in a single person who has also a share in the legislative, there that single person, in a very tolerable sense, may also be called supreme; not that he has in himself all the supreme power, which is that of law-making, but because he has in him the supreme execution from whom all inferior magistrates derive all their several subordinate powers, or, at least, the greatest part of them; having also no legislative superior to him, there being no law to be made without his consent, which cannot be expected should ever subject him to the other part of the legislative, he is properly enough in this sense supreme. But yet it is to be observed that though oaths of allegiance and fealty are taken to him, it is not to him as supreme legislator, but as supreme executor of the law made by a joint power of him with others, allegiance being nothing but an obedience according to law, which, when he violates, he has no right to obedience, nor can claim it otherwise than as the public person vested with the power of the law, and so is to be considered as the image, phantom, or representative of the commonwealth, acted by the will of the society declared in its laws, and thus he has no will, no power, but that of the law. But when he quits this representation, this public will, and acts by his own private will, he degrades himself, and is but a single private person without power and without will; the members owing no obedience but to the public will of the society.

152. The executive power placed anywhere but in a person that has also a share in the legislative is visibly subordinate and accountable to it, and may be at pleasure changed and displaced; so that it is not the supreme executive power that is exempt from subordination, but the supreme executive power vested in one, who having a share in the legislative, has no distinct superior legislative to be subordinate and accountable to, farther than he himself shall join and consent, so that he is no more subordinate than he himself shall think fit, which one may certainly conclude will be but very little. Of other ministerial and subordinate powers in a commonwealth we need not speak, they being so multiplied with infinite variety in the different customs and constitutions of distinct commonwealths, that it is impossible to give a particular account of them all. Only thus much which is necessary to our present purpose we may take notice of concerning them, that they have no manner of authority, any of them, beyond what is by positive grant and commission delegated to them, and are all of them accountable to some other power in the commonwealth.

153. It is not necessary—no, nor so much as convenient—that the legislative should be always in being; but absolutely necessary that the executive power should, because there is not always need of new laws to be made, but always need of execution of the laws that are made. When the legislative hath put the execution of the laws they make into other hands, they have a power still to resume it out of those hands when they find cause, and to punish for any mal-administration against the

laws. The same holds also in regard of the federative power, that and the executive being both ministerial and subordinate to the legislative, which, as has been shown, in a constituted commonwealth is the supreme, the legislative also in this case being supposed to consist of several persons; for if it be a single person it cannot but be always in being, and so will, as supreme, naturally have the supreme executive power, together with the legislative, may assemble and exercise their legislative at the times that either their original constitution or their own adjournment appoints, or when they please, if neither of these hath appointed any time, or there be no other way prescribed to convoke them. For the supreme power being placed in them by the people, it is always in them, and they may exercise it when they please, unless by their original constitution they are limited to certain seasons, or by an act of their supreme power they have adjourned to a certain time, and when that time comes they have a right to assemble and act again.

154. If the legislative, or any part of it, be of representatives, chosen for that time by the people, which afterwards return into the ordinary state of subjects, and have no share in the legislative but upon a new choice, this power of choosing must also be exercised by the people, either at certain appointed seasons, or else when they are summoned to it; and, in this latter case, the power of convoking the legislative is ordinarily placed in the executive, and has one of these two limitations in respect of time:—that either the original constitution requires their assembling and acting at certain intervals; and then the executive power does nothing but ministerially issue directions for their electing and assembling according to due forms; or else it is left to his prudence to call them by new elections when the occasions or exigencies of the public require the amendment of old or making of new laws, or the redress or prevention of any inconveniencies that lie on or threaten the people.

155. It may be demanded here, what if the executive power, being possessed of the force of the commonwealth, shall make use of that force to hinder the meeting and acting of the legislative, when the original constitution or the public exigencies require it? I say, using force upon the people, without authority, and contrary to the trust put in him that does so, is a state of war with the people, who have a right to reinstate their legislative in the exercise of their power. For having erected a legislative with an intent they should exercise the power of making laws, either at certain set times, or when there is need of it, when they are hindered by any force from what is so necessary to the society, and wherein the safety and preservation of the people consists, the people have a right to remove it by force. In all states and conditions the true remedy of force without authority is to oppose force to it. The use of force without authority always puts him that uses it into a state of war as the aggressor, and renders him liable to be treated accordingly.

156. The power of assembling and dismissing the legislative, placed in the executive, gives not the executive a superiority over it, but is a fiduciary trust placed in him for the safety of the people in a case where the uncertainty and variableness of human affairs could not bear a steady fixed rule. For it not being possible that the first framers of the government should by any foresight be so much masters of future events as to be able to prefix so just periods of return and duration to the assemblies of the legislative, in all times to come, that might exactly answer all the

exigencies of the commonwealth, the best remedy could be found for this defect was to trust this to the prudence of one who was always to be present, and whose business it was to watch over the public good. Constant, frequent meetings of the legislative, and long continuations of their assemblies, without necessary occasion, could not but be burdensome to the people, and must necessarily in time produce more dangerous inconveniencies, and yet the quick turn of affairs might be sometimes such as to need their present help; any delay of their convening might endanger the public; and sometimes, too, their business might be so great that the limited time of their sitting might be too short for their work, and rob the public of that benefit which could be had only from their mature deliberation. What, then, could be done in this case to prevent the community from being exposed some time or other to imminent hazard on one side or the other, by fixed intervals and periods set to the meeting and acting of the legislative, but to entrust it to the prudence of some who, being present and acquainted with the state of public affairs, might make use of this prerogative for the public good? And where else could this be so well placed as in his hands who was entrusted with the execution of the laws for the same end? Thus, supposing the regulation of times for the assembling and sitting of the legislative not settled by the original constitution, it naturally fell into the hands of the executive; not as an arbitrary power depending on his good pleasure, but with this trust always to have it exercised only for the public weal, as the occurrences of times and change of affairs might require. Whether settled periods of their convening, or a liberty left to the prince for convoking the legislative, or perhaps a mixture of both, hath the least inconvenience attending it, it is not my business here to inquire, but only to show that, though the executive power may have the prerogative of convoking and dissolving such conventions of the legislative, yet it is not thereby superior to it.

157. Things of this world are in so constant a flux that nothing remains long in the same state. Thus people, riches, trade, power, change their stations; flourishing mighty cities come to ruin, and prove in time neglected desolate corners, whilst other unfrequented places grow into populous countries filled with wealth and inhabitants. But things not always changing equally, and private interest often keeping up customs and privileges when the reasons of them are ceased, it often comes to pass that in governments where part of the legislative consists of representatives chosen by the people, that in tract of time this representation becomes very unequal and disproportionate to the reasons it was at first established upon. To what gross absurdities the following of custom when reason has left it may lead, we may be satisfied when we see the bare name of a town, of which there remains not so much as the ruins, where scarce so much housing as a sheepcote, or more inhabitants than a shepherd is to be found, send as many representatives to the grand assembly of law-makers as a whole country numerous in people and powerful in riches. This strangers stand amazed at, and every one must confess needs a remedy; though most think it hard to find one, because the constitution of the legislative being the original and supreme act of the society, antecedent to all positive laws in it, and depending wholly on the people, no inferior power can alter it. And, therefore, the people when the legislative is once constituted, having in such a government as we have been speaking of no power to act as long as the government stands, this inconvenience is thought incapable of a remedy.

158. *Salus populi suprema lex* is certainly so just and fundamental a rule, that he who sincerely follows it cannot dangerously err. If, therefore, the executive who has the power of convoking the legislative, observing rather the true proportion than fashion of representation, regulates not by old custom, but true reason, the number of members in all places, that have a right to be distinctly represented, which no part of the people, however incorporated, can pretend to, but in proportion to the assistance which it affords to the public, it cannot be judged to have set up a new legislative, but to have restored the old and true one, and to have rectified the disorders which succession of time had insensibly as well as inevitably introduced; for it being the interest as well as intention of the people to have a fair and equal representative, whoever brings it nearest to that is an undoubted friend to and establisher of the government, and cannot miss the consent and approbation of the community; prerogative being nothing but a power in the hands of the prince to provide for the public good in such cases which, depending upon unforeseen and uncertain occurrences, certain and unalterable laws could not safely direct. Whatsoever shall be done manifestly for the good of the people, and establishing the government upon its true foundations is, and always will be, just prerogative. The power of erecting new corporations, and therewith new representatives, carries with it a supposition that in time the measures of representation might vary, and those have a just right to be represented which before had none; and by the same reason, those cease to have a right, and be too inconsiderable for such a privilege, which before had it. It is not a change from the present state which, perhaps, corruption or decay has introduced, that makes an inroad upon the government, but the tendency of it to injure or oppress the people, and to set up one part or party with a distinction from an unequal subjection of the rest. Whatsoever cannot but be acknowledged to be of advantage to the society and people in general, upon just and lasting measures, will always, when done, justify itself; and whenever the people shall choose their representatives upon just and undeniably equal measures, suitable to the original frame of the government, it cannot be doubted to be the will and act of the society, whoever permitted or proposed to them so to do.

CHAP. XIV. OF PREROGATIVE

159. Where the legislative and executive power are in distinct hands, as they are in all moderated monarchies and well-framed governments, there the good of the society requires that several things should be left to the discretion of him that has the executive power. For the legislators not being able to foresee and provide by laws for all that may be useful to the community, the executor of the laws, having the power in his hands, has by the common law of Nature a right to make use of it for the good of the society, in many cases where the municipal law has given no direction, till the legislative can conveniently be assembled to provide for it; nay, many things there are which the law can by no means provide for, and those must necessarily be left to the discretion of him that has the executive power in his hands, to be ordered by him as the public good and advantage shall require; nay, it is fit that

the laws themselves should in some cases give way to the executive power, or rather to this fundamental law of Nature and government—vis., that as much as may be all the members of the society are to be preserved. For since many accidents may happen wherein a strict and rigid observation of the laws may do harm, as not to pull down an innocent man's house to stop the fire when the next to it is burning; and a man may come sometimes within the reach of the law, which makes no distinction of persons, by an action that may deserve reward and pardon; it is fit the ruler should have a power in many cases to mitigate the severity of the law, and pardon some offenders, since the end of government being the preservation of all as much as may be, even the guilty are to be spared where it can prove no prejudice to the innocent.

160. This power to act according to discretion for the public good, without the prescription of the law and sometimes even against it, is that which is called prerogative; for since in some governments the law-making power is not always in being and is usually too numerous, and so too slow for the dispatch requisite to execution, and because, also, it is impossible to foresee and so by laws to provide for all accidents and necessities that may concern the public, or make such laws as will do no harm, if they are executed with an inflexible rigour on all occasions and upon all persons that may come in their way, therefore there is a latitude left to the executive power to do many things of choice which the laws do not prescribe.

161. This power, whilst employed for the benefit of the community and suitably to the trust and ends of the government, is undoubted prerogative, and never is questioned. For the people are very seldom or never scrupulous or nice in the point of questioning of prerogative whilst it is in any tolerable degree employed for the use it was meant—that is, the good of the people, and not manifestly against it. But if there comes to be a question between the executive power and the people about a thing claimed as a prerogative, the tendency of the exercise of such prerogative, to the good or hurt of the people, will easily decide that question.

162. It is easy to conceive that in the infancy of governments, when commonwealths differed little from families in number of people, they differed from them too but little in number of laws; and the governors being as the fathers of them, watching over them for their good, the government was almost all prerogative. A few established laws served the turn, and the discretion and care of the ruler supplied the rest. But when mistake or flattery prevailed with weak princes, to make use of this power for private ends of their own and not for the public good, the people were fain, by express laws, to get prerogative determined in those points wherein they found disadvantage from it, and declared limitations of prerogative in those cases which they and their ancestors had left in the utmost latitude to the wisdom of those princes who made no other but a right use of it—that is, for the good of their people.

163. And therefore they have a very wrong notion of government who say that the people have encroached upon the prerogative when they have got any part of it to be defined by positive laws. For in so doing they have not pulled from the prince anything that of right belonged to him, but only declared that that power which they indefinitely left in his or his ancestors' hands, to be exercised for their good, was not

a thing they intended him, when he used it otherwise. For the end of government being the good of the community, whatsoever alterations are made in it tending to that end cannot be an encroachment upon anybody; since nobody in government can have a right tending to any other end; and those only are encroachments which prejudice or hinder the public good. Those who say otherwise speak as if the prince had a distinct and separate interest from the good of the community, and was not made for it; the root and source from which spring almost all those evils and disorders which happen in kingly governments. And, indeed, if that be so, the people under his government are not a society of rational creatures, entered into a community for their mutual good, such as have set rulers over themselves, to guard and promote that good; but are to be looked on as a herd of inferior creatures under the dominion of a master, who keeps them and works them for his own pleasure or profit. If men were so void of reason and brutish as to enter into society upon such terms, prerogative might indeed be, what some men would have it, an arbitrary power to do things hurtful to the people.

164. But since a rational creature cannot be supposed, when free, to put himself into subjection to another for his own harm (though where he finds a good and a wise ruler he may not, perhaps, think it either necessary or useful to set precise bounds to his power in all things), prerogative can be nothing but the people's permitting their rulers to do several things of their own free choice where the law was silent, and sometimes too against the direct letter of the law, for the public good and their acquiescing in it when so done. For as a good prince, who is mindful of the trust put into his hands and careful of the good of his people, cannot have too much prerogative—that is, power to do good, so a weak and ill prince, who would claim that power his predecessors exercised, without the direction of the law, as a prerogative belonging to him by right of his office, which he may exercise at his pleasure to make or promote an interest distinct from that of the public, gives the people an occasion to claim their right and limit that power, which, whilst it was exercised for their good, they were content should be tacitly allowed.

165. And therefore he that will look into the history of England will find that prerogative was always largest in the hands of our wisest and best princes, because the people observing the whole tendency of their actions to be the public good, or if any human frailty or mistake (for princes are but men, made as others) appeared in some small declinations from that end, yet it was visible the main of their conduct tended to nothing but the care of the public. The people, therefore, finding reason to be satisfied with these princes, whenever they acted without, or contrary to the letter of the law, acquiesced in what they did, and without the least complaint, let them enlarge their prerogative as they pleased, judging rightly that they did nothing herein to the prejudice of their laws, since they acted conformably to the foundation and end of all laws—the public good.

166. Such God-like princes, indeed, had some title to arbitrary power by that argument that would prove absolute monarchy the best government, as that which God Himself governs the universe by, because such kings partake of His wisdom and goodness. Upon this is founded that saying, "That the reigns of good princes have been always most dangerous to the liberties of their people." For when their

successors, managing the government with different thoughts would draw the actions of those good rulers into precedent and make them the standard of their prerogative—as if what had been done only for the good of the people was a right in them to do for the harm of the people, if they so pleased—it has often occasioned contest, and sometimes public disorders, before the people could recover their original right and get that to be declared not to be prerogative which truly was never so; since it is impossible anybody in the society should ever have a right to do the people harm, though it be very possible and reasonable that the people should not go about to set any bounds to the prerogative of those kings or rulers who themselves transgressed not the bounds of the public good. For "prerogative is nothing but the power of doing public good without a rule."

167. The power of calling parliaments in England, as to precise time, place, and duration, is certainly a prerogative of the king, but still with this trust, that it shall be made use of for the good of the nation as the exigencies of the times and variety of occasion shall require. For it being impossible to foresee which should always be the fittest place for them to assemble in, and what the best season, the choice of these was left with the executive power, as might be best subservient to the public good and best suit the ends of parliament.

168. The old question will be asked in this matter of prerogative, "But who shall be judge when this power is made a right use of?" I answer: Between an executive power in being, with such a prerogative, and a legislative that depends upon his will for their convening, there can be no judge on earth. As there can be none between the legislative and the people, should either the executive or the legislative, when they have got the power in their hands, design, or go about to enslave or destroy them, the people have no other remedy in this, as in all other cases where they have no judge on earth, but to appeal to Heaven; for the rulers in such attempts, exercising a power the people never put into their hands, who can never be supposed to consent that anybody should rule over them for their harm, do that which they have not a right to do. And where the body of the people, or any single man, are deprived of their right, or are under the exercise of a power without right, having no appeal on earth they have a liberty to appeal to Heaven whenever they judge the cause of sufficient moment. And therefore, though the people cannot be judge, so as to have, by the constitution of that society, any superior power to determine and give effective sentence in the case, yet they have reserved that ultimate determination to themselves which belongs to all mankind, where there lies no appeal on earth, by a law antecedent and paramount to all positive laws of men, whether they have just cause to make their appeal to Heaven. And this judgment they cannot part with, it being out of a man's power so to submit himself to another as to give him a liberty to destroy him; God and Nature never allowing a man so to abandon himself as to neglect his own preservation. And since he cannot take away his own life, neither can he give another power to take it. Nor let any one think this lays a perpetual foundation for disorder; for this operates not till the inconvenience is so great that the majority feel it, and are weary of it, and find a necessity to have it amended. And this the executive power, or wise princes, never need come in the danger of; and it is the thing of all others they have most need to avoid, as, of all others, the most perilous.

Baron de Montesquieu

Another influential political theorist whose ideas permeated the Philadelphia Convention was Charles de Secondat, Baron de Montesquieu. His book, *L'Espirit des Lois*, in French and in translation, was available to America before 1787, and there is considerable evidence that the leading figures at the Constitutional Convention had read it and were won over to its central doctrine. Montesquieu spent several years in England during the early part of the eighteenth century, and he became a great admirer of the British constitution and British parliamentary institutions. He was convinced that here was the soundest model for a political community which wanted to preserve its liberties. He believed that in the British constitutional system power was fairly evenly distributed among the King, the House of Commons and the House of Lords. Only by separating the various branches of government and giving them sufficient power to protect their independence could liberty be guaranteed:

> When the legislative and executive powers are united in the same person, or in the same body of magistrates, there can be no liberty; because apprehensions may arise, lest the same monarch or senate should enact tyrannical laws, to enact them in a tyrannical manner.[23]

James Madison used *L'Esprit des Lois* as a textbook at Princeton, where it provided the background for a series of lectures by the university president, Dr. John Witherspoon. Nine of the Constitutional Convention delegates were Princeton graduates, six had diplomas signed by Dr. Witherspoon. One writer has argued that the Witherspoon lectures inspired Madison to devote himself to public affairs. The knowledge of the "Father of the Constitution" of Montesquieu's work was so thorough that 20 years later he could quote from it by memory. When he was preparing materials for General Washington to study before embarking for the Convention, he relied heavily on Montesquieu. References to *L'Esprit des Lois* are also contained in his handwriting in his own notes, and he made use of them on the floor of the Convention. James Wilson was also familiar with the book, as was Hamilton, and they made references to Montesquieu or his theories when they spoke at the sessions.

The concept of the separation of powers which Montesquieu developed in *L'Esprit des Lois* found consensus in the expressed opinions of the delegates to the Convention, and finally in their handiwork, the Constitution itself. There was perhaps no other single idea which received such general approval. Some of the delegates, like Franklin, had long since perceived that significant changes had been generated in the British system which seriously damaged Montesquieu's theory, and that frequent and large scale corruption had made the principle honored more in the breach than in the practice. But these Americans were instinctive pragmatists who were quite willing to modify a theory in practice without feeling that they had abandoned it in principle. Madison demonstrated this in Federalist No. 47, where he argued that the Constitution is quite consistent with Montesquieu's popular maxim. The truth is that neither the American nor the British Executive was "separated" in theory or function from the other branches. The office of Prime

Minister had been emerging during the previous 50 years as the real Executive in the British system, responsible to, and in fact, elected by Parliament. He did possess a degree of independence which would help him to defend his position against encroachment, but he was anything but independent in the formal sense. All this was not yet cut and dried, and George III fought to retain many of his prerogatives and privileges; but, the real locus of power had shifted by the time the American Constitution was written, and with it the former "separateness" and independence of the King.

There is very little in the Second Article of the American Constitution that can be justifiably traced back to the singular influence of either Locke or Montesquieu. Both men endorsed what they thought were already existing provisions of the British constitution, such as the prerogative of the King to prorogue or dismiss Parliament, to veto bills, to serve as head of the army and navy and to be responsible for the conduct of foreign affairs. What is significant and distinctive about their contributions is that they attempted to present reasonable arguments as to why the King should possess such powers, and not simply to intone scripture based on authority, and these arguments were obviously influential with some of the delegates. In short, they hardly introduced new or revolutionary doctrines, but they tended to reinforce existing opinion, and to persuade others of its validity.

Americans did not, in the final analysis, want to duplicate the political system of their mother country, nor were they anxious to create institutions modeled after the British monarchy or the two houses of Parliament. Moreover, they were not about to accept any arguments based upon authority. But they did recognize many valuable aspects of this brilliant political system, and both Locke's and Montesquieu's analytical arguments were extremely helpful in this process, even if the French aristocrat's observations were somewhat obsolete before they were in print. [Editor's Note: See the interesting comments on Montesquieu's failure to comprehend the functional operations of the British system and the ambiguities involved in his influence upon the framers of the American Constitution, in Louis Fisher, *President and Congress: Power and Policy* (New York, 1972), 3-6; 244-51. Also note the excellent bibliography on the subject.]

Baron de Montesquieu
On Executive Powers
1748

Montesquieu, *The Spirit of the Laws*, in *Great Books of the Western World*, XXXVIII, 69-75.

6. Of the Constitution of England

In every government there are three sorts of power: the legislative; the executive in respect to things dependent on the law of nations; and the executive in regard to matters that depend on the civil law.

By virtue of the first, the prince or magistrate enacts temporary or perpetual laws, and amends or abrogates those that have been already enacted. By the second, he makes peace or war, sends or receives embassies, establishes the public security, and provides against invasions. By the third, he punishes criminals, or determines the disputes that arise between individuals. The latter we shall call the judiciary power, and the other simply the executive power of the state.

The political liberty of the subject is a tranquillity of mind arising from the opinion each person has of his safety. In order to have this liberty, it is requisite the government be so constituted as one man need not be afraid of another.

When the legislative and executive powers are united in the same person, or in the same body of magistrates, there can be no liberty; because apprehensions may arise, lest the same monarch or senate should enact tyrannical laws, to execute them in a tyrannical manner.

Again, there is no liberty, if the judiciary power be not separated from the legislative and executive. Were it joined with the legislative, the life and liberty of the subject would be exposed to arbitrary control; for the judge would be then the legislator. Were it joined to the executive power, the judge might behave with violence and oppression.

There would be an end of everything, were the same man or the same body, whether of the nobles or of the people, to exercise those three powers, that of enacting laws, that of executing the public resolutions, and of trying the causes of individuals.

Most kingdoms in Europe enjoy a moderate government because the prince who is invested with the two first powers leaves the third to his subjects. In Turkey, where these three powers are united in the Sultan's person, the subjects groan under the most dreadful oppression.

In the republics of Italy, where these three powers are united, there is less liberty than in our monarchies. Hence their government is obliged to have recourse to as violent methods for its support as even that of the Turks; witness the state inquisitors, and the lion's mouth into which every informer may at all hours throw his written accusations.

In what a situation must the poor subject be in those republics! The same body of magistrates are possessed, as executors of the laws, of the whole power they have given themselves in quality of legislators. They may plunder the state by their general determinations; and as they have likewise the judiciary power in their hands, every private citizen may be ruined by their particular decisions.

The whole power is here united in one body; and though there is no external pomp that indicates a despotic sway, yet the people feel the effects of it every moment.

Hence it is that many of the princes of Europe, whose aim has been levelled at arbitrary power, have constantly set out with uniting in their own persons all the branches of magistracy, and all the great offices of state.

I allow indeed that the mere hereditary aristocracy of the Italian republics does not exactly answer to the despotic power of the Eastern princes. The number of magistrates sometimes moderates the power of the magistracy; the whole body of the nobles do not always concur in the same design; and different tribunals are erected, that temper each other. Thus at Venice the legislative power is in the *council*, the executive in the *pregadi*, and the judiciary in the *quarantia*. But the mischief is, that these different tribunals are composed of magistrates all belonging to the same body; which constitutes almost one and the same power.

If the legislature leaves the executive power in possession of a right to imprison those subject who can give security for their good behaviour, there is an end of liberty; unless they are taken up, in order to answer without delay to a capital crime, in which case they are really free, being subject only to the power of the law.

But should the legislature think itself in danger by some secret conspiracy against the state, or by a correspondence with a foreign enemy, it might authorise the executive power, for a short and limited time, to imprison suspected persons, who in that case would lose their liberty only for a while, to preserve it for ever.

The executive power ought to be in the hands of a monarch, because this branch of government, having need of despatch, is better administered by one than by many: on the other hand, whatever depends on the legislative power is oftentimes better regulated by many than by a single person.

But if there were no monarch, and the executive power should be committed to a certain number of persons selected from the legislative body, there would be an end then of liberty; by reason the two powers would be united, as the same persons would sometimes possess, and would be always able to possess, a share in both.

Were the legislative body to be a considerable time without meeting, this would likewise put an end to liberty. For of two things one would naturally follow: either that there would be no longer any legislative resolutions, and then the state would fall into anarchy; or that these resolutions would be taken by the executive power, which would render it absolute.

It would be needless for the legislative body to continue always assembled. This would be troublesome to the representatives, and, moreover, would cut out too much work for the executive power, so as to take off its attention to its office, and oblige it to think only of defending its own prerogatives, and the right it has to execute.

Again, were the legislative body to be always assembled, it might happen to be kept up only by filling the places of the deceased members with new representatives; and in that case, if the legislative body were once corrupted, the evil would be past all remedy. When different legislative bodies succeed one another, the people who have a bad opinion of that which is actually sitting may reasonably entertain some hopes of the next: but were it to be always the same body, the people upon seeing it once corrupted would no longer expect any good from its laws; and of course they would either become desperate or fall into a state of indolence.

The legislative body should not meet of itself. For a body is supposed to have no will but when it is met; and besides, were it not to meet unanimously, it would be impossible to determine which was really the legislative body; the part assembled, or the other. And if it had a right to prorogue itself, it might happen never to be prorogued; which would be extremely dangerous, in case it should ever attempt to encroach on the executive power. Besides, there are seasons, some more proper than others, for assembling the legislative body: it is fit, therefore, that the executive power should regulate the time of meeting, as well as the duration of those assemblies, according to the circumstances and exigencies of a state known to itself.

Were the executive power not to have a right of restraining the encroachments of the legislative body, the latter would become despotic; for as it might arrogate to itself what authority it pleased, it would soon destroy all the other powers.

But it is not proper, on the other hand, that the legislative power should have a right to stay the executive. For as the execution has its natural limits, it is useless to confine it; besides, the executive power is generally employed in momentary operations. The power, therefore, of the Roman tribunes was faulty, as it put a stop not only to the legislation, but likewise to the executive part of government; which was attended with infinite mischief.

But if the legislative power in a free state has no right to stay the executive, it has a right and ought to have the means of examining in what manner its laws have been executed; an advantage which this government has over that of Crete and Sparta, where the Cosmi and the Ephori gave no account of their administration.

But whatever may be the issue of that examination, the legislative body ought not to have a power of arraigning the person, nor, of course, the conduct, of him who is entrusted with the executive power. His person should be sacred, because as it is necessary for the good of the state to prevent the legislative body from rendering themselves arbitrary, the moment he is accused or tried there is an end of liberty.

In this case the state would be no longer a monarchy, but a kind of republic, though not a free government. But as the person entrusted with the executive power cannot abuse it without bad counsellors, and such as have the laws as ministers, though the laws protect them as subjects, these men may be examined and punished—an advantage which this government has over that of Gnidus, where the law allowed of no such thing as calling the Amymones to an account, even after their administration; and therefore the people could never obtain any satisfaction for the injuries done them.

It is possible that the law, which is clear-sighted in one sense, and blind in another, might, in some cases, be too severe. But as we have already observed, the national judges are no more than the mouth that pronounces the words of the law, mere passive beings, incapable of moderating either its force or rigour. That part, therefore, of the legislative body, which we have just now observed to be a necessary tribunal on another occasion, is also a necessary tribunal in this; it belongs to its supreme authority to moderate the law in favour of the law itself, by mitigating the sentence.

It might also happen that a subject entrusted with the administration of public affairs may infringe the rights of the people, and be guilty of crimes which the ordinary magistrates either could not or would not punish. But, in general, the legislative power cannot try causes: and much less can it try this particular case, where it represents the party aggrieved, which is the people. It can only, therefore, impeach. But before what court shall it bring its impeachment? Must it go and demean itself before the ordinary tribunals, which are its inferiors, and, being composed, moreover, of men who are chosen from the people as well as itself, will naturally be swayed by the authority of so powerful an accuser? No: in order to preserve the dignity of the people, and the security of the subject, the legislative part which represents the people must bring in its charge before the legislative part which represents the nobility, who have neither the same interests nor the same passions.

Here is an advantage which this government has over most of the ancient republics, where this abuse prevailed, that the people were at the same time both judge and accuser.

The executive power, pursuant of what has been already said, ought to have a share in the legislature by the power of rejecting, otherwise it would soon be stripped of its prerogative. But should the legislative power usurp a share of the executive, the latter would be equally undone.

If the prince were to have a part in the legislature by the power of resolving, liberty would be lost. But as it is necessary he should have a share in the legislature for the support of his own prerogative, this share must consist in the power of rejecting.

The change of government at Rome was owing to this, that neither the senate, who had one part of the executive power, nor the magistrates, who were entrusted with the other, had the right of rejecting, which was entirely lodged in the people.

Here then is the fundamental constitution of the government we are treating of. The legislative body being composed of two parts, they check one another by the mutual privilege of rejecting. They are both restrained by the executive power, as the executive is by the legislative.

These three powers should naturally form a state of repose or inaction. But as there is a necessity for movement in the course of human affairs, they are forced to move, but still in concert.

As the executive power has no other part in the legislative than the privilege of rejecting, it can have no share in the public debates. It is not even necessary that it should propose, because as it may always disapprove of the resolutions that shall be taken, it may likewise reject the decisions on those proposals which were made against its will.

In some ancient commonwealths, where public debates were carried on by the people in a body, it was natural for the executive power to propose and debate in conjunction with the people, otherwise their resolutions must have been attended with a strange confusion.

Were the executive power to determine the raising of public money, otherwise than by giving its consent, liberty would be at an end; because it would become legislative in the most important point of legislation.

If the legislative power was to settle the subsidies, not from year to year, but for ever, it would run the risk of losing its liberty, because the executive power would be no longer dependent; and when once it was possessed of such a perpetual right, it would be a matter of indifference whether it held it of itself or of another. The same may be said if it should come to a resolution of entrusting, not an annual, but a perpetual command of the fleets and armies to the executive power.

To prevent the executive power from being able to oppress, it is requisite that the armies with which it is entrusted should consist of the people, and have the same spirit as the people, as was the case at Rome till the time of Marius. To obtain this end, there are only two ways, either that the persons employed in the army should have sufficient property to answer for their conduct to their fellow subjects, and be enlisted only for a year, as was customary at Rome; or if there should be a standing army, composed chiefly of the most despicable part of the nation, the legislative power should have a right to disband them as soon as it pleased; the soldiers should live in common with the rest of the people; and no separate camp, barracks, or fortress should be suffered.

When once an army is established, it ought not to depend immediately on the legislative, but on the executive, power; and this from the very nature of the thing, its business consisting more in action than in deliberation.

It is natural for mankind to set a higher value upon courage than timidity, on activity than prudence, on strength than counsel. Hence the army will ever despise a senate, and respect their own officers. They will naturally slight the orders sent them by a body of men whom they look upon as cowards, and therefore unworthy to command them. So that as soon as the troops depend entirely on the legislative body, it becomes a military government; and if the contrary has ever happened, it has been owing to some extraordinary circumstances. It is because the army was always kept divided; it is because it was composed of several bodies that depended each on a particular province; it is because the capital towns were strong places, defended by their natural situation, and not garrisoned with regular troops. Holland, for instance, is still safer than Venice; she might drown or starve the revolted troops; for as they are not quartered in towns capable of furnishing them with necessary subsistence, this subsistence is of course precarious.

In perusing the admirable treatise of Tacitus *On the Manners of the Germans*, we find it is from that nation the English have borrowed the idea of their political government. This beautiful system was invented first in the woods.

As all human things have an end, the state we are speaking of will lose its liberty, will perish. Have not Rome, Sparta, and Carthage perished? It will perish when the legislative power shall be more corrupt than the executive.

It is not my business to examine whether the English actually enjoy this liberty or not. Sufficient it is for my purpose to observe that it is established by their laws; and I inquire no further.

Neither do I pretend by this to undervalue other governments, nor to say that this extreme political liberty ought to give uneasiness to those who have only a moderate share of it. How should I have any such design, I who think that even the highest refinement of reason is not always desirable, and that mankind generally find their account better in mediums than in extremes?

Harrington, in his *Oceana*, has also inquired into the utmost degree of liberty to which the constitution of a state may be carried. But of him indeed it may be said that for want of knowing the nature of real liberty he busied himself in pursuit of an imaginary one; and that he built a Chalcedon, though he had a Byzantium before his eyes.

Sir William Blackstone

Of undoubtedly greater influence than the writings of the political theorists in framing the full structure of executive power in the American Constitution was the work of Sir William Blackstone, whose justly famous *Commentaries on the Laws of England* was published for the first time on this continent in Philadelphia in 1771-72. These four volumes by Blackstone rapidly became the standard reference work on the British constitution and the common law, and for the overwhelming number of delegates to the Philadelphia Convention who were born in this country and who had not lived in England, it provided the most reliable and detailed source of information on the British political system. In his famous "Speech on Conciliation with the Colonies," Edmund Burke pointed out that he had heard "that they have sold nearly as many of Blackstone's *Commentaries* in America as in England."[24] There is little doubt that most of the delegates at Philadelphia were familiar with the book.[25] Furthermore, many of the delegates were lawyers, and the impressive legal language and style of the *Commentaries* were bound to command their interest and respect.

Blackstone's chapter entitled "Of the King's Prerogative" was the most informative discussion of executive power available in that period, and much of the language and many of the provisions that found their way into Article II of the American Constitution traced their source to this book. It should be noted, however, that Blackstone's description of British institutions was somewhat dated even when it was written.

Although the forms had not changed, and indeed never really would, the nature of the relationship among Crown, Ministers, and Parliament was in the process of evolution, and one does not capture the impact of these changes in Blackstone's text. The real power for Blackstone still resided in the Crown (as indeed it did with George III) and both his Ministers and Parliament were expendable. In reality Parliament was beginning to encroach upon that power, and the Prime Minister was becoming the center of decision-making in the political process. It was perhaps decisive, as Bagehot later pointed out, that in the development of the American Constitution much of this was not understood. Exactly what changes in the British system were taking place at that time were still somewhat obscure, even to close students of the political process not inside the "magic circle." The value of Blackstone was that he set down in rich detail the framework of law and custom from which both the British and American systems evolved. Well-informed and experienced delegates to the Constitutional Convention, like Benjamin Franklin and James Wilson, however, understood the instances when his descriptions of power relationships departed from reality, and they pointed them out to their colleagues.

Some of the language and substantive provisions which are found in the *Commentaries* can be recognized in our Constitution. Such phrases as "*ex post facto* law," "due process," etc., appear throughout the document, and there are a number of provisions in Article II which appear to be heavily influenced by Blackstone's chapter on the King's prerogatives. The *Commentaries* present a Monarch who possesses close to absolute power in the realm of foreign policy as well as Commander in Chief of the Armed Forces, and who has the theoretical right at least to veto a provision of the Parliament, and to dismiss and prorogue it. Despite the Founding Fathers' denunciation of the unchecked power of the King, and their undisguised contempt for most of the trappings of royalty, they were obviously greatly influenced by Blackstone's definition of executive powers, and gave their democratic monarch many of the same responsibilities. Blackstone's biographer writes that his influence was "far greater in the United States than in England. The *Commentaries* arrived in the colonies at the right psychological moment, they supplied a pressing need which could *not* be filled by other texts. . . ."[26]

Sir William Blackstone
On the Powers of t.·.·King
1771-72

(Sir) William Blackstone, *Commentaries on the Laws of England,* Thomas M. Cooley, ed. (Chicago, 1884), 147-76.

CHAPTER VI
OF THE KING'S DUTIES

I proceed next to the duties, incumbent on the king by our constitution; in consideration of which duties his dignity and prerogatives are established by the laws of the land: it being a maxim in the law, that protection and subjection are reciprocal. And those reciprocal duties are what, I apprehend, were meant by the convention in 1688, when they declared that King James had broken the *original contract* between king and people. But, however, as the terms of that original contract were in some measure disputed, being alleged to exist principally in theory, and to be only deducible by reason and the rules of natural law; in which deduction different understandings might very considerably differ: it was, after the revolution, judged proper to declare these duties expressly, and to reduce that contract to a plain certainty. So that, whatever doubts might be formerly raised by weak and scrupulous minds about the existence of such an original contract, they must now entirely cease; especially with regard to every prince who hath reigned since the year 1688.

The principal duty of the king is, to govern his people according to law. *Nec regibus infinita aut libera potestas*, was the constitution of our German ancestors on the continent. And this is not only consonant to the principles of nature, of liberty, of reason, and of society, but has always been esteemed an express part of the common law of England, even when prerogative was at the highest. "The king," saith Bracton, who wrote under Henry III, "ought not to be subject to man, but to God, and to the law; for the law maketh the king. Let the king therefore render to the law, what the law has invested in him with regard to others; dominion and power for he is not truly king, where will and pleasure rules, and not the law." And again, "the king also hath a superior, namely God, and also the law, by which he was made a king." Thus Bracton: and Fortescue also, having first well distinguished between a monarchy absolutely and despotically regal, which is introduced by conquest and violence, and a political or civil monarchy which arises from mutual consent, (of which last species he asserts the government of England to be;) immediately lays it down as a principle, that "the king of England must rule his people according to the decrees of the laws thereof: insomuch that he is bound by an oath at his coronation to the observance and keeping of his own laws." But, to obviate all doubts and difficulties concerning this matter, it is expressly declared by statute 12 and 13 W.III,c.2, "that the laws of England are the birthright of the people thereof: and all the kings and queens who shall ascend the throne of this realm ought to administer the government of the same according to the said laws; and all their officers and ministers ought to serve them respectively according to the same: and therefore all the laws and statutes of this realm, for securing the established religion, and the rights and liberties of the people thereof, and all other laws and statutes of the same now in force, are ratified and confirmed accordingly."

And, as to the terms of the original contract between king and people, these I apprehend to be now couched in the coronation oath, which by the statute 1 W. and M. st. 1, c. 6, is to be administered to every king and queen, who shall succeed to the imperial crown of these realms, by one of the archbishops or bishops of the realm, in the presence of all the people; who on their parts do reciprocally take the oath of allegiance to the crown. This coronation oath is conceived in the following terms:

The archbishop or bishop shall say,—"Will you solemnly promise and swear to govern the people of this kingdom of England, and the dominions thereto belonging, according to the statutes in parliament agreed on, and the laws and customs of the same?"—*The king or queen shall say*, "I solemnly promise so to do."—*Archbishop or bishop*, "Will you to your power cause law and justice, in mercy, to be executed in all your judgments?"—*King or queen*, "I will."—*Archbishop or bishop*, "Will you to the utmost of your power maintain the laws of God, the true profession of the gospel, and the protestant reformed religion established by the law? And will you preserve unto the bishops and clergy of this realm, and to the churches committed to their charge, all such rights and privileges as by law do or shall appertain unto them or any of them?"—*King or queen*, "All this I promise to do."—*After this the king or queen, laying his or her hand upon the holy gospels, shall say*, "The things which I have herebefore promised I will perform and keep: so help me God:" and then shall kiss the book.

This is the form of the coronation oath, as is now prescribed by our laws; the principal articles of which appear to be at least as ancient as the mirror of justices, and even as the time of Bracton: but the wording of it was changed at the revolution, because (as the statute alleges) the oath itself has been framed in doubtful words and expressions, with relation to ancient laws and constitutions at this time unknown. However, in what form soever it be conceived, this is most undisputably a fundamental and original express contract, though doubtless the duty of protection is impliedly as much incumbent on the sovereign before coronation as after: in the same manner as allegiance to the king becomes the duty of the subject immediately on the descent of the crown, before he has taken the oath of allegiance, or whether he ever takes it at all. This reciprocal duty of the subject will be considered in its proper place. At present we are only to observe, that in the king's part of this original contract are expressed all the duties that a monarch can owe to his people, viz: to govern according to law; to execute judgment in mercy; and to maintain the established religion. And, with respect to the latter of these three branches, we may further remark, that by the act of union, 5 Ann., c. 8, two preceding statutes are recited and confirmed; the one of the parliament of Scotland, the other of the parliament of England; which enact: the former, that every king at his accession shall take and subscribe an oath, to preserve the protestant religion and presbyterian church government in Scotland; the latter, that at his coronation he shall take and subscribe a similar oath to preserve the settlement of the church of England within England, Ireland, Wales and Berwick, and the territories thereunto belonging.

CHAPTER VII
OF THE KING'S PREROGATIVE

It was observed in a former chapter, that one of the principal bulwarks of civil liberty, or, in other words, of the British constitution, was the limitation of the king's prerogative by bounds so certain and notorious, that it is impossible he should ever exceed them, without the consent of the people, on the one hand; or without, on the other, a violation of that original contract, which in all states impliedly, and in ours most expressly, subsists between the prince and the subject. It will now be our business to consider this prerogative minutely; to demonstrate its necessity in general; and to make out in the most important instances its particular extent and restrictions: from which considerations this conclusion will evidently follow, that the powers which are vested in the crown by the laws of England are necessary for the support of society; and do not intrench any farther on our *natural* liberties, than is expedient for the maintenance of our *civil*.

There cannot be a stronger proof of that genuine freedom, which is the boast of this age and country, than the power of discussing and examining, with decency and respect, the limits of the king's prerogative. A topic, that in some former ages was thought too delicate and sacred to be profaned by the pen of a subject. It was ranked among the *arcana imperii*: and, like the mysteries of the *bona dea*, was not suffered to be pried into by any but such as were initiated in its service: because perhaps the exertion of the one, like the solemnities of the other, would not bear the inspection of a rational and sober inquiry. The glorious Queen Elizabeth herself made no scruple to direct her parliaments to abstain from discoursing of matters of state; and it was the constant language of this favourite princess and her ministers, that even that august assembly "ought not to deal, to judge, or to meddle with her majesty's prerogative royal." And her successor, King James the First, who had imbibed high notions of the divinity of regal sway, more than once laid it down in his speeches, that, "as it is atheism and blasphemy in a creature to dispute what the Deity may do, so it is presumption and sedition in a subject to dispute what a king may do in the height of his power; good Christians," he adds, "will be content with God's will revealed in his word; and good subjects will rest in the king's will, revealed in *his* law."

By the word prerogative we usually understand that special pre-eminence, which the king hath over and above all other persons, and out of the ordinary course of the common law, in right of his regal dignity. It signifies, in its etymology (from *proe* and *rogo*,) something that is required or demanded before, or in preference to, all others. And hence it follows, that it must be in its nature singular and eccentrical; that it can only be applied to those rights and capacities which the king enjoys alone, in contradistinction to others, and not to those which he enjoys in common with any of his subjects: for if once any one prerogative of the crown could be held in common with the subject, it would cease to be prerogative any longer. And therefore Finch lays it down as a maxim, that the prerogative is that law in case of the king, which is law in no case of the subject.

Prerogatives are either *direct* or *incidental.* The *direct* are such positive substantial parts of the royal character and authority as are rooted in and spring from the king's political person, considered merely by itself, without reference to any other extrinsic circumstance; as, the right of sending embassadors, of creating peers, and of making war or peace. But such prerogatives as are *incidental* bear always a relation to something else, distinct from the king's person; and are indeed only exceptions, in favour of the crown, to those general rules that are established for the rest of the community; such as, that no costs shall be recovered against the king; that the king can never be a joint tenant; and that his debt shall be preferred before a debt to any of his subjects. These, and an infinite number of other instances, will better be understood, when we come regularly to consider the rules themselves, to which these incidental prerogatives are exceptions. And therefore we will at present only dwell upon the king's substantive or direct prerogatives.

These substantive or direct prerogatives may again be divided into three kinds: being such as regard, first, the king's royal *character*; secondly, his royal *authority*; and, lastly, his royal *income.* These are necessary to secure reverence to his person, obedience to his commands, and an affluent supply for the ordinary expenses of government; without all of which it is impossible to maintain the executive power in due independence and vigor. Yet, in every branch of this large and extensive dominion, our free constitution has interposed such reasonable checks and restrictions as may curb it from trampling on those liberties which it was meant to secure and establish. The enormous weight of prerogative, if left to itself, (as in arbitrary governments it is,) spreads havoc and destruction among all the inferior movements; but, when balanced and regulated (as with us) by its proper counterpoise, timely and judiciously applied, its operations are then equable and certain, it invigorates the whole machine, and enables every part to answer the end of its construction.

In the present chapter we shall only consider the two first of these divisions, which relate to the king's political *character* and *authority*; or, in other words, his *dignity* and regal *power*; to which last the name of prerogative is frequently narrowed and confined.

First, then, of the royal dignity. Under every monarchical establishment, it is necessary to distinguish the prince from his subjects, not only by the outward pomp and decorations of majesty, but also by ascribing to him certain qualities, as inherent in his royal capacity, distinct from and superior to those of any other individual in the nation. For though a philosophical mind will consider the royal person merely as one man appointed by mutual consent to preside over many others, and will pay him that reverence and duty which the principles of society demand; yet the mass of mankind will be apt to grow insolent and refractory, if taught to consider their prince as a man of no greater perfection than themselves. The law therefore ascribes to the king, in his high political character, not only large powers and emoluments, which form his prerogative and revenue, but likewise certain attributes of a great and transcendent nature; by which the people are led to consider him in the light of a superior being, and to pay him that awful respect, which may enable him with greater ease to carry on the business of government. This is what I understand by the royal dignity, the several branches of which we will now proceed to examine.

I. And, first, the law ascribes to the king the attribute of *sovereignty*, or pre-eminence. "*Rex est vicarius*," says Bracton, "*et minister Dei in terra: omnis quidem sub eo est, et ipse sub nullo, nisi tantum sub Deo.*" He is said to have *imperial* dignity; and in charters before the conquest is frequently styled *basileus* and *imperator*, the titles respectively assumed by the emperors of the east and west. His realm is declared to be an *empire*, and his crown *imperial*, by many acts of parliament, particularly the statutes 24 Hen. VIII, c. 12, and 25 Hen. VIII, c. 28; which at the same time declare the king to be the supreme head of the realm in matters both civil and ecclesiastical, and of consequence inferior to no man upon earth, dependent on no man, accountable to no man. Formerly there prevailed a ridiculous notion, propagated by the German and Italian civilians, that an emperor could do many things which a king could not, (as the creation of notaries and the like,) and that all kings were in some degree subordinate and subject to the emperor of Germany or Rome. The meaning, therefore, of the legislature, when it uses these terms of *empire* and *imperial*, and applies them to the realm and crown of England, is only to assert that our king is equally sovereign and independent within these his dominions, as any emperor is in his empire; and owes no kind of subjection to any other potentate upon earth. Hence it is, that no suit or action can be brought against the king even in civil matters, because no court can have jurisdiction over him. For all jurisdiction implies superiority of power: authority to try would be vain and idle, without an authority to redress; and the sentence of a court would be contemptible, unless that court had power to command the execution of it; but who, says Finch, shall command the king? Hence it is likewise, that by law the person of the king is sacred, even though the measures pursued in his reign be completely tyrannical and arbitrary: for no jurisdiction upon earth has power to try him in a criminal way; much less to condemn him to punishment. If any foreign jurisdiction had this power, as was formerly claimed by the pope, the independence of the kingdom would be no more; and, if such a power were vested in any domestic tribunal, there would soon be an end of the constitution, by destroying the free agency of one of the constituent parts of the sovereign legislative power.

Are then, it may be asked, the subjects of England totally destitute of remedy, in case the crown should invade their rights, either by private injuries or public oppression? To this we may answer, that the law has provided a remedy in both cases.

And, first, as to private injuries: if any person has, in point of property, a just demand upon the king, he must petition him in his court of chancery, where his chancellor will administer right as a matter of grace though not upon compulsion. And this is entirely consonant to what is laid down by the writers on natural law. "A subject," says Puffendorf, "so long as he continues a subject, hath no way to *oblige* his prince to give him his due, when he refuses it; though no wise prince will ever refuse to stand to a lawful contract. And, if the prince gives the subject leave to enter an action against him, upon such contract, in his own courts, the action itself proceeds rather upon natural equity, than upon the municipal laws." For the end of such action is not to *compel* the prince to observe the contract, but to *persuade* him. And, as to personal wrongs, it is well observed by Mr. Locke, "the harm which the sovereign can do in his own person not being likely to happen often, nor to extend itself far; nor being able by his single strength to subvert the laws, nor oppress the body of the people, (should any prince have so much weakness and ill-nature as to endeavour to do it)—the inconveniency therefore of some particular mischiefs, that may happen sometimes, when a heady prince comes to the throne, are well recompensed by the peace of the public and security of the government, in the person of the chief magistrate, being thus set out of the reach of danger."

Next, as to cases of ordinary public oppression, where the vitals of the constitution are not attacked, the law hath also assigned a remedy. For as a king cannot misuse his power, without the advice of evil counsellors, and the assistance of wicked ministers, these men may be examined and punished. The constitution has therefore provided, by means of indictments, and parliamentary impeachments, that no man shall dare to assist the crown in contradiction to the laws of the land. But it is at the same time a maxim in those laws, that the king himself can do no wrong: since it would be a great weakness and absurdity in any system of positive law, to define any possible wrong, without any possible redress.

For, as to such public oppressions as tend to dissolve the constitution, and subvert the fundamentals of government, they are cases, which the law will not, out of decency, suppose: being incapable of distrusting those whom it has invested with any part of the supreme power; since such distrust would render the exercise of that power precarious and impracticable. For, wherever the law expresses its distrust of abuse of power, it always vests a superior coercive authority in some other hand to correct it; the very notion of which destroys the idea of sovereignty. If therefore, for example, the two houses of parliament, or either of them, had avowedly a right to animadvert on the king, or each other, or if the king had a right to animadvert on either of the houses, that branch of the legislature, so subject to animadversion, would instantly cease to be a part of the supreme power; the balance of the constitution would be overturned; and that branch or branches, in which this jurisdiction resided, would be completely sovereign. The supposition of *law* therefore is, that neither the king nor either house of parliament, collectively taken, is capable of doing any wrong; since in such cases the law feels itself incapable of furnishing any adequate remedy. For which reason all oppressions which may happen to spring from any branch of the sovereign power, must necessarily be out of the reach of any *stated rule* or *express legal* provision; but, if ever they unfortunately happen, the prudence of the times must provide new remedies upon new emergencies.

Indeed, it is found by experience, that whenever the unconstitutional oppressions, even of the sovereign power, advance with gigantic strides, and threaten desolation to a state, mankind will not be reasoned out of the feelings of humanity; nor will sacrifice their liberty by a scrupulous adherence to those political maxims, which were originally established to preserve it. And therefore, though the positive laws are silent, experience will furnish us with a very remarkable case, wherein nature and reason prevailed. When King James the Second invaded the fundamental constitution of the realm, the convention declared an abdication, whereby the throne was rendered vacant, which induced a new settlement of the crown. And so far as this precedent leads, and no further, we may now be allowed to lay down the *law* of redress against public oppression. If, therefore, any future prince should endeavor to subvert the constitution by breaking the original contract between king and people, should violate the fundamental laws, and should withdraw himself out of the kingdom; we are now authorized to declare that this conjunction of circumstances would amount to an abdication, and the throne would be thereby vacant. But it is not for us to say that any one, or two, of these ingredients would amount to such a situation; for there our precedent would fail us. In these, therefore, or other circumstances, which a fertile imagination may furnish, since both law and history are silent, it becomes us to be silent too; leaving to future generations, whenever necessity and the safety of the whole shall require it, the exertion of those inherent, though latent, powers of society, which no climate, no time, no constitution, no contract, can ever destroy or diminish.

II. Besides the attribute of sovereignty, the law also ascribes to the king, in his political capacity, absolute *perfection*. The king can do no wrong; which ancient and fundamental maxim is not to be understood, as if every thing transacted by the government was of course just and lawful, but means only two things. First, that whatever is exceptionable in the conduct of public affairs, is not to be imputed to the king, nor is he answerable for it personally to his people: for this doctrine would totally destroy that constitutional independence of the crown, which is necessary for the balance of power in our free and active, and therefore compounded, constitution. And secondly, it means that the prerogative of the crown extends not to do any injury: it is created for the benefit of the people, and therefore cannot be exerted to their prejudice.

The king, moreover, is not only incapable of *doing* wrong, but even of *thinking* wrong: he can never mean to do an improper thing: in him is no folly or weakness. And, therefore, if the crown should be induced to grant any franchise or privilege to a subject contrary to reason, or in any wise prejudicial to the commonwealth or a private person, the law will not suppose the king to have meant either an unwise or an injurious action, but declares that the king was deceived in his grant; and thereupon such grant is rendered void, merely upon the foundation of fraud and deception, either by or upon those agents whom the crown has thought proper to employ. For the law will not cast an imputation on that magistrate whom it intrusts with the executive power, as if he was capable of intentionally disregarding his trust; but attributes to mere imposition (to which the most perfect of sublunary beings must still continue liable) those little inadvertencies, which, if charged on the will of the prince, might lessen him in the eyes of his subjects.

Yet still, notwithstanding this personal perfection, which the law attributes to the sovereign, the constitution has allowed a latitude of supposing the contrary, in respect to both houses of parliament, each of which in its turn, hath exerted the right of remonstrating and complaining to the king even of those acts of royalty, which are most properly and personally his own; such as messages signed by himself, and speeches delivered from the throne. And yet, such is the reverence which is paid to the royal person, that though the two houses have an undoubted right to consider these acts of state in any light whatever, and accordingly treat them in their addresses as personally proceeding from the prince, yet among themselves, (to preserve the more perfect decency, and for the greater freedom of debate) they usually suppose them to flow from the advice of the administration. But the privilege of canvassing thus freely the personal acts of the sovereign (either directly, or even through the medium of his reputed advisers) belongs to no individual, but is confined to those august assemblies; and there too the objections must be proposed with the utmost respect and deference. One member was sent to the Tower for suggesting that his majesty's answer to the address of the commons contained "high words to fright the members out of their duty;" and another, for saying that a part of the king's speech "seemed rather to be calculated for the meridian of Germany than Great Britain, and that the king was a stranger to our language and constitution."

In farther pursuance of this principle, the law also determines that in the king can be no negligence or *laches*, and therefore no delay will bar his right. *Nullum tempus occurrit regi* has been the standing maxim upon all occasions; for the law intends that the king is always busied for the public good, and therefore has not leisure to assert his right within the times limited to subjects. In the king also can be no stain or corruption of blood; for, if the heir to the crown were attainted of treason or felony, and afterwards the crown should descend to him, this would purge the attainder *ipso facto*. And therefore when Henry VII, who, as earl of Richmond, stood attainted, came to the crown, it was not thought necessary to pass an act of parliament to reverse this attainder; because, as Lord Bacon, in his history of that prince, informs us, it was agreed that the assumption of the crown had at once purged all attainders.

III. A third attribute of the king's majesty is his *perpetuity*. The law ascribes to him, in his political capacity, an absolute immortality. The king never dies. Henry, Edward, or George, may die; but the king survives them all. For immediately upon the decease of the reigning prince in his natural capacity, his kingship or imperial dignity, by act of law, without any *interregnum* or interval, is vested at once in his heir, who is, *eo instanti*, king to all intents and purposes. And so tender is the law of supposing even a possibility of his death, that his natural dissolution is generally called his *demise; demissio regis, vel coronoe*: an expression which signifies merely a transfer of property; for, as is observed in Plowden, when we say the demise of the crown, we mean only that, in consequence of the disunion of the king's natural body from his body politic, the kingdom is transferred or demised to his successor; and so the royal dignity remains perpetual. Thus too, when Edward the Fourth, in the tenth year of his reign, was driven from his throne for a few months, by the house of Lancaster, this temporary transfer of his dignity was denominated his *demise*; and all process was held to be discontinued, as upon a natural death of the king.

We are next to consider those branches of the royal prerogative, which invest thus our sovereign lord, thus all-perfect and immortal in his kingly capacity, with a number of authorities and powers; in the exertion whereof consists the executive part of government. This is wisely placed in a single hand by the British constitution, for the sake of unanimity, strength and dispatch. Were it placed in many hands, it would be subject to many wills: many wills, if disunited and drawing different ways, create weakness in a government; and to unite those several wills, and reduce them to one, is a work of more time and delay than the exigencies of state will afford. The king of England is therefore not only the chief, but properly the sole, magistrate of the nation, all others acting by commission from, and in due subordination to him: in like manner as, upon the great revolution in the Roman state, all the powers of the ancient magistracy of the commonwealth were concentrated in the new emperor: so that, as Gravina expresses it, "*in ejus unius persona veteris reipublicae vis atque majestas per cumulatas magistratuum potestates exprimebatur.*"

After what has been premised in this chapter, I shall not (I trust) be considered as an advocate for arbitrary power, when I lay it down as a principle, that in the exertion of lawful prerogative the king is and ought to be absolute; that is, so far absolute that there is no legal authority that can either delay or resist him. He may reject what bills, may make what treaties, may coin what money, may create what peers, may pardon what offences, he pleases; unless where the constitution hath expressly, or by evident consequence, laid down some exception, or boundary; declaring, that thus far the prerogative shall go, and no farther. For otherwise the power of the crown would indeed be but a name and a shadow, insufficient for the ends of government, if where its jurisdiction is clearly established and allowed, any man or body of men were permitted to disobey it, in the ordinary course of law: I say in the *ordinary* course of law; for I do not now speak of those *extraordinary* recourses to first principles, which are necessary when the contracts of society are in danger of dissolution, and the law proves too weak a defence against the violence of fraud or oppression. And yet the want of attending to this obvious distinction has occasioned these doctrines, of absolute power in the prince and of national resistance by the people, to be much misunderstood and perverted, by the advocates for slavery on the one hand, and the demagogues of faction on the other. The former, observing the absolute sovereignty and transcendent dominion of the crown laid down (as it certainly is) most strongly and emphatically in our law books, as well as our homilies, have denied that any case can be excepted from so general and positive a rule; forgetting how impossible it is, in any practical system of laws, to point out beforehand those eccentrical remedies, which the sudden emergence of national distress may dictate, and which that alone can justify. On the other hand, over-zealous republicans, feeling the absurdity of unlimited passive obedience, have fancifully (or sometimes factiously) gone over to the other extreme; and because resistance is justifiable to the person of the prince when the being of the state is endangered, and the public voice proclaims such resistance necessary, they have therefore allowed to every individual the right of determining this experience, and of employing private force to resist even private oppression. A doctrine productive of anarchy, and, in consequence, equally fatal to civil liberty, as tyranny itself. For civil liberty, rightly understood, consists in protecting the rights of individuals by the united force of society; society cannot be maintained, and of course can exert no protection, without obedience to some sovereign power; and obedience is an empty name, if every individual has a right to decide how far he himself shall obey.

In the exertion, therefore, of those prerogatives which the law has given him, the king is irresistible and absolute, according to the forms of the constitution. And yet, if the consequence of that exertion be manifestly to the grievance or dishonor of the kingdom, the parliament will call his advisers to a just and severe account. For prerogative consisting (as Mr. Locke has well defined it) in the discretionary power of acting for the public good, where the positive laws are silent; if that discretionary power be abused to the public detriment, such prerogative is exerted in an unconstitutional manner. Thus the king may make a treaty with a foreign state, which shall irrevocably bind the nation; and yet, when such treaties have been judged pernicious, impeachments have pursued those ministers, by whose agency or advice they were concluded.

The prerogatives of the crown (in the sense under which we are now considering them) respect either this nation's intercourse with foreign nations, or its own domestic government and civil polity.

With regard to foreign concerns, the king is the delegate or representative of his people. It is impossible that the individuals of a state, in their collective capacity, can transact the affairs of that state with another community equally numerous as themselves. Unanimity must be wanting to their measures, and strength to the execution of their counsels. In the king, therefore, as in a centre, all the rays of his people are united, and formed by that union, a consistency, splendor and power, that make him feared and respected by foreign potentates; who would scruple to enter into any engagement that must afterwards be revised and ratified by a popular assembly. What is done by the royal authority, with regard to foreign powers, is the act of the whole nation; what is done without the king's concurrence, is the act only of private men. And so far is this point carried by our law that it hath been held, that should all the subjects of England make war with a king in league with the king of England, without the royal assent, such war is no breach of the league. And, by the statute 2 Hen. V, c. 6, any subject committing acts of hostility upon any nation in league with the king was declared to be guilty of high treason; and, although that act was repealed by the statute 20 Hen. VI, c. 11, so far as relates to the making this offence high treason, yet still it remains a very great offence against the law of nations, and punishable by our laws, either capitally or otherwise, according to the circumstances of the case.

I. The king therefore, considered as the representative of his people, has the sole power of sending ambassadors to foreign states, and receiving ambassadors at home. This may lead us into a short digression, by way of inquiry, how far the municipal laws of England intermeddle with or protect the rights of these messengers from one potentate to another, whom we call ambassadors.

The rights, the powers, the duties, and the privileges of ambassadors are determined by the law of nature and nations, and not by any municipal constitutions. For, as they represent the persons of their respective masters, who owe no subjection to any laws but those of their own country, their actions are not subject to the control of the private law of that state wherein they are appointed to reside. He that is subject to the coercion of laws is necessarily dependent on that power by whom those laws were made: but an ambassador ought to be independent of every power except that by which he is sent, and of consequence ought not to be subject to the mere municipal laws of that nation wherein he is to exercise his functions. If he grossly offends, or makes an ill use of his character, he may be sent home and accused before his master; who is bound either to do justice upon him, or avow himself the accomplice of his crimes. But there is great dispute among the writers on the laws of nations, whether this exemption of ambassadors extends to all crimes, as well natural as positive; or whether it only extends to such as are *mala prohibita*, as coining, and not to those that are *mala in se*, as murder. Our law seems to have formerly taken in the restriction, as well as the general exemption. For it has been held, both by our common lawyers and civilians that an ambassador is privileged by the law of nature and nations; and yet, if he commits any offence against the law of reason and nature, he shall lose his privilege; and that therefore, if an ambassador conspires the death of the king in whose land he is, he may be condemned and executed for treason; but if he commits any other species of treason, it is otherwise, and he must be sent to his own kingdom. And these positions seem to be built upon good appearance of reason. For, since, as we have formerly shewn, all municipal laws act in subordination to the primary law of nature, and, where they annex a punishment to natural crimes, are only declaratory of, and auxiliary to, that law; therefore to this natural universal rule of justice, ambassadors, as well as other men, are subject in all countries; and of consequence, it is reasonable that, wherever they transgress it, they shall be liable to make atonement. But, however these principles might formerly obtain, the general practice of this country, as well as the rest of Europe, seems now to pursue the sentiments of the learned Grotius, that the security of ambassadors is or more importance than the punishment of a particular crime. And therefore few, if any, examples have happened within a century past, where an ambassador has been punished for any offence, however atrocious in its nature.

In respect to civil suits, all the foreign jurists agree that neither an ambassador, or any of his train or *comites* can be prosecuted for any debt or contract in the courts of that kingdom wherein he is sent to reside. Yet Sir Edward Coke maintains that, if an ambassador make a contract which is good *jure gentium*, he shall answer for it here. But the truth is, so few cases (if any) had arisen, wherein the privilege was either claimed or disputed, even with regard to civil suits, that our law books are (in general) quite silent upon it previous to the reign of Queen Anne; when an ambassador from Peter the Great, czar of Muscovy, was actually arrested and taken out of his coach in London, for a debt of fifty pounds which he had there contracted. Instead of applying to be discharged upon his privilege, he gave bail to the action, and the next day complained to the queen. The persons who were concerned in the arrest were examined before the privy council (of which the Lord Chief Justice Holt was at the same time sworn a member,) and seventeen were committed to prison; most of whom were prosecuted by information in the court of queen's bench, at the suit of the attorney general, and at their trial before the lord chief justice were convicted of the facts by the jury, reserving the question of law, how far those facts were criminal, to be afterwards argued before the judges; which question was never determined. In the meantime the czar resented this affront very highly, and demanded that the sheriff of Middlesex and all others concerned in the arrest should be punished with instant death. But the queen (to the amazement of that despotic court) directed her secretary to inform him, "that she could inflict no punishment upon any, the meanest, of her subjects, unless warranted by the law of the land; and therefore was persuaded that he would not insist upon impossibilities." To satisfy, however, the clamours of the foreign ministers, who made it a common cause, as well as to appease the wrath of Peter, a bill was brought into parliament, and afterwards passed into a law, to prevent and punish such outrageous insolence for the future. And with a copy of this act, elegantly engrossed and illuminated, accompanied by a letter from the queen, an ambassador extraordinary was commissioned to appear at Moscow, who declared "that though her majesty could not inflict such a punishment as was required, because of the defect in that particular of the former established constitutions of her kingdom, yet with the unanimous consent of the parliament she had caused a new act to be passed, to serve as a law for the future." This humiliating step was accepted as a full satisfaction by the czar; and the offenders, at his request, were charged from all farther prosecution.

This statute recites the arrest which had been made, "in contempt of the protection granted by her majesty, contrary to the law of nations, and in prejudice of the rights and privileges which ambassadors and other public ministers have at all times been thereby possessed of, and ought to be kept sacred and inviolable:" wherefore it enacts, that for the future all process whereby the person of any ambassador, or of his domestic or domestic servant, may be arrested, or his goods distrained or seized, shall be utterly null and void; and the persons prosecuting, soliciting, or executing such process, shall be deemed violators of the law of nations, and disturbers of the public repose; and shall suffer such penalties and corporal punishment as the lord chancellor and the two chief justices, or any two of them, shall think fit. But it is expressly provided, that no trader, within the description of the bankrupt laws, who shall be in the service of any ambassador, shall be privileged or protected by this act; nor shall any one be punished for arresting an ambassador's servant, unless his name be registered with the secretary of state, and by him strictly conformable to the rights of ambassadors, as observed in the most civilized countries. And, in consequence of this statute, thus declaring and enforcing the law of nations, these privileges are now held to be part of the law of the land, and are constantly allowed in the courts of common law.

II. It is also the king's prerogative to make treaties, leagues, and alliances with foreign states and princes. For it is by the law of nations essential to the goodness of a league, that it be made by the sovereign power; and then it is binding upon the whole community: and in England the sovereign power, *quoad hoc*, is vested in the person of the king. Whatever contracts therefore he engages in, no other power in the kingdom can legally delay, resist or annul. And yet, lest this plenitude of authority should be abused to the detriment of the public, the constitution (as we hinted before) hath here interposed a check, by the means of a parliamentary impeachment, for the punishment of such ministers as from criminal motives advise or conclude any treaty, which shall afterwards be judged to derogate from the honour and interest of the nation.

III. Upon the same principle the king has also the sole prerogative of making war and peace. For it is held by all the writers on the law of nature and nations, that the right of making war, which by nature subsisted in every individual, is given up by all private persons that enter into society, and is vested in the sovereign power: and this right is given up, not only by individuals, but even by the entire body of people, that are under the dominion of a sovereign. It would indeed be extremely improper, that any number of subjects should have the power of binding the supreme magistrate, and putting him against his will in a state of war. Whatever hostilities therefore may be committed by private citizens, the state ought not to be affected thereby; unless that should justify their proceedings, and thereby become partner in the guilt. Such unauthorized volunteers in violence are not ranked among open enemies, but are treated like pirates and robbers: according to that rule of the civil law; *hostes hi sunt qui nobis, aut quibus nos, publice bellum decrevimus: coeteri latrones aut proedones sunt.* And the reason which is given by Grotius, why according to the laws of nations a denunciation of war ought always to precede the actual commencement of hostilities, is not so much that the enemy may be put upon his guard (which is matter rather of magnanimity than right,) but that it may be certainly clear that the war is not undertaken by private persons, but by the will of the whole community; whose right of willing is in this case transferred to the supreme magistrate by the fundamental laws of society. So that, in order to make a war completely effectual, it is necessary with us in England that it be publicly declared and duly proclaimed by the king's authority; and, then, all parts of both the contending nations from the highest to the lowest, are bound by it. And wherever the right resides of beginning a national war, there also must reside the right of ending it, or the power of making peace. And the same check of parliamentary impeachment, for improper or inglorious conduct, in beginning, conducting, or concluding a national war, is in general sufficient to restrain the ministers of the crown from a wanton or injurious exertion of this great prerogative.

IV. But, as the delay of making war may sometimes be detrimental to individuals who have suffered by depredations from foreign potentates, our laws have in some respects armed the subject with powers to impel the prerogative; by directing the ministers of the crown to issue letters of marque and reprisal upon due demand; the prerogative of granting which is nearly related to, and plainly derived from, that other of making war; this being indeed only an incomplete state of hostilities, and generally ending in a formal declaration of war. These letters are grantable by the law of nations, whenever the subjects of one state are oppressed and injured by those of another; and justice is denied by that state to which the oppressor belongs. In this case letters of marque and reprisal (words used as synonymous; and signifying, the latter a taking in return, the former the passing the frontiers in order to such taking,) may be obtained, in order to seize the bodies or goods of the subjects of the offending state, until satisfaction be made, wherever they happen to be found. And indeed this custom of reprisals seems dictated by nature herself; for which reason we find in the most ancient times very notable instances of it. But here the necessity is obvious of calling in the sovereign power, to determine when reprisals may be made; else every private sufferer would be a judge in his own cause. In pursuance of which principle, it is with us declared by the statute 4 Hen. V, c. 7, that, if any subjects of the realm are oppressed in the time of truce by any foreigners, the king will grant marque in due form, to all that feel themselves grieved. Which form is thus directed to be observed: the sufferer must first apply to the lord privy-seal, and he shall make out letters of request under the privy seal; and if, after such request of satisfaction made, the party required do not within convenient time make due satisfaction or restitution to the party grieved, the lord chancellor shall make him out letters of marque under the great seal; and by virtue of these he may attack and seize the property of the aggressor nation, without hazard of being condemned as a robber or pirate.

V. Upon exactly the same reason stands the prerogative of granting safe-conducts, without which by the law of nations no member of one society has a right to intrude into another. And, therefore, Puffendorf very justly resolves, that it is left in the power of all states to take such measures about the admission of strangers as they think convenient; those being ever excepted who are driven on the coasts by necessity, or by any cause that deserves pity or compassion. Great tenderness is shown by our laws, not only to foreigners in distress (as will appear when we come to speak of shipwrecks,) but with regard also to the admission of strangers who come spontaneously. For so long as their nation continues at peace with ours, and they themselves behave peaceably, they are under the king's protection; though liable to be sent home whenever the king sees occasion. But no subject of a nation at war with us can, by the law of nations, come into the realm, nor can travel himself upon the high seas, or send his goods and merchandise from one place to another without danger of being seized by our subjects, unless he has letters of safe-conduct; which, by divers ancient statutes, must be granted under the king's great seal and enrolled in chancery, or else are of no effect: the king being supposed the best judge of such emergencies as may deserve exception from the general law of arms. But passports under the king's sign-manual, or licenses from his ambassadors abroad, are now more usually obtained, and are allowed to be of equal validity.

These are the principal prerogatives of the king respecting this nation's intercourse with foreign nations; in all of which he is considered as the delegate or representative of his people. But in domestic affairs he is considered in a great variety of characters, and from thence there arises an abundant number of other prerogatives.

I. First, he is a constituent part of the supreme legislative power; and, as such, has the prerogative of rejecting such provisions in parliament as he judges improper to be passed. The expediency of which constitution has before been evinced at large. I shall only farther remark, that the king is not bound by any act of parliament, unless he be named therein by special and particular words. The most general words that can be devised ("any person or persons, bodies politic or corporate, etc.") affect not him in the least, if they may tend to restrain or diminish any of his rights or interests. For it would be of most mischievous consequence to the public if the strength of the executive power were liable to be curtailed without its own express consent, by constructions and implications of the subject. Yet, where an act of parliament is expressly made for the preservation of public rights and the suppression of public wrongs, and does not interfere with the established rights of the crown, it is said to be binding as well upon the king as upon the subject: and, likewise, the king may take the benefit of any particular act, though he be not especially named.

II. The king is considered, in the next place, as the generalissimo, or the first in military command, within the kingdom. The great end of society is to protect the weakness of individuals by the united strength of the community; and the principal use of government is to direct that united strength in the best and most effectual manner to answer the end proposed. Monarchical government is allowed to be the fittest of any for this purpose: it follows therefore, from the very end of its institution, that in a monarchy the military power must be trusted in the hands of the prince.

In this capacity, therefore, of general of the kingdom, the king has the sole power of raising and regulating fleets and armies. Of the manner in which they are raised and regulated I shall speak more when I come to consider the military state. We are now only to consider the prerogative of enlisting and of governing them; which indeed was disputed and claimed, contrary to all reason and precedent, by the long parliament of King Charles I: but, upon the restoration of his son, was solemnly declared by the statute, 13 Car. II, c. 6, to be in the king alone: for that the sole supreme government and command of the militia within all his majesty's realms and dominions, and of all forces by sea and land, and of all forts and places of strength, ever was and is the undoubted right of his majesty, and his royal predecessors, kings and queens of England; and that both or either house of parliament cannot nor ought to pretend to the same.

This statute, it is obvious to observe, extends not only to fleets and armies, but also to forts and other places of strength within the realm; the sole prerogative as well of erecting as manning and governing of which, belongs to the king in his capacity of general of the kingdom: and all lands were formerly subject to a tax for building of castles wherever the king thought proper. This was one of the three things, from contributing to the performance of which no lands were exempted; and therefore called by our Saxon ancestors the *trinoda necessitas: sc. pontis reparatio, areis constructio, et expedito contra hostem.* And this they were called upon to do so often, that, as Sir Edward Coke from M. Paris assures us, there were, in the time of Henry II, 1115 castles subsisting in England. The inconveniences of which, when granted out to private subjects, the lordly barons of those times, were severely felt by the whole kingdom; for, as William of Newburgh remarks in the reign of King Stephen, "*erant in Anglia quodammodo tot reges vei potius tyranni quot domini castellorum:*" but it was felt by none more sensibly than by two succeeding princes, King John and King Henry III. And, therefore, the greatest part of them being demolished in the barons' wars, the kings of after-times have been very cautious of suffering them to be rebuilt in a fortified manner: and Sir Edward Coke lays it down, that no subject can build a castle, or house of strength embattled, or other fortress defensible, without the license of the king; for the danger which might ensue if every man at his pleasure might do it.

It is partly upon the same, and partly upon a fiscal foundation, to secure his marine revenue, that the king has the prerogative of appointing *ports* and *havens*, or such places only, for persons and merchandize to pass into and out of the realm, as he in his wisdom sees proper. By the feudal law all navigable rivers and havens were computed among the *regalia*, and were subject to the sovereign of the state. And in England it hath always been holden, that the king is lord of the whole shore, and particularly is the guardian of the ports and havens, which are the inlets and gates of the realm; and therefore, so early as the reign of King John, we find ships seized by the king's officers for putting in at a place that was not a legal port. These legal ports were undoubtedly at first assigned by the crown; since to each of them a court of portmote is incident, the jurisdiction of which must flow from the royal authority: the *great ports* of the sea are also referred to, as well known and established by statute 4 Hen. IV, c. 20, which prohibits the landing elsewhere under pain of confiscation; and the statute 1 Eliz. c. 11, recites, that the franchise of landing and discharging had been frequently granted by the crown.

But though the king had a power of granting the franchise of havens and ports, yet he had not the power of resumption, or of narrowing and confining their limits when once established; but any person had a right to load or discharge his merchandize in any part of the haven: whereby the revenue of the customs was much impaired and diminished by fraudulent landings in obscure and private corners. This occasioned the statutes of 1 Eliz. c. 11, and 13 and 14 Car. II, c. 11, § 14, which enable the crown by commission to ascertain the limits of all ports, and to assign proper wharfs and quays in each port for the exclusive landing and loading of merchandize.

The erection of beacons, light-houses and sea-marks is also a branch of the royal prerogative; whereof the first was anciently used in order to alarm the country, in case of the approach of an enemy; and all of them are signally useful in guiding and preserving vessels at sea, by night, as well as by day. For this purpose the king hath the exclusive power, by commission under his great seal, to cause them to be erected in fit and convenient places, as well upon the lands of the subject as upon the demesnes of the crown: which power is usually vested by letters patent in the office of lord high admiral. And by statute 8 Eliz. c. 13, the corporation of the trinity-house are impowered to set up any beacons or sea-marks wherever they shall think them necessary; and if the owner of the land, or any other person, shall destroy them, or shall take down any steeple, tree or other known sea-mark, he shall forfeit 100*l*, or in case of inability to pay it, shall be *ipso facto* outlawed.

To this branch of the prerogative may also be referred the power vested in his majesty by statutes 12 Car. II, c. 4, and 29 Geo. II, c. 16, of prohibiting the exportation of arms or ammunition out of this kingdom, under severe penalities: and likewise the right which the king has, whenever he sees proper, of confining his subjects to stay within the realm, or of recalling them when beyond the seas. By the common law, every man may go out of the realm for whatever cause he pleaseth, without obtaining the king's leave; provided he is under no injunction of staying at home: (which liberty was expressly declared in King John's great charter, though left out in that of Henry III,) but because that every man ought of right to defend the king and his realm, therefore, the king, at his pleasure, may command him by his writ that he go not beyond the seas, or out of the realm, without license; and, if he do the contrary, he shall be punished for disobeying the king's command. Some persons there anciently were, that, by reason of their stations, were under a perpetual prohibition of going abroad without license obtained; among which were reckoned all peers on account of their being counsellors of the crown; all knights, who were bound to defend the kingdom from invasions; all ecclesiastics, who were expressly confined by the fourth chapter of the constitutions of Clarendon, on account of their attachment in the times of popery to the see of Rome; all archers and other artificers, lest they should instruct foreigners to rival us in their several trades and manufactures. This was law in the times of Britton, who wrote in the reign of Edward I: and Sir Edward Coke gives us many instances to this effect in the time of Edward III. In the succeeding reign the affair of travelling wore a very different aspect; an act of parliament being made; forbidding all persons whatever to go abroad without license; *except* only the lords and other great men of the realm; and true and notable merchants; and the king's soldiers. But this act was repealed by the statute 4 Jac. I. c. 1. And at present everybody has, or at least assumes, the liberty of going abroad when he pleases. Yet, undoubtedly, if the king, by writ of *ne exeat regnum*, under his great seal, or privy seal, thinks proper to prohibit him from doing so; or if the king sends a writ to any man, when abroad, commanding his return; and, in either case, the subject disobeys; it is a high contempt of the king's prerogative, for which the offender's lands shall be seized till he return; and then he is liable to fine and imprisonment.

III. Another capacity, in which the king is considered in domestic affairs, is as the fountain of justice and general conservator of the peace of the kingdom. By the fountain of justice, the law does not mean the *author* or *original*, but only the *distributor*. Justice is not derived from the king, as from his *free gift*; but he is the steward of the public, to dispense it to whom it is *due*. He is not the spring, but the reservoir from whence right and equity are conducted, by a thousand channels, to every individual. The original power of judicature, by the fundamental principles of society, is lodged in the society at large: but as it would be impracticable to render complete justice to every individual, by the people in their collective capacity, therefore every nation has committed that power to certain select magistrates, who with more ease and expedition can hear and determine complaints; and in England this authority has immemorially been exercised by the king or his substitutes. He therefore has alone the right of erecting courts of judicature; for, though the constitution of the kingdom hath intrusted him with the whole executive power of the laws, it is impossible, as well as improper, that he should personally carry into execution this great and extensive trust: it is consequently necessary that courts should be erected, to assist him in executing this power; and equally necessary that, if erected, they should be erected by his authority. And hence it is, that all jurisdictions of courts are either mediately or immediately derived from the crown, their proceedings run generally in the king's name, they pass under his seal, and are excepted by his officers.

It is probable, and almost certain, that in very early times, before our constitution arrived at its full perfection, our kings in person often heard and determined causes between party and party. But at present, by the long and uniform usage of many ages, our kings have delegated their whole judicial power to the judges of their several courts; which are the grand depositaries of the fundamental laws of the kingdom, and have gained a known and stated jurisdiction, regulated by certain and established rules, which the crown itself cannot now alter but by act of parliament. And in order to maintain both the dignity and independence of the judges in the superior courts, it is enacted by the statute 13 Wm. III, c. 2, that their commissions shall be made (not, as formerly, *durante bene placito*, but) *quamdiu bene se gesserint*, and their salaries ascertained and established; but that it may be lawful to remove them on the address of both houses of parliament. And now, by the noble improvements of that law, in the statute of 1 Geo. III, c. 23, enacted at the earnest recommendation of the king himself from the throne, the judges are continued in their offices during their good behavior, notwithstanding any demise of the crown, (which was formerly held immediately to vacate their seats), and their full salaries are absolutely secured to them during the continuance of their commissions; his majesty having been pleased to declare, that "he looked upon the independence and uprightness of the judges as essential to the impartial administration of justice; as one of the best securities of the rights and liberties of his subjects; and as most conducive to the honor of the crown."

In criminal proceedings, or prosecutions for offences, it would be a still higher absurdity if the king personally sate in judgment; because, in regard to these, he appears in another capacity, that of *prosecutor*. All offences are either against the king's peace, or his crown and dignity; and are so laid in every indictment. For though in their consequences they generally seem (except in the case of treason, and a very few others,) to be rather offences against the kingdom than the king, yet as the public, which is an invisible body, has delegated all its power and rights, with regard to the execution of the laws, to one visible magistrate; all affronts to that power, and breaches of those rights are immediately offences against him, to whom they are so delegated by the public. He is therefore the proper person to prosecute for all public offences and breaches of the peace, being the person injured in the eye of the law. And this notion was carried so far in the old Gothic constitutions (wherein the king was bound by his coronation oath to conserve the peace,) that in case of any forcible injury offered to the person of a fellow-subject, the offender was accused of a kind of perjury, in having violated the king's coronation oath, *dicebatur fregisse jura mentum regis juratum*. And hence also arises another branch of the prerogative, that of *pardoning* offences; for it is reasonable that he only who is injured should have the power of forgiving. Of prosecutions and pardons I shall treat more at large hereafter: and only mention them here, in this cursory manner, to shew the constitutional grounds of this power of the crown, and how regularly connected all the links are in this vast chain of prerogative.

In this distinct and separate existence of the judicial power in a peculiar body of men, nominated indeed, but not removable at pleasure, by the crown, consists one main preservative of the public liberty which cannot subsist long in any state unless the administration of common justice be in some degree separated both from the legislative and also from the executive power. Were it joined with the legislative, the life, liberty, and property of the subject would be in the hands of arbitrary judges, whose decisions would be then regulated only by their own opinions, and not by any fundamental principles of law, which, though legislators may depart from, yet judges are bound to observe. Were it joined with the executive, this union might soon be an overbalance for the legislative. For which reason, by the statute of 16 Car. I, c. 10, which abolished the court of star chamber, effectual care is taken to remove all judicial power out of the hands of the king's privy council; who, as then was evident from recent instances, might soon be inclined to pronounce that for law which was most agreeable to the prince or his officers. Nothing, therefore, is more to be avoided, in a free constitution, than uniting the provinces of a judge and a minister of state. And, indeed, that the absolute power claimed and exercised in a neighboring nation is more tolerable than that of the eastern empires, is in great measure owing to their having vested the judicial power in their parliaments, a body separate and distinct from both the legislative and executive; and, if ever that nation recovers its former liberty, it will owe it to the efforts of those assemblies. In Turkey, where everything is centered in the sultan or his ministers, despotic power is in its meridian, and wears a more dreadful aspect.

A consequence of this prerogative is the legal *ubiquity* of the king. His majesty in the eye of the law is always present in all his courts, though he cannot personally distribute justice. His judges are the mirror by which the king's image is reflected. It is the regal office, and not the royal person, that is always present in court, always ready to undertake prosecutions, or pronounce judgment, for the benefit and protection of the subject. And from this ubiquity it follows, that the king can never be nonsuit; for a nonsuit is the desertion of the suit or action by the non-appearance of the plaintiff in court. For the same reason, also, in the forms of legal proceedings, the king is not said to appear *by his attorney*, as other men do: for in contemplation of law he is always present in court.

From the same original, of the king's being the fountain of justice, we may also deduce the prerogative of issuing proclamations, which is vested in the king alone. These proclamations have then a binding force, when, (as Sir Edward Coke observes,) they are grounded upon and enforce the laws of the realm. For, though the making of laws is entirely the work of a distinct part, the legislative branch of the sovereign power, yet the manner, time, and circumstances of putting those laws in execution must frequently be left to the discretion of the executive magistrate. And therefore his constitutions or edicts concerning these points, which we call proclamations, are binding upon the subject, where they do not either contradict the old laws or tend to establish new ones; but only enforce the execution of such laws as are already in being, in such manner as the king shall judge necessary. Thus the established law is, that the king may prohibit any of his subjects from leaving the realm: a proclamation therefore forbidding this in general for three weeks, by laying an embargo upon all shipping in time of war, will be equally binding as an act of parliament, because founded upon a prior law. But a proclamation to lay an embargo in time of peace upon all vessels laden with wheat (though in a time of a public scarcity) being contrary to law, and particularly to statute 22 Car. II, c. 13, the advisers of such a proclamation, and all persons acting under it, found it necessary to be indemnified by a special act of parliament. 7 Geo. III, c. 7. A proclamation for disarming papists is also binding, being only in execution of what the legislature has first ordained: but a proclamation for allowing arms to papists, or for disarming any protestant subjects will not bind; because the first would be to assume a dispensing power, the latter a legislative one; to the vesting of either of which in any single person the laws of England are absolutely strangers. Indeed by the statute 31 Hen. VIII, c. 8, it was enacted that the king's proclamations should have the force of acts of parliament; a statute which was calculated to introduce the most despotic tyranny, and which must have proved fatal to the liberties of this kingdom, had it not been luckily repealed in the minority of his successor, about five years after.

IV. The king is likewise the fountain of honour, of office, and of privilege; and this in a different sense from that wherein he is styled the fountain of justice; for here he is really the parent of them. It is impossible that government can be maintained without a due subordination of rank; that the people may know and distinguish such as are set over them, in order to yield them their due respect and obedience; and also that the officers themselves, being encouraged by emulation and the hopes of superiority, may the better discharge their functions; and the law supposes that no one can be so good a judge of their several merits and services, as the king himself who employs them. It has, therefore, intrusted him with the sole power of conferring dignities and honours, in confidence that he will bestow them upon none but such as deserve them. And therefore all degrees of nobility, of knighthood, and other titles, are received by immediate grant from the crown: either expressed in writing by writs or letters patent, as in the creation of peers and baronets, or by corporeal investiture, as in the creation of a simple knight.

From the same principle also arises the prerogative of erecting and disposing of offices; for honours and offices are in their nature convertible and synonymous. All offices under the crown carry in the eye of the law an honour along with them; because they imply a superiority of parts and abilities, being supposed to be always filled with those that are most able to execute them. And on the other hand, all honours in their original had duties or offices annexed to them; an earl, *comes*, was the conservator or governor of a county; and a knight, *miles*, was bound to attend the king in his wars. For the same reason, therefore, that honours are in the disposal of the king, offices ought to be so likewise; and as the king may create new titles, so may he create new offices: but with this restriction, that he cannot create new offices with new fees annexed to them, nor annex new fees to old offices; for this would be a tax upon the subject, which cannot be imposed but by act of parliament. Wherefore, in 13 Hen. IV, a new office being created by the king's letters patent for measuring cloths, with a new fee for the same, the letters patent were, on account of the new fee, revoked and declared void in parliament.

Upon the same, or a like reason, the king has also the prerogative of conferring privileges upon private persons. Such as granting place or precedence to any of his subjects, as shall seem good to his royal wisdom: or such as converting aliens, or persons born out of the king's dominions into denizens; whereby some very considerable privileges of natural-born subjects are conferred upon them. Such also is the prerogative of erecting corporations; whereby a number of private persons are united and knit together, and enjoy many liberties, powers and immunities in their politic capacity, which they were utterly incapable of in their natural. Of aliens, denizens, natural-born, and naturalized subjects, I shall speak more largely in a subsequent chapter; as also of corporations at the close of this book of our commentaries. I now only mention them incidentally, in order to remark the king's prerogative of making them; which is grounded upon this foundation, that the king, having the sole administration of the government in his hands, is the best and the only judge in what capacities, with what privileges, and under what distinctions, his people are the best qualified to serve and to act under him. A principle which was carried so far by the imperial law, that it was determined to be the crime of sacrilege, even to doubt whether the prince had appointed proper officers in the state.

V.   Another light in which the laws of England consider the king with regard to domestic concerns, is as the arbiter or commerce. By commerce, I at present mean domestic commerce only. It would lead me into too large a field, if I were to attempt to enter upon the nature of foreign trade, its privileges, regulations, and restrictions; and would be also quite beside the purpose of these commentaries, which are confined to the laws of England; whereas no municipal laws can be sufficient to order and determine the very extensive and complicated affairs of traffic and merchandise; neither can they have a proper authority for this purpose. For, as these are transactions carried on between subjects of independent states, the municipal laws of one will not be regarded by the other. For which reason the affairs of commerce are regulated by a law of their own, called the law merchant or *lex mercatoria*, which all nations agree in, and take notice of. And in particular it is held to be part of the law of England, which decides the causes of merchants by the general rules which obtain in all commercial countries; and that often, even in matters relating to domestic trade, as for instance, with regard to the drawing, the acceptance, and the transfer of inland bills of exchange.

With us in England, the king's prerogative, so far as it relates to mere domestic commerce, will fall principally under the following articles:

First, the establishment of public marts, or places of buying and selling, such as markets and fairs, with the tolls thereunto belonging. These can only be set up by virtue of the king's grant, or by long and immemorial usage and prescription, which presupposes such a grant. The limitation of these public resorts to such time and such place as may be most convenient for the neighbourhood, forms a part of economics, or domestic polity, which, considering the kingdom as a large family, and the king as the master of it, he clearly has a right to dispose and order as he pleases.

Secondly, the regulation of weights and measures. These, for the advantage of the public, ought to be universally the same throughout the kingdom; being the general criterions which reduce all things to the same or an equivalent value. But, as weight and measure are things in their nature arbitrary and uncertain, it is therefore expedient that they be reduced to some fixed rule or standard; which standard it is impossible to fix by any written law or oral proclamation; for no man can, by words only, give another an adequate idea of a foot-rule, or a pound-weight. It is therefore necessary to have recourse to some visible, palpable, material standard; by forming a comparison with which all weights and measures may be reduced to one uniform size: and the prerogative of fixing this standard our ancient law vested in the crown, as in Normandy it belonged to the duke. This standard was originally kept at Winchester; and we find in the laws of King Edgar, near a century before the conquest, an injunction that the one measure, which was kept at Winchester, should be observed throughout the realm. Most nations have regulated the standard of measures of length by comparison with the parts of the human body; as the palm, the hand, the span, the foot, the cubit, the ell, (*ulna*, or arm,) the pace, and the fathom. But, as these are of different dimensions in men of different proportions, our ancient historians inform us, that a new standard of longitudinal measure was ascertained by King Henry the First, who commanded that the *ulna*, or ancient ell, which answers to the modern yard, should be made of the exact length of his own arm. And, one standard of measures of length being gained, all others are easily derived from thence; those of greater length by multiplying, those of less by subdividing, that original standard. Thus, by the statute called *compositio ulnarum et perticarum*, five yards and a half make a perch; and the yard is subdivided into three feet, and each foot into twelve inches; which inches will be each of the length of three grains of barley. Superficial measures are derived by squaring those of length; and measures of capacity by cubing them. The standard of weights was originally taken from corns of wheat, whence the lowest denomination of weights we have is still called a grain; thirty-two of which are directed, by the statute called *compositio mensurarum*, to compose a penny-weight, whereof twenty make an ounce, twelve ounces a pound, and so upwards. And upon these principles the first standards were made; which, being originally so fixed by the crown, their subsequent regulations have been generally made by the king in parliament. Thus, under King Richard I, in his parliament holden at Westminster, A.D. 1197, it was ordained that there should be only one weight and one measure throughout the kingdom, and that the custody of the assize, or standard of weights and measures, should be committed to certain persons in every city and borough; from whence the ancient office of king's aulnager seems to have been derived, whose duty it was, for a certain fee, to measure all cloths made for sale, till the office was abolished by the statute 11 and 12 Wm. III, c. 20. In King John's time, this ordinance of King Richard was frequently dispensed with for money, which occasioned a provision to be made for enforcing it, in the great charters of King John and his son. These original standards were called *pondus regis*, and *mensura domini regis*: and are directed by a variety of subsequent statutes to be kept in the exchequer, and all weights and measures to be made conformable thereto. But, as Sir Edward Coke observes, though this hath so often by authority of parliament been enacted, yet it could never be effected; so forcible is custom with the multitude.

Thirdly, as money is the medium of commerce, it is the king's prerogative, as the arbiter of domestic commerce, to give it authority or make it current. Money is an universal medium, or common standard, by comparison with which the value of all merchandize may be ascertained; or it is a sign which represents the respective values of all commodities. Metals were well calculated for this sign, because they are durable and are capable of many subdivisions; and a precious metal is still better calculated for this purpose, because it is the most portable. A metal is also the most proper for a common measure, because it can easily be reduced to the same standard in all nations: and every particular nation fixes on it its own impression, that the weight and standard (wherein consists the intrinsic value) may both be known by inspection only.

As the quantity of previous metals increases, that is, the more of them there is extracted from the mine, this universal medium, or common sign, will sink in value, and grow less precious. Above a thousand millions of bullion are calculated to have been imported into Europe from America within less than three centuries; and the quantity is daily increasing. The consequence is, that more money must be given now for the same commodity that was given an hundred years ago. And, if any accident were to diminish the quantity of gold and silver, their value would proportionably rise. A horse, that was formerly worth ten pounds, is now perhaps worth twenty; and, by any failure of current specie, the price may be reduced to what it was. Yet is the horse in reality neither dearer nor cheaper at one time than another: for, if the metal which constitutes the coin was formerly twice as scarce as at present, the commodity was then as dear at half the price as now it is at the whole.

The coining of money is in all states the act of the sovereign power: for the reason just mentioned, that its value may be known on inspection. And with respect to coinage in general, there are three things to be considered therein; the materials, the impression and the denomination.

With regard to the materials, Sir Edward Coke lays it down, that the money of England must either be of gold or silver; and none other was ever issued by the royal authority till 1672, when copper farthings and half-pence were coined by King Charles the Second, and ordered by proclamation to be current in all payments, under the value of sixpence, and not otherwise. But this copper coin is not upon the same footing with the other in many respects, particularly with regard to the offence of counterfeiting it. And, as to the silver coin, it is enacted by statute 14 Geo. III, c. 42, that no tender of payment in silver money, exceeding twenty-five pounds at one time, shall be a sufficient tender in law for more than its value by weight, at the rate of 5s. 2d. an ounce.

As to the impression, the stamping thereof is the unquestionable prerogative of the crown: for, though divers bishops and monasteries had formerly the privilege of coining money, yet, as Sir Matthew Hale observes, this was usually done by special grant from the king or by prescription, which supposes one; and therefore was derived from, and not in derogation of, the royal prerogative. Besides that they had only the profit of the coinage, and not the power of instituting either the impression or denomination; but had usually the stamp sent them from the exchequer.

The denomination, or the value for which the coin is to pass current, is likewise in the breast of the king; and, if any unusual pieces are coined, that value must be ascertained by proclamation. In order to fix the value, the weight and the fineness of the metal are to be taken into consideration together. When a given weight of gold or silver is of a given fineness, it is then of the true standard, and called esterling or sterling metal; a name for which there are various reasons given, but none of them entirely satisfactory. And of this sterling or esterling metal all the coin of the kingdom must be made, by the statute 25 Edw. III, c. 13. So that the king's prerogative seemeth not to extend to the debasing or enhancing the value of the coin, below or above the sterling value, though Sir Matthew Hale appears to be of another opinion. The king may also, by his proclamation, legitimate foreign coin, and make it current here, declaring at what value it shall be taken in payments. But this, I apprehend, ought to be by comparison with the standard of our own coin; otherwise the consent of parliament will be necessary. There is at present no such legitimated money; Portugal coin being only current by private consent, so that any one who pleases may refuse to take it in payment. The king may also at any time decry, or cry down, any coin of the kingdom, and make it no longer current.

VI. The king is, lastly, considered by the laws of England as the head and supreme governor of the national church.

To enter into the reasons upon which this prerogative is founded is matter rather of divinity than of law. I shall therefore only observe that, by statute 26 Hen.

VIII, c. 1, (reciting that the king's majesty justly and rightfully is and ought to be the supreme head of the church of England; and so had been recognized by the clergy of this kingdom in their convocation,) it is enacted, that the king shall be reputed the only supreme head in earth of the church of England, and shall have, annexed to the imperial crown of this realm, as well the title and style thereof, as all jurisdictions, authorities and commodities, to the said dignity of the supreme head of the church appertaining. And another statute to the same purport, was made, 1 Eliz. c. 1.

In virtue of this authority the king convenes, prorogues, restrains, regulates, and dissolves all ecclesiastical synods or convocations. This was an inherent prerogative of the crown long before the time of Henry VIII, as appears by the statute 8 Hen. VI, c. 1, and the many authors, both lawyers and historians, vouched by Sir Edward Coke. So that the statute 25 Hen. VIII, c. 19, which restrains the convocation from making or putting in execution any canons repugnant to the king's prerogative, or the laws, customs and statutes of the realm, was merely declaratory of the old common law: that part of it only being new which makes the king's royal assent actually necessary to the validity of every canon. The convocation, or ecclesiastical synod, in England, differs considerably in its constitution from the synods of other Christian kingdoms: those consisting wholly of bishops; whereas with us the convocation is the miniature of a parliament wherein the archbishop presides with regal state; the upper house of bishops represents the house of lords; and the lower house, composed of representatives of the several dioceses at large, and of each particular chapter therein, resembles the house of commons, with its knights of the shire and burgesses. This constitution is said to be owing to the policy of Edward I, who thereby, at one and the same time, let in the inferior clergy to the privilege of forming ecclesiastical canons (which before they had not,) and also introduced a method of taxing ecclesiastical benefices, by consent of convocation.

From this prerogative also, of being the head of the church, arises the king's right of nomination to vacant bishoprics, and certain other ecclesiastical preferments; which will more properly be considered when we come to treat of the clergy. I shall only here observe that this is now done in consequence of the statute 25 Hen. VIII, c. 20.

As head of the church, the king is likewise the *dernier resort* in all ecclesiastical causes; an appeal lying ultimately to him in chancery from the sentence of every ecclesiastical judge: which right was restored to the crown by statute 25 Hen. VIII, c. 19, as will be more fully shown hereafter.

American Thought on Executive Power

The great harvest of early American political thinking concerned itself with the principles of representative government and did not spin out all the details of how such principles should be implemented. (This experience in America seems to have been paralleled in the French and Russian Revolutions, where a great deal of time and rhetoric were poured out denouncing the old order, but very little time was spent designing the shape of the new order.) One does not find much discussion about the power of the Executive in the early writings of the Founding Fathers. John Adams drafted some early outlines of his ideas, most of which appeared in the Massachusetts constitution, but he did not attend the Philadelphia Convention and his ideas were not particularly influential. James Madison, on the other hand, was perhaps the most active delegate to the Convention and the vagueness of his pre-Convention comments on executive power indicates how the clash of ideas can sometimes illuminate the mind and broaden the understanding.

In 1785 Madison was still undecided about such fundamental points as whether the Executive should be chosen by the legislature or the people, and whether, indeed, the executive power should be in the hands of one or many. He expressed these doubts in a letter to Caleb Wallace:

> *The Executive Department.* Though it claims the 2d place is not in my estimation entitled to it by its importance all the great powers which properly executive being transferred to the Federal Government. I have made up no final opinion whether the first Magistrate should be chosen by the Legislature or the people at large or whether power should be vested in one man assisted by a council or in a council of which the President shall be only *primus inter pares.* There are examples of each in the United States and probably advantages and disadvantages attending each. It is material I think that the number of members should be small & that their Salaries should be either unalterable by the Legislature or alterable only in such manner as will not affect any individual in place. Our Executive is the worst part of a bad Constitution. The Members of it are dependent on the Legislature not only for their wages but for their reputation and therefore are not likely to withstand usurpations of that branch; they are besides too numerous and expensive, their organization vague & perplexed & to crown the absurdity some of the members may without any new appointment continue in Office for life.[27]

Madison remained perplexed about these questions up to the eve of the Convention, and freely admitted as much. He outlined some general principles of government that he would like to see written into the new Constitution in a letter he wrote to Thomas Jefferson shortly before the Convention, but he had nothing to say about the powers and functions of the Executive. He was only certain that the existing government (the Confederation) was so deficient that substantial change was necessary:

What may be the result of this political experiment cannot be forseen. The difficulties which present themselves are, on the one side, almost sufficient to dismay the most sanguine, whilst on the other side the most timid are compelled to encounter them by the mortal diseases of the existing constitution. These diseases need not be pointed out to you, who so well understand them. Suffice it to say, that they are at present marked by symptoms which are truly alarming, which have tainted the faith of the most orthodox republicans, and which challenge from the votaries of liberty every concession in favor of stable Government not infringing fundamental principles, as the only security against an opposite extreme of our present situation.[28]

In a letter written a few days later to Edmund Randolph, head of the Virginia delegation to the Convention, Madison was still noncommital on the role of the Executive; he indicated only that:

A national Executive will also be necessary. I have scarcely ventured to form my own opinion yet, either of the manner in which it ought to be constituted, or the authorities with which it ought to be clothed.[29]

John Adams

John Adams was the only American political theorist who made a concrete and detailed contribution to the pre-Convention discussion of the executive office. He first expressed himself on the subject in a letter written to Richard Henry Lee in 1775. In it he sketched out the bare bones of a republican form of parliamentary government. In this very rough outline, the Executive was to be elected by a combined vote of the lower house, which he called "the house of commons," and the upper house, or "the council." The Executive or "governor" would have the power to appoint all civil and military officers and magistrates, with the advice and consent of the council, and also be in command of the army, militia and forts, etc.[30]

The following year he elaborated upon this outline in a far more detailed discussion of the problem in a work entitled, "Thoughts on Government." A much more sophisticated and flexible document than the first crude sketch, this essay provided many of the ideas that went into the Massachusetts constitution, which Adams drafted, and were later reflected in the federal Constitution drawn up in Philadelphia. In addition to those responsibilities outlined in the first document, Adams suggested that the state executive or governor should have a veto or "negative" power over the actions of the legislature, that he should be elected annually and should possess the power (together with the council) of granting pardons. A very healthy element of early American pragmatism was introduced when Adams also suggested, with respect to the mode of electing the "great offices of state" including the governor, that:

This mode of constituting the great offices of state will answer very well for the present; but if by experiment it should be found to be inconvenient, the legislature may, at its leisure, devise other methods of creating them, by elections of the people at large, as in Connecticut, or it may enlarge the term for which they shall be chosen to seven years, or three years, or for life, or make any other alterations which the society shall find productive of its ease, its safety, its freedom, or, in one word, its happiness.[31]

Adams was in London during the Constitutional Convention, serving as the first American ambassador to the Court of St. James. He and his family arrived there in the spring of 1785, and late in 1786 he set to work on a much larger treatise on government which was published in two volumes—*A Defence of the Constitutions of the United States of America.* The first volume was completed and printed early the following year and some have speculated that it was influential in swaying the delegates in the direction of forming a national government, but Adams's biographer, Page Smith, points out the unlikeliness of such an inference "in view of the fact that Adams supported Congress as a diplomatic rather than a legislative body and nowhere suggested that the Articles of Confederation be replaced by a constitution modeled along lines which he considered essential for state governments."[32] But when informed of the handiwork of the Founding Fathers at Philadelphia and the subsequent public discussion prior to its ratification, he wrote approvingly to Secretary of State John Jay:

> The public mind cannot be occupied about a nobler object than the proposed plan of government. It appears to be admirably calculated to cement all America in affection and interest, as one great nation. A result of accommodation and compromise cannot be supposed perfectly to coincide with every one's ideas of perfection. But, as all the great principles necessary to order, liberty, and safety, are respected in it, and provision is made for corrections and amendments, as they may be found necessary, I confess I hope to hear of its adoption by all the States.[33]

John Adams
Early Ideas on the Executive
November 15, 1775

John Adams, "From a Letter to Richard Henry Lee," in Charles Francis Adams, ed., *The Works of John Adams* (Boston, 1850) IV, 186-87.

A legislative, an executive, and a judicial power comprehend the whole of what is meant and understood by government. It is by balancing each of these powers against the other two, that the efforts in human nature towards tyranny can alone be checked and restrained, and any degree of freedom preserved in the constitution.

Let a full and free representation of the people be chosen for a house of commons.

Let the house choose, by ballot, twelve, sixteen, twenty-four, or twenty-eight persons, either members of the house, or from the people at large, as the electors please, for a council.

84

Let the house and council, by joint ballot, choose a governor, annually, triennially, or septennially, as you will.

Let the governor, council, and house, be each a distinct and independent branch of the legislature, and have a negative on all laws.

Let the governor, secretary, treasurer, commissary, attorney-general, and solicitor-general, be chosen annually, by joint ballot of both houses.

Let the governor, with seven counsellors, be a quorum.

Let all officers and magistrates, civil and military, be nominated and appointed by the governor, by and with the advice and consent of his council.

Let no officer be appointed but at a general council; and let notice be given to all the counsellors seven days, at least, before a general council.

Let the judges, at least of the supreme court, be incapacitated by law from holding any share in the legislative or executive power; let their commissions be during good behavior, and their salaries ascertained and established by law.

Let the governor have the command of the army, the militia, forts, etc.

Let the Colony have a seal, and affix it to all commissions.

In this way, a single month is sufficient, without the least convulsion, or even animosity, to accomplish a total revolution in the government of a colony. If it is thought more beneficial, a law may be made, by their new legislature, leaving to the people at large the privilege of choosing their governor and counsellors annually, as soon as affairs get into a more quiet course.

In adopting a plan in some respects similar to this, human nature would appear in its proper glory, asserting its own real dignity, pulling down tyrannies at a single exertion, and erecting such new fabrics as it thinks best calculated to promote its happiness.

As you were last evening polite enough to ask me for this model, if such a trifle will be of any service to you, or any gratification of curiosity, here you have it from, Sir,

Your friend and humble servant,

John Adams

John Adams
More Carefully Considered Definition
Of the Executive Role and Functions
January 1776

J. Adams, "Thoughts on Government," IV, 196-200.

4. A representative assembly, although extremely well qualified, and absolutely necessary, as a branch of the legislative, is unfit to exercise the executive power, for want of two essential properties, secrecy and despatch.

5. A representative assembly is still less qualified for the judicial power, because it is too numerous, too slow, and too little skilled in the laws.

6. Because a single assembly, possessed of all the powers of government, would make arbitrary laws for their own interest, execute all laws arbitrarily for their own interest, and adjudge all controversies in their own favor.

But shall the whole power of legislation rest in one assembly? Most of the foregoing reasons apply equally to prove that the legislative power ought to be more complex; to which we may add, that if the legislative power is wholly in one assembly, and the executive in another, or in a single person, these two powers will oppose and encroach upon each other, until the contest shall end in war, and the whole power, legislative and executive, be usurped by the strongest.

The judicial power, in such case, could not mediate, or hold the balance between the two contending powers, because the legislative would undermine it. And this shows the necessity, too, of giving the executive power a negative upon the legislative, otherwise this will be continually encroaching upon that.

To avoid these dangers, let a distinct assembly be constituted, as a mediator between the two extreme branches of the legislature, that which represents the people, and that which is vested with the executive power.

Let the representative assembly then elect by ballot, from among themselves or their constituents, or both, a distinct assembly, which for the sake of perspicuity, we will call a council. It may consist of any number you please, say twenty or thirty, and should have a free and independent exercise of its judgment, and consequently a negative voice in the legislature.

These two bodies, thus constituted, and made integral parts of the legislature, let them unite, and by joint ballot choose a governor, who, after being stripped of most of those badges of domination, called prerogatives, should have a free and independent exercise of his judgment, and be made also an integral part of the legislature. This, I know, is liable to objections; and, if you please, you may make him only president of the council, as in Connecticut. But as the governor is to be invested with the executive power, with consent of council, I think he ought to have a negative upon the legislative. If he is annually elective, as he ought to be, he will always have so much reverence and affection for the people, their representatives and counsellors, that, although you give him an independent exercise of his judgment, he will seldom use it in opposition to the two houses, except in cases the public utility of which would be conspicuous; and some such cases would happen.

In the present exigency of American affairs, when, by an act of Parliament, we are put out of the royal protection, and consequently discharged from our allegiance, and it has become necessary to assume government for our immediate security, the governor, lieutenant-governor, secretary, treasurer, commissary, attorney-general, should be chosen by joint ballot of both houses. And these and all other elections, especially of representatives and counsellors, should be annual, there not being in the whole circle of the sciences a maxim more infallible than this, "where annual elections end, there slavery begins."

These great men, in this respect, should be, once a year,
> Like bubbles on the sea of matter borne,
> They rise, they break, and to that sea return.

They will teach them the great political virtues of humility, patience, and moderation, without which every man in power becomes a ravenous beast of prey.

This mode of constituting the great offices of state will answer very well for the present; but if by experiment it should be found inconvenient, the legislature may, at its leisure, devise other methods of creating them, by elections of the people at large, as in Connecticut, or it may enlarge the term for which they shall be chosen to seven years, or three years, or for life, or make any other alterations which the society shall find productive of its ease, its safety, its freedom, or, in one word, its happiness.

A rotation of all offices, as well as of representatives and counsellors, has many advocates, and is contended for with many plausible arguments. It would be attended, no doubt, with many advantages; and if the society has a sufficient number of suitable characters to supply the great number of vacancies which would be made by such a rotation, I can see no objection to it. These persons may be allowed to serve for three years, and then be excluded three years, or for any longer or shorter term.

Any seven or nine of the legislative council may be made a quorum, for doing business as a privy council, to advise the governor in the exercise of the executive branch of power, and in all acts of state.

The governor should have the command of the militia and of all your armies. The power of pardons should be with the governor and council.

Judges, justices, and all other officers, civil and military, should be nominated and appointed by the governor, with the advice and consent of council, unless you choose to have a government more popular; if you do, all officers, civil and military, may be chosen by joint ballot of both houses; or, in order to preserve the independence and importance of each house, by ballot of one house, concurred in by the other. Sheriffs should be chosen by the freeholders of counties; so should registers of deeds and clerks of counties.

All officers should have commissions, under the hand of the governor and seal of the colony.

The dignity and stability of government in all its branches, the morals of the people, and every blessing of society depend so much upon an upright and skilful administration of justice, that the judicial power ought to be distinct from both the legislative and executive, and independent upon both, that so it may be a check upon both, as both should be checks upon that. The judges, therefore, should be always men of learning and experience in the laws, of exemplary morals, great patience, calmness, coolness, and attention. Their minds should not be distracted with jarring interests; they should not be dependent upon any man, or body of men. To these ends, they should hold estates for life in their offices; or, in other words, their commissions should be during good behavior, and their salaries ascertained and established by law. For misbehavior, the grand inquest of the colony, the house of representatives, should impeach them before the governor and council, where they should have time and opportunity to make their defence; but, if convicted, should be removed from their offices, and subjected to such other punishment as shall be thought proper.

A militia law, requiring all men, or with very few exceptions besides cases of conscience, to be provided with arms and ammunition, to be trained at certain seasons; and requiring counties, towns, or other small districts, to be provided with public stocks of ammunition and intrenching utensils, and with some settled plans for transporting provisions after the militia, when marched to defend their country against sudden invasions; and requiring certain districts to be provided with field-pieces, companies of matrosses, and perhaps some regiments of light-horse, is always a wise institution, and, in the present circumstances of our country, indispensable.

Laws for the liberal education of youth, especially of the lower class of people, are so extremely wise and useful, that, to a humane and generous mind, no expense for this purpose would be thought extravagant.

The very mention of sumptuary laws will excite a smile. Whether our countrymen have wisdom and virtue enough to submit to them, I know not; but the happiness of the people might be greatly promoted by them, and a revenue saved sufficient to carry on this war forever. Frugality is a great revenue, besides curing us of vanities, levities, and fopperies, which are real antidotes to all great, manly, and warlike virtues.

But must not all commissions run in the name of a king? No. Why may they not as well run thus, "the colony of   to A. B. greeting," and be tested by the governor?

Why may not writs, instead of running in the name of the king, run thus, "The colony of   to the sheriff," etc., and be tested by the chief justice?

Why may not indictments conclude, "against the peace of the colony of and the dignity of the same?"

A constitution founded on these principles introduces knowledge among the people, and inspires them with a conscious dignity becoming freemen; a general emulation takes place, which causes good humor, sociability, good manners, and good morals to be general. That elevation of sentiment inspired by such a government, makes the common people brave and enterprising. That ambition which is inspired by it makes them sober, industrious, and frugal. You will find among them some elegance, perhaps, but more solidity; a little pleasure, but a great deal of business; some politeness, but more civility. If you compare such a country with the regions of domination, whether monarchical or aristocratical, you will fancy yourself in Arcadia or Elysium.

If the colonies should assume governments separately, they should be left entirely to their own choice of the forms; and if a continental constitution should be formed, it should be a congress, containing a fair and adequate representation of the colonies, and its authority should sacredly be confined to these cases, namely, war, trade, disputes between colony and colony, the post-office, and the unappropriated lands of the crown, as they used to be called.

These colonies, under such forms of government, and in such a union, would be unconquerable by all the monarchies of Europe.

You and I, my dear friend, have been sent into life at a time when the greatest lawgivers of antiquity would have wished to live. How few of the human race have ever enjoyed an opportunity of making an election of government, more than of air, soil, or climate, for themselves or their children! When, before the present epocha, had three millions of people full power and a fair opportunity to form and establish the wisest and happiest government that human wisdom can contrive? I hope you will avail yourself and your country of that extensive learning and indefatigable industry which you possess, to assist her in the formation of the happiest governments and the best character of a great people. For myself, I must beg you to keep my name out of sight; for this feeble attempt, if it should be known to be mine, would oblige me to apply to myself those lines of the immortal John Milton, in one of his sonnets:—

> I did but prompt the age to quit their clogs
> By the known rules of ancient liberty,
> When straight a barbarous noise environs me
> Of owls and cuckoos, asses, apes, and dogs.

Thomas Paine

The literary and propaganda *tour de force* of the revolution, Tom Paine's *Common Sense*, covered the question briefly in a few sentences, merely outlining a procedure by which a "President" should be elected. Only the title "President" remained in anyone's memory, however, for Paine was probably the first person to suggest this title for the executive head of the new American government.

Thomas Paine
General References to the Executive Role
January 10, 1776

Philip Foner, ed., *The Complete Writings of Thomas Paine* (New York, 1945) I, 28-29.

Let the assemblies be annual, with a president only. The representation more equal, their business wholly domestic, and subject to the authority of a Continental Congress.

Let each colony be divided into six, eight, or ten, convenient districts, each district to send a proper number of delegates to Congress, so that each colony send at least thirty. The whole number in Congress will be at least 390. Each Congress to sit and to choose a President by the following method. When the delegates are met, let a colony be taken from the whole thirteen colonies by lot, after which let the Congress choose (by ballot) a President from out of the delegates of that province. In the next Congress, let a colony be taken by lot from twelve only, omitting that colony from which the president was taken in the former Congress, and so proceeding on till the whole thirteen shall have had their proper rotation. And in order that nothing may pass into a law but what is satisfactorily just, not less than three-fifths of the Congress to be called a majority. He that will promote discord, under a government so equally formed as this, would have joined Lucifer in his revolt.

But where, say some, is the king of America? I'll tell you, friend, he reigns above, and doth not make havoc of mankind like the royal brute of Great Britain. Yet that we may not appear to be defective even in earthly honors, let a day be solemnly set apart for proclaiming the charter; let it be brought forth placed on the divine law, the Word of God; let a crown be placed thereon, by which the world may know, that so far as we approve of monarchy, that in America the law is king. For as in absolute governments the king is law, so in free countries the law ought to be king; and there ought to be no other. But lest any ill use should afterwards arise, let the crown at the conclusion of the ceremony be demolished, and scattered among the people whose right it is.

Supporters and Critics of the British Constitutional System

The other political model to which the Founding Fathers constantly turned, though with very mixed opinions and emotions, was the British constitutional system, to which they could all trace their political lineage. The prerogatives of the King, the role of Parliament, the qualifications for the franchise, the corruption of the power of appointment, the treaty-making power, the power of impeachment—all of these questions which had originally emerged in a British context were brought out time and time again to the floor of the Constitutional Convention. Madison records instances where brief, or even in some cases extensive references were made to this significant landmark of constitutional government.[34] There were those like Alexander Hamilton and James Dickinson, and to a certain extent Charles Pinkney, who worshipped at the shrine of the British monarchy; others like Colonel George Mason and Benjamin Franklin consistently criticized it; and still others like Madison and James Wilson argued that different conditions in America required different, quite different solutions than those offered by the British system.

Perhaps one could describe the situation as something like the *identity crisis* of a child breaking away from his family ties, mixed emotions—both love and hate, pride and shame, approval and disapproval—were all manifested by the delegates. The British constitution was always in their minds, and it formed the background of their exploration of the major problems confronting them. Hamilton quoted Jacques Neckar, who described Britain as the only government in the world "which united public strength with individual security." Some approved and some disapproved of the British system, but no one could avoid considering it, and in a very significant sense it was the touchstone of the continuing discussion that went on through the hot summer of 1787 in Philadelphia.

Hamilton was the strongest supporter of the British constitutional system as it was presently operating, and he made this explicitly clear in his lengthy address to the Convention on Monday, June 18, 1787. His views on the executive office were extreme; he proposed an elective monarch to hold office for life. A delegate who was present and heard the speech, Dr. William Samual Johnson, remarked:

> The gentleman from New York is praised by all, but supported by no gentlemen.[35]

Madison's notes retain much of the flavor of Hamilton's remarks:

> This progress of the public mind led him to anticipate the time, when others as well as himself would join in the praise bestowed by Mr. Neckar on the British Constitution. . . . In every community where industry is encouraged, there will be a division of it into the few and the many. Hence separate interests will arise. There will be debtors and creditors, etc. Give all power to the many, they will oppress the few. Give all power to the few, they will oppress the many. Both therefore ought to have power, that each may defend itself against the other. To the want of this check we owe our paper money—installment laws, etc. To the proper adjustment of it the British owe the excellence of their Constitution. Their House of Lords is a most noble institution. Having nothing to hope for by a change, and a sufficient interest by means of their property, in being faithful to the National interest, they form a permanent barrier against every pernicious innovation, whether attempted on the part of the Crown or of the Commons. No temporary Senate will have firmness en'o' to answer the purpose. . . . Gentlemen differ in their opinions concerning the necessary checks, from different estimates they form of the human passions. They suppose seven years a sufficient period to give the Senate an adequate firmness, from not duly considering the amazing violence and turbulence of the democratic spirit. When a great object of government is pursued, which seizes the popular passions, they spread like wild fire, and become irresistible. He appealed to the gentlemen from the New England States whether experience had not there verified the remark. As to the Executive, it seemed to be admitted that no good one could be established on Republican principles. Was not this giving up the merits of the question; for can there be good Government without a good Executive. The English model was the only good one on this subject. The Hereditary interest of the King was so interwoven with that of the Nation, and his personal emoluments so great, that he was placed above the danger of being corrupted from abroad—and at the same time was both sufficiently independent and sufficiently controulled, to answer the purpose of the institution at home.[36]

Benjamin Franklin had been an American ambassador to Britain in the period before the American Constitution was written, and he was one of the few delegates who had any direct experience with the workings of the British constitution. He was disturbed by the amount of praise heaped upon the British system by admiring Americans during the discussions, and interjected his view of things from time to time in an effort to introduce a note of realism into the debates:

Sir, there are two passions which have a powerful influence on the affairs of men. These are ambition and avarice; the love of power, and the love of money. Separately each of these has great force in prompting men to action; but when united in view of the same object, they have in many minds the most violent effects. Place before the eyes of such men a post of honour that shall at the same time be a place of profit, and they will move heaven and earth to obtain it. The vast number of such places it is that renders the British Government so tempestuous. The struggles for them are the true sources of all those factions which are perpetually dividing the Nation, distracting its councils, hurrying sometimes into fruitless and mischievous wars, and often compelling a submission to dishonourable terms of peace.[37]

Much later in the discussion, Franklin continued his argument:

We seemed he said too much to fear cabals in appointment by a number, and to have too much confidence in those of single persons. Experience showed that caprice, the intrigues of favorites and mistresses, etc., were nevertheless the means most prevalent in monarchies. Among instances of abuse in such modes of appointment, he mentioned the many bad Governors appointed in Great Britain for the Colonies. He thought that a Council would not only be a check on a bad President but be a relief to a good one.[38]

James Wilson from Pennsylvania was brief in stating the case against transplanting either the prerogatives of the King or the British constitutional system to American soil:

He did not consider the prerogatives of the British Monarch as a proper guide in defining the Executive powers. Some of these prerogatives were of a Legislative nature. Among others that of war and peace, etc. The only powers he conceived strictly Executive were those of executing the laws, and appointing officers, not (appertaining to and) appointed by the Legislature. . . . He repeated that he was not governed by the British model which was inapplicable to the situation of this Country; the extent of which was so great, and manners so republican, that nothing but a great federated Republic would do for it.[39]

The Wilson arguments prevailed. Although the prerogatives of the British monarch may have served as the paradigm for the powers of the American Executive set forth in Article II of the United States Constitution, in almost every instance the actual definition or prescription of power indicated an arrangement whereby the executive's functions and powers were to be shared, and to some extent limited by the legislature. One can find little of this in the formal British constitution as set forth in Blackstone, but by the end of the eighteenth century the British system was in the process of a transition where legislative leaders in Parliament were informally being brought within the framework of the executive and the Crown. More and more, executive functions and responsibilities were being lodged in the persons of the leaders of the Parliament as advisors to the King.[40] The Americans struck out in a different direction, more in keeping with their traditionless society and the endless frontiers of their geography and their politics; but in their break with the past there were many residual legacies that were clearly traceable to the British system.

The Presidency at the Constitutional Convention

The Executive office which was created at the Constitutional Convention held in Philadelphia in the spring and summer of 1787 was clearly influenced by the early experiences of colonial and state governments and by the knowledge among the delegates of political theory and British constitutional history; but the debates at the long meetings themselves, stretching out over five months, sharpened the views of the delegates on the problems under discussion and brought about significant progress through compromise, resulting in a formidable initial profile of the presidential office. Many different proposals were presented and there was an ebb and flow of attitudes throughout the sessions with respect to presidential power and authority. It would be impossible to fully record here all of the discussion which took place touching upon these questions, for in truth all the major problems regarding the overall structure of the government, the form of representation, the interrelationship of all the branches of government to one another, would have some relevance to the presidency.

But if one were to select the most critical issues having extraordinary bearing upon the future of the presidential office, one could hardly avoid the question of a single or plural Executive which came up early in the convention. The second issue debated upon at the Convention was the manner in which the Executive would be selected. There was, of course, discussion and, at times, real conflict over the various powers the Executive should possess and whether or not his decisions should be subject to the review of an executive council which could serve as a check upon any form of tyrannical independence. But the Founding Fathers were too much under the influence of Montesquieu and his doctrine of division of power to let such an obvious threat to the independence of the Executive stand. The debates touching upon the nature of the office and the manner (and duration) of his selection are representative of the stimulating discussion which took place while the skeletal structure of the presidential office was being hammered out in 1787.

James Madison was the first delegate to arrive in Philadelphia in 1787 after a two day journey from New York. Ten days later General George Washington appeared and he was followed in the next few days by Governor Edmund Randolph and the other Virginia delegates. Soon the Virginians were caucusing at the India Queen Tavern, and out of these pre-convention discussions emerged the Virginia Plan, which, as historian James M. Burns has described it, was "essentially a recasting of the proposals Madison had sent from New York to Jefferson, Washington, and Randolph during the spring."[41]

The plan called for a national government with three branches. The legislature would be divided into two houses, one directly elected, the other indirectly. The executive was to be chosen by the national legislature, but he could have only one term. A national judiciary would have jurisdiction over questions involving the "national peace and harmony."[42]

The Virginia Plan became the working agenda of the Convention, and its proposal for the selection of a Chief Executive came dangerously close to winning the approval of the delegates. If it had, we would have experienced parliamentary government in the United States, because in essence that is what the proposal called for. It was presented in the form of a resolution to the Convention, by Governor Randolph on May 29, 1787, but Madison indicated on a number of occasions that it was the joint product of all seven of the Virginia delegates.

Two days after its introduction, the section of the Virginia Plan dealing with the national Executive came before the Committee of the Whole, thus initiating one of the most attenuated and controversial debates of the Convention.

The Edmund Randolph (Virginia) Proposal
For the Organization of the Executive Branch
May 29, 1787

Max Farrand, ed., *The Records of the Federal Convention* (New Haven, 1911) I, 21.

Resd. that a National Executive be instituted; to be chosen by the National Legislature for the term of   years, to receive punctually at stated times, a fixed compensation for the services rendered, in which no increase or diminution shall be made so as to affect the Magistracy, existing at the time of increase or diminution, and to be ineligible a second time; and that besides a general authority to execute the National laws, it ought to enjoy the Executive rights vested in Congress by the Confederation.

The discussion began over the question of whether the Executive should be a single person or more than one, and the debate became so heated on this point that it was finally agreed to postpone a vote until the body had further time to consider it. A discussion then followed concerning the length of the term the Executive would serve; the proposal that it should be a single term of seven years won by a majority of one vote. The following day the committee decided, by a vote of 8 to 2, that the Executive should be "chosen by the national legislature for a term of seven years." The only states to oppose the resolution were Pennsylvania and Maryland. But Elbridge Gerry of Massachusetts had serious doubts about such a procedure.

There would be a constant intrigue kept up for the appointment. The Legislature & the candidates wd. bargain & play into one another's hands. Votes would be given by the former under the promises or expectations from the latter, of recompensing them by services to members of the Legislature or to their friends. . . . He thought the Community not yet ripe for stripping the States of their powers, even such (as) might (not) be requisite for local purposes. He (was) for waiting till people (should) feel more the necessity of it. He seemed to prefer the taking the suffrages of the States instead of Electors, or letting the Legislature nominate, and the electors appoint. (He was) not clear that the people ought to act directly even in (the) choice of electors, being too little informed of personal characters in large districts and liable to deceptions.[43]

The same day James Wilson had tabled a substitute motion calling for the selection of an Executive by electors to be chosen by the people:

that the Executive Magistry be (elected) in the following manner: (That) the States be divided into   districts: (& that) the persons qualified (to vote in each) district for members of the first branch of the national Legislature elect   members for their respective districts to be electors of the Executive Magistracy. That the said Electors of the Executive magistry meet at   and they or any   of them so met shall proceed to elect by ballot, but not of their own body   person   in whom the Executive authority of the national Government shall be vested.[44]

This motion lost by the same margin by which the other motion had won, 8 to 2. It was forgotten for some time, but revived at a later date.

Elbridge Gerry then introduced an unpopular motion that the Executive should be "elected by the executives of the states," but this failed to carry a single state's vote in the committee. On the thirteenth of June the Committee of the Whole reported on its work of the previous two weeks. The parliamentary method of electing an Executive was firmly embedded in that report:

Resolved that a National Executive be instituted to consist of a single person, to be chosen by the Natl. Legislature for the term of seven years, with power to. . . .[45]

Two days later William Paterson of New Jersey presented an alternative to the Virginia proposal. He indicated that his plan had the backing of several of the other delegations which had participated in its preparation. In effect it was an attempt on the part of the smaller or less populous states (although New York was initially among them) to protect their interests and power in the new Constitution. They realized that under the provisions of the Virginia Plan the states with the largest populations would be able to control the government. By controlling the lower house, these states would also determine the majority in the upper house, and the Executive as well.

The New York delegates favored the Paterson proposal because they feared that all of the states would lose too much power if a new national government was created. They recognized that changes would have to be made in the existing government, but if its basic confederate structure could be retained, the states could continue to be the critical decision-makers on an equal basis. So the Paterson plan proposed the revision of the existing constitution by strengthening the powers of the

Confederation, eliminating some of its most obvious flaws and making it (hopefully) capable of governing. Under these changes the Congress could then impose decisions on the states, and an executive power was even proposed to carry out these decisions:

> Resd. that U. States in Congs. be authorized to elect a federal Executive to consist of   persons, to continue in office for the term of   years, to receive punctually at stated times a fixed compensation for their services, in which no increase or diminution shall be made so as to effect the persons composing the Executive at the time of such an increase or diminution, to be paid out of the federal treasury; to be incapable of holding any other office or appointment during their time of service and for   years thereafter; to be ineligible a second time, and removable by Congs. on application by a majority of the Executives of the several States, and that the. . . .[46]

The following Monday Alexander Hamilton delivered his famous Convention speech which lasted between five and six hours. In its course he argued that an Executive should serve "during good behavior," or, in other words, for life.

Alexander Hamilton
Major Constitutional Convention Speech
Sections Dealing With the Executive
June 18, 1787

Farrand, I, 289-92.

As to the Executive, it seemed to be admitted that no good one could be established on Republican principles. Was not this giving up the merits of the question; for can there be a good Govt. without a good Executive. The English model was the only good one on this subject. The Hereditary interest of the King was so interwoven with that of the Nation, and his personal emoluments so great, that he was placed above the danger of being corrupted from abroad—and at the same time was both sufficiently independent and sufficiently controuled, to answer the purpose of the institution at home. One of the weak sides of Republics was their being liable to foreign influence & corruption. Men of little character, acquiring great power become easily the tools of intermedling neibours. Sweeden was a striking instance. The French & English had each their parties during the late Revolution which was effected by the predominant influence of the former. What is the inference from all these observations? That we ought to go as far in order to attain stability and permanency, as republican principles will admit. Let one branch of the Legislature hold their places for life or at least during good-behaviour. Let the Executive also be for life. He appealed to the feelings of the members present whether a term of seven years, would induce the sacrifices of private affairs which an acceptance of public trust would require, so as to ensure the services of the best Citizens. On this plan we should have in the Senate a permanent will, a weighty interest, which would answer essential purposes. But is this a Republican Govt. it will be asked? Yes, if all the Magistrates are appointed, and vacancies are filled, by the people, or a process of election originating with the people. He was sensible that an Executive constituted as he proposed would have in fact but little of the power and independence that might be necessary. On the other plan of appointing him for 7 years, he thought the Executive ought to have but little power. He would be ambitious, with the means of making creatures; and as the object of his ambition wd. be to *prolong* his power, it is probable that in case of a war, he would avail himself of the emergence, to evade or refuse a degradation from his place. An Executive for life has not this motive for forgetting his fidelity, and will therefore be a safer depositary of power. It will be objected probably, that such an Executive will be an *elective Monarch*, and will give birth to the tumults which characterise that form of Govt. He wd. reply that *Monarch* is an indefinite term. It marks not either the degree or duration of power. If this Executive Magistrate wd. be a monarch for life—the other propd. by the Report from the Committee of the whole, wd. be a monarch for seven years. The circumstance of being elective was also applicable to both. It had been observed by judicious writers that elective monarchies wd. be the best if they could be guarded agst. the *tumults* excited by the ambition and intrigues of competitors. He was not sure that tumults were an inseparable evil. He rather thought this character of Elective Monarchies had been taken rather from particular cases than from general principles. The election of Roman Emperors was made by the *Army*. In *Poland* the election is made by great rival *princes* with independent power, and ample means, of raising commotions. In the German Empire, The appointment is made by the Electors & Princes, who have equal motives & means, for exciting cabals & parties. Might (not) such a mode of election be devised among ourselves as will defend the community agst. these effects in any dangerous degree? Having made these observations he would read to the Committee a sketch of a plan which he shd. prefer to either of those under consideration.

IV. The Supreme Executive authority of the United States to be vested in a Governour to be elected to serve during good behaviour—the election to be made by Electors chosen by the people in the Election Districts aforesaid— The authorities & functions of the Executive to be as follows: to have a negative on all laws about to be passed, and the execution of all laws passed, to have the direction of war when authorized or begun; to have with the advice and approbation of the Senate the power of making all treaties; to have the sole appointment of the heads or chief officers of the departments of Finance, War and Foreign Affairs; to have the nomination of all other officers (Ambassadors to foreign Nations included) subject to the approbation or rejection of the Senate; to have the power of pardoning all offences except Treason; which he shall not pardon without the approbation of the Senate.

V. On the death resignation or removal of the Governour his authorities to be exercised by the President of the Senate till a Successor be appointed.

Before he closed his speech, Hamilton outlined his proposed constitution. There is still considerable confusion and controversy over the various existing texts of these remarks, the difference existing mainly in the method of electing the Executive recorded in Madison's and the other delegate's notes on the one hand, and Hamilton's own copy found among his papers, which may have been changed at some later time by its author. In the Hamilton version there was a double set of presidential electors, the first chosen by the people, and the second set selected by the first electors.

Alexander Hamilton
Plan for the Election of the President
June 18, 1787

Farrand, III, 622-25

Article IV

1. The President of the United States of America, (except in the first instance) shall be elected in manner following——The Judges of the Supreme Court shall within sixty days after a vacancy shall happen, cause public notice to be given in each State, of such vacancy, appointing therein three several days for the several purposes following, to wit, a day for commencing the election of electors for the purposes hereinafter specified, to be called the first electors, which day shall not be less than forty, nor more than sixty days, after the day of the publication of the notice in each State——another day for the meeting of the electors not less than forty nor more than ninety days from the day for commencing their election—— another day for the meeting of electors to be chosen by the first electors, for the purpose hereinafter specified, and to be called the second Electors, which day shall be not less than forty nor more than sixty days after the meeting of the first electors.

2. After notice of a vacancy shall have been given there shall be chosen in each State a number of persons, as the first electors in the preceding section mentioned, equal to the whole number of the Representatives and Senators of such State in the Legislature of the United States; which electors shall be chosen by the Citizens of such State having an estate of inheritance or for three lives in land, or a clear personal estate of the value of one thousand Spanish milled dollars of the present Standard.

3. These first electors shall meet in their respective States at the time appointed, at one place; and shall proceed to vote by ballot for a President, who shall not be one of their own number, unless the Legislature upon experiment should hereafter direct otherwise. They shall cause two lists to be made of the name or names of the person or persons voted for, which they or the major part of them shall sign & certify. They shall then proceed each to nominate openly in the presence of the others, two persons as for second electors, and out of the persons who shall have the four highest numbers of Nominations, they shall afterwards by ballot by plurality of votes choose two who shall be the second electors, to each of whom shall

be delivered one of the lists before mentioned. These second electors shall not be any of the persons voted for as President. A copy of the same list signed and certified in like manner shall be transmitted by the first electors to the Seat of the Government of the United States, under a sealed cover directed to the President of the Assembly, which after the meeting of the second electors shall be opened for the inspection of the two House of the Legislature.

4. The second electors shall meet precisely on the day appointed and not on another day, at one place. The Chief Justice of the Supreme Court, or if there be no Chief Justice, the Judge senior in office in such Court, or if there be no one Judge senior in office, some other Judge of that Court, by the choice of the rest of the Judges or of a majority of them, shall attend at the same place and shall preside at the meeting, but shall have no vote. Two thirds of the whole number of the Electors shall constitute a sufficient meeting for the execution of their trust. At this meeting the lists delivered to the respective electors shall be produced and inspected, and if there be any person who has a majority of the whole number of votes given by the first electors, he shall be the President of the United States; but if there be no such person, the second electors so met shall proceed to vote, by ballot for one of the persons named in the lists who shall, have the three highest numbers of the votes of the first electors; and if upon the first or any succeeding ballot on the day of their meeting, either of those persons shall have a number of votes equal to a majority of the whole number of second electors chosen, he shall be the President. But if no such choice be made on the day appointed for the meeting either by reason of the nonattendance of the second electors, or their not agreeing, or any other matter, the person having the greatest number of votes of the first electors shall be the President.

5. If it should happen that the Chief Justice or some other Judge of the Supreme Court should not attend in due time, the second electors shall proceed to the execution of their trust without him.

6. If the Judges should neglect to cause the notice required by the first section of this article to be given within the time therein limited, they may nevertheless cause it to be afterwards given; but their neglect if wilful, is hereby declared to be an offence for which they may be impeached, and if convicted they shall be punished as in other cases of conviction on impeachment.

7. The Legislature shall by permanent laws provide such further regulations as may be necessary for the more orderly election of the President, not contravening the provisions herein contained.

8. The President before he shall enter upon the execution of his office shall take an oath or affirmation, faithfully to execute the same, and to the utmost of his Judgment & power to protect the rights of the people, and preserve the Constitution inviolate. This oath or affirmation shall be administered by the President of the Senate for the time being in the presence of both Houses of the Legislature.

9. The Senate and the Assembly shall always convene in Session on the day appointed for the meeting of the second electors and shall continue sitting till the President take the oath or affirmation of office. He shall hold his place during good behavior, removeable only by conviction upon an impeachment for some crime or misdemeanor.

10. The President at the beginning of every meeting of the Legislature as soon as they shall be ready to proceed to business, shall convene them together at the place where the Senate shall sit, and shall communicate to them all such matters as may be necessary for their information, or as may require their consideration. He may by message during the Session communicate all other matters which may appear to him proper. He may, whenever in his opinion the public business shall require it, convene the Senate and Assembly, or either of them, and may prorogue them for a time not exceeding forty days at one prorogation; and if they should disagree about their adjournment, he may adjourn them to such time as he shall think proper. He shall have a right to negative all bills, Resolutions or acts of the two Houses of the Legislature about to be passed into laws. He shall take care that the laws be faithfully executed. He shall be the commander in chief of the army and Navy of the United States and of the Militia within the several States, and shall have the direction of war when commenced, but he shall not take the actual command in the field of any army without the consent of the Senate and Assembly. All treaties, conventions and agreements with foreign nations shall be made by him, by and with the advice and consent of the Senate. He shall have the appointment of the principal or Chief officer of each of the departments of War, naval Affairs, Finance, and Foreign Affairs; and shall have the nomination; and by and with the Consent of the Senate, the appointment of all other officers to be appointed under the authority of the United States, except such for whom different provision is made by this Constitution; and provided that this shall not be construed to prevent the Legislature, from appointing by name in their laws, persons to special & particular trusts created in such laws, nor shall be construed to prevent principals in offices merely ministerial, from constituting deputies.—In the recess of the Senate he may fill vacancies in offices by appointments to continue in force until the end of the next Session of the Senate. And he shall commission all Officers. He shall have power to pardon all offences except treason, for which he may grant reprieves, until the opening of the Senate & Assembly can be had; and with their concurrence may pardon the same.

11. He shall receive a fixed compensation for his Services to be paid to him at stated times, and not to be increased nor diminished during his continuance in office—

12. If he depart out of the United States without the Consent of the Senate and Assembly, he shall thereby abdicate his office—

13. He may be impeached for any crime or misdemeanor by the two Houses of the Legislature, two thirds of each House concurring, and if convicted shall be removed from office. He may be afterwards tried & punished in the ordinary course of law—. His impeachment shall operate as a suspension from office until the determination thereof.

14. The President of the Senate shall be Vice President of the United States. On the death, resignation, impeachment, removal from office, or absence from the United States, of the President thereof, the Vice President shall exercise all the powers by this Constitution vested in the President, until another shall be appointed, or until he shall return within the United States, if his absence was with the Consent of the Senate and Assembly.

A whole month went by without any further serious debate on this question. The Convention was divided on the vital questions of power and representation, and this division was manifested in the struggle over the Virginia and the Paterson Plans. It was really not until "the Great Compromise"[47] was at least provisionally established on July 16 that the Convention was ready to return to the really unsettled question of the Executive. The term "unsettled" is used advisedly, for the Convention was to shift its position radically with respect to the selection of the Executive, but as late as July 17, the Committee of the Whole voted unanimously for the Executive "to be chosen by the national legislature." These votes took place by states, however, and there were an increasing number of articulate voices raised against that procedure. Gouverneur Morris and James Wilson both spoke out very strongly in favor of election by the people and not by the legislature.

Excerpts from the Convention Debate On the Election of the President
July 17, 1787

Farrand, II, 29-32.

MR. GOVERNR. MORRIS was pointedly agst. his being so chosen. He will be the mere creature of the Legisl: if appointed & impeachable by that body. He ought to be elected by the people at large, by the freeholders of the Country. That difficulties attend this mode, he admits. But they had been found superable in N.Y. & in Cont. and would he believed be found so, in the case of an Executive for the U. States. If the people should elect, they will never fail to prefer some man of distinguished character, or services; some man, if he might so speak, of continental reputation. If the Legislature elect, it will be the work of intrigue, of cabal, and of faction: it will be like the election of a pope by a conclave of cardinals; real merit will rarely be the title to the appointment. [He moved to strike out "National Legislature" & insert "citizens of U.S."]

MR. SHERMAN thought that the sense of the Nation would be better expressed by the Legislature, than by the people at large. The latter will never be sufficiently informed of characters, and besides will never give a majority of votes to any one man. They will generally vote for some man in their own State, and the largest State will have the best chance for the appointment. If the choice be made by the Legislre. A majority of voices may be made necessary to constitute an election.

MR. WILSON. Two arguments have been urged agst. an election of the Executive Magistrate by the people. 1. The example of Poland where an Election of the supreme Magistrate is attended with the most dangerous commotions. The cases he observed were totally dissimilar. The Polish nobles have resources & dependents which enable them to appear in force, and to threaten the Republic as well as each other. In the next place the electors all assemble in one place: which would not be the case with us. The 2d. argt. is that a *majority* of the people would never concur. It might be answered that the concurrence of a majority of people is not a necessary principle of election, nor required as such in any of the States. But allowing the objection all its force, it may be obviated by the expedient used in Masts. where the Legislature by majority of voices, decide in case a majority of people do not concur in favor of one of the candidates. This would restrain the choice to a good nomination at least, and prevent in a great degree intrigue & cabal. A particular objection with him agst. an absolute election by the Legislre. was that the Exec: in that case would be too dependent to stand the mediator between the intrigues & sinister views of the Representatives and the general liberties & interests of the people.

MR. PINKNEY did not expect this question would again have been brought forward; An Election by the people being liable to the most obvious & striking objections. They will be led by a few active & designing men. The most populous States by combining in favor of the same individual will be able to carry their points. The Natl. Legislature being most immediately interested in the laws made by themselves, will be most attentive to the choice of a fit man to carry them properly into execution.

MR. GOVR. MORRIS. It is said that in case of an election by the people the populous States will combine & elect whom they please. Just the reverse. The people of such States cannot combine. If their be any combination it must be among their representatives in the Legislature. It is said the people will be led by a few designing men. This might happen in a small district. It can never happen throughout the continent. In the election of a Govr. of N. York, it sometimes is the case in particular spots, that the activity & intrigues of little partizans are successful, but the general voice of the State is never influenced by such artifices. It is said the multitude will be uninformed. It is true they would be uninformed of what passed in the Legislative Conclave, if the election were to be made there; but they will not be uninformed of those great & illustrious characters which have merited their esteem & confidence. If the Executive be chosen by the Natl. Legislature, he will not be independent of it; and if not independent, usurpation & tyranny on the part of the Legislature will be the consequence. This was the case in England in the last Century. It has been the case in Holland, where their Senates have engrossed all power. It has been the case everywhere. He was surprised that an election by the people at large should ever have been likened to the Polish election of the first Magistrate. An election by the Legislature will bear a real likeness to the election by the Diet of Poland. The great must be the electors in both cases, and the corruption & cabal which are known to characterize the one would soon find their way into the other. Appointments made by numerous bodies, are always worse than those made by single responsible individuals, or by the people at large.

COL. MASON. It is curious to remark the different language held at different times. At one moment we are told that the Legislature is entitled to thorough confidence, and to indefinite power. At another, that it will be governed by intrigue & corruption, and cannot be trusted at all. But not to dwell on this inconsistency he would observe that a Government which is to last ought at least to be practicable. Would this be the case if the proposed election should be left to the people at large. He conceived it would be as unnatural to refer the choice of a proper character for chief Magistrate to the people, as it would, to refer a trial of colours to a blind man. The extent of the Country renders it impossible that the people can have the requisite capacity to judge of the respective pretensions of the Candidates.

MR. WILSON could not see the contrariety stated (by Col. Mason). The Legislre. might deserve confidence in some respects, and distrust in others. In acts which were to affect them & yr. Constituents precisely alike confidence was due. In others jealousy was warranted. The appointment to great offices, when the Legislre. might feel many motives, not common to the public confidence was surely misplaced. This branch of business it was notorious, was most corruptly managed of any that had been committed to legislative bodies.

When the question was put to a vote, however, only the Pennsylvania delegation (unquestionably influenced by Wilson) was in favor of popular election of the Executive. A proposal that the Executive be chosen by electors appointed by the legislatures of the individual states was defeated with only Maryland and Delaware supporting it. This again reflected the states' rights syndrome, the fear of the small states of the power of the larger ones in a government based essentially on the principle of proportional representation. The parliamentary government scheme, which was part of the original Virginia Plan, continued to be formally supported, although growing dissatisfaction was evident. Rossiter confidently assures us that the majority was "more clear than firm."[48] This was further illuminated in subsequent discussions on such topics as reeligibility and length of term, and the delegates began to discover that these three problems were inextricably mixed together, so much so that the debates on the subject have been described as similar to a three-dimensional game of chess. As one reads the debates, one can almost see the different minds changing. When it appeared that the delegates wanted to make the Executive eligible for reelection by the legislature for more than one (seven year) term, Madison became strongly opposed to the parliamentary procedure he had originally proposed. His reasoning was sound and consistent, though, for he thought that such reeligibility would threaten an even more basic principle—the doctrine of the separation of powers.

James Madison
Statement on Necessity of the
Independence of the President
July 17, 1787

Farrand, II, 34-35.

If it be essential to the preservation of liberty that the Legisl: Execut: & Judiciary powers be separate, it is essential to a maintenance of the separation, that they should be independent of each other. The executive could not be independent of the Legislure, if dependent on the pleasure of that branch for a re-appointment. Why was it determined that the Judges should not hold their places by such a tenure? Because they might be tempted to cultivate the Legislature, by an undue complaisance, and thus render the Legislature the virtual expositor, as well the maker of the laws. In like manner a dependence of the Executive on the Legislature, would render it the Executor as well as the maker of laws; & then according to the observation of Montesquieu, tyrannical laws may be made that they may be executed in a tyrannical manner. There was an analogy between the Executive & Judiciary departments in several respects. The latter executed the laws in certain cases as the former did in others. The former expounded & applied them for certain purposes, as the latter did for others. The difference between them seemed to consist chiefly in two circumstances—1. the collective interest & security were much more in the power belonging to the Executive than to the Judiciary department.—2. in the administration of the former much greater latitude is left to opinion and discretion than in the administration of the latter. But if the 2d. consideration proves that it will be more difficult to establish a rule sufficiently precise for trying the Execut: than the Judges, & forms an objection to the same tenure of office, both considerations prove that it might be more dangerous to suffer a Union between the Executive & Legisl: powers, than between the Judiciary & Legislative powers. He conceived it to be absolutely necessary to a well constituted Republic that the two first shd. be kept distinct & independent of each other. Whether the plan proposed by the motion was a proper one, was another question, as it depended on the practicability of instituting a tribunal for impeachmts. as certain & as adequate in the one case as in the other. On the other hand, respect for the mover entitled his proposition to a fair hearing & discussion, until a less objectionable expedient should be applied for guarding agst. a dangerous union of the Legislative & Executive departments.

Mr. Madison was not apprehensive of being thought to favor any step towards monarchy. The real object with him was to prevent its introduction. Experience had proved a tendency in our governments to throw all power into the Legislative vortex. The Executives of the States are in general little more than Cyphers; the legislatures omnipotent. If no effectual check be devised for restraining the instability & encroachments of the latter, a revolution of some kind or other would be inevitable. The preservation of Republican Govt. therefore required some expedient for the purpose, but required evidently at the same time that in devising it, the genuine principles of that form should be kept in view.

The following day Gouverneur Morris joined Madison in his attack upon the reeligibility provision which had been accepted earlier. Morris argued that such a limitation might help destroy the very Constitution it was created to protect. By this he meant that the forced retirement of a popular leader might lead to his subsequent return to power or his continued possession of it through unconstitutional means. It might also mean reliance upon the sword instead of the ballot. Morris was intent upon granting a great deal of power to the Chief Magistrate in order to give the executive branch energy and independence. He felt that the Executive could defend himself against the encroachment of the legislature only if he had both power and independence. If the Executive were subject to the legislature for periodic approval of tenure, the Executive would have neither. Morris saw only two alternatives: either the Executive be appointed for life or be elected by the people. For him the choice was simple. He wanted an elected magistrate, responsible to the people in order that their interests be protected, and independent of any power of the legislature to impeach or otherwise harass. His speech was one of the most decisive and persuasive performances of the Convention.

Gouverneur Morris
Speech on the Election of the President
July 19, 1787

Farrand, II, 52-54.

It is necessary to take into one view all that relates to the establishment of the Executive; on the due formation of which must depend the efficacy & utility of the Union among the present and future States. It has been a maxim in political Science that Republican Government is not adapted to a large extent of Country, because the energy of the Executive Magistracy can not reach the extreme parts of it. Our Country is an extensive one. We must either then renounce the blessing of the Union, or provide an Executive with sufficient vigor to pervade every part of it. This subject was of so much importance that he hoped to be indulged in an extensive view of it. One great object of the Executive is to controul the Legislature. The Legislature will continually seek to aggrandize & perpetuate themselves; and will seize those critical moments produced by war, invasion or convulsion for that purpose. It is necessary then that the Executive Magistrate should be the guardian of the people, even of the lower classes, agst. Legislative tyranny, against the Great & the wealthy who in the course of things will necessarily compose—the Legislative body. Wealth tends to corrupt the mind & to nourish its love of power, and to stimulate it to oppression. History proves this to be the spirit of the opulent. The check provided in the 2d. branch was not meant as a check on Legislative usurpations of power, but on the abuse of lawful powers, on the propensity in the 1st. branch to legislate too much to run into projects of paper money & similar expedients. It is no check on Legislative tyranny. On the contrary it may favor it, and if the 1st. branch can be seduced may find the means of success. The Executive therefore ought to be so constituted as to be the great protector of the Mass of the people.—It is the duty of the Executive to appoint the officers & to command the forces of the Republic: to appoint 1. ministerial officers for the administration of public affairs. 2. Officers for the dispensation of Justice—Who will be the best Judges whether these appointments be well made? The people at large, who will know, will see, will feel the effects of them—Again who can judge so well of the discharge of military duties for the protection & security of the people, as the people themselves who are to be protected & secured? He finds too that the Executive is not to be re-eligible. What effect will this have?—1. it will destroy the great incitement to merit public esteem by taking away the hope of being rewarded with a reappointment. It may give a dangerous turn to one of the strongest passions in the human breast. The love of fame is the great spring to noble & illustrious actions. Shut the Civil road to Glory & he may be compelled to seek it by the sword.—2. It will tempt him to make the most of the Short space of time allotted him, to accumulate wealth and provide for his friends.—3. It will produce violations of the very constitution it is meant to secure. In moments of pressing danger the tried abilities and established character of a favorite Magistrate will prevail over respect for the forms of the Constitution. The Executive is also to be impeachable. This is a dangerous part of the plan. It will hold him in such dependence that he will be no check on the Legislature, will not be a firm guardian of the people and of the public interest. He will be the tool of a faction, of some leading demagogue in the Legislature. These then are the faults of the Executive establishment as now proposed. Can no better establishmt. be devised? If he is to be the Guardian of the people let him be appointed by the people? If he is to be a check on the Legislature let him not be impeachable. Let him be of short duration, that he may with propriety be re-eligible.—It has been said that the candidates for this office will not be known to the people. If they be known to the Legislature, they must have such a notoriety and eminence of Character, that they cannot possibly be unknown to the people at large. It cannot be possible that a man shall have sufficiently distinguished himself to merit this high trust without having his character proclaimed by fame throughout the Empire. As to the danger from an unimpeachable magistrate he could not regard it as formidable. There must be certain great officers of State; a minister of finance, of war, of foreign affairs etc. These he presumes will exercise their functions in subordination to the Executive, and will be amenable by impeachment to the public Justice. Without these ministers the Executive can do nothing of consequence. He suggested a biennial election of the Executive at the time of electing the 1st. branch, and the Executive to hold over, so as to prevent any interregnum in the Administration. An election by the people at large throughout so great an extent of country could not be influenced, by those little combinations and those momentary lies which often decide popular elections within a narrow sphere. It will probably, be objected that the election will be influenced by the members of the Legislature; particularly of the 1st. branch, and that it will be nearly the same thing with an election by the Legislature itself. It could not be denied that such an influence would exist. But it might be answered that as the Legislature or the candidates for it would be divided, the enmity of one part would counteract the friendship of another; that if the administration of the Executive were good, it would be unpopular to oppose his re-election, if bad it ought to be opposed & a reappointmt. prevented; and lastly that in every view this indirect dependence on the favor of the Legislature could not be so mischievous as a direct dependence for his appointment. He saw no alternative for making the Executive independent of the Legislature but either to give him his office for life, or make him eligible by the people.—Again, it might be objected that two years would be too short a duration.

But he believes that as long as he should behave himself well, he would be continued in his place. The extent of the Country would secure his re-election agst. the factions & discontents of particular States. It deserved consideration also that such an ingredient in the plan would render it extremely palatable to the people. These were the general ideas which occurred to him on the subject, and which led him to wish & move that the (whole constitution of the Executive) might undergo reconsideration.

It was at this point that for the first time Madison threw his influence on the side of those who wanted to see the Executive elected by the people. Pointing out that the disenfranchisement of the Negroes in the South weakened its power in relation to the larger white population of the North, he accepted the principle of electors because "it obviated this difficulty and seemed on the whole to be liable to the fewest objections." Morris then moved to reconsider the method of election, and when this passed, Ellsworth moved to strike out election by the national legislature and proposed that the Executive "be chosen by electors appointed by the legislatures of the States in the following ratio; towit—one for each State not exceeding 200,000 inhabts., two for each yt. number & not exceeding 300,000, and, three for each State exceeding 300,000—Mr. Broome 2ded. the motion."[49]

After Elbridge Gerry, a last ditch opponent of the proposed strong national government, spoke up and said he preferred the plan for electors to the selection of an Executive by the national legislature, the matter went to a vote. The question was divided into two parts: 1) whether or not the Executive should be chosen by electors; 2) shall the electors be chosen by the state legislatures? Both measures passed: the first by a vote of 6 to 3 with one state divided, while the latter was endorsed by a margin of 8 to 2, again with one state divided. This was the first endorsement of the Electoral College, although not in the form in which it was ultimately adopted. The delegates continued to vacillate for the next few days and finally reversed this vote the following week, returning to the initial proposal contained in the Virginia Plan. In a mood of desperation James Wilson actually proposed that the Executive be chosen by electors "to be taken by lot from the national legislature," but this rash idea was sidetracked because the majority continued to support the plan so closely akin to the parliamentary form of government. On July 26, after two months of on-and-off debate, the Committee of the Whole endorsed the substance of the original proposal that the Executive be selected by the legislature for a term of seven years and that he be ineligible for a second term. The resolution was then turned over to the Committee on Detail as the Convention adjourned for ten days.

When the Convention reconvened the question was not seriously tackled again until August 24 when Gouverneur Morris mounted still another attack, attempting to substitute for election by the legislature the simple principle that the President "shall be chosen by the people of the several states." This time he carried Connecticut, New Jersey, Pennsylvania and Vermont with him, but the motion was defeated by a margin of one state. Time was running out. On a second vote on the first part of the Morris motion (that the President "shall be chosen by electors"), he picked up another state, Delaware, and the balloting was tied 4 to 4 with

Connecticut and Maryland divided, and Massachusetts absent. Defeat of the parliamentary form was now clearly in the offing, and when Roger Sherman proposed a new committee to settle postponed matters, a political resolution of this vexing question was in sight. John Roche has vividly described this major accomplishment by the committee, which reported to the Convention on September 4, 1787:

> The Brearley Committee on Postponed Matters was a superb aggregation of talent and its compromise on the Executive was a masterpiece of political improvisation. (The Electoral College, its creation, however, had little in its favor as an *institution*—as the delegates well appreciated.) The point of departure for all discussion about the presidency in the Convention was that in immediate terms, the problem was non-existent; in other words, everybody present knew that under any system devised, George Washington would be President. Thus they were dealing in the future tense and to a body of working politicians the merits of the Brearley proposal were obvious: everybody got a piece of cake. (Or to put it more academically, each viewpoint could leave the Convention and argue to its constituents that it had *really* won the day.) First, the state legislatures had the right to determine the mode of selection of the electors; second, the small states received a bonus in the Electoral College in the form of a guaranteed minimum of three votes while the big states got acceptance of the principle of proportional power; third, if the state legislatures agreed (as six did in the first presidential election), the people could be involved directly in the choice of electors; and finally, if no candidate received a majority in the College, the right of decision passed to the National Legislature with each state exercising equal strength. (In the Brearley recommendation, the election went to the Senate, but a motion from the floor substituted the House; this was accepted on the ground that the Senate already had enough authority over the executive in its treaty and appointment powers.)

This compromise was almost too good to be true, and the Framers snapped it up with little debate or controversy. No one seemed to think well of the College as an *institution*; indeed, what evidence there is suggests that there was an assumption that once Washington had finished his tenure as President, the electors would cease to produce majorities and the chief executive would usually be chosen in the House. George Mason observed casually that the selection would be made in the House nineteen times in twenty and no one seriously disputed this point. The vital aspect of the Electoral College was that it got the Convention over the hurdle and protected everybody's interests. The future was left to cope with the problem of what to do with this Rube Goldberg mechanism.

In short, the Framers did not in their wisdom endow the United States with a College of Cardinals—the Electoral College was neither an exercise in applied Platonism nor an experiment in indirect government based on elitist distrust of the masses. It was merely a jerry-rigged improvisation which has subsequently been endowed with a high theoretical content.

When an elector from Oklahoma in 1960 refused to cast his vote for Nixon (naming Byrd and Goldwater instead) on the ground that the Founding Fathers intended him to exercise his great independent wisdom, he was indulging in historical fantasy. If one were to indulge in counter-fantasy, he would be tempted to suggest that the Fathers would be startled to find the College still in operation—and perhaps even dismayed at their descendants' lack of judgment or inventiveness.[50]

From that point on it was all over, but the shouting. A major change was effected when some dissatisfaction was expressed with regard to the procedure of electing a President in the Senate in the event that no single candidate received a majority of the electoral votes. Roger Sherman finally proposed that such a run-off election be held in the House of Representatives, the representatives from each state having one vote. In the event that no candidate received a majority of electoral votes, the House would ballot immediately from the five highest candidates. If more than one were to obtain a majority, or two an equal number, the House would also vote in the same manner—a quorum consisting of representatives from two-thirds of the states, with any winning candidate receiving a concurrence of the majority of the states.

Other aspects of the presidential office were laboriously constructed at the Convention—issues such as the power of appointment, the desirability of an Executive Council, and even the right of the Congress to impeach the President—but no other question discussed or voted upon received such prolonged debate or was of such crucial importance as the method of selecting a President. If some variation of the Virginia Plan had been finally approved by the Convention, as it had been any number of times on a tentative basis, our present system of government would have been essentially parliamentary in character rather than presidential, as modern political scientists have begun to describe it.

The difference between the Chief Executive being answerable to a legislative body or to the people is enormous and has resulted in a significantly unique political system and political history for this country. Because of this the American presidency has emerged as the most powerful and interesting Executive office in the world. The presidency and the presidential system were born at the Constitutional Convention of 1787, but the modern office is a product of its own history and growth over a period of almost 200 years, when men and events have played equally important roles in determining the form and functions of this great office.

Before turning to this fascinating history, however, it would be prudent to record the results of the Philadelphia meeting—the final draft of Article II and the several other sections of the Constitution dealing with the executive powers as they emerged from the Constitutional Convention of 1787.

Provisions of the Constitution
Dealing With the Presidency
1787

United States Government Organization Manual, 1967-68, National Archives and Records Service, General Services Administration (Washington, D.C., 1967), 2-17.

Article I

Section 3

The Senate shall have the sole Power to try all Impeachments. When sitting for that Purpose, they shall be on Oath or Affirmation. When the President of the United States is tried, the Chief Justice shall preside: And no person shall be convicted without the Concurrence of two thirds of the Members present.

Judgement in Cases of Impeachment shall not extend further than to removal from Office, and disqualification to hold and enjoy any Office of honor, Trust or Profit under the United States: but the Party convicted shall nevertheless be liable and subject to Indictment, Trial, Judgement and Punishment, according to Law.

Article I

Section 7

Every Bill which shall have passed the House of Representatives and the Senate, shall, before it become a Law, be presented to the President of the United States; If he approve he shall sign it, but if not he shall return it, with his Objections to that House in which it shall have originated, who shall enter the Objections at large on their Journal, and proceed to reconsider it. If after such Reconsideration two thirds of that House shall agree to pass the Bill, it shall be sent, together with the Objections, to the other House, by which it shall likewise be reconsidered, and if approved by two thirds of that House, it shall become a Law. But in all such Cases the Votes of both Houses shall be determined by yeas and Nays, and the Names of the Persons voting for and against the Bill shall be entered on the Journal of each House respectively. If any Bill shall not be returned by the President within ten Days (Sundays excepted) after it shall have been presented to him, the Same shall be a Law, in like Manner as if he had signed it, unless the Congress by their Adjournment prevent its Return, in which Case it shall not be a Law.

Every Order, Resolution, or Vote to which the Concurrence of the Senate and House of Representatives may be necessary (except on a question of Adjournment) shall be presented to the President of the United States; and before the Same shall take Effect, shall be approved by him, or being disapproved by him, shall be repassed by two thirds of the Senate and House of Representatives, according to the Rules and Limitations prescribed in the Case of a Bill.

Article II

Section 1

The executive Power shall be vested in a President of the United States of America. He shall hold his Office during the Term of four Years, and, together with the Vice President, chosen for the same term, be elected, as follows.

Each State shall appoint, in such Manner as the Legislature thereof may direct, a Number of Electors, equal to the whole Number of Senators and Representatives to which the State may be entitled in the Congress: but no Senator or Representative, or Person holding an Office of Trust or Profit under the United States, shall be appointed an Elector.

The Electors shall meet in their respective States, and vote by Ballot for two Persons, of whom one at least shall not be an Inhabitant of the same State with themselves. And they shall make a List of all the Persons voted for, and of the Number of Votes for each; which List they shall sign and certify, and transmit sealed to the Seat of the Government of the United States, directed to the President of the Senate. The President of the Senate shall, in the Presence of the Senate and House of Representatives, open all the Certificates, and the Votes shall then be counted. The Person having the greatest Number of Votes shall be the President, if such Number be a Majority of the whole Number of Electors appointed; and if there be more than one who have such Majority, and have an equal Number of Votes, then the House of Representatives shall immediately chuse by Ballot one of them for President: and if no Person have a Majority, then from the five highest on the List the said House shall in like Manner chuse the President. But in chusing the President, the Votes shall be taken by States, the Representation from each State having one Vote; A quorum for this Purpose shall consist of a Member or Members from two thirds of the States, and a Majority of all the States shall be necessary to a Choice. In every Case, after the Choice of the President, the Person having the greatest Number of Votes of the Electors shall be the Vice President. But if there should remain two or more who have equal Votes, the Senate shall chuse from them by Ballot the Vice President.

The Congress may determine the Time of chusing the Electors, and the Day on which they shall give their Votes; which Day shall be the same throughout the United States.

No Person except a natural born Citizen, or a Citizen of the United States, at the time of the Adoption of this Constitution, shall be eligible to the Office of President; neither shall any Person be eligible to that Office who shall not have attained to the Age of thirty five Years, and been fourteen Years a Resident within the United States.

In Case of the Removal of the President from Office, or of his Death, Resignation, or Inability to discharge the Powers and Duties of the said Office, the Same shall devolve on the Vice President, and the Congress may by Law provide for the Case of Removal, Death, Resignation or Inability, both of the President and Vice President, declaring what Officer shall then act as President, and such Officer shall act accordingly, until the Disability be removed, or a President shall be elected.

The President shall, at stated Times, receive for his Services, a Compensation, which shall neither be encreased nor diminished during the Period for which he shall have been elected, and he shall not receive within that Period any other Emolument from the United States, or any of them.

Before he enter on the Execution of his Office, he shall take the following Oath or Affirmation:—"I do solemnly swear (or affirm) that I will faithfully execute the Office of President of the United States, and will to the best of my Ability, preserve, protect and defend the Constitution of the United States."

Section 2

The President shall be Commander in Chief of the Army and Navy of the United States, and of the Militia of the several States, when called into the actual Service of the United States; he may require the Opinion, in writing, of the principal Officer in each of the executive Departments, upon any Subject relating to the Duties of their respective Offices, and he shall have Power to grant Reprieves and Pardons for Offences against the United States, except in Cases of Impeachment.

He shall have Power, by and with the Advice and Consent of the Senate, to make Treaties, provided two thirds of the Senators present concur; and he shall nominate, and by and with the Advice and Consent of the Senate, shall appoint Ambassadors, other public Ministers and Consuls, Judges of the supreme Court, and all other Officers of the United States, whose Appointments are not herein otherwise provided for, and which shall be established by Law: but the Congress may by Law vest the Appointment of such inferior Officers, as they think proper, in the President alone, in the Courts of Law, or in the Heads of Departments.

The President shall have Power to fill up all Vacancies that may happen during the Recess of the Senate, by granting Commissions which shall expire at the End of their next Session.

Section 3

He shall from time to time give to the Congress Information of the State of the Union, and recommend to their Consideration such Measures as he shall judge necessary and expedient; he may, on extraordinary Occasions, convene both Houses, or either of them, and in Case of Disagreement between them, with Respect to the Time of Adjournment, he may adjourn them to such Time as he shall think proper; he shall receive Ambassadors and other public Ministers; he shall take Care that the Laws be faithfully executed, and shall Commission all the Officers of the United States.

Section 4

The President, Vice President and all civil Officers of the United States, shall be removed from Office on Impeachment for, and Conviction of, Treason, Bribery, or other High Crimes and Misdemeanors.

Defense of the New Constitution

In the period when the Constitution was under fire and awaiting ratification in several critical states, Madison, John Jay, and Hamilton wrote a series of essays in defense of the document which were published in the public press. They were later collected and published under the title of *The Federalist Papers*. Hamilton defended Article II, on the structure and powers of the President, in 11 of these articles, originally published in *The New York Packet* and *The Independent Journal*. In a systematic fashion he took up each of the major arguments raised against the method of selection, the nature of the office, the length of the term and the powers assigned to the office. In light of his speech on the Convention floor advocating a life term for the Chief Executive, Hamilton's later arguments in favor of the four-year term with the possibility of reelection indicated that he had made his peace with the compromises arrived at in Philadelphia and was prepared to battle just as ardently for the agreed upon procedures as he had for his own proposals. Hamilton was a political man, not an idealogue, and although he was a spirited fighter for the right as he saw it, this never precluded a political accommodation when he was convinced that his point would not carry the day.

The arguments Hamilton presented in favor of Article II were brilliantly conceived and altogether overwhelming in their persuasive style. In reading them, one would never think, if not otherwise informed, that the language and structure of Article II, and for that matter, the entire Constitution, were the products of numerous compromises which followed from long and elaborate debates begun in the spring of 1787 and stretched out over all of that summer. The procedure for electing the President was a case in point; the complex machinery that appears in Article II was proposed to accommodate both those who sought the direct election of the President by the people, and those who wanted him selected by the national or the state legislatures.

Hamilton's defense of Article II (this is hardly an accurate descriptive term, since his arguments suggested more of a ringing offensive) was quite sincere, although he had earlier wanted a considerably stronger or more absolute definition of the structure and power of the Chief Executive. Not only was Hamilton a political man, as I indicated above, and quite prepared to go along with the decision of his peers, but he had come to the conclusion by March 1788 that the compromise was a good one. Furthermore, he was convinced that he could accomplish everything he wanted in the Executive within the framework of its rather broad and still somewhat ambiguous definition of functions and powers. Hamilton believed in a strong executive leader, and he grasped very quickly, with almost prophetic insight, that the Constitution that was formulated at Philadelphia would permit such an Executive to develop and thrive if the political support for such an interpretation of the office existed among the leaders of the government. Rarely, if ever, have the subsequent believers in strong presidential leadership been able to equal his eloquent argument stated in Federalist No. 70:

There is an idea, which is not without its advocates, that a vigorous executive is inconsistent with the genius of republican government. The enlightened well wishers to this species of government must at least hope that the supposition is destitute of foundation; since they can never admit its truth, without at the same time admitting the condemnation of their own principles.

Energy in the executive is a leading character in the definition of good government. It is essential to the protection of the community against foreign attacks: it is not less essential to the steady administration of the laws, to the protection of property against those irregular and high handed combinations, which sometimes interrupt the ordinary course of justice, to the security of liberty against the enterprises and assaults of ambition, of faction and of anarchy. . . .[51]

Alexander Hamilton
The Federalist No. 67
March 11, 1788

Jacob E. Cooke, ed., *The Federalist* (New York, 1961), 452-57.

To the People of the State of New York   The Constitution of the executive department of the proposed government claims next our attention.

There is hardly any part of the system which could have been attended with greater difficulty in the arrangement of it than this; and there is perhaps none, which has been inveighed against with less candor, or criticised with less judgment.

Here the writers against the Constitution seem to have taken pains to signalize their talent of misrepresentation, calculating upon the aversion of the people to monarchy, they have endeavoured to inlist all their jealousies and apprehensions in opposition to the intended President of the United States; not merely as the embryo but as the full grown progeny of that detested parent. To establish the pretended affinity they have not scrupled to draw resources even from the regions of fiction. The authorities of a magistrate, in few instances greater, and in some instances less, than those of a Governor of New-York, have been magnified into more than royal prerogatives. He has been decorated with attributes superior in dignity and splendor to those of a King of Great-Britain. He has been shown to us with the diadem sparkling on his brow, and the imperial purple flowing in his train. He has been seated on a throne surrounded with minions and mistresses; giving audience to the envoys of foreign potentates, in all the supercilious pomp of majesty. The images of Asiatic despotism and voluptuousness have scarcely been wanting to crown the exaggerated scene. We have been almost taught to tremble at the terrific visages of murdering janizaries; and to blush at the unveiled mysteries of a future seraglio.

Attempts so extravagant as these to disfigure, or it might rather be said, to metamorphose the object, render it necessary to take an accurate view of its real nature and form; in order as well to ascertain its true aspect and genuine appearance, as to unmask the disingenuity and expose the fallacy of the counterfeit resemblances which have been so insidiously as well as industriously propagated.

In the execution of this task there is no man, who would not find it an arduous effort, either to behold with moderation or to treat with seriousness the devices, not less weak than wicked, which have been contrived to pervert the public opinion in relation to the subject. They so far exceed the usual, though unjustifiable, licenses of party-artifice, that even in a disposition the most candid and tolerant they must force the sentiments which favor an indulgent construction of the conduct of political adversaries to give place to a voluntary and unreserved indignation. It is impossible not to bestow the imputation of deliberate imposture and deception upon the gross pretence of a similitude between a King of Great-Britain and a magistrate of the character marked out for that of the President of the United States. It is still more impossible to withhold that imputation from the rash and barefaced expedients which have been employed to give success to the attempted imposition.

In one instance, which I cite as a sample of the general spirit, the temerity has proceeded so far as to ascribe to the President of the United States a power, which by the instrument reported is *expressly* allotted to the executives of the individual States. I mean the power of filling casual vacancies in the Senate.

This bold experiment upon the discernment of his countrymen, has been hazarded by a writer who (whatever may be his real merit) has had no inconsiderable share in the applauses of his party; and who upon this false and unfounded suggestion, has built a series of observations equally false and unfounded. Let him now be confronted with the evidence of the fact; and let him, if he be able, justify or extenuate the shameful outrage he has offered to the dictates of truth and to the rules of fair dealing.

The second clause of the second section of the second article empowers the President of the United States "to nominate, and by and with the advice and consent of the Senate to appoint ambassadors, other public ministers and consuls, judges of the Supreme Court, and all other *officers* of the United States, whose appointments are *not* in the Constitution *otherwise provided for*, and *which shall be established by law*." Immediately after this clause follows another in these words—"The President shall have power to fill up all *vacancies* that may happen *during the recess of the Senate*, by granting commissions which shall *expire at the end of their next session*." It is from this last provision that the pretended power of the President to fill vacancies in the Senate has been deduced. A slight attention to the connection of the clauses and to the obvious meaning of the terms will satisfy us that the deduction is not even colorable.

The first of these two clauses it is clear only provides a mode for appointing such officers, "whose appointments are *not otherwise provided for* in the Constitution, and which *shall be established by law*"; of course it cannot extend to the appointment of senators; whose appointments are *otherwise provided for* in the Constitution, [Article I. Sec. 3. Clause I. (Publius). Footnote in original.] and who are *established by the Constitution*, and will not require a future establishment by law. This position will hardly be contested.

The last of these two clauses, it is equally clear, cannot be understood to comprehend the power of filling vacancies in the Senate, for the following reasons—*First.* The relation in which that clause stands to the other, which declares the general mode of appointing officers of the United States, denotes it to be nothing more than a supplement to the other; for the purpose of establishing an auxiliary method of appointment in cases, to which the general method was inadequate. The ordinary power of appointment is confided to the President and Senate *jointly*, and can therefore only be exercised during the session of the Senate; but as it would have been improper to oblige this body to be continually in session for the appointment of officers; and as vacancies might happen *in their recess*, which it might be necessary for the public service to fill without delay, the succeeding clause is evidently intended to authorise the President *singly* to make temporary appointments "during the recess of the Senate, by granting commissions which should expire at the end of their next session." *Secondly.* If this clause is to be considered as supplementary to the one which precedes, the *vacancies* of which it speaks must be construed to relate to the "officers" described in the preceding one; and this we have seen excludes from its description the members of the Senate. *Thirdly.* The time within which the power is to operate "during the recess of the Senate" and the duration of the appointments "to the end of the next session" of that body, conspire to elucidate the sense of the provision; which if it had been intended to comprehend Senators would naturally have referred the temporary power of filling vacancies to the recess of the State Legislatures, who are to make the permanent appointments, and not to the recess of the national Senate, who are to have no concern in those appointments; and would have extended the duration in office of the temporary Senators to the next session of the Legislature of the State, in whose representation the vacancies had happened, instead of making it to expire at the end of the ensuing session of the national Senate. The circumstances of the body authorised to make the permanent appointments, would of course have governed the modification of a power which related to the temporary appointments; and as the national Senate is the body whose situation is alone contemplated in the clause upon which the suggestion under examination has been founded, the vacancies to which it alludes can only be deemed to respect those officers, in whose appointment that body has a concurrent agency with the President. But, *lastly*, the first and second clauses of the third section of the first article, not only obviate the possibility of doubt, but destroy the pretext of misconception. The former provides that "the Senate of the United States shall be composed of two Senators from each State, chosen *by the Legislature thereof* for six years," and the latter directs that "if vacancies in that body should happen by resignation or otherwise *during the recess of the Legislature of* any State, the Executive thereof may make temporary appointments until the *next meeting of the Legislature*, which shall then fill such vacancies." Here is an express power given, in clear and unambiguous terms, to the State executives to fill the casual vacancies in the Senate by temporary appointments; which not only invalidates the supposition, that the clause before considered could have been intended to confer that power upon the President of the United States; but proves that this supposition, destitute as it is even of the merit of plausibility, must have originated in an intention to deceive the people, too palpable to be obscured by sophistry, and too atrocious to be palliated by hypocrisy.

I have taken the pains to select this instance of misrepresentation, and to place it in a clear and strong light, as an unequivocal proof of the unwarrantable arts which are practised to prevent a fair and impartial judgment of the real merits of the constitution submitted to the consideration of the people. Nor have I scrupled in so flagrant a case to allow myself in a severity of animadversion little congenial with the general spirit of these papers. I hesitate not to submit it to the decision of any candid and honest adversary of the proposed government, whether language can furnish epithets of too much asperity for so shameless and so prostitute an attempt to impose on the citizens of America.

Publius

Alexander Hamilton
The Federalist No. 68
March 12, 1788

Cooke, 457-62.

To the People of the State of New York   The mode of appointment of the chief magistrate of the United States is almost the only part of the system, of any consequence, which has escaped without severe censure, or which has received the slightest mark of approbation from its opponents. The most plausible of these, who has appeared in print, has even deigned to admit, that the election of the president is pretty well guarded. I venture somewhat further; and hesitate not to affirm, that if the manner of it be not perfect, it is at least excellent. It united in an eminent degree all the advantages; the union of which was to be desired.

It was desireable, that the sense of the people should operate in the choice of the person to whom so important a trust was to be confided. This end will be answered by committing the right of making it, not to any pre-established body, but to men, chosen by the people for the special purpose, and at the particular conjuncture.

It was equally desirable, that the immediate election should be made by men most capable of analizing the qualities adapted to the station, and acting under circumstances favourable to deliberation and to a judicious combination of all the reasons and inducements, which were proper to govern their choice. A small number of persons, selected by their fellow citizens from the general mass, will be most likely to possess the information and discernment requisite to so complicated an investigation.

It was also peculiarly desirable, to afford as little opportunity as possible to tumult and disorder. This evil was not least to be dreaded in the election of a magistrate, who was to have so important an agency in the administration of the government, as the president of the United States. But the precautions which have been so happily concerted in the system under consideration, promise an effectual security against this mischief. The choice of *several* to form an intermediate body of electors, will be much less apt to convulse the community, with any extraordinary or violent movements, than the choice of *one* who was himself to be the final object of the public wishes. And as the electors, chosen in each state, are to assemble and vote in the state, in which they are chosen, this detached and divided situation will expose them much less to heats and ferments, which might be communicated from them to the people, than if they were all to be convened at one time, in one place.

Nothing was more to be desired, than that every practicable obstacle should be opposed to cabal, intrigue and corruption. These most deadly adversaries of republican government might naturally have been expected to make their approaches from more than one quarter, but chiefly from the desire in foreign powers to gain an improper ascendant in our councils. How could they better gratify this, than by raising a creature of their own to the chief magistracy of the union? But the convention have guarded against all danger of this sort with the most provident and judicious attention. They have not made the appointment of the president to depend on any pre-existing bodies of men who might be tampered with before hand to prostitute their votes; but they have referred it in the first instance to an immediate act of the people of America, to be exerted in the choice of persons for the temporary and sole purpose of making the appointment. And they have excluded from eligibility to this trust, all those who from situation might be suspected of too great devotion to the president in office. No senator, representative, or other person holding a place of trust or profit under the United States, can be of the number of the electors. Thus, without corrupting the body of the people, the immediate agents in the election will at least enter upon the task, free from any sinister bypass. Their transient existence, and their detached situation, already taken notice of, afford a satisfactory prospect of their continuing on, to the conclusion of it. The business of corruption, when it is to embrace so considerable a number of men, requires time, as well as means. Nor would it be found easy suddenly to embark them, dispersed as they would be over thirteen states, in any combinations, founded upon motives, which though they could not properly be denominated corrupt, might yet be of a nature to mislead them from their duty.

Another and no less important desideratum was, that the executive should be independent for his continuance in office on all, but the people themselves. He might otherwise be tempted to sacrifice his duty to his complaisance for those whose favor was necessary to the duration of his official consequence. This advantage will also be secured, by making his re-election to depend on a special body of representatives, deputed by the society for the single purpose of making the important choice.

All these advantages will be happily combined in the plan devised by the convention; which is, that the people of each state shall choose a number of persons as electors, equal to the number of senators and representatives of such state in the national government, who shall assemble within the state and vote for some fit person as president. Their votes, thus given, are to be transmitted to the seat of the national government, and the person who may happen to have a majority of the whole number of votes will be the president. But as a majority of the votes might not always happen to centre on one man and as it might be unsafe to permit less than a majority to be conclusive, it is provided, that in such a contingency, the house of representatives shall select out of the candidates, who shall have the five highest numbers of votes, the man who in their opinion may be best qualified for the office.

This process of election affords a moral certainty, that the office of president, will seldom fall to the lot of any man, who is not in an eminent degree endowed with the requisite qualifications. Talents for low intrigue and the little arts of popularity may alone suffice to elevate a man to the first honors in a single state; but it will require other talents and a different kind of merit to establish him in the esteem and confidence of the whole union, or of so considerable a portion of it as would be necessary to make him a successful candidate for the distinguished office of president of the United States. It will not be too strong to say, that there will be a constant probability of seeing the station filled by characters pre-eminent for ability and virtue. And this will be thought no inconsiderable recommendation of the constitution, by those, who are able to estimate the share, which the executive in every government must necessarily have in its good or ill administration. Though we cannot acquiesce in the political heresy of the poet who says—
    For forms of government let fools contest—
    That which is best administered is best.
—yet we may safely pronounce, that the true test of a good government is its aptitude and tendency to produce a good administration.

The vice-president is to be chosen in the same manner with the president; with this difference, that the senate is to do, in respect to the former, what is to be done by the house of representatives, in respect to the latter.

The appointment of an extraordinary person, as vice president, has been objected to as superfluous, if not mischievous. It has been alledged, that it would have been preferable to have authorised the senate to elect out of their own body an officer, answering that description. But two considerations seem to justify the ideas of the convention in this respect. One is, that to secure at all times the possibility of a definitive resolution of the body, it is necessary that the president should have only a casting vote. And to take the senator of any state from his seat as senator, to place him in that of president of the senate, would be to exchange, in regard to the state from which he came, a constant for a contingent vote. The other consideration is, that as the vice-president may occasionally become a substitute for the president, in the supreme executive magistracy, all the reasons, which recommend the mode of election prescribed for the one, apply with great, if not with equal, force to the manner of appointing the other. It is remarkable, that in this as in most other instances, the objection, which is made, would be against the constitution of this state. We have a Lieutenant Governor chosen by the people at large, who presides in the senate, and is the constitutional substitute for the Governor in casualties similar to those, which would authorise the vice-president to exercise the authorities and discharge the duties of the president.

Publius

Alexander Hamilton
The Federalist No. 69
March 14, 1788

Cooke, 462-70.

To the People of the State of New York   I proceed now to trace the real characters of the proposed executive as they are marked out in the plan of the Convention. This will serve tò place in a strong light the unfairness of the representations which have been made in regard to it.

The first thing which strikes our attention is that the executive authority, with few exceptions, is to be vested in a single magistrate. This will scarcely however be considered as a point upon which any comparison can be grounded; for if in this particular there be a resemblance to the King of Great-Britain, there is not less a resemblance to the Grand Signior, to the Khan of Tartary, to the man of the seven mountains, or to the Governor of New-York.

That magistrate is to be elected for *four* years; and is to be re-eligible as often as the People of the United States shall think him worthy of their confidence. In these circumstances, there is a total dissimilitude between *him* and a King of Great-Britain; who is an *hereditary* monarch, possessing the crown as a patrimony descendible to his heirs forever; but there is a close analogy between *him* and a Governor of New-York, who is elected for *three* years, and is re-eligible without limitation or intermission. If we consider how much less time would be requisite for establishing a dangerous influence in a single State, than for establishing a like influence throughout the United States, we must conclude that a duration of *four* years for the Chief Magistrate of the Union, is a degree of permanency far less to be dreaded in that office, than a duration of *three* years for a correspondent office in a single State.

The President of the United States would be liable to be impeached, tried, and upon conviction of treason, bribery, or other high crimes or misdemeanors, removed from office; and would afterwards be liable to prosecution and punishment in the ordinary course of law. The person of the King of Great-Britain is sacred and inviolable: There is no constitutional tribunal to which he is amenable; no punishment to which he can be subjected without involving the crisis of a national revolution. In this delicate and important circumstance or personal responsibility, the President of confederated America would stand upon no better ground than a Governor of New-York, and upon worse ground than the Governors of Virginia and Delaware.

The President of the United States is to h .ve power to return a bill, which shall have passed the two branches of the Legislature, for re-consideration; but the bill so returned is to become a law, if upon that re-consideration it be approved by two thirds of both houses. The King of Great-Britain, on his part, has an absolute negative upon the acts of the two houses of Parliament. The disuse of that power for a considerable time past, does not affect the reality of its existence; and is to be ascribed wholly to the crown's having found the means of substituting influence to authority, or the art of gaining a majority in one or the other of the two houses, to the necessity of exerting a prerogative which could seldom be exerted without hazarding some degree of national agitation. The qualified negative of the President differs widely from this absolute negative of the British sovereign; and tallies exactly with the revisionary authority of the Council of revision of this State, of which the Governor is a constituent part. In this respect, the power of the President would exceed that of the Governor of New-York; because the former would possess singly what the latter shares with the Chancellor and Judges: But it would be precisely the same with that of the Governor of Massachusetts, whose constitution, as to this article, seems to have been the original from which the Convention have copied.

The President is to be the "Commander in Chief of the army and navy of the United States, and of the militia of the several States, when called into the actual service of the United States. He is to have power to grant reprieves and pardons for offences against the United States, *except in cases of impeachment*; to recommend to the consideration of Congress such measures as he shall judge necessary and expedient; to convene on extraordinary occasions both houses of the Legislature, or either of them, and in case of disagreement between them *with respect to the time of adjournment*, to adjourn them to such time as he shall think proper; to take care that the laws be faithfully executed; and to commission all officers of the United States." In most of these particulars the power of the President will resemble equally that of the King of Great-Britain and of the Governor of New-York. The most material points of difference are these—First; the President will have only the occasional command of such part of the militia of the nation, as by legislative provision may be called into the actual service of the Nation. The King of Great-Britain and the Governor of New-York have at all times the entire command of all the militia within their several jurisdictions. In this article therefore the power of the President would be inferior to that of either the Monarch or the Governor. Secondly; the President is to be Commander in Chief of the army and navy of the United States. In this respect his authority would be nominally the same with that of the King of Great-Britain, but in substance much inferior to it. It would amount to nothing more than the supreme command and direction of the military and naval forces, as first General and Admiral of the confederacy; while that of the British King extends to the *declaring* of war and to the *raising* and *regulating* of fleets and armies; all which by the Constitution under consideration would appertain to the Legislature. The Governor of New-York on the other hand, is by the Constitution of the State vested only with the command of its militia and navy. But the Constitutions of several of the States, expressly declare their Governors to be the Commanders in Chief as well of the army as navy; and it may well be a question whether those of New-Hampshire and Massachusetts, in particular, do not in this instance confer larger powers upon their respective Governors, than could be claimed by a President of the United States. Thirdly; the power of the President in respect to pardons would extend to all cases, *except those of impeachment*. The Governor of New-York may pardon in all cases, even in those of impeachment, except for treason and murder. Is not the power of the Governor in this article, on a calculation of political consequences, greater than that of the President? All conspiracies and plots against the government, which have not been matured into actual treason, may be screened from punishment of every kind, by the interposition of the prerogative of pardoning. If a Governor of New-York therefore should be at the head of any such conspiracy, until the design had been ripened into actual hostility, he could ensure his accomplices and adherents an entire impunity. A President of the Union on the other hand, though he may even pardon treason, when prosecuted in the ordinary course of law, could shelter no offender in any degree from the effects of impeachment & conviction. Would not the prospect of a total indemnity for all the preliminary steps be a greater temptation to undertake and persevere in an enterprise against the public liberty than the mere prospect of an exemption from death and confiscation, if the final execution of the design, upon an actual appeal to arms, should miscarry? Would this last expectation have any influence at all, when the probability was computed that the person who was to afford that exemption might himself be involved in the consequences of the measure; and might be incapacitated by his agency in it, from affording the desired impunity? The better to judge of this matter, it will be necessary to recollect that by the proposed Constitution the offence of treason is limited "to levying war upon the United States, and adhering to their enemies, giving them aid and comfort," and that by the laws of New-York it is confined within similar bounds. Fourthly; the President can only adjourn the national Legislature in the single case of disagreement about the time of adjournment. The British monarch may prorogue or even dissolve the Parliament. The Governor of New-York may also prorogue the Legislature of this State for a limited time; a power which in certain situations may be employed to very important purposes.

The President is to have power with the advice and consent of the Senate to make treaties; provided two thirds of the Senators present concur. The King of Great-Britain is the sole and absolute representative of the nation in all foreign transactions. He can of his own accord make treaties of peace, commerce, alliance, and of every other description. It has been insinuated, that his authority in this respect is not conclusive, and that his conventions with foreign powers are subject to the revision, and stand in need of the ratification of Parliament. But I believe this doctrine was never heard of 'till it was broached upon the present occasion. Every jurist of that kingdom, and every other man acquainted with its constitution knows, as an established fact, that the prerogative of making treaties exists in the crown in its utmost plenitude; and that the compacts entered into by the royal authority have the most complete legal validity and perfection, independent of any other sanction. The Parliament, it is true, is sometimes seen employing itself in altering the existing laws to conform them to the stipulations in a new treaty; and this may have possibly given birth to the imagination that its co-operation was necessary to the obligatory efficacy of the treaty. But this parliamentary interposition proceeds from a different cause; from the necessity of adjusting a most artificial and intricate system of revenue and commercial laws to the changes made in them by the operation of the treaty; and of adapting new provisions and precautions to the new state of things, to keep the machine from running into disorder. In this respect therefore, there is no comparison between the intended power of the President, and the actual power of the British sovereign. The one can perform alone, what the other can only do with the concurrence of a branch of the Legislature. It must be admitted that in this instance the power of the federal executive would exceed that of any State executive. But this arises naturally from the exclusive possession by the Union of that part of the sovereign power, which relates to treaties. If the confederacy were to be dissolved, it would become a question, whether the executives of the several States were not solely invested with that delicate and important prerogative.

The President is also to be authorised to receive Ambassadors and other public Ministers. This, though it has been a rich theme of declamation, is more a matter of dignity than of authority. It is a circumstance, which will be without consequence in the administration of the government; and it was far more convenient that it should be arranged in this manner, than that there should be a necessity of convening the Legislature, or one of its branches, upon every arrival of a foreign minister; though it were merely to take the place of a departed predecessor.

The President is to nominate and *with the advice and consent of the Senate* to appoint Ambassadors and other public Ministers, Judges of the Supreme Court and in general all officers of the United States established by law and whose appointments are not otherwise provided for by the Constitution. The King of Great-Britain is emphatically and truly stiled the fountain of honor. He not only appoints to all offices, but can create offices. He can confer titles of nobility at pleasure; and has the disposal of an immense number of church preferments. There is evidently a great inferiority, in the power of the President in this particular, to that of the British King; nor is it equal to that of the Governor of New-York, if we are to interpret the meaning of the constitution of the State by the practice which has obtained under it. The power of appointment is with us lodged in a Council composed of the Governor and four members of the Senate chosen by the Assembly. The Governor *claims* and has frequently *exercised* the right of nomination, and is *entitled* to a casting vote in the appointment. If he really has the right of nominating, his authority is in this respect equal to that of the President, and exceeds it in the article of the casting vote. In the national government, if the Senate should be divided, no appointment could be made: In the government of New-York, if the Council should be divided the Governor can turn the scale and confirm his own nomination. [Candor however demands an acknowledgment; that I do not think the claim of the Governor to a right of nomination well founded. Yet it is always justifiable to reason from the practice of a government till its propriety has been constitutionally questioned. And independent of this claim, when we take into view the other considerations and pursue them through all their consequences, we shall be inclined to draw much the same conclusion. (Publius). Footnote in original.] If we compare the publicity which must necessarily attend the mode of appointment by the President and an entire branch of the national Legislature, with the privacy in the mode of appointment by the Governor of New-York, closeted in a secret apartment with at most four, and frequently with only two persons; and if we at the same time consider how much more easy it must be to influence the small number of which a Council of Appointment consist than the considerable number of which the national Senate would consist, we cannot hesitate to pronounce, that the power of the Chief Magistrate of this State in the disposition of offices must in practice be greatly superior to that of the Chief Magistrate of the Union.

Hence it appears, that except as to the concurrent authority of the President in the article of treaties, it would be difficult to determine whether that Magistrate would in the aggregate, possess more or less power than the Governor of New-York. And it appears yet more unequivocally that there is no pretence for the parallel which has been attempted between him and the King of Great-Britain. But to render the contrast, in this respect, still more striking, it may be of use to throw the principal circumstances of dissimilitude into a closer groupe.

The President of the United States would be an officer elected by the people for *four* years. The King of Great-Britain is a perpetual and *hereditary* prince. The one would be amenable to personal punishment and disgrace: The person of the other is sacred and inviolable. The one would have a *qualified* negative upon the acts of the legislative body: The other has an *absolute* negative. The one would have a right to command the military and naval forces of the nation: The other in addition to this right, possesses that of *declaring* war, and of *raising* and *regulating* fleets and armies by his own authority. The one would have a concurrent power with a branch of the Legislature in the formation of treaties: The other is the *sole possessor* of the power of making treaties. The one would have a like concurrent authority in appointing to offices: The other is the sole author of all appointments. The one can infer no privileges whatever: The other can make denizens of aliens, noblemen of commoners, can erect corporations with all the rights incident to corporate bodies. The one can prescribe no rules concerning the commerce or currency of the nation: The other is in several respects the arbiter of commerce, and in this capacity can establish markets and fairs, can regulate weights and measures, can lay embargoes for a limited time, can coin money, can authorise or prohibit the circulation of foreign coin. The one has no particle of spiritual jurisdiction: The other is the supreme head and Governor of the national church! What answer shall we give to those who would persuade us that things so unlike resemble each other! The same that ought to be given to those who tell us, that a government, the whole power of which would be in the hands of the elective and periodical servants of the people, is an aristocracy, a monarchy, and a despotism.

Publius

Alexander Hamilton
The Federalist No. 70
March 15, 1788

Cooke, 471-80.

To the People of the State of New York   There is an idea, which is not without its advocates, that a vigorous executive is inconsistent with the genius of republican government. The enlightened well wishers to the species of government must at least hope that the supposition is destitute of foundation; since they can never admit its truth, without at the same time admitting the condemnation of their own principles. Energy in the executive is a leading character in the definition of good government. It is essential to the protection of the community against foreign attacks: It is not less essential to the stead administration of the laws, to the protection of property against those irregular and high handed combinations, which sometimes interrupt the ordinary course of justice, to the security of liberty against the enterprises and assaults of ambition, of faction and of anarchy. Every man the least conversant in Roman story knows how often that republic was obliged to take refuge in the absolute power of a single man, under the formidable title of dictator, as well as against the intrigues of ambitious individuals, who aspired to the tyranny, and the seditions of whole classes of the community, whose conduct threatened the existence of all government, as against the invasions of external enemies, who menaced the conquest and destruction of Rome.

There can be no need however to multiply arguments or examines on this head. A feeble executive implies a feeble execution of the government. A feeble execution is but another phrase for a bad execution: And a government ill executed, whatever it may be in theory, must be in practice a bad government.

Taking it for granted, therefore, that all men of sense will agree in the necessity of an energetic executive; it will only remain to inquire, what are the ingredients which constitute this energy—how far can they be combined with those other ingredients which constitute safety in the republican sense? And how far does this combination characterise the plan, which has been reported by the convention?

The ingredients, which constitute energy in the executive, are first unity, secondly duration, thirdly an adequate provision for its support, fourthly competent powers.

The circumstances which constitute safety in the republican sense are, 1st. a due dependence on the people, secondly a due responsibility.

Those politicians and statesmen, who have been the most celebrated for the soundness of their principles, and for the justness of their views, have declared in favor of a single executive and a numerous legislature. They have with great propriety considered energy as the most necessary qualification of the former, and have regarded this as most applicable to power in a single hand; while they have with equal propriety considered the latter as best adapted to deliberation and wisdom, and best calculated to conciliate the confidence of the people and to secure their privileges and interests.

That unity is conducive to energy will not be disputed. Decision, activity, secrecy, and dispatch will generally characterise the proceedings of one man, in a much more eminent degree, than the proceedings of any greater number; and in proportion as the number is increased, these qualities will be diminished.

This unity may be destroyed in two ways; either by vesting the power in two or more magistrates of equal dignity and authority; or by vesting it ostensibly in one man, subject in whole or in part to the controul and co-operation of others, in the capacity of counsellors to him. Of the first the two consuls of Rome may serve as an example; of the last we shall find examples in the constitutions of several of the states. New-York and New-Jersey, if I recollect right, are the only states, which have entrusted the executive authority wholly to single men. [New-York has no council except for the single purpose of appointing to offices; New-Jersey has a council, whom the governor may consult. But I think from the terms of the constitution their resolutions do not bind him. (Publius). Footnote in original.] Both these methods of destroying the unity of the executive have their partisans; but the votaries of an executive council are the most numerous. They are both liable, if not to equal, to similar objections; and may in most lights be examined in conjunction.

The experience of other nations will afford little instruction on this head. As far however as it teaches any thing, it teaches us not to be inamoured of plurality in the executive. We have seen that the Achaeans on an experiment of two Praetors, were induced to abolish one. The Roman history records many instances of mischiefs to the republic from the dissentions between the consuls, and between the military tribunes, who were at times substituted to the consuls. But it gives us no specimens of any peculiar advantages derived to the state, from the circumstance of the plurality of those magistrates. That the dissentions between them were not more frequent, or more fatal, is matter of astonishment; until we advert to the singular position in which the republic was almost continually placed and to the prudent policy pointed out by the circumstances of the state, and pursued by the consuls, of making a division of the government between them. The Patricians engaged in a perpetual struggle with the Plebians for the preservation of their antient authorities and dignities; the consuls, who were generally chosen out of the former body, were commonly united by the personal interest they had in the defence of the privileges of their order. In addition to this motive of union, after the arms of the republic had considerably expanded the bounds of its empire, it became an established custom with the consuls to divide the administration between themselves by lot; one of them remaining at Rome to govern the city and its environs; the other taking the command in the more distant provinces. This expedient must no doubt have had great influence in preventing those collisions and rivalships, which might otherwise have embroiled the peace of the republic.

But quitting the dim light of historical research, and attaching ourselves purely to the dictates of reason and good sense, we shall discover much greater cause to reject than to approve the idea of plurality in the executive, under any modification whatever.

Wherever two or more persons are engaged in any common enterprize or pursuit, there is always danger of difference of opinion. If it be a public trust or office in which they are cloathed with equal dignity and authority, there is peculiar danger of personal emulation and even animosity. From either and especially from all these causes, the most bitter dissentions are apt to spring. Whenever these happen, they lessen the respectability, weaken the authority, and distract the plans and operations of those whom they divide. If they should unfortunately assail the supreme executive magistracy of a country, consisting of a plurality of persons, they might impede or frustrate the most important measures of the government, in the most critical emergencies of the state. And what is still worse, they might split the community into the most violent and irreconcilable factions, adhering differently to the different individuals who composed the magistracy.

Men often oppose a thing merely because they have had no agency in planning it, or because it may have been planned by those whom they dislike. But if they have been consulted and have happened to disapprove, opposition then becomes in their estimation an indispensable duty of self love. They seem to think themselves bound in honor, and by all the motives of personal infallibility to defeat the success of what has been resolved upon, contrary to their sentiments. Men of upright, benevolent tempers have too many opportunities of remarking with horror, to what desperate lengths this disposition is sometimes carried, and how often the great interests of society are sacrificed to the vanity, to the conceit and to the obstinacy of individuals, who have credit enough to make their passions and their caprices interesting to mankind. Perhaps the question now before the public may in its consequences afford melancholy proofs of the effects of this despicable frailty, or rather detestable vice in the human character.

Upon the principles of a free government, inconveniencies from the source just mentioned must necessarily be submitted to in the formation of the legislature; but it is unnecessary and therefore unwise to introduce them into the constitution of the executive. It is here too that they may be most pernicious. In the legislature, promptitude of decision is oftener an evil than a benefit. The differences of opinion, and the jarrings of parties in that department of the government, though they may sometimes obstruct salutary plans, yet often promote deliberation and circumspection; and serve to check excesses in the majority. When a resolution too is once taken, the opposition must be at an end. That resolution is a law, and resistance to it punishable. But no favourable circumstances palliate or atone for the disadvantages of dissention in the executive department. Here they are pure and unmixed. There is no point at which they cease to operate. They serve to embarrass and weaken the execution of the plan or measure, to which they relate, from the first step to the final conclusion of it. They constantly counteract those qualities in the executive, which are the most necessary ingredients in its composition, vigour and expedition, and this without any counterballancing good. In the conduct of war, in which the energy of the executive is the bulwark of the national security, every thing would be to be apprehended from its plurality.

It must be confessed that these observations apply with principal weight to the first case supposed, that is to a plurality of magistrates of equal dignity and authority; a scheme the advocates for which are not likely to form a numerous sect: But they apply, though not with equal, yet with considerable weight, to the project of a council, whose concurrence is made constitutionally necessary to the operations of the ostensible executive. An artful cabal in that council would be able to distract and to enervate the whole system of administration. If no such cabal should exist, the mere diversity of views and opinions would alone be sufficient to tincture the exercise of the executive authority with a spirit of habitual feebleness and dilatoriness.

But one of the weightiest objections to a plurality in the executive, and which lies as much against the last as the first plan, is that it tends to conceal faults, and destroy responsibility. Responsibility is of two kinds, to censure and to punishment. The first is the most important of the two; especially in an elective office. Man, in public trust, will much oftener act in such a manner as to render him unworthy of being any longer trusted, than in such a manner as to make him obnoxious to legal punishment. But the multiplication of the executive adds to the difficulty of detection in either case. If often becomes impossible, amidst mutual accusations, to determine on whom the blame or the punishment of a pernicious measure, or series of pernicious measures ought really to fall. It is shifted from one to another with so much dexterity, and under such plausible appearances, that the public opinion is left in suspense about the real author. The circumstances which may have led to any national miscarriage or misfortune are sometimes so complicated, that where there are a number of actors who may have had different degrees and kinds of agency, though we may clearly see upon the whole that there has been mismanagement, yet it may be impracticable to pronounce to whose account the evil which may have been incurred is truly chargeable.

"I was overruled by my council. The council were so divided in their opinions, that it was impossible to obtain any better resolution on the point." These and similar pretexts are constantly at hand, whether true or false. And who is there that will either take the trouble or incur the odium of a strict scrutiny into the secret springs of the transaction? Should there be found a citizen zealous enough to undertake the unpromising task, if there happen to be a collusion between the parties concerned, how easy is it to cloath the circumstances with so much ambiguity, as to render it uncertain what was the precise conduct of any of those parties?

In the single instance in which the governor of this state is coupled with a council, that is in the appointment to offices, we have seen the mischiefs of it in the view now under consideration. Scandalous appointments to important offices have been made. Some cases indeed have been so flagrant, that all parties have agreed in the impropriety of the thing. When enquiry has been made, the blame has been laid by the governor on the members of the council; who on their part have charged it upon his nomination: While the people remain altogether at a loss to determine by whose influence their interests have been committed to hands so unqualified, and so manifestly improper. In tenderness to individuals, I forbear to descend to particulars.

It is evident from these considerations, that the plurality of the executive tends to deprive the people of the two greatest securities they can have for the faithful exercise of any delegated power; first, the restraints of public opinion, which lose their efficacy as well on account of the division of the censure attendant on bad measures among a number, as on account of the uncertainty on whom it ought to fall; and secondly, the opportunity of discovering with facility and clearness the misconduct of the persons they trust, in order either to their removal from office, or to their actual punishment, in cases which admit of it.

In England the king is a perpetual magistrate; and it is a maxim, which has obtained for the sake of the public peace, that he is unaccountable for his administration, and his person sacred. Nothing therefore can be wiser in that kingdom than to annex to the king a constitutional council, who may be responsible to the nation for the advice they give. Without this there would be no responsibility whatever in the executive department; an idea inadmissible in a free government. But even there the king is not bound by the resolutions of his council, though they are answerable for the advice they give. He is the absolute master of his own conduct, in the exercise of his office; and may observe or disregard the council given to him at his sole discretion.

But in a republic, where every magistrate ought to be personally responsible for his behaviour in office, the reason which in the British constitution dictates the propriety of a council not only ceases to apply, but turns against the institution. In the monarchy of Great-Britain, it furnishes a substitute for the prohibited responsibility of the chief magistrate; which serves in some degree as a hostage to the national justice for his good behaviour. In the American republic it would serve to destroy, or would greatly diminish the intended and necessary responsibility of the chief magistrate himself.

The idea of a council to the executive, which has so generally obtained in the state constitutions, has been derived from that maxim of republican jealousy, which considers power as safer in the hands of a number of men than of a single man. If the maxim should be admitted to be applicable to the case, I should contend that the advantage on that side would not counterballance the numerous disadvantages on the opposite side. But I do not think the rule at all applicable to the executive power. I clearly concur in opinion in this particular with a writer whom the celebrated Junius pronounces to be "deep, solid and ingenious," that, "the executive power is more easily confined when it is one": That it is far more safe there should be a single object for the jealousy and watchfulness of the people; and in a word that all multiplication of the executive is rather dangerous than friendly to liberty.

A little consideration will satisfy us, that the species of security sought for in the multiplication of the executive is unattainable. Numbers must be so great as to render combination difficult; or they are rather a source of danger than of security. The united credit and influence of several individuals must be more formidable to liberty than the credit and influence of either of them separately. When power therefore is placed in the hands of so small a number of men, as to admit of their interests and views being easily combined in a common enterprise, by an artful leader, it becomes more liable to abuse the more dangerous when abused, than if it be lodged in the hands of one man; who from the very circumstance of his being alone will be more narrowly watched and more readily suspected, and who cannot unite so great a mass of influence as when he is associated with others. The Decemvirs of Rome, whose name denotes their number, were more to be dreaded in their usurpation than any one of them would have been. No person would think of proposing an executive much more numerous than that body, from six to a dozen have been suggested for the number of the council. The extreme of these numbers is not too great for an easy combination; and from such a combination America would have more to fear, than from the ambition of any single individual. A council to a magistrate, who is himself responsible for what he does, are generally nothing better than a clog upon his good intentions; are often the instruments and accomplices of his bad, and are almost always a cloak to his faults.

I forbear to dwell upon the subject of expence; though it be evident that if the council should be numerous enough to answer the principal end, aimed at by the institution, the salaries of the members, who must be drawn from their homes to reside at the seat of government, would form an item in the catalogue of public expenditures, too serious to be incurred for an object of equivocal utility.

I will only add, that prior to the appearance of the constitution, I rarely met with an intelligent man from any of the states, who did not admit as the result of experience, that the unity of the Executive of this state was one of the best of the distinguishing features of our constitution.

Publius

Alexander Hamilton
The Federalist No. 71
March 18, 1788

Cooke, 481-86.

To the People of the State of New York   Duration in office has been mentioned as the second requisite to the energy of the executive authority. This has relation to two objects: To the personal firmness of the Executive Magistrate in the employment of his constitutional powers; and to the stability of the system of administration which may have been adopted under his auspices. With regard to the first, it must be evident, that the longer the duration in office, the greater will be the probability of obtaining so important an advantage. It is a general principle of human nature, that a man will be interested in whatever he possesses, in proportion to the firmness or precariousness of the tenure, by which he holds it; will be less attached to what he holds by a momentary or uncertain title, than to what he enjoys by a durable or certain title; and of course will be willing to risk more for the sake of the one, than for the sake of the other. This remark is not less applicable to a political privilege, or honor, or trust, than to any article of ordinary property. The inference from it is, that a man acting in the capacity of Chief Magistrate, under a consciousness, that in a very short time he *must* lay down his office, will be apt to feel himself too little interested in it, to hazard any material censure or perplexity, from the independent exertion of his powers, or from encountering the ill-humors, however transient, which may happen to prevail either in a considerable part of the society itself, or even in a predominant faction in the legislative body. If the case should only be, that he *might* lay it down, unless continued by a new choice; and if he should be desirous of being continued, his wishes conspiring with his fears would tend still more powerfully to corrupt his integrity, or debase his fortitude. In either case feebleness and irresolution must be the characteristics of the station.

There are some, who would be inclined to regard the servile pliancy of the executive to a prevailing current, either in the community, or in the Legislature, as its best recommendation. But such men entertain very crude notions, as well of the purposes for which government was instituted, as of the true means by which the public happiness may be promoted. The republican principle demands, that the deliberate sense of the community should govern the conduct of those to whom they entrust the management of their affairs; but it does not require an unqualified complaisance to every sudden breese of passion, or to every transient impulse which the people may receive from the arts of men, who flatter their prejudices to betray their interests. It is a just observation, that the people commonly *intend* the public good. This often applies to their very errors. But their good sense would despise the adulator, who should pretend that they always *reason right* about the *means* of promoting it. They know from experience, that they sometimes err; and the wonder is, that they so seldom err as they do; beset as they continually are by the wiles of parasites and sycophants, by the snares of the ambitious, the avaricious, the desperate; by the artifices of men, who possess their confidence more than they deserve it, and of those who seek to possess, rather than to deserve it. When occasions present themselves in which the interests of the people are at variance with their inclinations, it is the duty of the persons whom they have appointed to be the guardians of those interests, to withstand the temporary delusion, in order to give them time and opportunity for more cool and sedate reflection. Instances might be cited, in which a conduct of this kind has saved the people from very fatal consequences of their own mistakes, and has procured lasting monuments of their gratitude to the men, who had courage and magnanimity enough to serve them at the peril of their displeasure.

But however inclined we might be to insist upon an unbounded complaisance in the executive to the inclinations of the people, we can with no propriety contend for a like complaisance to the humors of the Legislature. The latter may sometimes stand in opposition to the former; and at other times the people may be entirely neutral. In either supposition, it is certainly desirable that the executive should be in a situation to dare to act his own opinion with vigor and decision.

The same rule, which teaches the propriety of a partition between the various branches of power, teaches us likewise that this partition ought to be so contrived as to render the one independent of the other. To what purpose separate the executive, or the judiciary, from the legislative, if both the executive and the judiciary are so constituted as to be at the absolute devotion of the legislative? Such a separation must be merely nominal and incapable of producing the ends for which it was established. It is one thing to be subordinate to the laws, and another to be dependent on the legislative body. The first comports with, the last violates, the fundamental principles of good government; and whatever may be the forms of the Constitution, unites all power in the same hands. The tendency of the legislative authority to absorb every other, has been fully displayed and illustrated by examples, in some preceding numbers. In governments purely republican, this tendency is almost irresistible. The representatives of the people, in a popular assembly, seem sometimes to fancy that they are the people themselves; and betray strong symptoms of impatience and disgust at the least sign of opposition from any other quarter; as if the exercise of its rights by either the executive or judiciary, were a breach of their privilege and an outrage to their dignity. They often appear disposed to exert an imperious controul over the other departments; and as they commonly have the people on their side, they always act with such momentum as to make it very difficult for the other members of the government to maintain the balance of the Constitution.

It may perhaps be asked how the shortness of the duration in office can affect the independence of the executive on the legislature, unless the one were possessed of the power of appointing or displacing the other? One answer to this enquiry may be drawn from the principle already remarked, that is from the slender interest a man is apt to take in a short lived advantage, and the little inducement it affords him to expose himself on account of it to any considerable inconvenience or hazard. Another answer, perhaps more obvious, though not more conclusive, will result from the consideration of the influence of the legislative body over the people, which might be employed to prevent the re-election of a man, who by an upright resistance to any sinister project of that body, should have made himself obnoxious to its resentment.

It may be asked also whether a duration of four years would answer the end proposed, and if it would not, whether a less period which would at least be recommended by greater security against ambitious designs, would not for that reason be preferable to a longer period, which was at the same time too short for the purpose of inspiring the desired firmness and independence of the magistrate?

It cannot be affirmed, that a duration of four years or any other limited duration would completely answer the end proposed; but it would contribute towards it in a degree which would have a material influence upon the spirit and character of the government. Between the commencement and termination of such a period there would always be a considerable interval, in which the prospect of annihilation would be sufficiently remote not to have an improper effect upon the conduct of a man endued with a tolerable portion of fortitude; and in which he might reasonably promise himself, that there would be time enough, before it arrived, to make the community sensible of the propriety of the measures he might incline to pursue. Though it be probable, that as he approached the moment when the public were by a new election to signify their sense of his conduct, his confidence and with it, his firmness would decline; yet both the one and the other would derive support from the opportunities, which his previous continuance in the station had afforded him of establishing himself in the esteem and good will of his constituents. He might then hazard with safety, in proportion of the proofs he had given of his wisdom and integrity, and to the title he had acquired to the respect and attachment of his fellow citizens. As on the one hand, a duration of four years will contribute to the firmness of the executive in a sufficient degree to render it a very valuable ingredient in the composition; so on the other, it is not long enough to justify any alarm for the public liberty. If a British House of Commons, from the most feeble beginnings, *from the mere power of assenting or disagreeing to the imposition of a new tax*, have by rapid strides, reduced the prerogatives of the crown and the privileges of the nobility within the limits they conceived to be compatible with the principles of a free government; while they raised themselves to the rank and consequence of a coequal branch of the Legislature; if they have been able in one instance to abolish both the royalty and the aristocracy, and to overturn all the ancient establishments as well in the church as State; if they have been able on a recent occasion to make the monarch tremble at the prospect of an innovation attempted by them; what would be to be feared from an elective magistrate of four years duration, with the confined authorities of a President of the United States? What but that he might be unequal to the task which the Constitution assigns him? I shall only add that if his duration be such as to leave a doubt of his firmness, that doubt is inconsistent with a jealousy of his encroachments.

Publius

Alexander Hamilton
The Federalist No. 72
March 19, 1788

Cooke, 486-92.

To the People of the State of New York   The administration of government, in its largest sense, comprehends all the operations of the body politic, whether legislative, executive or judiciary, but in its most usual and perhaps in its most precise signification, it is limited to executive details, and falls peculiarly within the province of the executive department. The actual conduct of foreign negotiations, the preparatory plans of finance, the application and disbursement of the public monies, in conformity to the general appropriations of the legislature, the arrangement of the army and navy, the direction of the operations of war; these and other matters of a like nature constitute what seems to be most properly understood by the administration of government. The persons therefore, to whose immediate management these different matters are committed, ought to be considered as the assistants or deputies of the chief magistrate; and, on this account, they ought to derive their offices from his appointment, at least from his nomination, and ought to be subject to his superintendence. This view of the subject will at once suggest to us the intimate connection between the duration of the executive magistrate in office, and the stability of the system of administration. To reverse and undo what has been done by a predecessor is very often considered by a successor, as the best proof he can give of his own capacity and desert; and, in addition to this propensity, where the alteration has been the result of public choice, the person substituted is warranted in supposing, that the dismission of his predecessor has proceeded from a dislike to his measures, and that the less he resembles him the more he will recommend himself to the favor of his constituents. These considerations, and the influence of personal confidences and attachments, would be likely to induce every new president to promote a change of men to fill the subordinate stations; and these causes together could not fail to occasion a disgraceful and ruinous mutability in the administration of the government.

With a positive duration of considerable extent, I connect the circumstance of re-eligibility. The first is necessary to give to the officer himself the inclination and the resolution to act his part well, and to the community time and leisure to observe the tendency of his measures, and thence to form an experimental estimate of their merits. The last is necessary to enable the people, when they see reason to approve of his conduct, to continue him in the station, in order to prolong the utility of his talents and virtues, and to secure to the government, the advantage of permanency in a wise system of administration.

Nothing appears more plausible at first sight, nor more ill founded upon close inspection, than a scheme, which in relation to the present point has had some respectable advocates—I mean that of continuing the chief magistrate in office for a certain time, and then excluding him from it, either for a limited period, or for ever after. This exclusion whether temporary or perpetual would have nearly the same effects; and these effects would be for the most part rather pernicious than salutary. One ill effect of the exclusion would be a diminution of the inducements to good behaviour. There are few men who would not feel much less zeal in the discharge of a duty, when they were conscious that the advantages of the station, with which it was connected, must be relinquished at a determinate period, then when they were permitted to entertain a hope of *obtaining* by *meriting* a continuance of them. This position will not be disputed, so long as it is admitted that the desire of reward is one of the strongest incentives of human conduct, or that the best security for the fidelity of mankind is to make their interest coincide with their duty. Even the love of fame, the ruling passion of the noblest minds, which would prompt a man to plan and undertake extensive and arduous enterprises for the public benefit, requiring considerable time to mature and perfect them, if he could flatter himself with the prospect of being allowed to finish what he had begun, would on the contrary deter him from the undertaking, when he foresaw that he must quit the scene, before he could accomplish the work, and must commit that, together with his own reputation, to hands which might be unequal or unfriendly to the task. The most to be expected from the generality of men, in such a situation, is the negative merit of not doing harm instead of the positive merit of doing good.

Another ill effect of the exclusion would be the temptation to sordid views, to peculation, and in some instances, to usurpation. An avaricious man, who might happen to fill the offices, looking forward to a time when he must at all events yield up the emoluments he enjoyed, would feel a propensity, not easy to be resisted by such a man, to make the best use of the opportunity he enjoyed, while it lasted; and might not scruple to have recourse to the most corrupt expedients to make the harvest as abundant as it was transitory; though the same man probably, with a different prospect before him, might content himself with the regular perquisites of his station, and might even be unwilling to risk the consequences of an abuse of his opportunities. His avarice might be a guard upon his avarice. Add to this, that the same man might be vain or ambitious as well as avaricious. And if he could expect to prolong his honors, by his good conduct, he might hesitate to sacrifice his appetite for them to his appetite for gain. But with the prospect before him of approaching and inevitable annihilation, his avarice would be likely to get the victory over his caution, his vanity or his ambition.

An ambitious man too, when he found himself seated on the summit of his country's honors, when he looked forward to the time at which he must descend from the exalted eminence forever; and reflected that no exertion of merit on his part could save him from the unwelcome reverse: Such a man, in such a situation, would be much more violently tempted to embrace a favorable conjuncture for attempting the prolongation of his power, at every personal hazard, then if he had the probability of answering the same end by doing his duty.

Would it promote the peace of the community, or the stability of the government, to have half a dozen men who had had credit enough to be raised to the seat of the supreme magistracy, wandering among the people like discontented ghosts, and sighing for a place which they were destined never more to possess?

A third ill effect of the exclusion would be the depriving the community of the advantage of the experience gained by the chief magistrate in the exercise of his office. That experience is the parent of wisdom is an adage, the truth of which is recognized by the wisest as well as the simplest of mankind. What more desirable or more essential than this quality in the governors of nations? Where more desirable or more essential than in the first magistrate of a nation? Can it be wise to put this desirable and essential quality under the ban of the constitution; and to declare that the moment it is acquired, its possessor shall be compelled to abandon the station in which it was acquired, and to which it is adapted? This nevertheless is the precise import of all those regulations, which exclude men from serving their country, by the choice of their fellow citizens, after they have, by a course of service fitted themselves for doing it with a greater degree of utility.

A fourth ill effect of the exclusion would be the banishing men from stations, in which in certain emergencies of the state their presence might be of the greatest moment to the public interest or safety. There is no nation which has not at one period or another experienced an absolute necessity of the services of particular men, in particular situations, perhaps it would not be too strong to say, to the preservation of its political existence. How unwise therefore must be every such self-denying ordinance, as serves to prohibit a nation from making use of its own citizens, in the manner best suited to its exigences and circumstances! Without supposing the personal essentiality of the man, it is evident that a change of the chief magistrate, at the breaking out of a war, or at any similar crisis, for another even of equal merit, would at all times be detrimental to the community; inasmuch as it would substitute inexperience to experience and would tend to unhinge and set afloat the already settled train of the administration.

A fifth ill effect of the exclusion would be, that it would operate as a constitutional interdiction of stability in the administration. *By necessitating* a change of men, in the first office in the nation, it would necessitate a mutability of measures. It is not generally to be expected, that men will vary; and measures remain uniform. The contrary is the usual course of things. And we need not be apprehensive there will be too much stability, while there is even the option of changing; nor need we desire to prohibit the people from continuing their confidence, where they think it may be safely placed, and where by constancy on their part they may obviate the fatal inconveniences of fluctuating councils and a variable policy.

These are some of the disadvantages, which would flow from the principle of exclusion. They apply most forcibly to the scheme of a perpetual exclusion; but when we consider that even a partial exclusion would always render the re-admission of the person a remote and precarious object, the observations which have been made will apply nearly as fully to one case as to the other.

What are the advantages promised to counterballance these disadvantages? They are represented to be 1st. Greater independence in the magistrate: 2dly. Greater security to the people. Unless the exclusion be perpetual there will be no pretence to infer the first advantage. But even in that case, may he have no object beyond his present station to which he may sacrifice his independence? May he have no connections, no friends, for whom he may sacrifice it? May he not be less willing, by a firm conduct, to make personal enemies, when he acts under the impression, that a time is fast approaching, on the arrival of which he not only may, but must be exposed to their resentments, upon an equal, perhaps upon an inferior footing? It is not an easy point to determine whether his independence would be most promoted or impaired by such an arrangement.

As to the second supposed advantage, there is still greater reason to entertain doubts concerning it. If the exclusion were to be perpetual, a man of irregular ambition, of whom alone there could be reason in any case to entertain apprehensions, would with infinite reluctance yield to the necessity of taking his leave forever of a post, in which his passion for power and pre-eminence had acquired the force of habit. And if he had been fortunate or adroit enough to conciliate the good will of people he might induce them to consider as a very odious and unjustifiable restraint upon themselves, a provision which was calculated to debar them of the right of giving a fresh proof of their attachment to a favorite. There may be conceived circumstances, in which this disgust of the people, seconding the thwarted ambition of such a favourite, might occasion greater danger to liberty, than could ever reasonably be dreaded from the possibility of a perpetuation in office, by the voluntary suffrages of the community, exercising a constitutional privilege.

There is an excess of refinement in the idea of disabling the people to continue in office men, who had entitled themselves, in their opinion, to approbation and confidence; the advantages of which are at best speculative and equivocal; and are over-balanced by disadvantages far more certain and decisive.

Publius

Alexander Hamilton
The Federalist No. 73
March 21, 1788

Cooke, 492-99.

To the People of the State of New York   The third ingredient towards constituting the vigor of the executive authority is an adequate provision for its support. It is evident that without proper attention to this article, the separation of the executive from the legislative department would be merely nominal and nugatory. The Legislature, with a discretionary power over the salary and emoluments of the Chief Magistrate, could render him as obsequious to their will, as they might think proper to make him. They might in most cases either reduce him by famine, or tempt him by largesses, to surrender at discretion his judgment to their inclinations. These expressions taken in all the latitude of the terms would no doubt convey more than is intended. There are men who could neither be distressed nor won into a sacrifice of their duty; but this stern virtue is the growth of few soils: And in the main it will be found, that a power over a man's support is a power over his will. If it were necessary to confirm so plain a truth by facts, examples would not be wanting, even in this country, of the intimidation or seduction of the executive by the terrors, or allurements, of the pecuniary arrangements of the legislative body.

It is not easy therefore to commend too highly the judicious attention which has been paid to this subject in the proposed Constitution. It is there provided that "The President of the United States shall, at stated times, receive for his services a compensation, *which shall neither be increased nor diminished, during the period for which he shall have been elected,* and he shall *not receive within that period any other emolument* from the United States or any of them." It is impossible to imagine any provision which would have been more eligible than this. The Legislature on the appointment of a President is once for all to declare what shall be the compensation for his services during the time for which he shall have been elected. This done, they will have no power to alter it either by increase or diminution, till a new period of service by a new election commences. They can neither weaken his fortitude by operating upon his necessities; nor corrupt his integrity, by appealing to his avarice. Neither the Union nor any of its members will be at liberty to give, nor will he be at liberty to receive any other emolument, than that which may have been determined by the first act. He can of course have no pecuniary inducement to renounce or desert the independence insured for him by the Constitution.

The last of the requisites to energy which have been enumerated are competent powers. Let us proceed to consider those which are proposed to be vested in the President of the United States.

The first thing that offers itself to our observation, is the qualified negative of the President upon the acts or resolutions of the two Houses of the Legislature; or in other words his power of returning all bills with objections; to have the effect of preventing their becoming laws, unless they should afterwards be ratified by two thirds of each of the component members of the legislative body.

The propensity of the legislative department to intrude upon the rights and to absorb the powers of the other departments, has been already suggested and repeated; the insufficiency of a mere parchment delineation of the boundaries of each, has also been remarked upon; and the necessity of furnishing each with constitutional arms for its own defence, has been inferred and proved. From these clear and indubitable principles results the propriety of a negative, either absolute or qualified, in the executive, upon the acts of the legislative branches. Without the one or the other the former would be absolutely unable to defend himself against the depredations of the latter. He might gradually be stripped of his authorities by successive resolutions, or annihilated by a single vote. And in the one mode or the other, the legislative and executive powers might speedily come to be blended in the same hands. If even no propensity had ever discovered itself in the legislative body, to invade the rights of the executive, the rules of just reasoning and theoretic propriety would of themselves teach us, that the one ought not to be left at the mercy of the other, but ought to possess a constitutional and effectual power of self defence.

But the power in question has a further use. It not only serves as a shield to the executive, but it furnishes an additional security against the enaction of improper laws. It establishes a salutary check upon the legislative body calculated to guard the community against the effects of faction, precipitancy, or of any impulse unfriendly to the public good, which may happen to influence a majority of that body.

The propriety of a negative, has upon some occasions been combated by an observation, that it was not to be presumed a single man would possess more virtue or wisdom, than a number of men; and that unless this presumption should be entertained, it would be improper to give the executive magistrate any species of controul over the legislative body.

But this observation when examined will appear rather specious than solid. The propriety of the thing does not turn upon the supposition of superior wisdom or virtue in the executive: But upon the supposition that the legislative will not be infallible: That the love of power may sometimes betray it into a disposition to encroach upon the rights of the other members of the government; that a spirit of faction may sometimes pervert its deliberations; that impressions of the moment may sometimes hurry it into measures which itself on maturer reflection would condemn. The primary inducement to conferring the power in question upon the executive, is to enable him to defend himself; the secondary one is to encrease the chances in favor of the community, against the passing of bad laws, through haste, inadvertence, or design. The oftener a measure is brought under examination, the greater the diversity in the situations of those who are to examine it, the less must be the danger of those errors which flow from want of due deliberation, or of those missteps which proceed from the contagion of some common passion or interest. It is far less probable, that culpable views of any kind should infect all the parts of the government, at the same moment and in relation to the same object, than that they should be turns govern and mislead every one of them.

It may perhaps be said, that the power of preventing bad laws includes that of preventing good ones; and may be used to the one purpose as well as to the other. But this objection will have little weight with those who can properly estimate the mischiefs of that inconstancy and mutability in the laws, which form the greatest blemish in the character and genius of our governments. They will consider every institution calculated to restrain the excess of law making, and to keep things in the same state, in which they may happen to be at any given period, as much more likely to do good than harm; because it is favorable to greater stability in the system of legislation. The injury which may possibly be done by defeating a few good laws will be amply compensated by the advantage of preventing a number of bad ones.

Nor is this all. The superior weight and influence of the legislative body in a free government, and the hazard to the executive in a trial of strength with that body, afford a satisfactory security, that the negative would generally be employed with great caution, and that there would oftener be room for a charge of timidity than of rashness, in the exercise of it. A King of Great-Britain, with all his train of sovereign attributes, and with all the influence he draws from a thousand sources, would at this day hesitate to put a negative upon the joint resolutions of the two houses of Parliament. He would not fail to exert the utmost resources of that influence to strangle a measure disagreeable to him, in its progress to the throne, to avoid being reduced to the dilemma of permitting it to take effect, or of risking the displeasure of the nation, by an opposition to the sense of the legislative body. Nor is it probable that he would ultimately venture to exert his prerogative, but in a case of manifest propriety, or extreme necessity. All well informed men in that kingdom will accede to the justness of this remark. A very considerable period has elapsed since the negative of the crown has been exercised.

If a magistrate, so powerful and so well fortified as a British monarch, would have scruples about the exercise of the power under consideration, how much greater caution may be reasonably expected in a President of the United States, cloathed for the short period of four years with the executive authority of a government wholly and purely republican?

It is evident that there would be greater danger of his not using his power when necessary, than of his using it too often, or too much. An argument indeed against its expediency has been drawn from this very source. It has been represented on this account as a power odious in appearance; useless in practice. But it will not follow, that because it might be rarely exercised, it would never be exercised. In the case for which it is chiefly designed, that of an immediate attack upon the constitutional rights of the executive, or in a case in which the public good was evidently and palpably sacrificed, a man of tolerable firmness would avail himself of his constitutional means of defence, and would listen to the admonitions of duty and responsibility. In the former supposition, his fortitude would be stimulated by his immediate interest in the power of his office; in the latter by the probability of the sanction of his constituents; who though they would naturally incline to the legislative body in a doubtful case, would hardly suffer their partiality to delude them in a very plain case. I speak now with an eye to a magistrate possessing only a common share of firmness. There are men, who under any circumstances will have the courage to do their duty at every hazard.

But the Convention have pursued a mean in this business; which will both facilitate the exercise of the power vested in this respect in the executive magistrate, and make its efficacy to depend on the sense of a considerable part of the legislative body. Instead of an absolute negative, it is proposed to give the executive the qualified negative already described. This is a power, which would be much more readily exercised than the other. A man who might be afraid to defeat a law by his single veto, might not scruple to return it for re-consideration; subject to being finally rejected only in the event of more than one third of each house concurring in the sufficiency of his objections. He would be encouraged by the reflection, that if his opposition should prevail, it would embark in it a very respectable proportion of the legislative body, whose influence would be united with his in supporting the propriety of his conduct, in the public opinion. A direct and categorical negative has something in the appearance of it more harsh, and more apt to irritate, than the mere suggestion of argumentative objections to be approved or disapproved, by those to whom they are addressed. In proportion as it would be less apt to offend, it would be more apt to be exercised; and for this very reason it may in practice be found more effectual. It is to be hoped that it will not often happen, that improper views will govern so large a proportion as two-thirds of both branches of the Legislature at the same time; and this too in defiance of the counterpoising weight of the executive. It is at any rate far less probable, that this should be the case, than that such views should taint the resolutions and conduct of a bare majority. A power of this nature, in the executive, will often have a silent and unperceived though forcible operation. When men engaged in unjustifiable pursuits are aware, that obstructions may come from a quarter which they cannot controul, they will often be restrained, by the bare apprehension of opposition, from doing what they would with eagerness rush into, if no such external impediments were to be feared.

This qualified negative, as has been elsewhere remarked, is in this State vested in a council, consisting of the Governor, with the Chancellor and Judges of the

Supreme Court, or any two of them. [Mr. Abraham Yates, a warm opponent of the plan of the Convention, is of this number. (Publius). Footnote in original.] It has been freely employed upon a variety of occasions, and frequently with success. And its utility has become so apparent, that persons who in compiling the Constitution were violent opposers of it, have from experience become its declared admirers.

I have in another place remarked, that the Convention in the formation of this part of their plan, had departed from the model of the Constitution of this State, in favor of that of Massachusetts—two strong reasons may be imagined for this preference. One is that the Judges, who are to be the interpreters of the law, might receive an improper bias from having given a previous opinion in their revisionary capacities. The other is that by being often associated with the executive they might be induced to embark too far in the political views of that magistrate, and thus a dangerous combination might by degrees be cemented between the executive and judiciary departments. It is impossible to keep the Judges too distinct from every other avocation than that of expounding the laws. It is peculiarly dangerous to place them in a situation to be either corrupted or influenced by the executive.

Publius

Alexander Hamilton
The Federalist No. 74
March 25, 1788

Cooke, 500-03.

To the People of the State of New York   The President of the United States is to be "Commander in Chief of the army and navy of the United States, and of the militia of the several States *when called into the actual service* of the United States." The propriety of this provision is so evident in itself; and it is at the same time so consonant to the precedents of the State constitutions in general, that little need be said to explain or enforce it. Even those of them, which have in other respects coupled the Chief Magistrate with a Council, have for the most part concentred the military authority in him alone. Of all the cares or concerns of government, the direction of war most peculiarly demands those qualities which distinguish the exercise of power by a single hand. The direction of war implies the direction of the common strength; and the power of directing and employing the common strength, forms an usual and essential part in the definition of the executive authority.

"The President may require the opinion in writing of the principal officer in each of the executive departments upon any subject relating to the duties of their respective offices." This I consider as a mere redundancy in the plan; as the right for which it provides would result of itself from the office.

He is also to be authorised "to grant reprieves and pardons for offences against the United States *except in cases of impeachment.*" Humanity and good policy conspire to dictate, that the benign prerogative of pardoning should be as little as possible fettered or embarrassed. The criminal code of every country partakes so much of necessary severity, that without an easy access to exceptions in favor of unfortunate guilt, justice would wear a countenance too sanguinary and cruel. As the sense of responsibility is always strongest in proportion as it is undivided, it may be inferred that a single man would be most ready to attend to the force of those motives, which might plead for a mitigation of the right of the law, and least apt to yield to considerations, which were calculated to shelter a fit object of its vengeance. The reflection, that the fate of a fellow creature depended on his *sole fiat*, would naturally inspire scrupulousness and caution: The dread of being accused of weakness or connivance would beget equal circumspection, though of a different kind. On the other hand, as men generally derive confidence from their numbers, they might often encourage each other in an act of obduracy, and might be less sensible to the apprehension of suspicion or censure for an injudicious or affected clemency. On these accounts, one man appears to be a more eligible dispenser of the mercy of the government than a body of men.

The expediency of vesting the power of pardoning in the President has, if I mistake not, been only contested in relation to the crime of treason. This, it has been urged, ought to have depended upon the assent of one or both of the branches of the legislative body. I shall not deny that there are strong reasons to be assigned for requiring in this particular the concurrence of that body or of a part of it. As treason is a crime levelled at the immediate being of the society, when the laws have once ascertained the guilt of the offender, there seems a fitness in refering the expediency of an act of mercy towards him to the judgment of the Legislature. And this ought the rather to be the case, as the supposition of the connivance of the Chief Magistrate ought not to be entirely excluded. But there are also strong objections to such a plan. It is not to be doubted that a single man of prudence and good sense, is better fitted, in delicate conjunctures, to balance the motives, which may plead for and against the remission of the punishment, than any numerous body whatever. It deserves particular attention, that treason will often be connected with seditions, which embrace a large proportion of the community; as lately happened in Massachusetts. In every such case, we might expect to see the representation of the people tainted with the same spirit, which had given birth to the offense. And when parties were pretty equally matched, the secret sympathy of the friends and favorers of the condemned person, availing itself of the good nature and weakness of others, might frequently bestow impunity where the terror of an example was necessary. On the other hand, when the sedition had proceeded from causes which had inflamed the resentments of the major party, they might often be found obstinate and inexorable, when policy demanded a conduct of forbearance and clemency. But the principal arguments for reposing the power of pardoning in this case in the Chief Magistrate is this—In seasons of insurrection or rebellion, there are often critical moments, when a well timed offer of pardon to the insurgents or rebels may restore the tranquility of the commonwealth; and which, if suffered to pass unimproved, it may never be possible afterwards to recall. The dilatory process of convening the Legislature, or one of its branches, for the purpose of obtaining its sanction to the measure, would frequently be the occasion of letting slip the golden opportunity. The loss of a week, a day, an hour, may sometimes be fatal. If it should be observed that a discretionary power with a view to such contingencies might be occasionally conferred upon the President; it may be answered in the first place, that it is questionable whether, in a limited constitution, that power could be delegated by law; and in the second place, that it would generally be impolitic before-hand to take any step which might hold out the prospect of impunity. A proceeding of this kind, out of the usual course, would be likely to be construed into an argument of timidity or of weakness, and would have a tendency to embolden guilt.

Publius

Alexander Hamilton
The Federalist No. 75
March 26, 1788

Cooke, 503-09.

To the People of the State of New York   The president is to have power "by and with the advice and consent of the senate, to make treaties, provided two-thirds of the senators present concur." Though this provision has been assailed on different grounds, with no small degree of vehemence, I scruple not to declare my firm persuasion, that it is one of the best digested and most unexceptionable parts of the plan. One ground of objection is, the trite topic of the intermixture of powers; some contending that the president ought alone to possess the power of making treaties; and others, that it ought to have been exclusively deposited in the senate. Another source of objection is derived from the small number of persons by whom a treaty may be made: Of those who espouse this objection, a part are of opinion that the house of representatives ought to have been associated in the business, while another part seem to think that nothing more was necessary than to have substituted two-thirds of *all* the members of the senate to two-thirds of the members *present*. As I flatter myself the observations made in a preceding number, upon this part of the plan, must have sufficed to place it to a discerning eye in a very favourable light, I shall here content myself with offering only some supplementary remarks, principally with a view to the objections which have been just stated.

  With regard to the intermixture of powers, I shall rely upon the explanations already given, in other places of the true sense of the rule, upon which that objection is founded; and shall take it for granted, as an inference from them, that the union of the executive with the senate, in the article of treaties, is no infringement of that rule. I venture to add that the particular nature of the power of making treaties indicates a peculiar propriety in that union. Though several writers on the subject of government place that power in the class of executive authorities, yet this is evidently an arbitrary disposition: For if we attend carefully to its operation, it will be found to partake more of the legislative than of the executive character, though it does not seem strictly to fall within the definition of either of them. The essence of the legislative authority is to enact laws, or in other words to prescribe rules for the regulation of the society. While the execution of the laws and the employment of the common strength, either for this purpose or for the common defence, seem to comprise all the functions of the executive magistrate. The power of making treaties is plainly neither the one nor the other. It relates neither to the execution of the subsisting laws, nor to the enaction of new ones, and still less to an exertion of the common strength. Its objects are contracts with foreign nations, which have the force of law, but derive it from the obligations of good faith. They are not rules prescribed by the sovereign to the subject, but agreements between sovereign and sovereign. The power in question seems therefore to form a distinct department, and to belong properly neither to the legislative nor to the executive. The qualities elsewhere detailed, as indispensable in the management of foreign negotiations, point out the executive as the most fit agent in those transactions; while the vast importance of the trust, and the operation of treaties as laws, plead strongly for the participation of the whole or a part of the legislative body in the office of making them.

However proper or safe it may be in governments where the executive magistrate is an hereditary monarch, to commit to him the entire power of making treaties, it would be utterly unsafe and improper to entrust that power to an elective magistrate of four years duration. It has been remarked upon another occasion, and the remark is unquestionably just, that an hereditary monarch, though often the oppressor of his people, has personally too much at stake in the government to be in any material danger of being corrupted by foreign powers. But a man raised from the station of a private citizen to the rank of chief magistrate, possessed of but a moderate or slender fortune, and looking forward to a period not very remote, when he may probably be obliged to return to the station from which he was taken, might sometimes be under temptations to sacrifice his duty to his interest, which it would require superlative virtue to withstand. An avaricious man might be tempted to betray the interests of the state to the acquisition of wealth. An ambitious man might make his own aggrandizement, by the aid of a foreign power, the price of his treachery to his constituents. The history of human conduct does not warrant that exalted opinion of human virtue which would make it wise in a nation to commit interests of so delicate and momentous a kind as those which concern its intercourse with the rest of the world to the sole disposal of a magistrate, created and circumstanced, as would be a president of the United States.

To have entrusted the power of making treaties to the senate alone, would have been to relinquish the benefits of the constitutional agency of the president, in the conduct of foreign negotiations. It is true, that the senate would in that case have the option of employing him in this capacity; but they would also have the option of letting it alone; and pique or cabal might induce the latter rather than the former. Besides this, the ministerial servant of the senate could not be expected to enjoy the confidence and respect of foreign powers in the same degree with the constitutional representative of the nation; and of course would not be able to act with an equal degree of weight or efficacy. While the union would from this cause lose a considerable advantage in the management of its external concerns, the people would lose the additional security, which would result from the co-operation of the executive. Though it would be imprudent to confide in him solely so important a trust; yet it cannot be doubted, that his participation in it would materially add to the safety of the society. It must indeed be clear to a demonstration, that the joint possession of the power in question by the president and senate would afford a greater prospect of security, than the separate possession of it by either of them. And whoever has maturely weighed the circumstances, which must concur in the appointment of a president will be satisfied, that the office will always bid fair to be filled by men of such characters as to render their concurrence in the formation of treaties peculiarly desirable, as well on the score of wisdom as on that of integrity.

The remarks made in a former number, which has been alluded to in an other part of this paper, will apply with conclusive force against the admission of the house of representatives to a share in the formation of treaties. The fluctuating, and taking its future increase into the account, the multitudinous composition of that body, forbid us to expect in it those qualities which are essential to the proper execution of such a trust. Accurate and comprehensive knowledge of foreign politics; a steady and systematic adherence to the same views; a nice and uniform sensibility to national character, decision, *secrecy* and dispatch; are incompatible with the genius of a body so variable and so numerous. The very complication of the business by introducing a necessity of the concurrence of so many different bodies, would of itself afford a solid objection. The greater frequency of the calls upon the house of representatives, and the greater length of time which it would often be necessary to keep them together when convened, to obtain their sanction in the progressive stages of a treaty, would be source of so great inconvenience and expense, as alone ought to condemn the project.

The only objection which remains to be canvassed is that which would substitute the proportion of two thirds of all the members composing the senatorial body to that of two thirds of the members *present*. It has been shewn under the second head of our inquiries that all provisions which require more than the majority of any body to its resolutions have a direct tendency to embarrass the operations of the government and an indirect one to subject the sense of the majority to that of the minority. This consideration seems sufficient to determine our opinion, that the convention have gone as far in the endeavour to secure the advantage of numbers in the formation of treaties as could have been reconciled either with the activity of the public councils or with a reasonable regard to the major sense of the community. If two thirds of the whole number of members had been required, it would in many cases from the non attendance of a part amount in practice to a necessity of unanimity. And the history of every political establishment in which this principle has prevailed is a history of impotence, perplexity and disorder. Proofs of this position might be adduced from the examples of the Roman tribuneship, the Polish diet and the states general of the Netherlands; did not an example at home render foreign precedents unnecessary.

To require a fixed proportion of the whole body would not in all probability contribute to the advantages of a numerous agency, better than merely to require a proportion of the attending members. The former by making a determinate number at all times requisite to a resolution diminishes the motives to punctual attendance. The latter by making the capacity of the body to depend on a *proportion* which may be varied by the absence or presence of a single member, has the contrary effect. And as, by promoting punctuality, it tends to keep the body complete, there is great likelihood that its resolutions would generally be dictated by as great a number in this case as in the other; while there would be much fewer occasions of delay. It ought not to be forgotten that under the existing confederation two members *may* and usually *do* represent a state; whence it happens that Congress, who now are solely invested with *all the powers* of the union, rarely consists of a greater number of persons than would compose the intended senate. If we add to this, that as the members vote by states, and that where there is only a single member present from a state, his vote is lost, it will justify a supposition that the active voices in the senate, where the members are to vote individually, would rarely fall short in number of the active voices in the existing Congress. When in addition to these considerations we take into view the co-operation of the president, we shall not hesitate to infer that the people of America would have greater security against an improper use of the power of making treaties, under the new constitution, than they now enjoy under the confederation. And when we proceed still one step further, and look forward to the probable augmentation of the senate, by the erection of new states, we shall not only perceive ample ground of confidence in the sufficiency of the numbers, to whose agency that power will be entrusted; but we shall probably be led to conclude that a body more numerous than the senate would be likely to become, would be very little fit for the proper discharge of the trust.

Publius

Alexander Hamilton
The Federalist No. 76
April 1, 1788

Cooke, 509-15.

To the People of the State of New York   The President is "to *nominate* and by and with the advice and consent of the Senate to appoint Ambassadors, other public Ministers and Consuls, Judges of the Supreme Court, and all other officers of the United States, whose appointments are not otherwise provided for in the Constitution. But the Congress may by law vest the appointment of such inferior officers as they think proper in the President alone, or in the Courts of law, or in the heads of departments. The President shall have power to fill up *all vacancies* which may happen *during the recess of the Senate*, by granting commissions which shall *expire* at the end of their next session."

It has been observed in a former paper, "that the true test of a good government is its aptitude and tendency to produce a good administration." If the justness of this observation be admitted, the mode of appointing the officers of the United States contained in the foregoing clauses, must when examined be allowed to be entitled to particular commendation. It is not easy to conceive a plan better calculated than this, to produce a judicious choice of men for filling the offices of the Union; and it will not need proof, that on this point must essentially depend the character of its administration.

It will be agreed on all hands, that the power of appointment in ordinary cases ought to be modified in one of three ways. It ought either to be vested in a single man—or in a *select* assembly of a moderate number—or in a single man with the concurrence of such an assembly. The exercise of it by the people at large, will be readily admitted to be impracticable; as, waving every other consideration it would leave them little time to do any thing else. When therefore mention is made in the subsequent reasonings of an assembly or body of men, what is said must be understood to relate to a select body or assembly of the description already given. The people collectively from their number and from their dispersed situation cannot be regulated in their movements by that systematic spirit of cabal and intrigue, which will be urged as the chief objections to reposing the power in question in a body of men.

Those who have themselves reflected upon the subject, or who have attended to the observations made in other parts of these papers, in relation to the appointment of the President, will I presume agree to the position that there would always be great probability of having the place supplied by a man of abilities, at least respectable. Premising this, I proceed to lay it down as a rule, that one man of discernment is better fitted to analise and estimate the peculiar qualities adapted to particular offices, than a body of men of equal, or perhaps even of superior discernment.

The sole and undivided responsibility of one man will naturally beget a livelier sense of duty and a more exact regard to reputation. He will on this account feel himself under stronger obligations, and more interested to investigate with care the qualities requisite to the stations to be filled, and to prefer with impartiality the persons who may have the fairest pretentions to them. He will have *fewer* personal attachments to gratify than a body of men, who may each be supposed to have an equal number, and will be so much the less liable to be misled by the sentiments of friendship and of affection. A single well directed man by a single understanding, cannot be distracted and warped by that diversity of views, feelings and interests, which frequently distract and warp the resolutions of a collective body. There is nothing so apt to agitate the passions of mankind as personal considerations, whether they relate to ourselves or to others, who are to be the objects of our choice or preference. Hence, in every exercise of the power of appointing to offices by an assembly of men, we must expect to see a full display of all the private and party likings and dislikes, partialities and antipathies, attachments and animosities, which are felt by those who compose the assembly. The choice which may at any time happen to be made under such circumstances will of course be the result either of a victory gained by one party over the other, or of a compromise between the parties. In either case, the intrinsic merit of the candidate will be too often out of sight. In the first, the qualifications best adapted to uniting the suffrages of the party will be more considered than those which fit the person for the station. In the last the coalition will commonly turn upon some interested equivalent—"Give us the man we wish for this office, and you shall have the one you wish for that." This will be the usual condition of the bargain. And it will rarely happen that the advancement of the public service will be the primary object either of party victories or of party negociations.

The truth of the principles here advanced seems to have been felt by the most intelligent of those who have found fault with the provision made in this respect by the Convention. They contend that the President ought solely to have been authorized to make the appointments under the Federal Government. But it is easy to shew that every advantage to be expected from such an arrangement would in substance be derived from the power of *nomination*, which is proposed to be conferred upon him; while several disadvantages which might attend the absolute power of appointment in the hands of that officer, would be avoided. In the act of nomination his judgment alone would be exercised; and as it would be his sole duty to point out the man, who with the approbation of the Senate should fill an office, his responsibility would be as complete as if he were to make the final appointment. There can in this view be no difference between nominating and appointing. The same motives which would influence a proper discharge of his duty in one case would exist in the other. And as no man could be appointed, but upon his previous nomination, every man who might be appointed would be in fact his choice.

But might not his nomination be overruled? I grant it might, yet this could only be to make place for another nomination by himself. The person ultimately appointed must be the object of his preference, though perhaps not in the first degree. It is also not very probable that his nomination would often be overruled. The Senate could not be tempted by the preference they might feel to another to reject the one proposed; because they could not assure themselves that the person they might wish would be brought forward by a second or by any subsequent nomination. They could not even be certain that a future nomination would present a candidate in any degree more acceptable to them: And as their dissent might cast a kind of stigma upon the individual rejected; and might have the appearance of a reflection upon the judgment of the chief magistrate; it is not likely that their sanction would often be refused, where there were not special and strong reasons for the refusal.

To what purpose then require the co-operation of the Senate? I answer that the necessity of their concurrence would have a powerful, though in general a silent operation. It would be an excellent check upon a spirit of favoritism in the President, and would tend greatly to preventing the appointment of unfit characters from State prejudice, from family connection, from personal attachment, or from a view to popularity. And, in addition to this, it would be an efficacious source of stability in the administration.

It will readily be comprehended, that a man, who had himself the sole disposition of offices, would be governed much more by his private inclinations and interests, than when he was bound to submit the propriety of his choice to the discussion and determination of a different and independent body; and that body an entire branch of the Legislature. The possibility of rejection would be a strong motive to care in proposing. The danger to his own reputation, and, in the case of an elective magistrate, to his political existence, from betraying a spirit of favoritism, or an unbecoming pursuit of popularity, to the observation of a body, whose opinion would have great weight in forming that of the public, could not fail to operate as a barrier to the one and to the other. He would be both ashamed and afraid to bring forward for the most distinguished or lucrative stations, candidates who had no other merit, than that of coming from the same State to which he particularly belonged, or of being in some way or other personally allied to him, or of possessing the necessary insignificance and pliancy to render them the obsequious instruments of his pleasure.

To this reasoning, it has been objected, that the President by the influence of the power of nomination may secure the compliance of the Senate to his views. The supposition of universal venality in human nature is little less an error in political reasoning than the supposition of universal rectitude. The institution of delegated power implies that there is a portion of virtue and honor among mankind, which may be a reasonable foundation of confidence. And experience justifies the theory: It has been found to exist in the most corrupt periods of the most corrupt governments. The venality of the British House of Commons has been long a topic of accusation against that body, in the country to which they belong, as well as in this; and it cannot be doubted that the charge is to a considerable extent well founded. But it is as little to be doubted that there is always a large proportion of the body, which consists of independent and public spirited men, who have an influential weight in the councils of the nation. Hence it is (the present reign not excepted) that the sense of that body is often seen to controul the inclinations of the monarch, both with regard to men and to measures. Though it might therefore be allowable to suppose, that the executive might occasionally influence some individuals in the Senate; yet the supposition that he could in general purchase the integrity of the whole body would be forced and improbable. A man disposed to view human nature as it is, without either flattering its virtues or exaggerating its vices, will see sufficient ground of confidence in the probity of the Senate, to rest satisfied not only that it will be impracticable to the Executive to corrupt or seduce a majority of its members; but that the necessity of its co-operation in the business of appointments will be a considerable and salutary restraint upon the conduct of that magistrate. Nor is the integrity of the Senate the only reliance. The constitution has provided some important guards against the danger of executive influence upon the legislative body: It declares that "No Senator, or representative shall, during the time *for which he was elected*, be appointed to any civil office under the United States, which shall have been created, or the emoluments whereof shall have been encreased during such time; and no person holding any office under the United States shall be a member of either house during his continuance in office."

Publius

Alexander Hamilton
The Federalist No. 77
April 2, 1788

Cooke, 515-21.

To the People of the State of New York   It has been mentioned as one of the advantages to be expected from the co-operation of the senate, in the business of appointments, that it would contribute to the stability of the administration. The consent of that body would be necessary to displace as well as to appoint. A change of the chief magistrate therefore would not occasion so violent or so general a revolution in the officers of the government, as might be expected if he were the sole disposer of offices. Where a man in any station had given satisfactory evidence of his fitness for it, a new president would be restrained from attempting a change, in favour of a person more agreeable to him, by the apprehension that the discountenance of the senate might frustrate the attempt, and bring some degree of discredit upon himself. Those who can best estimate the value of a steady administration will be most disposed to prize a provision, which connects the official existence of public men with the approbation or disapprobation of that body, which from the greater permanency of its own composition, will in all probability be less subject to inconstancy, than any other member of the government.

To this union of the senate with the president, in the article of appointments, it has in some cases been objected, that it would serve to give the president an undue influence over the senate; and in others, that it would have an opposite tendency; a strong proof that neither suggestion is true.

To state the first in its proper form is to refute it. It amounts to this—The president would have an improper *influence over* the senate; because the senate would have the power of *restraining* him. This is an absurdity in terms. It cannot admit of a doubt that the intire power of appointment would enable him much more effectually to establish a dangerous empire over that body, than a mere power of nomination subject to their controul.

Let us take a view of the converse of the proposition—"The senate would influence the executive." As I have had occasion to remark in several other instances, the indistinctness of the objection forbids a precise answer. In what manner is this influence to be exerted? In relation to what objects? The power of influencing a person, in the sense in which it is here used, must imply a power of conferring a benefit upon him. How could the senate confer a benefit upon the president by the manner of employing their right of negative upon his nominations? If it be said they might sometimes gratify him by an acquiescence in a favorite choice, when public motives might dictate a different conduct; I answer that the instances in which the president could be personally interested in the result, would be too few to admit of his being materially affected by the compliances of the senate. The power which can *originate* the disposition of honors and emoluments, is more likely to attract than to be attracted by the power which can merely obstruct their course. If by influencing the president be meant *restraining* him, this is precisely what must have been intended. And it has been shewn that the restraint would be salutary, at the same time that it would not be such as to destroy a single advantage to be looked for from the uncontrouled agency of that magistrate. The right of nomination would produce all the good of that of appointment and would in a great measure avoid its ills.

Upon a comparison of the plan for the appointment of the officers of the proposed government with that which is established by the constitution of this state a decided preference must be given to the former. In that plan the power of nomination is unequivocally vested in the executive. And as there would be a necessity for submitting each nomination to the judgment of an entire branch of the legislature, the circumstances attending an appointment, from the mode of conducting it, would naturally become matters of notoriety; and the public would be at no loss to determine what part had been performed by the different actors. The blame of a bad nomination would fall upon the president singly and absolutely. The censure of rejecting a good one would lie entirely at the door of the senate; aggravated by the consideration of their having counteracted the good intentions of the executive. If an ill appointment should be made the executive for nominating and the senate for approving would participate though in different degrees in the opprobrium and disgrace.

The reverse of all this characterises the manner of appointment in this state. The council of appointment consists of from three to five persons, of whom the governor is always one. This small body, shut up in a private apartment, impenetrable to the public eye, proceed to the execution of the trust committed to them. It is known that the governor claims the right of nomination, upon the strength of some ambiguous expressions in the constitution; but it is not known to what extent, or in what manner he exercises it; nor upon what occasions he is contradicted or opposed. The censure of a bad appointment, on account of the uncertainty of its author, and for want of a determinate object, has neither poignancy nor duration. And while an unbounded field for cabal and intrigue lies open, all idea of responsibility is lost. The most that the public can know is, that the governor claims the right of nomination: That *two* out of the considerable number of *four* men can too often be managed without much difficulty: That if some of the members of a particular council should happen to be of an uncomplying character, it is frequently not impossible to get rid of their opposition, by regulating the times of meeting in such a manner as to render their attendance inconvenient: And that, from whatever cause it may proceed, a great number of very improper appointments are from time to time made. Whether a governor of this state avails himself of the ascendant he must necessarily have, in this delicate and important part of the administration, to prefer to offices men who are best qualified for them: Or whether he prostitutes that advantage to the advancement of persons, whose chief merit is their implicit devotion to his will, and to the support of a despicable and dangerous system of personal influence, are questions which unfortunately for the community can only be the subjects of speculation and conjecture.

Every mere council of appointment, however constituted, will be a conclave, in which cabal and intrigue will have their full scope. Their number, without an unwarrantable increase of expence, cannot be large enough to preclude a facility of combination. And as each member will have his friends and connections to provide for, the desire of mutual gratification will beget a scandalous bartering of votes and bargaining for places. The private attachments of one man might easily be satisfied; but to satisfy the private attachments of a dozen, or of twenty men, would occasion a monopoly of all the principal employments of the government, in a few families, and would lead more directly to an aristocracy or an oligarchy, than any measure that could be contrived. If to avoid an accumulation of offices, there was to be a frequent change in the persons, who were to compose the council, this would involve the mischiefs of a mutable administration in their full extent. Such a council would also be more liable to executive influence than the senate, because they would be fewer in number, and would act less immediately under the public inspection. Such a council in fine as a substitute for the plan of the convention, would be productive of an increase of expence, a multiplication of the evils which spring from favouritism and intrigue in the distribution of the public honors, a decrease of stability in the administration of the government, and a diminution of the security against an undue influence of the executive. And yet such a council has been warmly contended for as an essential amendment in the proposed constitution.

I could not with propriety conclude my observations on the subject of appointments, without taking notice of a scheme, for which there has appeared some, though by a few advocates; I mean that of uniting the house of representatives in the power of making them. I shall however do little more than mention it, as I cannot imagine that it is likely to gain the countenance of any considerable part of the community. A body so fluctuating, and at the same time so numerous, can never be deemed proper for the exercise of that power. Its unfitness will appear manifest to all, when it is recollected that in half a century it may consist of three or four hundred persons. All the advantages of the stability, both of the executive and of the senate, would be defeated by this union; and infinite delays and embarrassments would be occasioned. The example of most of the states in their local constitutions, encourages us to reprobate the idea.

The only remaining powers of the executive, are comprehended in giving information to congress of the state of the union; in recommending to their consideration such measures as he shall judge expedient; in convening them, or either branch, upon extraordinary occasions; in adjourning them when they cannot themselves agree upon the time of adjournment; in receiving ambassadors and other public ministers; in faithfully executing the laws; and in commissioning all the officers of the United States.

Except some cavils about the power of convening *either* house of the legislature and that of receiving ambassadors, no objection has been made to this class of authorities; nor could they possibly admit of any. It required indeed an insatiable avidity for censure to invent exceptions to the parts which have been excepted to. In regard to the power of convening either house of the legislature, I shall barely remark, that in respect to the senate at least, we can readily discover a good reason for it. As this body has a concurrent power with the executive in the article of treaties, it might often be necessary to call it together with a view to this object, when it would be unnecessary and improper to convene the house of representatives. As to the reception of ambassadors, what I have said in a former paper will furnish a sufficient answer.

We have now compleated a survey of the structure and powers of the executive department, which, I have endeavoured to show, combines, as far as republican principles would admit, all the requisites to energy. The remaining enquiry is: does it also combine the requisites to safety in the republican sense—a due dependence on the people—a due responsibility? The answer to this question has been anticipated in the investigation of its other characteristics, and is satisfactorily deducible from these circumstances, the election of the president once in four years by persons immediately chosen by the people for that purpose; and from his being at all times liable to impeachment, trial, dismission from office, incapacity to serve in any other;

and to the forfeiture of life and estate by subsequent prosecution in the common course of law. But these precautions, great as they are, are not the only ones, which the plan of the convention has provided in favor of the public security. In the only instances in which the abuse of the executive authority was materially to be feared, the chief magistrate of the United States would by that plan be subjected to the controul of a branch of the legislative body. What more could be desired by an enlightened and reasonable people?

Publius

The new Constitution was adopted by the necessary nine states eight months after the Philadelphia Convention, and by the end of July 1788, two more states had joined the Union. It had been rough going at some of the ratifying conventions, particularly Virginia, Massachusetts, New Hampshire and New York; and Patrick Henry fired salvo after salvo at the presidential office, as if it was modeled directly after the British King. The truth is that the Constitution sketched only a very faint image of the office of the President of the United States, and it would take another century and a half, perhaps more, before its physiognomy, its bone structure, nerve and muscular tissues would be fully developed. The fortunate thing about the provisions of the American Constitution dealing with the Executive was that it allowed for necessary growth, its very general grants of power inviting expanded definitions when the situations arose to demand such development. The major contours of the presidential office still remained to be drawn after 1787; indeed they could not be drawn until the various men who achieved that high office molded the framework of presidential power by responding to the problems and crises that confronted them. But that, of course, is the story of the growth of presidential power and will be the subject matter of the rest of this book.

NOTES

1. Bernard Bailyn, *The Ideological Origins of the American Revolution* (Cambridge, Massachusetts, 1967).
2. Bailyn, 299-300.
3. John P. Roche, "The Founding Fathers: A Reform Caucus in Action," in *American Political Science Review,* LV (December 1961), 799-816.
4. Clinton Rossiter, *1787: The Grand Convention* (New York, 1966), 15.
5. Percy Lewis Kaye, *The Colonial Executive Prior to the Restoration* (Baltimore, Maryland, 1900), 11.
6. Kaye, 64-65.
7. Jack P. Greene, *The Quest for Power: The Lower Houses of Assembly in the Southern Royal Colonies, 1689-1776.* (Chapel Hill, North Carolina, 1963), 221-22.
8. Kaye, 69.
9. Evarts Boutell Greene, *The Provincial Governor in the English Speaking Colonies* (New York, 1966), 194-95.
10. Allan Nevins, *The American States, During and After the Revolution* (New York, 1924), 166.
11. Charles C. Thach, *The Creation of the Presidency, 1775-1789* (Baltimore, Maryland, 1922), 29. (My emphasis.)

12. Thach, 29.
13. Quoted in Thach, 30.
14. Nevins, 183.
15. Merrill Jensen, *The New Nation: A History of the United States During the Confederation, 1781-1789* (New York, 1950), 424-25.
16. Jensen, 425.
17. Jensen, 425-26.
18. Harold C. Syrett and Jacob Cooke, ed., *The Papers of Alexander Hamilton* (New York, 1961) II, 404.
19. John Locke, "Concerning Civil Government, Second Essay," in *Great Books of the Western World* (Chicago, 1952) XXXV, 58, paragraph 144.
20. Locke, XXXV, 59, paragraph 148.
21. Locke, XXXV, 62, paragraph 160.
22. Locke, XXXV, 62-63, paragraph 161.
23. Charles de Secondat, Baron de Montesquieu, "The Spirit of the Laws," in *Great Books of the Western World* (Chicago, 1952) XXXVIII, 70.
24. David A. Lockmiller, *Sir William Blackstone* (Chapel Hill, North Carolina, 1938), 172, footnote 8.
25. Lockmiller, 174. Gareth Jones points out that this claim had a solid basis in fact. The imported English editions of the *Commentaries* simply could not keep up with the demand, so in 1771-72 a Philadelphia publisher printed an edition of 1400 volumes, which sold for £3 a set, and he had to print a second edition later at an increased price. (Gareth Jones, *The Sovereignty of the Law* (Toronto, 1973), xlvii.)
26. Lockmiller, 182.
27. James Madison to Caleb Wallace, August 23, 1785. Gaillard Hunt, ed., *The Writings of James Madison* (New York, 1901) II, 168-69.
28. James Madison to Thomas Jefferson, March 19, 1787. Hunt, II, 326.
29. James Madison to Edmund Randolph, April 8, 1787. Hunt, II, 339-40.
30. Charles Francis Adams, ed., *The Works of John Adams* (Boston, 1851) IV, 185-86.
31. Adams, IV, 197.
32. Page Smith, *John Adams* (Garden City, New York, 1962).
33. C. F. Adams, VIII, 467.
34. Madison took notes and kept a daily diary in Philadelphia which recorded the Convention discussions, and although there are other records, such as an official journal, I have relied upon Madison almost completely as a documentary source, because his record is more complete. See Max Farrand, ed., *The Records of the Federal Convention* (New Haven, Connecticut, 1911), 3 Vols.
35. Charles Warren, *The Making of the Constitution* (Cambridge, Massachusetts, 1947), 228, footnote 2.
36. Farrand, I, 288-89.
37. Farrand, I, 82.
38. Farrand, II, 542.
39. Farrand, I, 65-66.
40. Sir Lewis Namier, *Crossroads of Power* (New York, 1962), Chapter 7.
41. James MacGregor Burns, *The Deadlock of Democracy* (Englewood Cliffs, New Jersey, 1963), 15.
42. Burns, 15.
43. Farrand, I, 80.
44. Farrand, I, 80.
45. Farrand, I, 236.
46. Farrand, I, 244.
47. The so called "Great Compromise" was a compromise resolution of the struggle that had gone on for weeks between the delegates of the large and the small states with respect to representation. The Randolph Plan obviously gave greater power to the larger states by allocating representation in the lower house according to population, while the New Jersey or Paterson Plan preserved the power of the smaller states by giving each state equal representation, regardless of population. The "Great Compromise" proposed by Connecticut simply incorporated both principles in a separate house of the legislature, the House of Representatives being based on the Randolph Plan proposal, and the Senate on the Paterson Plan.
48. Rossiter, 198.
49. Farrand, II, 57.
50. Roche, 810-11.
51. Jacob E. Cooke, ed., *The Federalist* (New York, 1961), 471.

Bibliography

Adams, John. *The Works of John Adams*. Charles Francis Adams, ed. Vol. IV. Boston: Charles C. Little and James Brown, 1851.

Blackstone, (Sir) William. *Commentaries on the Laws of England*. Thomas M. Cooley, ed. Chicago: Callaghan and Company, 1884.

Burns, James MacGregor. *The Deadlock of Democracy*. Englewood Cliffs, New Jersey: Prentice-Hall, Inc., 1963.

Cooke, Jacob E., ed. *The Federalist*. New York: World Publishing Company, Meridian Books, 1961.

Farrand, Max, ed. *The Records of the Federal Convention of 1787*. 3 Vols. New Haven, Connecticut: Yale University Press, 1911.

Foner, Philip, ed. *The Complete Writings of Thomas Paine*. Vol. I. New York: Citadel Press, 1945.

Hunt, Gaillard, ed. *The Writings of James Madison*. Vol. II. New York: G. P. Putnam's Sons, 1901.

Jensen, Merrill. *The Articles of Confederation*. Madison, Wisconsin: University of Wisconsin Press, 1948.

  The New Nation: A History of the United States During the Confederation, 1781-1789. New York: Alfred A. Knopf, 1950.

Jones, Gareth, ed. *The Sovereignty of the Law*. Toronto, Canada: University of Toronto Press, 1973.

Kaye, Percy Lewis. *The Colonial Executive Prior to the Restoration*. Baltimore, Maryland: Johns Hopkins Press, 1900.

Locke, John. "Concerning Civil Government, Second Essay." *Great Books of the Western World*. Vol. XXXV. Chicago: Encyclopaedia Britannica, Inc., 1952.

Lockmiller, David A. *Sir William Blackstone*. Chapel Hill, North Carolina: University of North Carolina Press, 1938.

Montesquieu, Charles de Secondat, Baron de. *The Spirit of the Laws. Great Books of the Western World.* Vol. XXXVIII. Chicago: Encyclopaedia Britannica, Inc., 1952.

Namier, (Sir) Louis. *Crossroads of Power.* New York: The Macmillan Company, 1962.

Nevins, Allan. *The American States, During and After the Revolution.* New York: The Macmillan Company, 1924.

Roche, John P. "The Founding Fathers: A Reform Caucus in Action." *American Political Science Review.* LV (December, 1961).

Rossiter, Clinton. *1787: The Grand Convention.* New York: The Macmillan Company, 1966.

Thach, Charles C. *The Creation of the Presidency, 1775-1789.* Baltimore, Maryland: Johns Hopkins Press, 1922.

Thorpe, Francis Newton. *The Federal and State Constitutions, Colonial Charters and Other Organic Laws.* Vols. III, IV, V. Washington, D.C.: U.S. Government Printing Office, 1909.

II. The President
as Administrative Head
of the Government

THE PRESIDENT AS ADMINISTRATIVE HEAD OF THE GOVERNMENT

The Power of Appointment

When George Washington crossed the harbor from the New Jersey side to Manhattan Island in the spring of 1789 for his inauguration as the first President of the United States, he faced a range of administrative problems unique in his time. The man to whom the country had turned to head the new government was certainly a unique figure in a unique nation-state. A large man standing over six feet in height, Washington commanded the kind of respect from his countrymen that no other American at that time could approach. Without doubt, his popularity was due, in part, to his military accomplishments, first in the war against the French and the Indians, and later as Commanding General of the American Revolutionary army. In the latter capacity, Washington's reputation assumed mythical proportions, and although the American forces suffered many defeats and were forced to fight a delaying and defensive war, General Washington's reknown as a patient and courageous leader emerged stronger than ever when the long order ended.

Washington was not a person of intellectual distinction, but was rather a cautious and balanced man, conservative in his approach to any problem, somewhat shy and very conscious of his unusual role and of the problems which lay before him. His commitment was unquestioned, and he was voted into office unanimously by the first electoral college, even though the voting for Vice President was scattered among a handful of aspirants. John Adams received more than three times as many votes as his closest opponent, but that was still less than one-half the number of votes tallied by Washington. Perhaps the best indication of what would be the first President's behavior once in the Executive office is found in his perception of the goals of the Constitutional Convention:

> To please all is impossible, and to attempt it would be vain. The only way, therefore, is . . . to form such a government as will bear the scrutiny of criticism, and trust to it the good sense and patriotism of the people to carry it into effect. . . .
> Let us raise a standard to which the wise and honest can repair.[1]

There were in existence at that time three administrative departments which had functioned under the almost powerless Articles of Confederation: the Department of Foreign Affairs, the Department of Finance and the Department of War. A fourth, the Department of Marine, had been initially anticipated, but was later merged with the Department of Finance. Both the Departments of Foreign

Affairs and War were directed by a single head, and after 1784 the Department of Finance was run by a board of three.

Washington inherited this already inadequate administrative structure when he became President, and he quickly obtained from the heads of these agencies a written analysis of their mode of operation. The Departments of Finance, under Robert Morris, and Foreign Affairs, under John Jay, were directed with great skill, but they nevertheless lacked the power to impose their policies upon the constituent member states. In other words, the pre-Constitutional period had produced several brilliant administrators, but the administrative structure within which they operated was a dismal failure.

The new President had to wait until nearly the end of the summer of 1789 before Congress created the major new executive departments—State, War, the Treasury and the office of the attorney general—and obviously he could not make any appointments until the positions were established. The Constitution was very clear on the power of the President to appoint such administrative officers; he did so with the advice and consent of the Senate, of course. The President's power to remove such officials was seriously challenged from the very beginning, but the appointive power was always formally acknowledged, even though in periods of extreme tension between the two branches it too was disputed on a *de facto*, if not a *de jure* basis.

When Congress finally established the major departments of government, President Washington appointed Alexander Hamilton as his secretary of the treasury, Thomas Jefferson as secretary of state, and Major General Henry Knox as secretary of war. The last of the four key positions in the new administration was filled when Washington named Edmund Randolph of Virginia attorney general.

There had been support at the Convention for an executive council, patterned on the model of the advisory councils attached to the colonial governors. Roger Sherman, for example, expressed the hope that such a council would limit the arbitrary character of a single Executive. The proposal by Gouverneur Morris which the Convention finally accepted called for a Council of State made up of the chief justice of the Supreme Court and the heads of the five major departments. Morris's draft proposed that the President "may from time to time submit any matter to the discussion of the Council of State, and he may require the written opinions of any one or more of the Members; But he shall in all cases exercise his own judgment, and either conform to such opinions or not as he may think proper."[2] When this proposal emerged from both the Committee on Detail and the final Committee on Style which produced the draft of the Constitution ultimately accepted by the delegates, it had been reduced to a clause empowering the President to "require the opinion, in writing, of the principal officers in each of the executive departments, upon any subject relating to the duties of their respective offices."

Washington used this injunction freely and often, and after the first few years in office, he began to meet with his advisors, particularly during crises, when, as Jefferson has indicated, they met almost daily. The President's cabinet, then, although not created specifically by constitutional fiat, followed mainly from the general intent of the Convention's discussion of the role of presidential advisors, as well as from those sections of the Constitution which suggested the appointment of department heads and indicated their advisory role. Finally, it arose from the increasingly more important functional need that the first President had for the advice and assistance of his department heads. Although a great authority on presidential power has argued that the institution of the cabinet could be declared "unconstitutional," since Washington's time it has flourished, and by custom and precedent, it has become a very significant element of the American political system.[3]

Washington established the procedure of determining decisions by a vote of his cabinet, and Jefferson indicated that he followed the same practice, though the results were very different. Washington appointed what he considered to be the best men available for the position at hand, and gave no thought to their political predispositions. The break-up of his official family, however, brought on by the continuous dispute between Hamilton and Jefferson, led him to the conclusion in his second term not to appoint individuals to his administration who were strongly adverse to his policies:

> I shall not, while I have the honor to administer the government, bring a man into an office of consequence knowingly, whose political tenets are adverse to the measures which the general government are pursuing; for this, in my opinion, would be a sort of political suicide.[4]

Jefferson, on the other hand, surrounded himself from the very beginning with close party colleagues: James Madison, as secretary of state; Albert Gallatin, secretary of the treasury; a series of able attorney generals: Levi Lincoln (1801-05), John Breckenridge (1805-06) and Ceasar A. Rodney (1807-09); General Henry Dearborn, secretary of war; and Robert Smith, secretary of the navy. All acknowledged Jefferson's leadership, and the inner core of the cabinet which met and was consulted frequently—Jefferson, Madison and Gallatin—made up one of the most brilliant and effective cabinets in the history of our government. If they did adhere to a democratic vote on all issues, as Jefferson has indicated, this did not diminish his leadership one bit; for despite the others' individual brilliance and abilities, they looked to Jefferson as their natural leader and their intellectual and political superior.

The right of the President to appoint the major department heads and advisors has continued down through the years and has only been seriously challenged on a few occasions. No cabinet level appointment of the first six Presidents was defeated by the Senate, but during the administration of James Madison, legislative pressures were exerted which forced the President to change his mind with respect to his initial appointments, and he was later forced to drop a member of his cabinet because of congressional opposition. The Senate actually did defeat Andrew Jackson's nomination of Rober B. Taney for secretary of the treasury, but this defeat came only as a result of a much more significant struggle between the President and Congress (Taney was also involved) over the Second Bank of the United States and its deposits. Although the Senate succeeded in defeating Taney for the Treasury position, Jackson later nominated him as chief justice of the Supreme Court, and the new Jackson majority in the Senate confirmed the appointment.

While George Washington was prevented from appointing his chief advisors before the Congress acted to create the various departments and to define the responsibilities of their top officials or secretaries, as they were to be called, nothing stopped him from going ahead in the appointment of many positions which were not on the level of the President's cabinet. Revenues had to be collected, routine business conducted, and other basic functions of the national government carried on. The constitutional mandate was reasonably clear in this respect, for it specified that the President shall:

> nominate, and by and with the Advice and Consent of the Senate, shall appoint Ambassadors, other public ministers and Consuls, Judges of the Supreme Court and all other officers of the United States, whose Appointments are not herein otherwise provided for, and which shall be established by Law. . . .

The Constitution further provided that the "Congress may by Law vest Appointment of such inferior Officers, as they think proper, in the President alone, in the Courts of Law, or in the Heads of Departments." This constitutional language established the perimeters within which many complex questions remained unanswered. It did not define, for example, the dividing line between major administrative officers and "inferior officers," nor did it state precisely whether or not the President, the Congress, or both should be involved in the removal of any or all of these appointees. Many years would go by and a great deal of debate would take place before such questions would ultimately be solved, but apart from these problems the Constitution did provide the President (without further action from Congress) with the authority to appoint certain officers with the "Advice and Consent of the Senate."

Washington had some very clear ideas of his own with regard to the appointment of public officials. Even before arriving in New York, the nation's capital at that time, he wrote:

> I have no conception of a more delicate task, than, that which is imposed by the Constitution on the Executive. It is the nature of Republicans, who are nearly in a state of equality, to be extremely jealous as to disposal of all honorary or lucrative appointments. Perfectly convinced I am, that, if injudicious or unpopular measures should be taken by the Executive under the new Government with regard to appointments, the Government itself would be in the utmost danger of being utterly subverted by those measures. So necessary is it, at this crisis, to conciliate the good will of the People; and so impossible is it, in my judgment, to build the ediface of public happiness, but upon their affections.[5]

He went on to summarize the general principles he planned to apply in the appointment of individuals for positions:

(1) to enter office without any engagements.
(2) not to be influenced by motives of amity or blood.
(3) to take into account three principle factors:
    a) fitness;

b) comparative claims "from the former merits and sufferings in service;"

c) equal distribution among the states.[6]

Washington decided to submit all of his nominations in writing, because he indicated that if he were to present the candidate's name in person to the Senate, it might be embarrassing for him to hear the merits of the appointment discussed, and perhaps somewhat intimidating to the senators to have to make such a decision in his presence. Several weeks later the wisdom of this judgment was borne out by his first and last humiliating confrontation with the Senate in the process of seeking its ratification of a treaty.

The President established an excellent record with respect to Senate approval of his nominations, however, maintaining his objective principles and attempting to bring into public office the best qualified individuals he could find. He was quite willing to receive suggestions for nominations from members of Congress, and he indicated that he considered both geography and political point of view in his selections.

In the final analysis, however, he refused to be badgered, and he resisted all efforts to persuade him against his better judgment. His prestige was so enormous that only on rare occasions were his nominations turned down. The first was the rejection of Benjamin Fishbourne as naval officer in the Port of Savannah. Fishbourne had been one of about a hundred nominations that the President had submitted for posts as collectors, naval officers and surveyors. Washington quickly proposed a different candidate after Colonel Fishbourne's rejection, but he took the occasion to remind the Senate in detail of the rejected nominee's high qualifications for the office, and tartly suggested that in the future, if the Senate was disposed to question the propriety of a nomination, it would be expedient "to communicate that circumstance to me, and thereby avail yourselves of the information which led me to make them (appointments), and which I would with pleasure lay before you."[7] Later the Senate refused to confirm a more important appointment, that of John Rutledge of South Carolina as chief justice of the Supreme Court, and it was clear to Jefferson and others that the rejection was based upon Rutledge's political views. At the time of his consideration by the Senate he had strongly attacked the Jay Treaty, which was more or less the touchstone of the majority Federalist point of view in the Senate.

During the administration of John Adams, the already discernible tendency of members of Congress to press their selections upon the Chief Executive increased, although the total number of appointments was small. Long before he was elected President, Adams had suggested the potential difficulties involved in this problem in a brilliant and prophetic passage of a letter written to Roger Sherman in 1789.

John Adams
Letter to Roger Sherman
On the Appointing Power of the President
July 17, 1789

C. F. Adams, *The Works of John Adams*, VI, 432-36.

The negative of the senate upon appointments is liable to the following objections:

1. It takes away, or, at least, it lessens the responsibility of the executive. Our constitution obliges me to say, that it lessens the responsibility of the president. The blame of an injudicious, weak, or wicked appointment, is shared so much between him and the senate, that his part of it will be too small. Who can censure him, without censuring the senate, and the legislatures who appoint them? All their friends will be interested to vindicate the president, in order to screen them from censure. Besides, if an impeachment against an officer is brought before them, are they not interested to acquit him, lest some part of the odium of his guilt should fall upon them, who advised to his appointment?

2. It turns the minds and attention of the people to the senate, a branch of the legislature, in executive matters. It interests another branch of the legislature in the management of the executive. It divides the people between the executive and the senate; whereas, all the people ought to be united to watch the executive, to oppose its encroachments, and resist its ambition. Senators and representatives, and their constituents, in short, the aristocratical and democratical divisions of society ought to be united on all occasions to oppose the executive or the monarchical branch, when it attempts to overleap its limits. But how can this union be effected, when the aristocratical branch has pledged its reputation to the executive, by consenting to an appointment?

3. It has a natural tendency to excite ambition in the senate. An active, ardent spirit, who is rich and able, and has a great reputation and influence, will be solicited by candidates for office. Not to introduce the idea of bribery, because, though it certainly would force itself in, in other countries, and will probably here, when we grow populous and rich, it is not yet to be dreaded, I hope, ambition must come in already. A senator of great influence will be naturally ambitious and desirous of increasing his influence. Will he not be under a temptation to use his influence with the president as well as his brother senators, to appoint persons to office in the several states, who will exert themselves in elections, to get out his enemies or opposers, both in senate and house of representatives, and to get in his friends, perhaps his instruments? Suppose a senator to aim at the treasury office for himself, his brother, father, or son. Suppose him to aim at the president's chair, or vice-president's, at the next election, or at the office of war, foreign, or domestic affairs. Will he not naturally be tempted to make use of his whole patronage, his whole influence, in advising to appointments, both with president and senators, to get such

persons nominated as will exert themselves in elections of president, vice-president, senators, and house of representatives, to increase his interest and promote his views? In this point of view, I am very apprehensive that this defect in our constitution will have an unhappy tendency to introduce corruption of the grossest kinds, both of ambition and avarice, into all our elections, and this will be the worst of poisons to our constitution. It will not only destroy the present form of government, but render it almost impossible to substitute in its place any free government, even a better limited-monarchy, or any other than a despotism or a simple monarchy.

4. To avoid the evil under the last head, it will be in danger of dividing the continent into two or three nations, a case that presents no prospect but of perpetual war.

5. This negative on appointments is in danger of involving the senate in reproach, censure, obloquy, and suspicion, without doing any good. Will the senate use their negative or not? If not, why should they have it? Many will censure them for not using it; many will ridicule them, and call them servile, etc. If they do use it, the very first instance of it will expose the senators to the resentment of not only the disappointed candidate and all his friends, but of the president and all his friends, and these will be most of the officers of government, through the nation.

6. We shall very soon have parties formed; a court and country party, and these parties will have names given them. One party in the house of representatives will support the president and his measures and ministers; the other will oppose them. A similar party will be in the senate; these parties will study with all their arts, perhaps with intrigue, perhaps with corruption, at every election to increase their own friends and diminish their opposers. Suppose such parties formed in the senate, and then consider what factious divisions we shall have there upon every nomination.

7. The senate have not time. The convention and Indian treaties. . .

You are of opinion "that the concurrence of the senate in the appointments to office, will strengthen the hands of the executive, and secure the confidence of the people, much better than a select council, and will be less expensive."

But in every one of these ideas, I have the misfortune to differ from you.

It will weaken the hands of the executive, by lessening the obligation, gratitude, and attachment of the candidate to the president, by dividing his attachment between the executive and legislative, which are natural enemies. Officers of government, instead of having a single eye and undivided attachment to the executive branch, as they ought to have, consistent with law and the constitution, will be constantly tempted to be factious with their factious patrons in the senate. The president's own officers, in a thousand instances, will oppose his just and constitutional exertions, and screen themselves under the wings of their patrons and party in the legislature. Nor will it secure the confidence of the people. The people will have more confidence in the executive, in executive matters, than in the senate. The people will be constantly jealous of factious schemes in the senators to unduly influence the executive, to serve each other's private views. The people will also be jealous that the influence of the senate will be employed to conceal, connive at, and defend guilt in executive officers, instead of being a guard and watch upon them, and a terror to them. A council, selected by the president himself, at his pleasure, from among the senators, representatives, and nation at large, would be purely responsible. In that case, the senate would be a terror to privy counsellors; its honor would never be pledged to support any measure or instrument of the executive beyond justice, law, and the constitution. Nor would a privy council be more expensive. The whole senate must now deliberate on every appointment, and if they ever find time for it, you will find that a great deal of time will be required and consumed in this service. Then, the president might have a constant executive council; now, he has none.

I said, under the seventh head, that the senate would not have time. You will find that the whole business of this government will be infinitely delayed by this negative of the senate on treaties and appointments. Indian treaties and consular conventions have been already waiting for months, and the senate have not been able to find a moment of time to attend to them; and this evil must constantly increase. So that the senate must be constantly sitting, and must be paid as long as they sit. . .

But I have tired your patience. Is there any truth in these broken hints and crude surmises, or not? To me they appear well founded and very important.

I am, with usual affection, yours,

John Adams

The Republicans in Office

Thomas Jefferson was the first President to justify the placing of his political supporters in governmental positions; his explanation was so candidly expressed and so eloquently phrased that it caused no undue alarm at the time, and most writers on the subject continue to attribute the introduction of the "spoils system" to Andrew Jackson. Of course there were extenuating circumstances that led to its development under Jefferson. The Federalists had been in power for 12 years when Jefferson came to the White House, and at the end of the Adams administration they had rather shamelessly entrenched their own followers in office. In fact, it would probably be correct to attribute to John Adams the beginning of the "spoils system," because his "midnight appointments" created the need for Jefferson's innovation.

Jefferson was confronted with an executive branch staffed almost entirely by Federalist supporters, and although he wanted to calm the factious spirit alive in the country and stressed national unity, he did not conceive that it was his duty to preserve jobs in government for politicians who had opposed him. In removing the tax collector in the city of New Haven, Connecticut, a Federalist in a Federalist stronghold, Jefferson explained his actions and defended the principle upon which he acted. Adams had appointed the tax collector a week before Jefferson's inauguration, but Jefferson, instead of dismissing the man in question, refused to acknowledge the legality of the appointment and proceeded to appoint a new tax collector.

A howl of criticism went up over this and other similar appointments enacted in the wake of Jefferson's appeal for national unity and conciliation in his first inaugural address ("We are all Republicans, we are all Federalists.") He answered with a brilliant and ringing defense:

> Declarations by myself in favor of *political tolerance*, exhortations to *harmony* and affection in social intercourse, and to respect for the *equal rights* of the minority, have, on certain occasions, been quoted and misconstrued into assurances that the tenure of offices was to be undisturbed. But could candor apply such a construction?[8]

He went on to point out that the Federalists had excluded everyone but their own party from office during their more than a decade in power, and as a consequence of this, public office had become a monopoly of the minority:

> Does it violate their equal rights to assert some rights in the majority also? Is it *political intolerance* to claim a proportionate share in the direction of public affairs . . .? If the will of the nation, manifested by their various elections, calls for an administration of government according with the opinions of those elected; if, for the fulfillment of that will, displacements are necessary, with whom can they so justly begin as with the persons appointed in the last moments of an administration, not for its own aid, but to begin a career at the same time with their successors?
>
> If due participation of office is a matter of right, how are vacancies to be obtained? Those by death are few; by resignation, none. Can any other mode than that of removal be proposed? This is a painful office; but it is made my duty, and I meet it as such. I proceed in the operation with deliberation and inquiry, that it may injure the best man least, and effect the purposes of justice and public utility with the least private distress; that it may be thrown, as much as possible, on delinquency, on oppression, on intolerance, on ante-revolutionary adherence to our enemies. It would have been to me a circumstance of great relief, had I found a moderate participation of office in the hands of the majority. I would gladly have left to time and accident to raise them to their just share. But their total exclusion calls for prompter corrections. I shall correct the procedure; but that done, return with joy to that state of things when the only questions concerning a candidate shall be, is he honest? Is he capable? Is he faithful to the Constitution?[9]

In addition to his eloquence and philosophical train of thought, Jefferson was an exceptionally able politician, and he accomplished his purpose in the area of appointments with consummate artistry and ease. During his first term as President he initiated a change in almost half of the presidential offices without destroying the equilibrium of the government. Perhaps this was because the total number of presidentially appointed positions was small (334), or because Jefferson was so quietly efficient in carrying out his political objectives. A leading student of this aspect of administrative behavior has concluded:

> It is evident that, in spite of favoritism and politics, Jefferson succeeded in

the main object which he placed before himself in dealing with the patronage—that of satisfying the people. In this, as in many other cases, his sympathetic response to popular desire gave him unexpected victory; to satisfy his own followers, and at the same time not to alienate the masses of the opposition, was indeed a wonderful feat. So cleverly did Jefferson steer his bark that the patronage had ceased to be an issue by 1809.[10]

James Madison's weakness in his relations with Congress resurrected the problem that Jefferson's adroit leadership had buried—the spectre of Congress controlling the power not only of deciding who would be the next President, but also, what his policies would be. Madison was not even sure of getting Senate approval for the cabinet of his choice, and was finally forced to accept the nominee of several powerful senators for one critical cabinet post in order to prevent them from eliminating his other selections. He was thus compelled to reshuffle his cabinet in order to make Albert Gallatin secretary of the treasury, rather than secretary of state as he had planned.

The Senate rejected Madison's nomination of John Quincy Adams as ambassador to Russia the first time it was presented, and also turned down the nomination of Gallatin as a special peace conference envoy when it was first presented. Adding insult to injury, Gallatin's enemies in the Senate succeeded in pushing through a resolution declaring that the duties of a special envoy were incompatible with the position of secretary of the treasury, a move Gallatin had anticipated when he agreed to take the diplomatic assignment.[11] As a result of all this maneuvering, Madison was forced to appoint another head of the Treasury and to drop his own choice for that position.

During this period Congress exploited its newly acquired power by extending its influence in the executive branch. Congressmen and senators increasingly interfered in the appointment process, and although the number of positions was not very large, such an invasion of executive prerogatives further jeopardized the independence of the President as an administrator. The number of congressmen acquiring positions in the executive branch also greatly increased during this period. But when the Senate tried to interfere to the extent of attempting to remove the most reliable and important member of his cabinet, Madison finally reacted strongly.

The President had appointed his secretary of the treasury to be one of the special envoys sent to negotiate a peace treaty with the British in St. Petersburg at the request of the Czar. Madison had no grounds for conjecture that such an appointment would cost Gallatin his job at the Treasury, for there had been ample precedents where government officials had accepted such special assignments without jeopardizing their other posts. The Senate thought differently, however, passing a resolution which declared that "in the opinion of the Senate, the powers and duties of the Secretary of the Department of the Treasury, and those of an Envoy Extraordinary to a foreign power, are so incompatible, that they ought not to be, and remain united in the same person."[12] The Senate then instructed the committee considering Gallatin's appointment as envoy "to communicate this resolution to the President of the United States, and respectfully to confer with him upon the matter thereof."[13] Madison attempted to prevent such a meeting by firing off a quick rebuke to the Senate:

> The executive and the Senate in the case of appointments to office, and of treaties, are to be considered as independent of and coordinate with each other. If they agree, the appointments or treaties are made. If the Senate disagrees, they fail. If the Senate wish (sic) information previous to their final decision, the practice . . . has been either to request the Executive to furnish it, or to refer the subject to a committee of their body to communicate either formally or informally, with the head of the proper department. The appointment of a committee of the Senate to confer immediately with the Executive himself appears to lose sight of the coordinate relation between the Executive and the Senate, which the Constitution has established, and which ought therefore to be maintained.[14]

When the Senate committee persisted the President did meet with them, but it was a chilly occasion and he refused to provide any further information. Madison had finally taken a firm stand on the question, but his defiance had come too late to defend an executive prerogative long since relinquished by default. While it was an impressive statement when viewed in historical perspective, it accomplished very little for Madison; the legislature had already invaded his executive domain and trampled upon the powers and independence which his predecessors had been able to maintain.

James Monroe and John Quincy Adams did somewhat better than Madison in defending the independence of the executive branch against the encroachment of Congress in the appointment process. This problem became significantly more important with the passage of the Tenure of Office Act in 1820, which greatly increased the potentiality for national patronage. The act stipulated that the "principal officers concerned with the collection or disbursement of money should henceforth be appointed for fixed terms of four years, and that the commissions of present incumbents should expire at stated intervals, not later than September 30, 1821."[15] The ostensible objective of the act was to introduce a systematic review of financial responsibility in the national service. In fact the principle of "rotation in office," which the act supported, had a long and ideologically democratic history in the various states. But although it was initially introduced in the states as a means of cultivating democratic values and responsibility in office, it quickly became recognized as a means of perpetuating a system of political patronage. When introduced into national affairs in 1820 its patrons, particularly Secretary of the Treasury William H. Crawford, obviously had increased patronage in mind.[16] Jefferson, now at home in Monticello, was apprehensive about this and strongly opposed the act:

> It [the Law] saps the constitutional and salutary functions of the President, and introduces a principle of intrigue and corruption, which will soon leaven the mass, not only of Senators, but of citizens. It is more baneful than the attempt which failed at the beginning of the government to make all officers irremovable, but with the consent of the Senate. This

places, every four years, all appointments under their power and obliges them to act on every one nomination. It will keep in constant excitement all the hungry cormorants for office, render them, as well as those in place, sycophants to their senators, engage these in eternal intrigue to turn one out and put in another, in cabals to swap work, and make of them what all executive directories become, mere sinks of corruption and faction.[17]

The first two Presidents who were charged with administering the act tended to agree with Jefferson and to blunt its impact. James Monroe refused to exploit or to allow Congress to exploit this law which he had unfortunately signed, and John Quincy Adams following directly in his footsteps, was perhaps even more aware than his predecessor of its insidious potential for corrupting and weakening the Executive. "The Senate," Adams complained, "was conciliated by the permanent increase of their power, which was the principle ultimate effect of the act, and every senator was flattered by the power conferred upon himself of multiplying chances to provide for his friends and dependents."[18] Adams was as effective as Monroe in preventing this from happening:

I have proceeded upon the principle established by Mr. Monroe, and have renominated every officer, friend or foe, against whom no specific charge of misconduct has been brought.[19]

So strongly did Adams hold to this conviction that Leonard White has speculated that it might have cost him a second term in the White House.[20]

The Jacksonian Impact

The election of Andrew Jackson as President in 1828 marked an important turning point in our national affairs and was a major landmark in the development of presidential power. It certainly brought to a close one period of American life, generally referred to as the era of "good feeling," and began another, rich in contrast and pregnant with new ideas and very different forms of political behavior and institutions.

The early years of the republic had been dominated by the Virginia dynasty and the New England Puritans, national politics and the presidency being rigidly controlled by a legislative political obligarchy in Washington. When Jefferson was elected in 1800, the Republican party came into a position of power which it did not relinquish for the next 25 years. During that period the Federalists had less and less influence on national affairs. The Republicans provided all of the national leadership, setting the tone and style of the institution of the presidency as well as the political structure over which it presided.

Up until the presidential election of 1828, however, the electorate remained relatively small, and by and large political life and institutions were dominated by the more economically and culturally advantaged members of the community. Before the election of 1828 six states did not even conduct a popular election for presidential electors, and in those that did, increasing apathy over national elections had reduced the voting population to approximately one quarter of those eligible to cast their ballots. A number of converging factors changed all of this after the election of 1824, however, and four years later voters went to the polls in greater numbers than ever before in American history.

The explanation for this dynamic development of interest in the political franchise, an interest which continued to grow fantastically for the next decade or more, is of course not simple. Through 1828 one of the reasons eligible voters had not flocked to the polls was that there was little or no significant competition for many national electoral offices. With the failure of the Federalist party in the election of 1800, the Republicans continued to gain support and influence while the Federalists generally receded into obscurity in the ensuing presidential elections. The critical choices involving nominations and electoral support came essentially from the legislative caucus in Washington, a gathering of Republicans from both houses of Congress, which met early in the presidential election year to name the candidate who would receive its active endorsement. Their decision then went out to the legislators' party allies on the state level, where additional caucuses were frequently held, and the verdicts of the Washington body were endorsed and implemented.

The caucus was a central factor in American politics from the very earliest days. As John Adams wrote:

> Our revolution was effected by caucuses. The federal constitution was formed by caucuses, and the federal administrations, for twenty years, have been supported or subverted by caucuses . . . Alexander Hamilton was the greatest organist that ever played upon this instrument.[21]

But by the mid-1820s the congressional caucus in Washington and the various state and legislative caucuses were becoming an anathema to many Americans who felt they were being denied a significant role in the electoral process. The functions of this elite political mechanism had taken the quadrennial election of a President of the United States from a constitutionally defined democratic procedure to an oligarchical field day. Once the senators and representatives in Washington had determined who they wanted to see as President, their decision was almost automatically accepted in the various states by their faithful constituents.

However, opposition to the procedure was growing. The greater part of the press was antagonistic to the activities of the caucus. According to Niles' *Register*, 32 out of 35 journals in one state, and 47 out of 48 in another, opposed the caucus.[22] One famous editor indicated that he would "rather learn that the halls of Congress were converted into common brothels than that caucuses . . . should be held in them. . . . The great mass of the American people feel that they are able to judge for themselves; they do not want a master to direct them how they shall vote."[23] The congressional caucus was also denounced in several state legislatures, and in the Senate itself. One of the Founding Fathers, Rufus King, characterized it as a "new, extraordinary self-created central power, stronger than that of the Constitution, which threatens to overturn the balance of power proceeding from its division and distribution between the states and the United States."[24]

The question was thrashed out in the Senate and after three days of acrimonious debate in March 1824, it was clear that the legislative caucus was doomed. In the election of that same year only one of the three candidates sought its endorsement, and he (William Harris Crawford) received the least number of votes. At the caucus meeting endorsing his candidacy two-thirds of the Republican members were absent. "King Caucus" had been overthrown, and although it took until the following election for the impact of this development to be felt in the electoral process, its democratizing influence was inevitable.

The striking fact is that in the election of 1828 three times as many Americans participated as in any previous presidential election. Jackson swept everything except New England and three middle Atlantic states, from his opponent, John Quincy Adams, polling 647,276 popular votes to Adams' 508,064. Even when one allows for the fact that six states did not hold a popular election for presidential electors in 1824, but named them through the state legislatures instead, the 1828 results were still impressive. Adams did not win a single southern or western state and succeeded in holding Jackson's lead down to a respectable margin in only two, Louisiana and Ohio. Moreover, General Jackson won every one of the ten states which had more than doubled their 1824 vote, and in most cases by a very large margin. Most of Adams' strength was in his own, fairly static (in terms of population) native New England, while Jackson made his largest gains in the new western states and in states with expanding western boundaries and populations like Pennsylvania and Virginia. It is clear that something quite new and different happened to the presidential electoral process in this election, something which eventually would have significant impact upon the function and role of the President in American life and the power which the bearer of that office possessed.

A number of factors contributed to this dramatically changing situation. First there was the revolt against the congressional caucus described above. Voters were not simply rejecting an outmoded procedure but rather protesting against its undemocratic character and moving to establish more representative methods of selecting the Chief Executive. The country was growing, property restrictions on the franchise were disappearing and the old aristocratic leaders no longer commanded the respect that heretofore they could rely upon. The familiar myths of freedom from tyranny and dedication to liberty were no longer sufficient in themselves to trigger automatic patriotic support. Men were finding new problems and new vistas, the frontier was already pushing forward and the people sought new symbols and new goals by which to live.

The symbolic heroes of the earlier days were all well-established leaders of their communities, men of substantial background and education as well as (in most cases) property. General Jackson, on the other hand, was a frontier hero; he was a man who had emerged from the humblest circumstances, having been orphaned at 14 when the plague struck down his mother as she nursed his cousins wounded in the Revolutionary War. He managed to pick up enough education to read and write, and after a short apprenticeship with a distinguished lawyer, was accredited by the court as a full-fledged attorney. Shortly thereafter he migrated west into Tennessee where he distinguished himself as a frontier lawyer and later as a military hero in the successive wars against the Indians and the British at New Orleans.

Andrew Jackson became a legend in his own time; a national hero by virtue of his stunning military victory over the British in the War of 1812, he also served at various times as a local attorney general, judge, United States congressman, senator, major general of both the Tennessee Reserves and the United States Army and governor of the Florida Territory. No other American by background or even by conviction was so well suited to serve as both a symbol and an actual leader of a society beginning to realize its expanding horizons, geographically, socially, economically and politically. By the end of the first quarter of the nineteenth century the United States had reached the stage in its development where its independence and security as a nation were taken for granted and its attention had shifted from the early and tentative steps toward nationhood to a period of rapid strides towards expansion and growth, where domestic problems and possibilities took precedence over diplomacy and any uneasiness concerning America's unsettled and unprotected international situation. In this sense, and in many others, Jackson was truly a man of his age.

And yet this should not be simply interpreted as heralding the pure democratic revolution, as several prominent historians have attempted to argue. Growth and expansion also offered great opportunities for behavior which was not so much democratic as it was self-serving and opportunistic. The frontiersman was not simply the hero paving the way for future civilization but also the entrepreneur, the greedy land developer, the get-rich-quick sucker, the man on-the-make. There was much of this in the Jacksonian revolution and the fervor of its attack upon the eastern commercial establishment stemmed not so much from a principled criticism of its materialism, but from a sense of jealousy and bitterness on the part of those who aspired to the same goals but who had arrived too late to taste the early fruits of hard work and exploitation.

Andrew Jackson received the largest number of popular votes in the presidential election of 1824, but as none of the candidates had a majority of electoral votes, the election was referred to the House of Representatives. There Jackson lost. The general and his supporters charged that a deal had been made between the other two leading candidates, John Quincy Adams and Henry Clay. They suggested that the Kentuckian (Clay) had swung his support behind Adams in exchange for a commitment from Adams that he would appoint Clay secretary of state (the traditional stepping-stone position to the presidency). Adams denied the validity of the charge and yet it plagued him for the duration of his public life. Jackson, on the other hand, convinced that he had been defrauded of his rightful claim to the presidency, not only continued to harbor a grudge against both Adams and Clay, but was determined to even the score by turning both of them out of office. His campaign for the next presidential election began soon after he returned to his home in Nashville, Tennessee in 1825, while the anger and bitterness that he and his supporters felt over what they considered to be the "corrupt deal," provided a great deal of the energy and inspiration for the successful and revolutionary campaign of 1828.

Some of Jackson's success in the election campaign of 1828 can also be credited to the aspiring politicians and entrepreneurs who hitched their wagons to his rising star because they desired the power which had thus far been beyond their grasp.

They included not only recent frontier settlers in Tennessee, Kentucky, and Ohio, but also land-poor Jeffersonian democrats, rural and urban politicians, highly mobile and aspiring journalists, mechanics and journeymen hungering for their own stake in the new America and even well-established businessmen who longed for more effective levers of power. Jackson's astute political managers stirred up layers of social, economic and political discontent, and for the first time in 25 years political life came alive with the bustle of activity and invective which usually accompanies the rising expectations of new converts to the promised land.

Much of this eventually was bound to have its impact upon the political institutions of the country and of course upon the office which motivated all of this activity. The political mechanics of the 1828 campaign were unlike those of any previous presidential campaign in American history. Under the astute direction of Martin Van Buren, senator from New York and leader of a vast political apparatus in his own state, a national political network in support of Jackson was gradually put together over a period of four years. Newspapers and communication played an unprecedented role in Jackson's election. Correspondence committees were created in the various states and connected with a central committee made up of Jackson's friends and supporters in Nashville. Editors of established papers were won over to Jackson's position or new journals were created to spread the important word of Jackson's campaign. Democratic congressmen promised to create a vast "chain of newspaper posts, from the New England states to Louisiana, and branching through Lexington to the western states."[25]

> North Carolina politicians, for instance, started nine new Jackson sheets by the summer of 1827, and in Ohio eighteen were added to the five that existed in 1824. During a single six-month period three papers were founded in Indiana and several were organized in Pennsylvania, Massachusetts, New Jersey, and Illinois. . . .[26]

Jackson supporters propped up dying newspapers with ads and loans, and congressmen cooperated by using their franking privileges to mail out important reprints of speeches and other campaign material. The great outpouring of literature and enthusiastic word of mouth contact had a profound effect upon many people. Among some of them it created an interest in politics for the first time; at the same time it also forced out for public discussion the critical issues involved in the campaign.

There was considerable activity on the Washington front where supporters of Jackson were in the majority in Congress. They succeeded in electing their candidate for Speaker of the House—Andrew Stevenson, a Virginian—and they secured control of the powerful House committees, mobilizing still greater support in Congress.

A central Washington campaign committee was created to become a clearing house for the distribution of campaign material. The experienced editor Duff Green was brought to Washington to edit a national newspaper favorable to the candidacy of Andrew Jackson and to provide a continuous source of attack upon the candidacy and character of his opponent. Green also supplied the correspondence committees with a weekly edition of his paper which provided them with all of the arguments and campaign information they might need. Additional material such as badges, posters and flags were also distributed by these committees.[27] One historian of the period estimates that in the neighborhood of $1,000,000 was spent on the campaign.

> During the summer, mass meetings were organized, militia musters were utilized, barbecues and fish fries were staged as political rallies. Songs were composed. Hickory trees were planted. In the cities Jackson committees were set up by wards. . . . Money became easier to raise. . . . The story of the hero cheated by the negotiators of a corrupt bargain was taking hold.[28]

This flowering of various forms of communication had real impact on the level of the political consciousness operative in the country at that time and made inevitable new and responsive changes in the procedure of nominating candidates for the presidency and ultimately in the demeanor of those candidates when secured in the White House office.

Reflected in this energetic concentration upon organization was a new politics, but it represented deeper currents flowing in the country. Resentment was growing against old elites. In the cities and on the frontier men who had never participated in politics before were stirring, restless and eager for power. The Jackson candidacy appealed to many of these changing attitudes.

As more people became involved in the nomination and election of the President, the demand that the presidency become an office much more responsive to the people was inevitable. There was a remoteness and complexity about the legislature which was counterbalanced by the unity and drama of the presidency, and the new voters and mass campaign techniques tended to exphasize this aspect of the office, even before Andrew Jackson was forced (although willingly) to demonstrate just those qualities in his two terms in office.

Even prior to the collapse of the congressional caucus there had been some defection from the national pattern on the state level. In 1822 the Tennessee state caucus did not wait obediently to be instructed from Washington as it had done in previous years, but took the initiative two years before the congressional caucus met and enthusiastically nominated General Jackson for the presidency. Later the Tennessee state legislature condemned the congressional caucus and transmitted the texts of its resolution to the legislatures of the other states in the Union. The action was not particularly well received at the time, but the ground swell of opposition followed rapidly on the heels of the attempt by the congressional caucus in 1824 to implement its minority decision.

There had been earlier developments on the local level to make the state caucus more representative of the voters in the area. This resulted in the practice in a number of states of electing delegates to the caucus from local areas not represented in the state legislature by an elected member of the party. This came to be known as the mixed caucus. The first appeared in Rhode Island in 1807. In Pennsylvania ten years later non-legislators outnumbered legislators, legislators being allowed to participate only if no regularly elected delegate was present from their district. Particularly after the collapse of the national caucus, the mixed caucus gave way to the mixed convention, as Ostrogorski has put it, "the principle and basis of which were of a popular nature, and to which the members of the legislature were admitted on a subsidiary footing only."[29]

It came to pass that legislators gained access to these conventions only when local areas were not interested enough in sending an elected delegate that they merely authorized the representative from the district to sit instead. Gradually but irresistibly the convention based upon representation by elected delegates only became the fixed form of nominating or endorsing state and national candidates for office. During Jackson's first term this more democratic and representative form of designating party candidates was established on a national level, following the state pattern. In 1832 after being challenged by a national convention of the Anti-Masonic party which had met in Philadelphia in 1830 and nominated opposition candidates for President and Vice President, the major figures among the National Republicans opposed to Jackson and Jackson's supporters themselves, met in separate national conventions in Baltimore. They duly nominated Clay and Jackson as their candidates for the presidential election to be held later that year. These national conventions were made up of delegates elected at state and district conventions who in turn had been selected at county conventions. The delegates at this lower level had emerged directly from the primary associations and groups which were loosely organized in the cities and in rural areas.

The rise of both the state and national conventions contributed substantially to a more representative selection of presidential candidates and also strengthened the democratic ties between the people and the President. In time the national nominating convention would become a substantial factor in the emergence of national parties and the means of focusing national attention upon the presidential nominees and the development of party platforms. As Ostrogorski has indicated, the "active campaign conducted on behalf of Jackson during the years 1825-1828, gave a great stimulus to the movement. . . . Established at first in a more or less sporadic fashion, the conventions became general and spread throughout the country, falling according to the territorial units and electoral divisions into state, district, county conventions, etc., and ended up by covering the whole Union in a regular and exhaustive manner."[30]

> The new democratic structure thus erected, from base to summit, in place of the old shattered party apparatus, was on much broader lines and far more comprehensive; but it nevertheless brought about a concentration of power and a compression of public opinion and of its preoccupations, which increased at each stage of the Organization.[31]

The Chief Executive now became a national figure in fact as well as in theory, a leader who had been selected by the will of the people to represent all of their interests, if indeed that was possible. But this is getting ahead of our story. Jackson's new national constituency had already become evident in his stunning victory in 1828, prior to the existence of the national conventions. Such a constituency was bound to feel entitled to a greater role in government than they had previously held, and they were not at all tardy or reticent in presenting their demands.

Anticipating radical developments, but not knowing exactly what to expect, Daniel Webster nervously recorded his thoughts in Washington:

General Jackson will be here abt. 15. of Feb.——
Nobody knows what he will do.
Many letters are sent to him; he answers none of them.
His friends here pretend to be very knowing; but. . . .
Great efforts are being made to put him up to a general sweep as to
    all offices. . . .
My opinion is
That when he comes he will bring a breeze with him.
Which way it will blow I cannot tell.[32]

The breeze certainly came, and so did the office seekers. The throng took possession of Washington "in the assured manner of an army of occupation." Jackson's major biographer (Marquis James) wrote:

Night and day applicants for an audience [with Jackson's representatives, who set up their office in a small hotel] filled lobby, stairways, corridors, pressing and jostling until nervous persons feared for the safety of the building. . . . "It was like the inundation of northern barbarians into Rome . . . Strange faces filled every public place, and every face seemed to bear defiance on its brow." Tennessee backwoodsmen and pioneers from the Northwest mingled with Irish immigrants from the seaboard cities, old soldiers, politicians of high and low degree, editors, adventurers, schemers. . . . They roamed the streets, surging in and out of taprooms until the spectre of a whiskey famine contributed to an outlook already unsettled. They overflowed Washington into Georgetown and Alexandria, sleeping five in a bed or on billiard tables, or on floors, or apparently not at all.[33]

The symbolic event heralding the new era was the traditional presidential reception after the inaugural ceremony:

In the stately East Room long tables were spread with cakes and ice cream and orange punch for the officially and socially eligible as defined by precedent. Precedent? The mob . . . swept through the Mansion gates and through the portals, leaving the "eligible" to shift for themselves. Representative and Mrs. John Floyd whose "two stout sons" cleaved a path, remained long enough to see clothing torn, women faint, glasses and china broken. "One hundred and fifty dollar chairs (were) profaned by the feet of clod-hoppers" anxious for a glimpse of the President. "A regular Saturnalia," a South Carolinian informed Mr. Van Buren, happily detained at Albany. . . . Locking arms, men threw a cordon about the President enabling him to escape by the backway. As Old Hickory retreated . . . the departure of the White House guests was facilitated by placing tubs of punch on the lawn.[34]

In his First Annual Message President Jackson offered an eloquent defense for the principle of "rotation in office," suggesting that the application of the principle in the executive branch of the national government would result in positive accomplishments.

President Andrew Jackson
First Annual Message
Excerpt Extolling the Virtues of Rotation in Office
December 8, 1829

James D. Richardson, ed., *Messages and Papers of the Presidents* (New York, 1897) III, 1011-12.

There are, perhaps, few men who can for any great length of time enjoy office and power without being more or less under the influence of feelings unfavorable to the faithful discharge of their public duties. Their integrity may be proof against improper considerations immediately addressed to themselves, but they are apt to acquire a habit of looking with indifference upon the public interests and of tolerating conduct from which an unpracticed man would revolt. Office is considered as a species of property, and government rather as a means of promoting individual interests than as an instrument created solely for the service of the people. Corruption in some and in others a perversion of correct feelings and principles divert government from its legitimate ends and make it an engine for the support of the few at the expense of the many. The duties of all public officers are, or at least admit of being made, so plain and simple that men of intelligence may readily qualify themselves for their performance; and I can not but believe that more is lost by the long continuance of men in office than is generally to be gained by their experience. I submit, therefore, to your consideration whether the efficiency of the Government would not be promoted and official industry and integrity better secured by a general extension of the law which limits appointments to four years.

In a country where offices are created solely for the benefit of the people no one man has any more intrinsic right to official station than another. Offices were not established to give support to particular men at the public expense. No individual wrong is, therefore, done by removal, since neither appointment to nor continuance in office is matter of right. The incumbent became an officer with a view to public benefits, and when these require his removal they are not to be sacrificed to private interests. It is the people, and they alone, who have a right to complain when a bad officer is substituted for a good one. He who is removed has the same means of obtaining a living that are enjoyed by the millions who never held office. The proposed limitation would destroy the idea of property now so generally connected with official station, and although individual distress may be sometimes produced, it would, by promoting that rotation which constitutes a leading principle in the republican creed, give healthful action to the system.

It is not clear how well informed the new President was of the fact that the new practice of "rotation" in office had been in effect in most of the states for some time, or that although it had initially been introduced as a means of democratizing aristocratic strongholds, it had ended up in practically every case providing a foundation for political patronage (sometimes corrupt), without which the party organizations would have had difficulty operating. John Quincy Adams expected no better from the policy when applied to the national government:

> Everyone is in breathless expectation, trembling at heart, and afraid to speak. Some of the dismissions are deserved, from age, from incapacity, from intemperance, from irregularities of private life; and these are made on the pretext for justifying all the removals. The persons appointed are of equally various character—some good, the greater part indifferent, some notoriously bad—on the average much less respectable than those dismissed.[35]

Jackson's associates were more conscious of the more tangible and immediate advantages of "rotation" than of his "principled" approach. His postmaster general, William T. Barry, argued that ". . . it is right and politic to reward and encourage your friends. . . . Public employments must necessarily and ought to be on the principle of 'rotation' in office."[36] A Jackson supporter, New York Senator William L. Marcy, later made the classical defense of the spoils system in a speech delivered to his colleagues on the floor of the Senate:

> It may be, sir, that the politicians of the United States are not so fastidious as some gentlemen are, as to disclosing the principles on which they act. They boldly preach what they practice. When they are contending for victory, they avow their intention of enjoying the fruits of it. If they are defeated, they expect to retire from office. If they are successful, they claim, as a matter of right, the advantages of success. They see nothing wrong in the rule, that to the victor belongs the spoils of the enemy.[37]

Within several years of his inauguration, however, the President was able to observe, rather pessimistically, that "rotation" in practice fell short of the principled objectives he had outlined in his speech:

> It appeared that instead of love of principle it was love of office that had induced many of them to support the good cause as they pleased to term it, . . . that self-exertion was about to be abandoned and dependence for a livelihood placed upon the government.[38]

How bad was it? The recorded figure is 252 removals out of 610 offices.[39] These figures do not include deputy postmasters, but somewhere between 400 and 600 out of a total of 8,000 of them were also removed.[40] All told the number constitutes roughly ten percent of the posts available to presidential appointment. The turnover was much larger on the local level. But on the whole the number was low when one considers it in the context of the traditional discussion of how Jackson opened the "pandora's box" of public service as a political reward for his supporters. Under Whig Presidents William Henry Harrison and Zachary Taylor the number of removals increased by 100 percent, although the total number of jobs only increased from 619 in 1829 to 929 in 1849.[41] Again, these figures also do not include the deputy postmasters.

What was far more appalling than the numbers involved was the precedent that was established and the designs of congressmen and senators in quest for future offices that were set in motion. Jackson was a strong enough Executive not to be fazed by the eagerness of the members of the legislature to encroach upon the Executive's prerogatives with respect to appointments, but many who came after him were not. For the next 40 or 50 years the power of American Presidents with respect to their administrative control of the executive departments declined in direct ratio to the influence and control which the Congress achieved by its intrusion into the nominating and appointive process. Appointed government officials reasoned that they owed their loyalty and obedience to the individual(s) responsible for their appointments, and to the extent to which this responsibility passed out of the hands of the Chief Executive and his department heads and into the hands of legislators and state and local politicians, administrative strength and power at the center of the government was obviously dispersed and weakened. Realistically, this development must be evaluated as one of the major negative legacies of the Jacksonian era. It contributed immeasurably to the weakening of presidential power during the rest of the century and became a source of contention and increasing strife between the executive and legislative branches of the national government.

The Removal Power of the President

The President's power to remove an appointed official from office, in contrast to the general acceptance of his appointing power, was bitterly challenged almost from the very beginning, and became in time a critical nexus of dispute between the executive and legislative branches of the government. For most of the nineteenth century, the failure to reach agreement on this important administrative power resulted in immeasurable harm to the effective operation of the American political system. During the second half of the century the Congress succeeded for the most part in dominating the Executive, and by so doing, drained significant powers from the President and crippled his operating strength in other areas by consuming his time and energy in attempting to first defend and then to win back this necessary and essential administrative prerogative.

The constitutional question here is extremely confusing because Article II fails to outline this procedure and the Constitutional Convention did not even discuss it. Yet the power to remove an appointed official is the key to the President's command of his own household. Without this power he could exert little control over the heads of executive departments, or, for that matter, any of their subordinates. Without this authority a President would be powerless to implement national policies and to enforce the law. No wonder that every President from George Washington on has tried to defend this power, some in the face of frustrating congressional opposition. The struggle between the President and Congress over the removal power was one of the major factors to weaken the Executive office during a significant part of its early history.

Discussion in the First Congress

When the first session of the First Congress turned its attention to this problem, the President was already installed in office, waiting to fill out his executive family. Action by the Congress was necessary to establish both the great departments and the positions of those who would lead them. In the process of creating the offices of secretary of state, secretary of the treasury, and secretary of war, the House of Representatives turned to the problem of how these officials would be removed, if necessary, from office. The Constitution provided that the President "shall nominate, and by and with the Advice and Consent of the Senate, shall appoint Ambassadors, other public Ministers and Consuls . . ." but it provided no specific instructions as to how and by whom these officials should be removed from office, except in the case of impeachment.

On Tuesday, May 19, 1789, the House of Representatives resolved itself into a Committee of the Whole to consider this question. Congressman Elias Boudinot of New Jersey opened the discussion, urging the necessity of acting promptly with regard to this problem since the old departments of the confederation were no longer able to serve the administration of President Washington's government. After some parliamentary jostling, James Madison introduced a substitute motion which called for the establishment of an "Executive Department, to be denominated the Department of Foreign Affairs, at the head of which there shall be an officer, to be called the Secretary of the Department of Foreign Affairs, who shall be appointed by the President, by and with the advice and consent of the Senate; and to be removable by the President."[42]

The objection was raised that specifying the mode of appointment was unnecessary because the Constitution had already defined such a procedure, and with Madison's agreement the committee voted to strike out the words "who shall be appointed by the President, by and with the advice and consent of the Senate." For the rest of that day the power of the President to remove such an executive officer was debated and the motion was finally carried by a "considerable majority." Almost a month later the House again took up the question in the Committee of the Whole; and this time the debate lasted for six solid days, and all aspects of the question were fully explored.

The members of the House were fully aware that their discussion and subsequent decision were of great importance and would probably settle the question for future generations. One student of this period has argued that "when this Congress in its first session organized the administrative departments, it was sitting as a constitutional convention, so far as subject matter is a criterion, just as certainly as the Convention, *par excellence* was."[43] Madison certainly reflected this concern when he argued that:

> The decision that is at this time made, will become the permanent exposition of the constitution; and on a permanent exposition of the

constitution will depend the genius and character of the whole government. It will depend, perhaps, on this decision whether the Government shall retain that equilibrium which the constitution intended, or take a direction toward aristocracy or anarchy among members of the Government. Hence, how careful ought we to be to give a true direction to a power so critically circumstanced. It is incumbent upon us to weigh with particular attention, the arguments which have been advanced in support of the various opinions with cautious deliberation. I own to you, Mr. Chairman, that I feel great anxiety, because I am called upon to give a decision in a case that may affect the fundamental principles of the Government under which we act, and liberty itself.[44]

"Cautious deliberation" there was. Eight members of the House had been delegates to the Founding Convention in Philadelphia, including Madison, who had taken perhaps the most active role at that meeting and has always been considered the major architect of the Constitution.[45] In the Senate, where the debates on this question were held in executive session, and not recorded, one-half of the 20 members who sat in that body at the time had been Constitutional Convention delegates.[46]

Those opposed to granting the President the independent power to remove executive officers who in his opinion had become detrimental to his administration advanced several different arguments against his possessing such a potent executive power. Perhaps the easiest to dismiss was the opinion advanced by Congressman Smith of South Carolina, who argued that he had "doubts the officer could be removed by the President. He apprehended that he could only be removed by an impeachment before the Senate, and that, being once in office, he must remain there until convicted upon impeachment."[47]

Madison and others quickly pointed out how powerless this would leave the government if it had no machinery to dismiss any appointed official unless the individual had committed acts which would qualify him for impeachment. But the major objections to the President's removal power centered around a number of congressmen's concern that:

1. There was no specific Constitutional provision for such a power.

2. That if such a power were to be inferred from constitutional language, it would have to be based upon the appointing power, which required both presidential and Senate approval.

3. The independent power to remove all appointive officers from their high positions in the government granted unwarranted and dangerous power to the elected head of state, and made him more of a monarch than the elected leader of a republic.

The first argument proved very little, for both those in favor of granting independent removal power to the President and those who opposed it agreed that such was the case. But since there was no specific assignment of this power to the President both groups were forced to establish their constitutional arguments upon inferences drawn from Article II of that document. Those who were opposed based their case upon the inference that the constitutional provision linking the President and the Senate in the appointing power implied that both the President and the Senate should also participate in the removal procedure. As Congressman White put it bluntly:

> The Constitution gives the President the power of nominating, and, by and with the advice and consent of the Senate, appointing to office. As I conceive the power of appointing and dismissing to be united in their natures, and a principle that never was called in question in any Government, I am averse to that part of the clause which subjects the Secretary of Foreign Affairs to be removed at the will of the President.[48]

One of the strongest arguments that proponents of this point of view could produce were the supporting words of Publius (Alexander Hamilton) in Federalist No. 1. In one of his many speeches during the debate, Congressman Smith argued that "it has been the opinion of sensible men that the power was lodged in this manner [removal requiring joint endorsement of the President and the Senate]. A publication of no inconsiderable eminence in the class of political writings on the constitution, has advanced this sentiment. . . ."[49] The passage by Hamilton which indicated this interpretation of the Constitution was then read into the record:

> It has been mentioned as one of the advantages to be expected from the co-operation of the Senate in the business of appointments, that it would contribute to the stability of the administration. The consent of that body would be necessary to displace as well as appoint. A change of the Chief Magistrate, therefore, would not occasion so violent or so general a revolution in the officers of the Government, as might be expected if he were the sole disposer of offices. Where a man in any station has given satisfactory evidence of his fitness for it, a new President would be restrained from attempting a change in favor of a person more agreeable to him, by the apprehension that the discountenance of the Senate might frustrate the attempt, and bring some degree of discredit upon himself. Those who can best estimate the value of a steady administration, will be most disposed to prize a provision which connects the official existence of public men with the approbation or disapprobation of that body, which, from the greater permancy of its own composition, will, in all probability, be less subject to inconstancy than any other member of the Government.[50]

Justice William Howard Taft, a former President, was so disturbed at having Alexander Hamilton placed on what he considered to be the wrong side of this question that in his famous decision on the removal power in the *Myers* case he pointed out that Hamilton had later rejected this view and embraced the doctrine of independent executive removal. Hamilton asserted this view, he said, in his advisory memorandum written for President Washington on the question of the President's power to issue a neutrality proclamation:

> The general doctrine of our Constitution then is, that the executive power of the nation is vested in the President; subject only to the exceptions and qualifications, which are expressed in the instrument.

Two of these have already been noticed; the participation of the Senate in the appointment of officers, and in the making of treaties. A third remains to be mentioned; the right of the legislature to "declare war and grant letters of marque and reprisal."

With these exceptions, the executive power of the United States is completely lodged in the President. This mode of construing the Constitution has indeed been recognized by Congress in formal acts upon full consideration and debate; of which the power of removal from office is an important instance.[51]

It is clear from this statement that Hamilton had changed his mind in four years time and was not satisfied to go along with the final decision of the Congress on the removal power. It is therefore rather astonishing to note that in a rather vehement book attacking Taft's decision in the *Myers* case, the great presidential scholar and professor of jurisprudence at Princeton University, Edward S. Corwin, used this same quotation to argue the opposite position. He stated that Hamilton did not change his opinion on this question. Unfortunately, and reprehensibly, Professor Corwin omitted the last sentence in Hamilton's quotation, which, of course, is decisive to the argument.[52]

From time to time in this initial debate members of the House expressed some alarm over the implications of the concentration of the removal power in the hands of a single Executive. Congressman Jackson warned:

Let it be remembered, that the constitution gives the President the command of the military. If you give him complete power over the men with the strong box, he will have the liberties of America under his thumb. . . . It is easy to see the evil which may result.[53]

It fell to James Madison, a future President, with able assistance from Fisher Ames, George Clymer and Theodore Sedgewick, to demonstrate the flaws in the opposition arguments and the political and administrative necessity of granting the President the independent removal power. Madison spoke 11 times in the course of the seven-day debate on this question. He made his first major speech on the subject at the June 16 session, when Congress returned to consideration of this matter after almost a month's lapse of time.

James Madison
First Major Statement on the Removal Power
June 16, 1789

Joseph Gales, ed., *Debates and Proceedings in the Congress of the United States* (Washington, D.C., 1834) I, 479-82.

If the construction of the constitution is to be left to its natural course with respect to the executive powers of this Government, I own that the insertion of this sentiment in law may not be of material importance, though, if it is nothing more than a mere declaration of a clear grant made by the constitution, it can do no harm; but if it relates to a doubtful part of the constitution, I suppose an exposition of the constitution may come with as much propriety from the Legislature, as any other department of the Government. If the power naturally belongs to the Government, and the constitution is undecided, as to the body which is to exercise it, it is likely that it is submitted to the discretion of the Legislature, and the question will depend upon its own merits.

I am clearly of opinion with the gentleman from South Carolina, (Mr. Smith,) that we ought in this, and every other case, to adhere to the constitution, so far as it will serve as a guide to us, and that we ought not to be swayed in our decisions by the splendor of the character of the present Chief Magistrate, but to consider it with respect to the merit of men who, in the ordinary course of things, may be supposed to fill the chair. I believe the power here declared is a high one, and, in some respects, a dangerous one; but, in order to come to a right decision on this point, we must consider both sides of the question; the possible abuses which may spring from the single will of the First Magistrate, and the abuse which may spring from the combined will of the Executive and the Senatorial disqualification.

When we consider that the First Magistrate is to be appointed at present by the suffrages of three millions of people, and in all human probability in a few years' time by double that number, it is not to be presumed that a vicious or bad character will be selected. If the Government of any country on the face of the earth was ever effectually guarded against the election of ambitious or designing characters to the first office of the State, I think it may with truth be said to be the case under the constitution of the United States. With all the infirmities incident to a popular election, corrected by the particular mode of conducting it, as directed under the present system, I think we may fairly calculate that the instances will be very rare in which an unworthy man will receive that mark of the public confidence which is required to designate the President of the United States. Where the people are disposed to give so great an elevation to one of their fellow-citizens, I own that I am not afraid to place my confidence in him, especially when I know he is impeachable for any crime or misdemeanor before the Senate, at all times; and that, at all events, he is impeachable before the community at large every four years, and liable to be displaced if his conduct shall have given umbrage during the time he has been in office. Under these circumstances, although the trust is a high one, and in some degree, perhaps, a dangerous one, I am not sure but it will be safer here than placed where some gentlemen suppose it ought to be.

It is evidently the intention of the constitution, that the first Magistrate should be responsible for the executive department; so far therefore as we do not make the officers who are to aid him in the duties of that department responsible to him, he is not responsible to his country. Again, is there no danger that an officer, when he is appointed by the concurrence of the Senate. and has friends in that body, may choose rather to risk his establishment on the favor of that branch, than rest it upon the discharge of his duties to the satisfaction of the executive branch, which is constitutionally authorized to inspect and control his conduct? And if it should happen that the officers connect themselves with the Senate, they may mutually support each other, and for want of efficacy reduce the power of the President to a mere vapor; in which case, his responsibility would be annihilated, and the expectation of it unjust. The high executive officers, joined in cabal with the Senate, would lay the foundation of discord, and end in an assumption of the executive power, only to be removed by a revolution in the Government. I believe no principle is more clearly laid down in the constitution than that of responsibility. After premising this, I will proceed to an investigation of the merits of the question upon constitutional ground.

I have, since the subject was last before the House, examined the constitution with attention, and I acknowledge that it does not perfectly correspond with the ideas I entertained of it from the first glance. I am inclined to think, that a free and systematic interpretation of the plan of Government will leave us less at liberty to abate the responsibility than gentlemen imagine. I have already acknowledged that the powers of the Government must remain as apportioned by the constitution. But it may be contended, that where the constitution is silent, it becomes a subject of legislative discretion; perhaps, in the opinion of some, an argument in favor of the clause may be successfully brought forward on this ground: I, however, leave it for the present untouched.

By a strict examination of the constitution, on what appears to be its true principles, and considering the great departments of the Government in the relation they have to each other, I have my doubts whether we are not absolutely tied down to the construction declared in the bill. In the first section of the first article, it is said, that all legislative powers herein granted shall be vested in a Congress of the United States. In the second article, it is affirmed that the executive power shall be vested in a President of the United States of America. In the third article, it is declared that the judicial power of the United States shall be vested in one Supreme Court, and in such Inferior Courts as Congress may, from time to time, ordain and establish. I suppose it will be readily admitted, that so far as the constitution has separated the powers of these great departments, it would be improper to combine them together; and so far as it has left any particular department in the entire possession of the powers incident to that department, I conceive we ought not to qualify them further than they are qualified by the constitution. The legislative powers are vested in Congress, and are to be exercised by them uncontrolled by any other department, except the constitution has qualified it otherwise. The constitution has qualified the legislative power, by authorizing the President to object to any act it may pass, requiring, in this case, two-thirds of both Houses to concur in making a law; but still the absolute legislative power is vested in the Congress with this qualification alone.

The constitution affirms, that the executive power shall be vested in the President. Are there exceptions to this proposition? Yes, there are. The constitution says, that in appointing to office, the Senate shall be associated with the President, unless in the case of inferior officers, when the law shall otherwise direct. Have we a right to extend this exception? I believe not. If the constitution has invested all executive power in the President, I venture to assert that the Legislature has no right to diminish or modify his executive authority.

The question now resolves itself into this, Is the power of displacing, an executive power? I conceive that if any power whatsoever is in its nature executive, it is the power of appointing, overseeing, and controlling those who execute the laws. If the constitution had not qualified the power of the President in appointing to office, by associating the Senate with him in that business, would it not be clear that he would have the right, by virtue of his executive power, to make such appointment? Should we be authorized, in defiance of that clause in the constitution, "The executive power shall be vested in a President," to unite the Senate with the President in the appointment to office? I conceive not. If it is admitted that we should not be authorized to do this, I think it may be disputed whether we have a right to associate them in removing persons from office, the one power being as much of an executive nature as the other; and the first one is authorized by being excepted out of the general rule established by the constitution, in these words, "the executive power shall be vested in the President."

The judicial power is vested in a Supreme Court; but will gentlemen say the judicial power can be placed elsewhere, unless the constitution has made an exception? The constitution justifies the Senate in exercising a judiciary power in determining on impeachments; but can the judicial power be further blended with the powers of that body? They cannot. I therefore say it is incontrovertible, if neither the legislative nor judicial powers are subjected to qualifications, other than those demanded in the constitution, that the executive powers are equally unabateable as either of the others; and inasmuch as the power of removal is of an executive nature, and not affected by any constitutional exception, it is beyond the reach of the legislative body.

If this is the true construction of this instrument, the clause in the bill is nothing more than explanatory of the meaning of the constitution, and therefore not liable to any particular objection on that account. If the constitution is silent, and it is a power the Legislature have a right to confer, it will appear to the world, if we strike out the clause, as if we doubted the propriety of vesting it in the President of the United States. I therefore think it best to retain it in the bill.

The future President addressed himself to the problem in even greater detail on the following day, June 17. After this thorough exposition of both the constitutional and practical aspects of the question, Madison rested his case and rose again only to speak on technical matters involving the eventual vote.

James Madison
Final Arguments in Favor of the President's
Independent Possession of the Removal Power
June 17, 1789

Gales, I, 514-21.

However various the opinions which exist upon the point now before us, it seems agreed on all sides, that it demands a careful investigation and full discussion.

I feel the importance of the question, and know that our decision will involve the decision of all similar cases. The decision that is at this time made, will become the permanent exposition of the constitution; and on a permanent exposition of the constitution will depend the genius and character of the whole Government. It will depend, perhaps, on this decision, whether the Government shall retain that equilibrium which the constitution intended, or take a direction towards aristocracy or anarchy among the members of the Government. Hence, how careful ought we to be to give a true direction to a power so critically circumstanced! It is incumbent on us to weigh with particular attention, the arguments which have been advanced in support of the various opinions with cautious deliberation. I own to you, Mr. Chairman, that I feel great anxiety upon this question; I feel an anxiety, because I am called upon to give a decision in a case that may affect the fundamental principles of the Government under which we act, and liberty itself. But all that I can do on such an occasion is, to weigh well every thing advanced on both sides, with the purest desire to find out the true meaning of the constitution, and to be guided by that, and an attachment to the true spirit of liberty, whose influence I believe strongly predominates here.

Several constructions have been put upon the constitution relative to the point in question. The gentleman from Connecticut (Mr. Sherman) has advanced a doctrine which was not touched upon before. He seems to think (if I understood him rightly) that the power of displacing from office is subject to legislative discretion; because it having a right to create, it may limit or modify as it thinks proper. I shall not say but at first view this doctrine may seem to have some plausibility. But when I consider, that the constitution clearly intended to maintain a marked distinction between the legislative, executive, and judicial powers of Government; and when I consider, that if the Legislature has a power, such as contended for, they may subject and transfer at discretion powers from one department of our Government to another; they may, on that principle, exclude the President altogether from exercising any authority in the removal of officers; they may give it to the Senate alone, or the President and Senate combined; they may vest it in the whole Congress; or they may reserve it to be exercised by this House. When I consider the consequences of this doctrine, and compare them with the true principles of the constitution, I own that I cannot subscribe to it.

Another doctrine, which has found very respectable friends, has been particularly advocated by the gentleman from South Carolina. (Mr. Smith.) It is this: when an officer is appointed by the President and Senate, he can only be displaced for malfeasance in his office by impeachment. I think this would give a stability to the executive department, so far as it may be described by the heads of departments, which is more incompatible with the genius of republican Governments in general, and this constitution in particular, than any doctrine which has yet been proposed. The danger to liberty, the danger of mal-administration, has not yet been found to lie so much in the facility of introducing improper persons into office, as in the difficulty of displacing those who are unworthy of the public trust. If it is said, that an officer once appointed shall not be displaced without the formality required by impeachment, I shall be glad to know what security we have for the faithful administration of the Government? Every individual, in the long chain which extends from the highest to the lowest link of the Executive Magistracy, would find a security in his situation which would relax his fidelity and promptitude in the discharge of his duty.

The doctrine, however, which seems to stand most in opposition to the principles I contend for, is, that the power to annul an appointment is, in the nature of things, incidental to the power which makes the appointment. I agree that if nothing more was said in the constitution than that the President, by and with the advice and consent of the Senate, should appoint to office, there would be great force in saying that the power of removal resulted by a natural implication from the power of appointing. But there is another part of the constitution, no less explicit than the one on which the gentleman's doctrine is founded; it is that part which declares that the executive power shall be vested in a President of the United States. The association of the Senate with the President in exercising that particular function, is an exception to this general rule; and exceptions to general rules, I conceive, are ever to be taken strictly. But there is another part of the constitution which inclines, in my judgment, to favor the construction I put upon it; the President is required to take care that the laws be faithfully executed. If the duty to see the laws faithfully executed be required at the hands of the Executive Magistrate, it would seem that it was generally intended he should have that species of power which is necessary to accomplish that end. Now, if the officer when once appointed is not to depend upon the President for his official existence, but upon a distinct body, (for where there are two negatives required, either can prevent the removal,) I confess I do not see how the President can take care that the laws be faithfully executed. It is true, by a circuitous operation, he may obtain an impeachment, and even without this it is possible he may obtain the concurrence of the Senate for the purpose of displacing an officer; but would this give that species of control to the Executive Magistrate which seems to be required by the constitution? I own, if my opinion was not contrary to that entertained by what I suppose to be the minority on this question, I should be doubtful of being mistaken, when I discovered how inconsistent that construction would make the constitution with itself. I can hardly bring myself to imagine the wisdom of the convention who framed the constitution contemplated such incongruity.

There is another maxim which ought to direct us in expounding the constitution, and is of great importance. It is laid down, in most of the constitutions or bills of rights in the republics of America; it is to be found in the political writings of the most celebrated civilians, and is every where held as essential to the preservation of liberty, that the three great departments of Government be kept separate and distinct; and if in any case they are blended, it is in order to admit a partial qualification, in order more effectually to guard against an entire, consolidation. I think, therefore, when we review the several parts of this constitution, when it says that the legislative powers shall be vested in a Congress of the United States under certain exceptions, and the executive power vested in the President with certain exceptions, we must suppose they were intended to be kept separate in all cases in which they are not blended, and ought, consequently, to expound the constitution so as to blend them as little as possible.

Every thing relative to the merits of the question as distinguished from a constitutional question, seems to turn on the danger of such a power vested in the President alone. But when I consider the checks under which he lies in the exercise of this power, I own to you I feel no apprehensions but what arise from the dangers incidental to the power itself; for dangers will be incidental to it, vest it where you please. I will not reiterate what was said before with respect to the mode of election, and the extreme improbability that any citizen will be selected from the mass of citizens who is not highly distinguished by his abilities and worth; in this alone we have no small security for the faithful exercise of this power. But, throwing that out of the question, let us consider the restraints he will feel after he is placed in that elevated station. It is to be remarked, that the power in this case will not consist so much in continuing a bad man in office, as in the danger of displacing a good one. Perhaps the great danger, as has been observed, of abuse in the executive power, lies in the improper continuance of bad men in office. But the power we contend for will not enable him to do this; for if an unworthy man be continued in office by an unworthy President, the House of Representatives can at any time impeach him, and the Senate can remove him, whether the President chooses or not. The danger then consists merely in this: the President can displace from office a man whose merits require that he should be continued in it. What will be the motives which the President can feel for such abuse of his power, and the restraints that operate to prevent it? In the first place, he will be impeachable by this House, before the Senate, for such an act of mal-administration; for I contend that the wanton removal of meritorious officers would subject him to impeachment and removal from his own high trust. But what can be his motives for displacing a worthy man? It must be that he may fill the place with an unworthy creature of his own. Can he accomplish this end? No; he can place no man in the vacancy whom the Senate shall not approve; and if he could fill the vacancy with the man he might choose, I am sure he would have little inducement to make an improper removal. Let us consider the consequences. The injured man will be supported by the popular opinion; the community will take side with him against the President; it will facilitate those combinations, and give success to those exertions which will be pursued to prevent his re-election. To displace a man of high merit, and who from his station may be supposed a man of extensive influence, are considerations which will excite serious reflections beforehand in the mind of any man who may fill the Presidential chair. The friends of those individuals and the public sympathy will be against him. If this should not produce his impeachment before the Senate, it will amount to an impeachment before the community, who will have the power of punishment, by refusing to re-elect him. But suppose this persecuted individual cannot obtain revenge in this mode; there are other modes in which he could make the situation of the President very inconvenient, if you suppose him resolutely bent on executing the dictates of resentment. If he had not influence enough to direct the vengeance of the whole community, he may probably be able to obtain an appointment in one or the other branch of the Legislature; and being a man of weight, talents, and influence, in either case he may prove to the President troublesome indeed. We have seen examples in the history of other nations, which justifies the remark I now have made. Though the prerogatives of the British King are great as his rank, and it is unquestionably known that he has a positive influence over both branches of the legislative body, yet there have been examples in which the appointment and removal of ministers have been found to be dictated by one or other of those branches. Now if this be the case with an hereditary Monarch, possessed of those high prerogatives and furnished with so many means of influence; can we suppose a President, elected for four years only, dependent upon the popular voice, impeachable by the Legislature, little, if at all, distinguished for wealth, personal talents or influence from the head of the department himself; I say, will he bid defiance to all these considerations, and wantonly dismiss a meritorious and virtuous officer? Such abuse of power exceeds my conception. If any thing takes place in the ordinary course of business of this kind, my imagination cannot extend to it on any rational principle. But let us not consider the question on one side only; there are dangers to be contemplated on the other. Vest this power in the Senate jointly with the President, and you abolish at once that great principle of unity and responsibility in the executive department, which was intended for the security of liberty and the public good. If the President should possess alone the power of removal from office, those who are employed in the execution of the law will be in their proper situation, and the chain of dependence be preserved; the lowest officers, the middle grade, and the highest, will depend, as they ought, on the President, and the President on the community. The chain of dependence therefore terminates in the supreme body, namely, in the people, who will possess, besides, in aid of their original power, the decisive engine of impeachment. Take the other supposition; that the power should be vested in the Senate, on the principle that the power to displace is necessarily connected with the power to appoint. It is declared by the constitution, that we may by law vest the appointment of inferior officers in the heads of departments; the power of removal being incidental, as stated by some gentlemen. Where does this terminate? If you begin with the subordinate officers, they are dependent on their superior, he on the next superior, and he on—whom? On the Senate, a permanent body, a body, by its particular mode of election, in reality existing forever; a body possessing that proportion of aristocratic power which the constitution no doubt thought wise to be established in the system, but which some have strongly excepted against. And let me ask gentlemen, is there equal security in this case as in the other? Shall we trust the Senate, responsible to individual Legislatures, rather than the person who is responsible to the whole community? It is true, the Senate do not hold their offices for life, like aristocracies recorded in the historic page; yet the fact is, they will not possess that responsibility for the exercise of Executive powers which would render it safe for us to vest such powers in them. But what an aspect will this give to the Executive? Instead of keeping the departments of Government distinct, you make an Executive out of one branch of the Legislature; you make the Executive a two-headed monster, to use the expression of the gentleman from New Hampshire, (Mr. Livermore,) you destroy the great principle of responsibility, and perhaps have the creature divided in its will, defeating the very purposes for which a unity in the Executive was instituted. These objections do not lie against such an arrangement as the bill establishes. I conceive that the President is sufficiently accountable to the community; and if this power is vested in him, it will be vested where its nature requires it should be vested; if any thing in its nature is executive, it must be that power which is employed in superintending and seeing that the laws are faithfully executed. The laws cannot be executed but by officers appointed for that purpose; therefore, those who are over such officers naturally possess the executive power. If any other doctrine be admitted, what is the consequence? You may set the Senate at the head of the executive department, or you may require that the officers hold their places during the pleasure of this branch of the Legislature, if you cannot go so far as to say we shall appoint them; and by this means, you link together two branches of the Government which the preservation of liberty requires to be constantly separated.

Another species of argument has been urged against this clause. It is said, that it is improper, or at least unnecessary, to come to any decision on this subject. It has been said by one gentleman, that it would be officious in this branch of the Legislature to expound the constitution, so far as it relates to the division of power between the President and Senate; it is incontrovertibly of as much importance to this branch of the Government as to any other, that the constitution should be preserved entire. It is our duty, so far as it depends upon us, to take care that the powers of the constitution be preserved entire to every department of Government; the breach of the constitution in one point, will facilitate the breach in another; a breach in this point may destroy that equilibrium by which the House retains its consequence and share of power; therefore we are not chargeable with an officious interference. Besides, the bill, before it can have effect, must be submitted to both those branches who are particularly interested in it; the Senate may negative, or the President may object, if he thinks it unconstitutional.

But the great objection drawn from the source to which the last arguments would lead us is, that the Legislature itself has no right to expound the constitution; that wherever its meaning is doubtful, you must leave it to take its course, until the Judiciary is called upon to declare its meaning. I acknowledge, in the ordinary course of Government, that the exposition of the laws and constitution devolves upon the Judiciary. But, I beg to know, upon what principle it can be contended, that any one department draws from the constitution greater powers than another, in marking out the limits of the powers of the several departments? The constitution is the charter of the people to the Government; it specifies certain great powers as absolutely granted, and marks out the departments to exercise them. If the constitutional boundary of either be brought into question, I do not see that any one of these independent departments has more right than another to declare their sentiments on that point.

Perhaps this is an omitted case. There is not one Government on the face of the earth, so far as I recollect, there is not one in the United States, in which provision is made for a particular authority to determine the limits of the constitutional division of power between the branches of the Government. In all systems there are points which must be adjusted by the departments themselves, to which no one of them is competent. If it cannot be determined in this way, there is no resource left but the will of the community, to be collected in some mode to be provided by the constitution, or one dictated by the necessity of the case. It is therefore a fair question, whether this great point may not as well be decided, at least by the whole Legislature as by a part, by us as well as by the Executive or Judiciary? As I think it will be equally constitutional, I cannot imagine it will be less safe, that the exposition should issue from the legislative authority than any other; and the more so, because it involves in the decision the opinions of both those departments, whose powers are supposed to be affected by it. Besides, I do not see in what way this question could come before the judges, to obtain a fair and solemn decision; but even if it were the case that it could, I should suppose, at least while the Government is not led by passion, disturbed by faction, or deceived by any discolored medium of sight, but while there is a desire in all to see and be guided by the benignant ray of truth, that the decision may be made with the most advantage by the Legislature itself.

My conclusion from these reflections is, that it will be constitutional to retain the clause; that it expresses the meaning of the constitution as must be established by fair construction, and a construction which, upon the whole, not only consists with liberty, but is more favorable to it than any one of the interpretations that have been proposed.

By the time Madison's second speech was finished, the majority of members of the House probably had made up their minds on the question; nevertheless the debate continued for another four days. On June 23, Madison and most of the other supporters of the removal power voted for Congressman Benson's motion to strike out of the main motion the clause "to be removable by the President." Madison's reasoning here was that eliminating this clause would mollify those who did not think that the House of Representatives had the "legislative discretion" to rule on such a question. Furthermore, since they were insisting that the Chief Executive's removal power was clearly the intent of the Constitution, there was no point complicating the question by introducing congressional sanction. The vote to eliminate the clause won 31 to 19. The following day the amended version of the bill passed by a vote of 29 to 22, with a clear understanding that its failure to carry any directive with respect to removal indicated that the removal power constitutionally resided within the scope of the independent powers of the President.[54]

The debate in the Senate was not officially recorded, nor in all probability was it as brilliantly argued as its counterpart in the House, but the results were favorable to the President's removal power. The private journal of the debates of the first session of Congress kept by an eccentric and cynical participant, William Maclay, and the correspondence of the presiding officer, Vice President John Adams, have left some record of the proceedings. Opinion was evenly divided among the 20 senators then in attendance. Here again, ten of this number had been delegates to the Constitutional Convention, and six out of the ten favored the removal power being granted exclusively to the President. Among the six favoring this principle were Oliver Ellsworth and William Patterson, two of the most active and respected men at the Philadelphia Convention, and Robert Morris, the banker who raised most of the money that supported the American Revolution. Vice President Adams, who was already on record in support of the removal power being vested in the Chief Executive, voted to break the 10-10 tie, giving the principle a victory in both houses of the legislature.

Madison's constitutional arguments and practical considerations were so persuasive that it is difficult to understand how such doubts could have arisen in the first place. If any of the alternative proposals had been adopted, the new government would have been in chaos in short order. Curiously, the disastrous implications of the President not having such essential executive powers seem not to have occurred to the opponents of the principle. Congressman Bland actually argued:

> What would be the consequence of the removal by the President alone, he had already mentioned, and need not repeat. A new President might, by turning out the great officers, bring about a change of the ministry, and throw affairs of the Union into disorder: would not this, in fact, make the President a monarch, and give him absolute power over all the great departments of Government?[55]

In other words, each successive administration would inherit, and presumably have to accept, all the holdover appointments from the previous administration, regardless of whether or not they were from the same political party. If the removal required Senate approval and the Senate was under control of the opposition party (which frequently was the case), then the Senate could block the removal of any and all executive officers and paralyze the effectiveness of the President.

Despite such views, which, if successful, would have radically transformed the political system as it stands today, the House did acknowledge the President's right to remove his appointed officers, and this helped establish the basis for both a stable and united executive branch and also provided for a normal changeover of administrations whenever the electorate determined to vote a new President or a new party into office. But although the President's removal power was firmly established as an operating principle of the new government by this exhaustive and thorough debate and by subsequent decisions, this power would be challenged time and again by a jealous and misguided Congress in the future. It would take almost another full century to lay its effective opponents to rest, and nearly another 45 years beyond that date to arrive at a decision by the Supreme Court which would endorse the principle by the orderly process of judicial review.

Madison's construction of the Constitution was not seriously challenged for the next 45 years, but in 1820 Congress passed the first Tenure of Office Act, which further complicated the question of the removal power of the President. As previously indicated the statute provided that the principal officers of the executive branch involved in the collection or disbursement of money should be appointed for fixed terms of four years, and that the tenure of the present officeholders in these positions should expire at stated intervals, not later than September 30, 1821. President Monroe signed the bill making it law, but later, upon greater reflection, he regretted his action, considering the bill unconstitutional. John Quincy Adams wrote in his memoirs:

> Mr. Monroe unwarily signed the bill without adverting to its real character. He told me that Mr. Madison considered it as in principle unconstitutional. . . . Mr. Monroe himself inclined to the same opinion, but the question had not occurred to him when he signed the bill.[56]

Both Jefferson and Madison were extremely apprehensive about the measure and its constitutionality and were gloomily prophetic about the implications of imposing such limitations upon the President's removal power. John Quincy Adams' condemnation rounded out the rejection of the law by every living President or ex-President: "A more pernicious expedient could scarcely have been devised," he declared.[57]

The resolute opposition of both Monroe and Adams together removed only 34 officials from office in their 12 years in the White House.

The First Confrontation

The Jacksonian "revolution" brought many changes to the American political system, and one of the most significant was the development of considerable friction between Congress and the President. Jackson was the first President since Washington to be nominated and elected by the people and not by the congressional caucus or the House of Representatives. Congress, at least since Madison's administration, had considered itself the center of the political system, and had been the decisive force first in selecting a President for nomination, and then in influencing his election. The free political wind that blew Andrew Jackson into office swept away the remnants of the past practice which had made the President obligated to Congress for his presence in office. Jackson had been elected by a popular political movement and he was already embittered against many of the members of Congress who had blocked his election in 1824, when he had received the highest number of electoral votes, but had been defeated by an alliance of his enemies in the House of Representatives. Once in office he did not court congressional leaders, nor try to manipulate them as had Jefferson. Jackson developed his policy positions in consultation with a number of close advisors, none of whom were members of Congress, with the exception of Senator Thomas Hart Benton and Congressman James Polk.

Jackson's break with his Vice President, John C. Calhoun, on the nullification issue further exacerbated his relationship with the Senate, for Calhoun resigned as Vice President and was quickly named to replace Senator Robert Y. Hayne, who had resigned his Senate seat to become governor of South Carolina. Calhoun soon joined other powerful Senate figures such as Daniel Webster and Henry Clay to oppose Jackson on the issue of rechartering the Bank of the United States. The President first publicly indicated his opposition to the Bank in his message to Congress in 1829 when he suggested that the Bank had not succeeded in "establishing a uniform and sound currency,"[58] and the people ought to begin to consider whether another agency might be devised to replace it rather than renew its charter in 1836.

But Jackson was not ready to act on the Bank question at this time. He had enough trouble trying to keep peace in his own cabinet, which was almost at swords' points over the social slights administered to the famous Peggy Eaton, wife of the secretary of war. The cabinet was divided on the question of the Bank, and before 1832 Jackson leaned towards accepting some reforms which would create greater control and responsibility on the part of the government for the Bank's policies and restrictions and limitations which would prevent the Bank from ever utilizing its considerable power to jeopardize or to act against the public interest.

The President was something of a populist at heart. He mistrusted the eastern establishment, and, like other westerners and planters, balked at the tight money restrictions sometimes imposed by the Bank of the United States. He resented its extra-governmental power, its ability to determine national economic policy, by and large dictated, he thought, by considerations of the private profit of its stockholders and directors. Jackson was surrounded by men who shared his opposition to the Bank in his Kitchen Cabinet, an informal and unofficial body made up of personal friends and supporters who saw a great deal of the President and assisted him with many of his statutory tasks. Together with his attorney general, Roger B. Taney, another avowed opponent of the Bank, they helped sharpen Jackson's opposition to the point where he became consummately obsessed with the problem.

But President Jackson would probably not have moved precipitately against the Bank if the action of its president, Nicholas Biddle, had not forced him to take strong retaliatory action. Biddle was alarmed by the continued warnings uttered by Jackson in his Annual Messages, but he was also perplexed by confidential assurances from some of the President's intimate colleagues that the President had no intention of taking any overt steps against the Bank, or of attempting to deny its recharter. Finally, he probably shared the opinion of Henry Clay, an announced candidate for the presidency in 1832, who looked at the Bank issue as a trap which was bound to embarrass Jackson in the coming election. Clay was completely wrong in this conclusion, thus revealing how lacking he was in the intuitive insight that makes for a successful national leader.

In early January 1832 Nicholas Biddle requested that the Congress consider the Bank's application for recharter, a full four years ahead of its statutory renewal date. His associates had carefully assessed the votes, and Biddle knew that he would win in both houses. He was not confident, however, that he could command the votes necessary to overcome a presidential veto. And he had reason to be insecure. The President was angered at Biddle's premature proposal, and although neither he nor his advisors had as yet fully determined their policy on the Bank, he saw this move as a challenge or a test of strength. He promptly vetoed the bill to recharter the Bank after it had passed both houses of Congress in early July 1832. When the Congress failed to override the President's veto the future of the Bank was determined, although all of the subsequent events following upon the veto were certainly not anticipated at that time. Jackson had defeated the Bank in this first major encounter between Congress and the President and the die was now cast for an all-out battle to the finish.

Biddle's political instinct failed him a second time when he speculated that Jackson's veto message would backfire and work against the President's interests in the upcoming election. The Philadelphia banker considered the message to be a demagogic appeal to the masses, full of contradictions and errors, which all intelligent Americans would be able to quickly ascertain. He had 30,000 copies of the veto message printed and distributed as an anti-Jackson political broadside but many who read it liked what it said and voted instead for Jackson. There is no question that the veto message turned out to be Jackson's most effective campaign document.

The following spring the President submitted a paper to his cabinet (and to several members of his Kitchen Cabinet) outlining what he considered to be the desired policy that his administration should pursue regarding the Bank of the United States, dealing particularly with the subject of the removal of the government's funds from the Bank of the United States.

President Andrew Jackson
Outline of Bank Policy to His Cabinet
March 20, 1833

John Spencer Basset, ed., *Correspondence of Andrew Jackson* (Washington, D.C., 1931) V, 42-43.

A few days ago I took the liberty of submitting to the Secretary of the Treasury somewhat at large, my views on this and other points, a copy of which I send herewith for your perusal. I will only add on this point, that if the people of the United States are so corrupt or deluded, that they will not sustain their government in taking the public money out of the hands of an institution proved by indubitable evidence to be guilty of almost every crime which a Bank can commit, they are prepared for the yoke of a master. But we have no right, notwithstanding the resolution of the House of Representatives, to distrust the purity and intelligence of the people. If, however, I knew that the measure would lead to a doubtful conflict, I would take the public deposits out of that Bank. It is better to fail in an attempt to put down corruption and preserve the purity of our institutions, than enjoy ease and office under a heartless Bank government.

The more I see of the present Bank, the less I like a national Bank of any sort. It impairs the morals of our people, corrupts our statesmen and is dangerous to liberty. If it can be effected, therefore, I would prefer the employment of the state institutions in the service of the Treasury to the reestablishment of any national Bank. I have great confidence, that, through the agency of a few state banks, the revenue may be collected, the money transferred and every necessary aid afforded to the Treasury as cheaply and as safely as by the present bank of the United States. Entertaining this belief, I suggest the following outline of the policy which I think would at this moment most redound to the interest of the country and the honor and strength of the administration:

1. That steps be immediately taken to ascertain what state banks are best managed, most safe and most willing to aid the government in effecting its views and policy; and that such an understanding be formed between them as will produce in the collection and distribution of the public revenue the same beneficial results as are now produced by the Bank of the United States and Branches.

2. That as soon as an arrangement can be matured with a few Banks at the most important points the Collectors and others receiving public moneys be directed to deposit them in the selected Banks.

3. That the Commissioners of Loans be forthwith directed to deposit to the credit of the Treasurer all moneys set apart for the payment of the public debt and not now applied, forward their amounts and Books to the Treasury Department, and that notice be given that the public debt will hereafter be paid only at the Treasury.

4. That the public money now in the Bank of the United States be drawn upon by the usual warrants of the Treasury for the ordinary expenditures of the government and the payment of the public debt until it be exhausted, before any warrant shall be drawn on the new deposit in the state Banks.

5. That all public officers be instructed to transfer their amounts to the state banks when they shall receive the first warrants on those institutions.

6. That there be an understanding with the state banks employed by the government, that they shall extend all reasonable and safe indulgence to the other state banks and such accommodations to the debtors of the government as necessity and sound policy may, from time to time, require.

Immediate reactions came from two advisors who were the most bitter opponents of the Bank of the United States. Attorney General Taney wrote a long paper reiterating his opposition to the Bank and advocating the removal of the government's funds to the state banks. In the course of responding to Jackson's fourth interrogatory—should a new national bank be formed?—the attorney general supported the President's position strongly:

A Bank of the United States cannot be justified under the constitution if the fiscal operations of the government can be carried on with safety and convenience without it. And a full and fair experiment ought to be made before the General Government can be warranted in assuming that a Bank chartered by the United States is a necessary and an indispensable agent of the Treasury. The history of the financial concerns of this Government by no means prove the necessity of such a Bank.[59]

In endorsing the President's intention to rely on the state banks for the federal deposits, Taney concluded:

The remaining enquiry is what system ought to be adopted for the deposite (sic) and distribution of the revenue?

The one you have proposed appears to me to be the best, and I think on experiment will be found to be quite safe and convenient as the Bank of the United States without being attended with any of the evils and dangers which always arise out of an institution of that description. The state banks judiciously selected and arranged will, I have no doubt, be able to perform all the duties of fiscal agents and be able to furnish a general currency as wholesome and stable as that of the United States Bank. . . .

I do not conceal from myself the fierce and desperate struggle which the Bank will make to maintain its monopoly and procure a restoration of the deposites (sic). Nor am I insensible of its power. But I sincerely believe that the purity of our institutions and the best interests of the country call for prompt, firm and decisive measures on the part of the Executive, and I rely for support on the intelligence and patriotism of the people. . . .[60]

Amos Kendall, the *eminence grise* of the Kitchen Cabinet, also answered the President in quick order and did not hedge in his advice:

I entirely concur with you in the opinion that it ought not under any circumstances to be rechartered. Its abuses and corruptions are too notorious and too flagrant to entitle it to the least favor, and much less to a renewal of its privileges and immunities. But if its management had been unexceptionable, the power it concentrates, the encroachments it covers on the rights of the States and its incompatibility with the Constitution, constitute insurmountable objections. . . .

I look upon this as a critical moment. Upon the determination at which you and your cabinet shall now arrive, depend, in my opinion, the character of this government for years to come. A new scheme to govern the American people by fraud and corruption, has been matured. The means of execution are the Bank, the Public lands, an overflowing Treasury and Internal Improvements. The projectors can do nothing but arrange their plans and marshall their forces while you hold the veto power. But they look beyond your term of service and expect to elect as your successor some one and any one who will agree to be their creature and instrument. To you, sir, the friends of a good and pure government look to settle the remaining great questions of national policy and strike from the hands of corruption its means to do mischief. The most effectual blow which can now be struck is, by a removal of the public deposites, to cripple the Bank of the United States and deprive the conspirators of the aid they expect from its money power. By one act you would weaken if not destroy a powerful enemy and raise up powerful friends; the Bank managers would have full employment in maintaining their own defences instead of affording the administration any annoyance; and I doubt whether their utmost exertions could save the institution from a sudden ruin. Deprived of this powerful auxiliary, I think the other weapons of the corrupt league might easily be parried or turned against them.[61]

Against this kind of inflamed rhetoric and reasoning the milder members of the cabinet, opposed to removing the deposits, made little headway with the President who was already sufficiently convinced to move the national funds from the state banks. But Jackson proceeded with due caution and tried to establish a solid constitutional and administrative foundation for his later actions.

Seven weeks after the President had received replies from Taney and Kendall, he received a 91-page manuscript response from his secretary of the treasury, Louis McLane. The secretary had moderate views on the Bank question. He wanted to introduce modest reforms which would make the Bank more responsible to the government of the United States and would reduce its independent power to manipulate economic policy. But he did not believe that the Bank was unconstitutional; he recognized the important regulating and stabilizing function it carried on and he realized the disastrous effects to which its sweeping elimination would probably lead. In his answer to the President he made these points quite effectively, and warned against the removal of the deposits without first establishing an institutional equivalent to the Bank which could take over its normal and essential functions. McLane had warned Biddle earlier not to inject the Bank issue into the election of 1832, and when he did, the secretary became convinced that the Bank of the United States should not be rechartered, and looked instead towards the establishment of a government-controlled substitute in Washington.

Although Jackson described McLane's views as "strong points," and "ably discussed," the President's other advisors quickly supplied him with harsh rebuttals to these arguments; his mind was not changed. McLane had seen the impasse coming, and arrangements had been made previously to switch him to the post of secretary of state when the incumbent, Edward Livingston, went to France as United States ambassador. The office of secretary of the treasury was critical to the actual removal or transfer of the government's funds from the Bank of the United States because the Bank's charter, drawn up by the Congress of the United States, carefully stipulated that the secretary was the only official authorized to withdraw these funds, after giving his reasons to the Congress.

William J. Duane, the man Andrew Jackson selected to succeed Secretary McLane, was a Philadelphia lawyer, the son of the celebrated editor of the Jeffersonian *Aurora*, and a long-time active supporter of the President. Duane had not sought public office and had twice refused positions offered by the President, one of them ironically being director of the Bank of the United States, an appointment to which the Senate had consented but which Duane had declined. The President had finally persuaded him to accept a diplomatic commission, after being confirmed by the Senate without his knowledge. He consented under pressure from Jackson who argued that another refusal would cost the administration extreme embarrassment.

Before the Philadelphia lawyer could assume his duties in this last post, however, he was invited in December 1832 to replace McLane in the cabinet as secretary of the treasury. Secretary McLane personally came to Philadelphia to advise Duane of the proposed appointment and to persuade him to accept the offer. The shift of offices was being made with pleasure by the present secretary, who was moving over (or up, as some would interpret it) to the State Department, and Duane was promised he would not have to move to Washington to assume the duties of the job until the following spring.

Duane indicated that he was reluctant to accept the cabinet position, but he finally did so on January 30, 1833; he assumed the duties of office on the first day of June 1833. The new secretary of the treasury was visited that same evening by an official in the Treasury Department, Reuben Whitney, who led him to believe that he was an emissary of the President, and who reviewed for him the present state of the Bank controversy. Duane assumed that this was more or less of an official briefing. He was informed by his visitor that the President, after seeking and receiving divided cabinet advice on the question, had decided to assume personally the responsibility of directing the secretary of the treasury to remove the public deposits from the Bank of the United States. Whitney even brought along correspondence with various state banks, indicating their willingness to accept the deposits. When he returned the following evening, accompanied by President Jackson's confidential advisor, Amos Kendall, also technically a Treasury official, the new secretary could not conceal his mortification at what he considered "an attempt, apparently with the sanction of the President, to reduce me to a mere cipher in the administration."[62] Kendall explained at that time that he was already actively engaged in negotiating with various state banks to arrange for the transfer of the government's funds. The new secretary of the treasury was furious and quickly dismissed his uninvited guests.

When Secretary Duane met with the President the following day Jackson denied sending these emissaries, but since both men enjoyed his confidence, such a denial hardly explained the incident. Unfortunately this situation set the tone of the relationship between the President and his secretary of the treasury from that point on. Jackson, whose impatience with the Bank was growing every day, had assumed that an old opponent of the Bank of the United States like Duane would naturally go along with him on any program aimed at destroying its power. He had not even bothered to consult the new secretary on this matter before his official appointment, although it is clear that the President's mind was firmly fixed on the question.

This great tactical error on Jackson's part stemmed from his oversimplified views of the Bank question. He looked upon the Bank as a great evil dragon and justified using any weapon to slay it. But the function and operation of such a central banking system or a national bank is not a simple problem. The Bank of the United States was the heart of the credit and monetary system of the United States and tampering with it ran the risk of exposing the national economy to peril. Both Secretary Duane and former Secretary McLane understood this and they were alarmed at the essentially clumsy and political approach the administration was making to the Bank. They were not in favor of rechartering the old Bank of the United States and shared most of the President's critical views with respect to its policies and his apprehension over the Bank's tremendous economic powers, unrestrained by any public body. But the President and his advisors were ready to crush the Bank and experiment with any sort of replacement, even if it were questionable that it could assume the functions and responsibilities which the Bank of the United States had conducted, functions which, as most authorities would argue, must be assumed by some responsible central agency in order to avoid pure chaos in the economic life of the nation. Duane did not buy their approach.

The President clearly had made a serious mistake in the manner in which he handled the Duane appointment. After his difficulties with Secretary McLane he should have taken the time to explore the problem thoroughly with his successor before appointing him. A public position in opposition to the rechartering of the Bank was not assurance that the individual holding that position would go along with any plan to destroy the Bank, particularly if in his position as secretary of the treasury he was responsible to Congress to explain any such action. Not only did Jackson fail to discuss the matter with Duane before his appointment, but he very thoughtlessly permitted his underlings to confront the new secretary of the treasury with the full-blown plans for withdrawal of the deposits. The secretary was presented with a *fait accompli* before he had been interviewed by the President or spent more than a full day in office. Duane, a proud and dignified individual, was outraged at this treatment, and from that point on, approached the whole problem in a very negative frame of mind.

To compound the difficulties both Duane and Jackson put so much down on paper in their lengthy exchanges during the summer of 1833 that they both trapped themselves in commitments which they could not fulfill. The President was at first very patient with his secretary and attempted to soothe his wounded feelings and to win him over to his opinion through persuasion. But even here Jackson handled the situation awkwardly, reflecting his insensitivity to Duane's situation. In a long letter in July he told Duane that "the circumstances of your differing in opinion from me upon this point, and the failure to communicate your views at an earlier period required no apologies."[63]

Duane must have been furious upon reading that passage. But in an earlier letter Jackson made the fatal slip that provided Duane with the defense for his later actions. In a letter written from Boston in June, in which he outlined his position in favor of withdrawing the government's deposits from the Bank of the United States, President Jackson explained:

> In making to you, my dear Sir, this frank and explicit avowal of my opinions and feelings, *it is not my intention to interfere with the independent exercise of the discretion committed to you by law over the subject.* I have thought it however, due to you, under any circumstances, to place before you, with this restriction, my sentiments upon the subject, to the end that you may upon my responsibility allow them to enter into your decision on the subject, and into my future exposition of it as far as you may deem proper.[64]

This was all the encouragement Duane needed. He shortly replied to the President, seizing upon this very explicit statement:

> In the conclusion of the President's letter, he has the goodness to say, that, while he frankly avows his own opinions and feelings, he does not intend to interfere with the independent exercise of the discretion, committed to the undersigned by law, over the subject; and the undersigned may adopt, on the President's responsibility, the sentiments expressed by him, in his letter, as the basis in part of his own decision. The undersigned, therefore, concludes, that he has not received the direction of the chief magistrate, to perform an act of executive duty; but that the President believes, that congress (sic) had a right to direct and hold responsible, an executive agent. And, accordingly, without expressing a doubt on that point, that might be thought presumptuous, the undersigned will decide on his responsibility to congress, and that decision shall be the same, as if he received an executive order.[65]

This is precisely the course which Secretary Duane followed until removed from office by the President on September 23, 1833. The argument continued all of that summer, Duane maintaining that the withdrawal of the government's funds would endanger the financial stability of the country and that he was not warranted by law in performing such a task, while the President argued that the real danger was the continued existence of the Bank and that the removal of the deposits was the only practical method of protecting the government's funds and crushing the Bank. Jackson (and his ghost writers) harped upon the abuses of the public trust which Biddle and the Bank had engaged in, and Duane stressed the arguments that the President should press charges in the courts for such violation, and wait for the Congress to legislate a final solution to the whole problem.

But as indicated above, Duane wrote so much that he too presented the President with a written promise which contradicted his later actions, and very possibly his intentions. Later in July when the President challenged his secretary with the charge that in a recent document Duane had seemed to be saying that under no circumstances would he consider withdrawing the deposits, Duane replied that his mind was always open to new evidence and arguments, and was capable of embracing the President's position if he were convinced of its validity. He went on to say that:

> I shall also be ready to enter into a full examination of the whole subject, when you shall, as you propose, bring it before your cabinet. But if, after receiving the information, and hearing the discussions, I shall not consider it my duty, as the responsible agent of the law, to carry into effect the decision that you make, I will, from my respect for you and myself, promptly afford you the opportunity to select a successory, whose views may accord with your own on the important subject in contemplation.[66]

In early September, President Jackson came to a final decision to withdraw the deposits from the Bank of the United States; he called a cabinet meeting and distributed a report made under his supervision on the feasibility of having the state banks receive the funds. With it he distributed copies of his extensive correspondence with Duane and asked the cabinet to study this material and to come to a conclusion on the matter.

They came together a week later and the President requested that they express their individual opinions on the question. Two members of the cabinet, the secretaries of state and of the treasury, were firmly opposed; the secretary of war was of the opinion that the matter should be left entirely in the hands of the secretary of the treasury (which was a roundabout form of disagreeing with the President, since he certainly knew of Duane's strong opposition). The attorney general and the secretary of the navy supported the President in his already expressed intention to withdraw the funds.

Jackson thanked them and asked the members of the cabinet to gather for a third time the following day to hear his decision in the case. At that time his private secretary read a state paper which reviewed many of the familiar arguments and concluded that the secretary should remove the funds under the direct order of the President. Jackson had written the first draft of this paper earlier in the summer when he was vacationing at Rips Raps, Virginia; Taney polished it up at a later date. The document that emerged was a well-rounded denouncement of the Bank of the United States, utilizing all the arguments which had appeared in earlier cabinet papers and in letters sent back and forth between the President and his subordinates. It denounced the Bank as an incipient aristocratic evil in the society and enlarged upon the dangers inherent in its great power and pervasive influence in the body politic. It did not reflect, however, any basic understanding of the functional role which the Bank played in the economic life of the country and assumed that the decentralized and weaker state banks could take over this role. Jackson and his close associates in this contention were actually not wholly confident that the new arrangements would work out for the benefit of the country, but they were willing to take a chance on the assumption that anything would be better than the system existing under the Bank of the United States.

At the close of the cabinet meeting Secretary Duane approached Jackson and asked him if the President was directing him to remove the deposits. Jackson replied that it was his desire that the secretary should remove them, but upon the President's responsibility; he added with great emphasis that "if I would stand by him, it would be the happiest day of his life."[67] Duane has described his state of indecision at that point:

> When I retired, I had to consider, not merely whether I ought to remove the deposits, but whether I should resign. I was sensible that I had erred in giving any assurance on the latter point, and doubted whether subsequent occurrences had not absolved me from all obligation to respect it.[68] I decided to avoid a surrender of an important post, and yet wished to part from the President without unkind feeling. It had occurred to me, that I might accomplish both these ends by asking for a written expression of the President's wish that I should retire; and, in giving me such a memorandum, I did not perceive that there would be any committal of himself. It seemed to me that, assailed as I had been and menaced with new attacks, the President, if really my friend, would not desire to tie my hands.[69]

The President was in no mood to wait upon Duane's prolonged delays, however, and he sent a message to him after several days had passed, inquiring whether he had come to a decision. Duane replied that he would give the President an answer two days hence (September 21). Jackson still displayed commendable patience with his secretary's delaying tactics, and wrote to Vice President Van Buren on the same day, indicating his confidence that Duane would either agree or resign:

> Mr. Duane says the exposé [the cabinet paper] has put me on strong grounds, and has entirely presented the case in a new form to his mind. I have thought it right to indulge him and I expect *now* he will act with energy, or retire friendly, which to me is desirable.[70]

It is quite clear Duane had no intent to choose either alternative; he was going to persuade or force the President to remove him. There is no indication that he wanted to cling to the office, but his own sense of honor required him to stick to his position and retain his post until the President was forced to remove him.

The next day Jackson went ahead and published his decision to remove the deposits in *The Globe* (the administration newspaper, edited by the President's confidant, Frank Blair). Since it was published before any final determination was made in the Duane case, the secretary considered this to be inexcusable and still another slight on the part of the administration. The day following the publication of the President's intentions Secretary Duane called upon him at the White House, delivered a formal refusal to remove the deposits or to resign, and had a final personal interview with the President (recorded by the secretary).

Final Interview
Between William J. Duane and
President Andrew Jackson
September 21, 1833

William J. Duane, *Narrative and Correspondence Concerning the Removal of Deposites (sic) and Occurrences Connected Therewith* (Philadelphia, Pennsylvania, 1838), 102-03.

SECRETARY. I have, at length, waited upon you, sir, with this letter.
PRESIDENT. What is it?
S. It respectfully and finally makes known my decision, not to remove the deposites, or resign.
P. Then you do not mean, that we shall part as friends.
S. The reverse, sir, is my desire; but I must protect myself.
P. But you said you would retire, if we could not finally agree.
S. I indiscreetly said so, sir; but I am now compelled to take this course.
P. I have been under an impression that you would resign, even as an act of friendship to me.
S. Personal wishes, sir, must give way. The true question is, which must I observe, my promise to execute my duty faithfully, or my agreement to retire, when the latter conflicts with the former?
P. I certainly never expected that any such difficulties could arise between us; and think you ought still to consider the matter.
S. I have painfully considered it; and hope you will not ask me to make a sacrifice. All that you need is a successor, and him you may have at once.
P. But I do not wish to dismiss you. I have too much regard for yourself, your family and friends, to take that course.
S. Excuse me, sir, you may only do now what you said, in your letter of the 22d of July, it would be your duty to do, if I then said I would not thereafter remove the deposites.
P. It would be at any time disagreeable to do what might be injurious to you.
S. A resignation, I think, would be more injurious. And permit me to say, that the publication in yesterday's Globe removes all delicacy. A worm if trodden upon will turn. I am assailed in all the leading papers of the administration; and if my friend, you will not tie up my hands.
P. Then, I suppose you mean to come out against me.
S. Nothing is further from my thoughts. I barely desire to do what is now my duty; and to defend myself if assailed hereafter.

[Here the President expatiated on the late disclosures in relation to the bank, the corruptibility of congress, etc.; and at length taking a paper from his drawer said]

P. You have been all along mistaken in your views. Here is a paper that will show you your obligations—that the executive must protect you.

S. I will read it, sir, if such is your wish, but I cannot anticipate a change of opinion.

P. A secretary, sir, is merely an executive agent, a subordinate, and you may say so in self-defence.

S. In this particular case, congress confers a discretionary power, and requires reasons if I exercise it. Surely this contemplates responsibility on my part.

P. This paper will show you, that your doubts are wholly groundless.

S. As to the deposites, allow me, sir, to say, my decision is positive. The only question is as to the mode of my retirement.

P. My dear Mr. Duane; we must separate as friends. Far from desiring, that you should sustain any injury, you know I have intended to give you the highest appointment now in my gift. You shall have the mission to Russia. I would have settled this matter before, but for the delay or difficulty [as I understood the President] in relation to Mr. Buchanan.

S. I am sincerely thankful to you, sir, for your kind disposition, but I beg you to serve me in a way that will be truly pleasing. I desire no new station, and barely wish to leave my present one blameless, or free from apprehension as to the future. Favour me with a written declaration of your desire, that I should leave office, as I cannot carry out your views as to the deposites, and I will take back this letter [the one I had just presented].

P. Never have I had any thing, that has given me more mortification than this whole business. I had not the smallest notion that we could differ.

S. My principles and opinions, sir, are unchanged. We differ only about time—you are for acting now, I am for waiting for congress.

P. How often have I told you, that congress cannot act until the deposites are removed.

S. I am unable, sir, to change my opinion at will upon that point.

P. You are altogether wrong in your opinion, and I thought Mr. Taney would have convinced you that you are.

S. Mr. Taney, sir, endeavoured to prevail on me to adopt his views, but failed. As to the deposites, I barely desired a delay of about ten weeks.

P. Not a day—not an hour; recent disclosures banish all doubt, and I do not see how you can hesitate.

S. I have often stated my reasons. Surely, sir, it is enough that were I to act, I could not give reasons satisfactory to myself.

P. My reasons, lately read in the cabinet, will release you from complaint.

S. I am sorry I cannot view the subject in the same light.

Our conversation was further extended, under varying emotions on both sides; but without any change of opinion or decision—at length I retired.

From that point on it was simply a matter of compounded recriminations. Duane wrote a series of notes to the President, and Jackson returned them (as he had done with Duane's final refusal), charging that they contained inadmissable and improper statements. On September 22 the President formally dismissed the secretary of the treasury, after reminding him of his earlier promise to resign whenever his personal decision was in flat contradiction to the President's wishes. Jackson had finally lost all patience with Duane, and also his confidence in the secretary's judgment and loyalty to his administration. On the day of the removal the President poured out his true feelings in a letter to Van Buren.

President Andrew Jackson
Letter to Martin Van Buren
September 23, 1833

Basset, V, 206-07.

my D'r sir,   I have this morning, from imperious necessity been compelled to dismiss Mr. Duane from the Treasury department. His conduct has been such of late that would induce a belief that he came into the Dept. as the secrete agent of the Bank, to disclose the cabinet secretes for its benefit, rather than to aid the Executive in the administration of the Government.

I had a hope after the pledge he had given in his letter of july, that if he could not finally agree with me, that he would retire and give room for me to appoint a secretary who would act agreable to my views. Contrary, to this pledge, he took the stand that he would not resign and in a very indecorous letter told me I *must remove him before he would leave the office*. This was returned to him with a calm dignified note informing him of his pledge; that I could not now hold a correspondence with one of my secretaries on a subject on which I had decided, aluded to the indecorum of his letter and concluded by adding that all I wished *now* to know from him was, whether he would aid me in carrying into effect the measures which I had decided on, or not. Mr. Duane addressed me another letter equally indecorous but professing the greatest personal regard etc. Before I had time to act upon this, he sent a note to Major Donelson requesting my permission to withdraw it etc. etc. in the course of the day, yesterday, he wrote me two letters, and altho couched in more decorous language, equally offensive, containing palpable untruths and misrepresentations. These of course lay over for action until this morning, yesterday being sunday. This morning I inclosed them back to him with a very dignified note which I thought suitable for the occasion, concluding by telling him that *I had no further use for him at the head of the Treasury*, appointed Mr. Taney, who accepted, resigning the atto. Genls office, and unites with me heart in hand to meet the crisis. Mr. Taney is commissioned, sworn into office, and the business of the Treasury is progressing as tho Mr. Duane had never been born. In his appointment I surely caught a tarter in disguise, but I have got rid of him. His father is here and if [I] can judge correctly, the papers that were so indecorous were withdrawn and others written for publication hereafter. Believing this, as I had him in the wrong, I have kept him so—therefore he must come forth himself, and if his letters are published by him it must destroy him. The blame that can attach to me is, that I did not dismiss him long before.

I have been a good deal indisposed, would no doubt have been much worse, if it had not been for the *exciting* pills administered by Doctor Duane. But my friend how humiliating to me to be so much disappointed in a man whose purity of principle and politics I had so much confided, one who was always opposed to the Bank, who I had every confidence in when I appointed him that he would go hand and hand with me in carrying into effect a measure that I had called for the written opinion of my cabinet in last month. Professions will not do to be relied on now a days where the *power of the Bank* comes in question—hereafter I will have a Pledge. Who shall I take to fill the atto. Genls place? He ought to be right upon the Indian and Bank questions, and possessing legal talents and weight of character. Mr. Woodbury says he ought to come from the south, who can we choose in the south to fill the character, Judge Parker. Some say Mr. Dallas. Write me freely and confidentially on this subject.

In haste yr friend.

P.S. I send you no Globe as I expect the major has. When read give me your views of it. I now begin my message—it must be carefully adapted to the crisis. I will have a rough draft made for your examination when you come on.

A. J.

When Congress met in December, the anti-Jackson forces did not take long to denounce his actions and to try to develop a strategy to defeat him in the next election. Henry Clay led off with a three-day speech just after Christmas in support of two resolutions which he introduced, one censuring the President for exceeding his constitutional authority in the dismissal of Duane for his refusal to adhere to the President's decision to remove the government's deposits from the Bank of the United States, the other rejecting Taney's (and, of course, Jackson's too) reasons for withdrawing the deposits:

> Resolved, that by dismissing the late Secretary of the Treasury, because he would not, contrary to his sense of his own duty, remove the money of the United States in deposit with the Bank of the United States and its branches, in conformity with the President's opinion; and by appointing his successor to effect such removal, which has been done, the President has assumed the exercise of a power over the Treasury of the United States not granted to him by the Constitution and laws, and dangerous to the liberties of the people.
>
> Resolved, that the reasons assigned by the Secretary of the Treasury for the removal of the money of the United States, deposited in the Bank of

the United States and its branches, communicated to Congress on the 3rd December, 1833, are unsatisfactory and insufficient.[71]

Clay's attack did not concentrate upon the removal itself, but criticized the illegality of the entire action, arguing that the President had usurped the statutory function of the Congress and without legal sanction had ordered an action which in itself was illegal. The secretary of the treasury, the Kentuckian argued, is "the agent of Congress" according to the congressional charter of the Bank of the United States, and the President had no constitutional or statutory authority to direct this "agent of Congress" to withdraw the governmental funds from the Bank. Clay's argument was long-winded and, although apparently greeted with wild cheers from the Senate gallery, was ineffective in crystallizing any effective action against the President or his administration.

Webster and Calhoun also attacked the President's actions in the course of a long and acrimonious debate stretching out over the next few months. Both senators spoke out frequently against Jackson, as did Clay, but they failed to unite in a specific program or policy in opposition to the President. Calhoun and Webster were interested in rechartering the Bank of the United States, but they both had different proposals and neither could come into agreement with Clay, who was mainly interested in attacking the President for political advantage, rather than in solving any specific problems.

The Clay resolutions, substantially modified, were voted on by the Senate on March 5, 1834. In the resolution condemning the President, the specific charges were removed, and the resolution was rewritten to read:

Resolved, that the President, in the late Executive proceedings in relation to the public revenue, has assumed upon himself authority and power not conferred by the Constitution and laws, but in derogation of both.[72]

In supporting the modification of the original resolution, Clay must have realized the weakness of his case on constitutional grounds. He therefore agreed to transform the unsupportable specific charges, while retaining the vague and general condemnation.

President Jackson's principal supporter in the Senate, Thomas Benton of Missouri, pointed out at the time that the case against the President, if valid, was rightfully punishable by impeachment proceedings. Jackson took the same high ground in a "Protest" sent to the Senate on April 15 in answer to the humiliating resolution passed by that body in March. The President commented upon the extraordinary nature of this action in which one of the major branches of the government had publicly accused the Chief Executive of violating the Constitution and the laws of the land. This necessitated that he defend himself against such charges.

The Jackson paper is a superb argument on constitutional law, exposing the weakness of the Senate case and pointing out the unconstitutional character of its action. To accuse the President of violating the Constitution and not to impeach him for such a crime, Jackson pointed out, is in itself a derogation of duty. The Constitution carefully prescribes a judicial role for the Senate in the case where the President or any other high governmental official has committed such a crime, and yet the Senate violated the Constitution, usurped the constitutional role of the House in initiating such a procedure and itself violated the Constitution by transforming its proper role of an impeachment jury into that of a prosecutor. The fact that the House of Representatives voted against this same resolution strengthened the President's case further still.

In the body of his "Protest," the President went on to defend the action of removing both his secretary of the treasury and the deposits from the Bank of the United States on strict constitutional grounds. No stronger case has been made for the removal power of the President, with the exception of Madison's initial defense in the first session of Congress; the resolute temper and style of the document reinforced the prestige and standing of the man who delivered it to the Senate. This was necessary at the time, for Biddle and the Bank of the United States were hitting at the President with every economic weapon at their disposal. Credit was tightened, some banks floundered, and the public suffered from the effects of this retaliatory attack upon the economic life of the nation.

President Andrew Jackson
Protest to the Senate
April 15, 1834

Richardson, III, 1288-1311.

It appears by the published Journal of the Senate that on the 26th of December last a resolution was offered by a member of the Senate, which after a protracted debate was on the 28th day of March last modified by the mover and passed by the votes of twenty-six Senators out of forty-six who were present and voted, in the following words, viz:

Resolved,

That the President, in the late Executive proceedings in relation to the public revenue, has assumed upon himself authority and power not conferred by the Constitution and laws, but in derogation of both.

Having had the honor, through the voluntary suffrages of the American people, to fill the office of President of the United States during the period which may be presumed to have been referred to in this resolution, it is sufficiently evident that the censure it inflicts was intended for myself. Without notice, unheard and untried, I thus find myself charged on the records of the Senate, and in a form hitherto unknown in our history, with the high crime of violating the laws and Constitution of my country.

It can seldom be necessary for any department of the Government, when assailed in conversation or debate or by the strictures of the press or of popular assemblies, to step out of its ordinary path for the purpose of vindicating its conduct or of pointing out any irregularity or injustice in the manner of the attack; but when the Chief Executive Magistrate is, by one of the most important branches of the

Government in its official capacity, in a public manner, and by its recorded sentence, but without precedent, competent authority, or just cause, declared guilty of a breach of the laws and Constitution, it is due to his station, to public opinion, and to a proper self-respect that the officer thus denounced should promptly expose the wrong which has been done.

In the present case, moreover, there is even a stronger necessity for such a vindication. By an express provision of the Constitution, before the President of the United States can enter on the execution of his office he is required to take an oath or affirmation in the following words:

> I do solemnly swear (or affirm) that I will faithfully execute the office of President of the United States and will to the best of my ability preserve, protect, and defend the Constitution of the United States.

The duty of defending so far as in him lies the integrity of the Constitution would indeed have resulted from the very nature of his office, but by thus expressing it in the official oath or affirmation, which in this respect differs from that of any other functionary, the founders of our Republic have attested their sense of its importance and have given to it a peculiar solemnity and force. Bound to the performance of this duty by the oath I have taken, by the strongest obligations of gratitude to the American people, and by the ties which unite my every earthly interest with the welfare and glory of my country, and perfectly convinced that the discussion and passage of the above-mentioned resolution were not only unauthorized by the Constitution, but in many respects repugnant to its provisions and subversive of the rights secured by it to other coordinate departments, I deem it an imperative duty to maintain the supremacy of that sacred instrument and the immunities of the department intrusted to my care by all means consistent with my own lawful powers, with the rights of others, and with the genius of our civil institutions. To this end I have caused this my *solemn protest* against the aforesaid proceedings to be placed on the files of the executive department and to be transmitted to the Senate.

It is alike due to the subject, the Senate, and the people that the views which I have taken of the proceedings referred to, and which compel me to regard them in the light that has been mentioned, should be exhibited at length, and with the freedom and firmness which are required by an occasion so unprecedented and peculiar.

Under the Constitution of the United States the powers and functions of the various departments of the Federal Government and their responsibilities for violation or neglect of duty are clearly defined or result by necessary inference. The legislative power is, subject to the qualified negative of the President, vested in the Congress of the United States, composed of the Senate and House of Representatives; the executive power is vested exclusively in the President, except that in the conclusion of treaties and in certain appointments to office he is to act with the advice and consent of the Senate; the judicial power is vested exclusively in the Supreme and other courts of the United States, except in cases of impeachment, for which purpose the accusatory power is vested in the House of Representatives and that of hearing and determining in the Senate. But although for the special purposes which have been mentioned there is an occasional intermixture of the powers of the different departments, yet with these exceptions each of the three great departments is independent of the others in its sphere of action, and when it deviates from that sphere is not responsible to the others further than it is expressly made so in the Constitution. In every other respect each of them is the coequal of the other two, and all are the servants of the American people, without power or right to control or censure each other in the service of their common superior, save only in the manner and to the degree which that superior has prescribed.

The responsibilities of the President are numerous and weighty. He is liable to impeachment for high crimes and misdemeanors, and on due conviction to removal from office and perpetual disqualification; and notwithstanding such conviction, he may also be indicted and punished according to law. He is also liable to the private action of any party who may have been injured by his illegal mandates or instructions in the same manner and to the same extent as the humblest functionary. In addition to the responsibilities which may thus be enforced by impeachment, criminal prosecution, or suit at law, he is also accountable at the bar of public opinion for every act of his Administration. Subject only to the restraints of truth and justice, the free people of the United States have the undoubted right, as individuals or collectively, orally or in writing, at such times and in such language and form as they may think proper, to discuss his official conduct and to express and promulgate their opinions concerning it. Indirectly also his conduct may come under review in either branch of the Legislature, or in the Senate when acting in its executive capacity, and so far as the executive or legislative proceedings of these bodies may require it, it may be exercised by them. These are believed to be the proper and only modes in which the President of the United States is to be held accountable for his official conduct.

Tested by these principles, the resolution of the Senate is wholly unauthorized by the Constitution, and in derogation of its entire spirit. It assumes that a single branch of the legislative department may for the purposes of a public censure, and without any view to legislation or impeachment, take up, consider, and decide upon the official acts of the Executive. But in no part of the Constitution is the President subjected to any such responsibility, and in no part of that instrument is any such power conferred on either branch of the Legislature.

The justice of these conclusions will be illustrated and confirmed by a brief analysis of the powers of the Senate and a comparison of their recent proceedings with those powers.

The high functions assigned by the Constitution to the Senate are in their nature either legislative, executive, or judicial. It is only in the exercise of its judicial powers, when sitting as a court for the trial of impeachments, that the Senate is expressly authorized and necessarily required to consider and decide upon the conduct of the President or any other public officer. Indirectly, however, as has already been suggested, it may frequently be called on to perform that office. Cases may occur in the course of its legislative or executive proceedings in which it may be indispensable to the proper exercise of its powers that it should inquire into and decide upon the conduct of the President or other public officers, and in every such case its constitutional right to do so is cheerfully conceded. But to authorize the

Senate to enter on such a task in its legislative or executive capacity the inquiry must actually grow out of and tend to some legislative or executive action, and the decision, when expressed, must take the form of some appropriate legislative or executive act.

The resolution in question was introduced, discussed, and passed not as a joint but as a separate resolution. It asserts no legislative power, proposes no legislative action, and neither possesses the form nor any of the attributes of a legislative measure. It does not appear to have been entertained or passed with any view or expectation of its issuing in a law or joint resolution, or in the repeal of any law or joint resolution, or in any other legislative action.

Whilst wanting both the form and substance of a legislative measure, it is equally manifest that the resolution was not justified by any of the executive powers conferred on the Senate. These powers relate exclusively to the consideration of treaties and nominations to office, and they are exercised in secret session and with closed doors. This resolution does not apply to any treaty or nomination, and was passed in a public session.

Nor does this proceeding in any way belong to that class of incidental resolutions which relate to the officers of the Senate, to their Chamber and other appurtenances, or to subjects of order and other matters of the like nature, in all which either House may lawfully proceed without any cooperation with the other or with the President.

On the contrary, the whole phraseology and sense of the resolution seem to be judicial. Its essence, true character, and only practical effect are to be found in the conduct which it charges upon the President and in the judgment which it pronounces on that conduct. The resolution, therefore, though discussed and adopted by the Senate in its legislative capacity, is in its office and in all its characteristics essentially judicial.

That the Senate possesses a high judicial power and that instances may occur in which the President of the United States will be amenable to it is undeniable; but under the provisions of the Constitution it would seem to be equally plain that neither the President nor any other officer can be rightfully subjected to the operation of the judicial power of the Senate except in the cases and under the forms prescribed by the Constitution.

The Constitution declares that "the President, Vice-President, and all civil officers of the United States shall be removed from office on impeachment for and conviction of treason, bribery, or other high crimes and misdemeanors;" that the House of Representatives "shall have the sole power of impeachment;" that the Senate "shall have the sole power to try all impeachments;" that "when sitting for that purpose they shall be on oath or affirmation;" that "when the President of the United States is tried the Chief Justice shall preside;" that "no person shall be convicted without the concurrence of two-thirds of the members present," and that "judgment shall not extend further than to removal from office and disqualification to hold and enjoy any office of honor, trust, or profit under the United States."

The resolution above quoted charges, in substance, that in certain proceedings relating to the public revenue the President has usurped authority and power not conferred upon him by the Constitution and laws, and that in doing so he violated both. Any such act constitutes a high crime—one of the highest, indeed, which the President can commit—a crime which justly exposes him to impeachment by the House of Representatives, and, upon due conviction, to removal from office and to the complete and immutable disfranchisement prescribed by the Constitution. The resolution, then, was in substance an impeachment of the President, and in its passage amounts to a declaration by a majority of the Senate that he is guilty of an impeachable offense. As such it is spread upon the journals of the Senate, published to the nation and to the world, made part of our enduring archives, and incorporated in the history of the age. The punishment of removal from office and future disqualification does not, it is true, follow this decision, nor would it have followed the like decision if the regular forms of proceeding had been pursued, because the requisite number did not concur in the result. But the moral influence of a solemn declaration by a majority of the Senate that the accused is guilty of the offense charged upon him has been as effectually secured as if the like declaration had been made upon an impeachment expressed in the same terms. Indeed, a greater practical effect has been gained, because the votes given for the resolution, though not sufficient to authorize a judgment of guilty on an impeachment, were numerous enough to carry that resolution.

That the resolution does not expressly allege that the assumption of power and authority which it condemns was intentional and corrupt is no answer to the preceding view of its character and effect. The act thus condemned necessarily implies volition and design in the individual to whom it is imputed, and, being unlawful in its character, the legal conclusion is that it was prompted by improper motives and committed with an unlawful intent. The charge is not of a mistake in the exercise of supposed powers, but of the assumption of powers not conferred by the Constitution and laws, but in derogation of both, and nothing is suggested to excuse or palliate the turpitude of the act. In the absence of any such excuse or palliation there is only room for one inference, and that is that the intent was unlawful and corrupt. Besides, the resolution not only contains no mitigating suggestions, but, on the contrary, it holds up the act complained of as justly obnoxious to censure and reprobation, and thus as distinctly stamps it with impurity of motive as if the strongest epithets had been used.

The President of the United States, therefore, has been by a majority of his constitutional triers accused and found guilty of an impeachable offense, but in no part of this proceeding have the directions of the Constitution been observed.

The impeachment, instead of being preferred and prosecuted by the House of Representatives, originated in the Senate, and was prosecuted without the aid or concurrence of the other House. The oath or affirmation prescribed by the Constitution was not taken by the Senators, the Chief Justice did not preside, no notice of the charge was given to the accused, and no opportunity afforded him to respond to the accusation, to meet his accusers face to face, to cross-examine the witnesses, to procure counteracting testimony, or to be heard in his defense. The safeguards and formalities which the Constitution has connected with the power of impeachment were doubtless supposed by the framers of that instrument to be essential to the protection of the public servant, to the attainment of justice, and to the order, impartiality, and dignity of the procedure. These safeguards and formalities were not only practically disregarded in the commencement and conduct of these proceedings, but in their result I find myself convicted by less than two-thirds of the members present of an impeachable offense.

In vain may it be alleged in defense of this proceeding that the form of the resolution is not that of an impeachment or of a judgment thereupon, that the punishment prescribed in the Constitution does not follow its adoption, or that in this case no impeachment is to be expected from the House of Representatives. It is because it did not assume the form of an impeachment that it is the more palpably repugnant to the Constitution, for it is through that form only that the President is judicially responsible to the Senate; and though neither removal from office nor future disqualification ensues, yet it is not to be presumed that the framers of the Constitution considered either or both of those results as constituting the whole of the punishment they prescribed. The judgment of *guilty* by the highest tribunal in the Union, the stigma it would inflict on the offender, his family, and fame, and the perpetual record on the Journal, handing down to future generations the story of his disgrace, were doubtless regarded by them as the bitterest portions, if not the very essence, of that punishment. So far, therefore, as some of its most material parts are concerned, the passage, recording, and promulgation of the resolution are an attempt to bring them on the President in a manner unauthorized by the Constitution. To shield him and other officers who are liable to impeachment from consequences so momentous, except when really merited by official delinquencies, the Constitution has most carefully guarded the whole process of impeachment. A majority of the House of Representatives must think the officer guilty before he can be charged. Two-thirds of the Senate must pronounce him guilty or he is deemed to be innocent. Forty-six Senators appear by the Journal to have been present when the vote on the resolution was taken. If after all the solemnities of an impeachment thirty of those Senators had voted that the President was guilty, yet would he have been acquitted; but by the mode of proceeding adopted in the present case a lasting record of conviction has been entered up by the votes of twenty-six Senators without an impeachment or trial, whilst the Constitution expressly declares that to the entry of such a judgment an accusation by the House of Representatives, a trial by the Senate, and a concurrence of two-thirds in the vote of guilty shall be indispensable prerequisites.

Whether or not an impeachment was to be expected from the House of Representatives was a point on which the Senate had no constitutional right to speculate, and in respect to which, even had it possessed the spirit of prophecy, its anticipations would have furnished no just ground for this procedure. Admitting that there was reason to believe that a violation of the Constitution and laws had been actually committed by the President, still it was the duty of the Senate, as his sole constitutional judges, to wait for an impeachment until the other House should think proper to prefer it. The members of the Senate could have no right to infer that no impeachment was intended. On the contrary, every legal and rational presumption on their part ought to have been that if there was good reason to believe him guilty of an impeachable offense the House of Representatives would perform its constitutional duty by arraigning the offender before the justice of his country. The contrary presumption would involve an implication derogatory to the integrity and honor of the representatives of the people. But suppose the suspicion thus implied were actually entertained and for good cause, how can it justify the assumption by the Senate of powers not conferred by the Constitution?

It is only necessary to look at the condition in which the Senate and the President have been placed by this proceeding to perceive its utter incompatibility with the provisions and the spirit of the Constitution and with the plainest dictates of humanity and justice.

If the House of Representatives shall be of opinion that there is just ground for the censure pronounced upon the President, then will it be the solemn duty of that House to prefer the proper accusation and to cause him to be brought to trial by the constitutional tribunal. But in what condition would he find that tribunal? A majority of its members have already considered the case, and have not only formed but expressed a deliberate judgment upon its merits. It is the policy of our benign systems of jurisprudence to secure in all criminal proceedings, and even in the most trivial litigations, a fair, unprejudiced, and impartial trial, and surely it can not be less important that such a trial should be secured to the highest officer of the Government.

The Constitution makes the House of Representatives the exclusive judges, in the first instance, of the question whether the President has committed an impeachable offense. A majority of the Senate, whose interference with this preliminary question has for the best of all reasons been studiously excluded, anticipate the action of the House of Representatives, assume not only the function which belongs exclusively to that body, but convert themselves into accusers, witnesses, counsel, and judges, and prejudge the whole case, thus presenting the appalling spectacle in a free State of judges going through a labored preparation for an impartial hearing and decision by a previous *ex parte* investigation and sentence against the supposed offender.

There is no more settled axiom in that Government whence we derived the model of this part of our Constitution than that "the lords can not impeach any to themselves, nor join in the accusation, *because they are judges*." Independently of the general reasons on which this rule is founded, its propriety and importance are greatly increased by the nature of the impeaching power. The power of arraigning the high officers of government before a tribunal whose sentence may expel them from their seats and brand them as infamous is eminently a popular remedy—a remedy designed to be employed for the protection of private right and public liberty against the abuses of injustice and the encroachments of arbitrary power. But the framers of the Constitution were also undoubtedly aware that this formidable instrument had been and might be abused, and that from its very nature an impeachment for high crimes and misdemeanors, whatever might be its result, would in most cases be accompanied by so much of dishonor and reproach, solicitude and suffering, as to make the power of preferring it one of the highest solemnity and importance. It was due to both these considerations that the impeaching power should be lodged in the hands of those who from the mode of their election and the tenure of their offices would most accurately express the popular will and at the same time be most directly and speedily amenable to the people. The theory of these wise and benignant intentions is in the present case effectually defeated by the proceedings of the Senate. The members of that body represent not the people, but the States; and though they are undoubtedly responsible to the States, yet from their extended term of service the effect of that responsibility during the whole period of that term must very much depend upon their own impressions of its obligatory force. When a body thus constituted expresses beforehand its opinion in a particular case, and thus indirectly invites a prosecution, it not only assumes a power intended for wise reasons to be confined to others, but it shields the latter from that exclusive and personal responsibility under which it was intended to be exercised, and reverses the whole scheme of this part of the Constitution.

Such would be some of the objections to this procedure, even if it were admitted that there is just ground for imputing to the President the offenses charged in the resolution. But if, on the other hand, the House of Representatives shall be of opinion that there is no reason for charging them upon him, and shall therefore deem it improper to prefer an impeachment, then will the violation of privilege as it respects that House, of justice as it regards the President, and of the Constitution as it relates to both be only the more conspicuous and impressive.

The constitutional mode of procedure on an impeachment has not only been wholly disregarded, but some of the first principles of natural right and enlightened jurisprudence have been violated in the very form of the resolution. It carefully abstains from averring in *which* of "the late proceedings in relation to the public revenue the President has assumed upon himself authority and power not conferred by the Constitution and laws." It carefully abstains from specifying *what laws* or *what parts* of the Constitution have been violated. Why was not the certainty of the offense—"the nature and cause of the accusation"—set out in the manner required in the Constitution before even the humblest individual, for the smallest crime, can be exposed to condemnation? Such a specification was due to the accused that he might direct his defense to the real points of attack, to the people that they might clearly understand in what particulars their institutions had been violated, and to the truth and certainty of our public annals. As the record now stands, whilst the resolution plainly charges upon the President at least one act of usurpation in "the late Executive proceedings in relation to the public revenue," and is so framed that those Senators who believed that one such act, and only one, had been committed could assent to it, its language is yet broad enough to include several such acts, and so it may have been regarded by some of those who voted for it. But though the accusation is thus comprehensive in the censures it implies, there is no such certainty of time, place, or circumstance as to exhibit the particular conclusion of fact or law which induced any one Senator to vote for it; and it may well have happened that whilst one Senator believed that some particular act embraced in the resolution was an arbitrary and unconstitutional assumption of power, others of the majority may have deemed that very act both constitutional and expedient, or, if not expedient, yet still within the pale of the Constitution; and thus a majority of the Senators may have been enabled to concur in a vague and undefined accusation that the President, in the course of "the late Executive proceedings in relation to the public revenue," had violated the Constitution and laws, whilst if a separate vote had been taken in respect to each particular act included within the general terms the accusers of the President might on any such vote have been found in the minority.

Still further to exemplify this feature of the proceeding, it is important to be remarked that the resolution as originally offered to the Senate specified with adequate precision certain acts of the President which it denounced as a violation of the Constitution and laws, and that it was not until the very close of the debate, and when perhaps it was apprehended that a majority might not sustain the specific accusation contained in it, that the resolution was so modified as to assume its present form. A more striking illustration of the soundness and necessity of the rules which forbid vague and indefinite generalities and require a reasonable certainty in all judicial allegations, and a more glaring instance of the violation of those rules, has seldom been exhibited.

In this view of the resolution it must certainly be regarded not as a vindication of any particular provision of the law or the Constitution, but simply as an official rebuke or condemnatory sentence, too general and indefinite to be easily repelled, but yet sufficiently precise to bring into discredit the conduct and motives of the Executive. But whatever it may have been intended to accomplish, it is obvious that the vague, general, and abstract form of the resolution is in perfect keeping with those other departures from first principles and settled improvements in jurisprudence so properly the boast of free countries in modern times. And it is not too much to say of the whole of these proceedings that if they shall be approved and sustained by an intelligent people, then will that great contest with arbitrary power which had established in statutes, in bills of rights, in sacred charters, and in constitutions of government the right of every citizen to a notice before trial, to a hearing before conviction, and to an impartial tribunal for deciding on the charge have been waged in vain.

If the resolution had been left in its original form it is not to be presumed that it could ever have received the assent of a majority of the Senate, for the acts therein specified as violations of the Constitution and laws were clearly within the limits of the Executive authority. They are the "dismissing the late Secretary of the Treasury because he would not, contrary to his sense of his own duty, remove the money of the United States in deposit with the Bank of the United States and its branches in conformity with the President's opinion, and appointing his successor to effect such removal, which has been done." But as no other specification has been substituted, and as these were the "Executive proceedings in relation to the public revenue" principally referred to in the course of the discussion, they will doubtless be generally regarded as the acts intended to be denounced as "an assumption of authority and power not conferred by the Constitution or laws, but in derogation of both." It is therefore due to the occasion that a condensed summary of the views of the Executive in respect to them should be here exhibited.

By the Constitution "the executive power is vested in a President of the United States." Among the duties imposed upon him, and which he is sworn to perform, is that of "taking care that the laws be faithfully executed." Being thus made responsible for the entire action of the executive department, it was but reasonable that the power of appointing, overseeing, and controlling those who execute the laws—a power in its nature executive—should remain in his hands. It is therefore not only his right, but the Constitution makes it his duty, to "nominate and, by and with the advice and consent of the Senate, appoint" all "officers of the United States whose appointments are not in the Constitution otherwise provided for," with a proviso that the appointment of inferior officers may be vested in the President alone, in the courts of justice, or in the heads of Departments.

The executive power vested in the Senate is neither that of "nominating" nor "appointing." It is merely a check upon the Executive power of appointment. If individuals are proposed for appointment by the President by them deemed incompetent or unworthy, they may withhold their consent and the appointment can not be made. They check the action of the Executive, but can not in relation to those very subjects act themselves nor direct him. Selections are still made by the President, and the negative given to the Senate, without diminishing his responsibility, furnishes an additional guaranty to the country that the subordinate executive as well as the judicial offices shall be filled with worthy and competent men.

The whole executive power being vested in the President, who is responsible for its exercise, it is a necessary consequence that he should have a right to employ agents of his own choice to aid him in the performance of his duties, and to discharge them when he is no longer willing to be responsible for their acts. In strict accordance with this principle, the power of removal, which, like that of appointment, is an original executive power, is left unchecked by the Constitution in relation to all executive officers, for whose conduct the President is responsible, while it is taken from him in relation to judicial officers, for whose acts he is not responsible. In the Government from which many of the fundamental principles of our system are derived the head of the executive department originally had power to appoint and remove at will all officers, executive and judicial. It was to take the judges out of this general power of removal, and thus make them independent of the Executive, that the tenure of their offices was changed to good behavior. Nor is it conceivable why they are placed in our Constitution upon a tenure different from that of all other officers appointed by the Executive unless it be for the same purpose.

But if there were any just ground for doubt on the face of the Constitution whether all executive officers are removable at the will of the President, it is obviated by the cotemporaneous construction of the instrument and the uniform practice under it.

The power of removal was a topic of solemn debate in the Congress of 1789 while organizing the administrative departments of the Government, and it was finally decided that the President derived from the Constitution the power of removal so far as it regards that department for whose acts he is responsible. Although the debate covered the whole ground, embracing the Treasury as well as all the other Executive Departments, it arose on a motion to strike out of the bill to establish a Department of Foreign Affairs, since called the Department of State, a clause declaring the Secretary "to be removable from office by the President of the United States." After that motion had been decided in the negative it was perceived that these words did not convey the sense of the House of Representatives in relation to the true source of the power of removal. With the avowed object of preventing any future inference that this power was exercised by the President in virtue of a grant from Congress, when in fact that body considered it as derived from the Constitution, the words which had been the subject of debate were struck out, and in lieu thereof a clause was inserted in a provision concerning the chief clerk of the Department, which declared that "whenever the said principal officer shall be removed from office by the President of the United States, or in any other case of vacancy," the chief clerk should during such vacancy have charge of the papers of the office. This change having been made for the express purpose of declaring the sense of Congress that the President derived the power of removal from the Constitution, the act as it passed has always been considered as a full expression of the sense of the Legislature on this important part of the American Constitution.

Here, then, we have the concurrent authority of President Washington, of the Senate, and the House of Representatives, numbers of whom had taken an active part in the convention which framed the Constitution and in the State conventions which adopted it, that the President derived an unqualified power of removal from that instrument itself, which is "beyond the reach of legislative authority." Upon this principle the Government has now been steadily administered for about forty-five years, during which there have been numerous removals made by the President or by his direction, embracing every grade of executive officers from the heads of Departments to the messengers of bureaus.

The Treasury Department in the discussions of 1789 was considered on the same footing as the other Executive Departments, and in the act establishing it were incorporated the precise words indicative of the sense of Congress that the President derives his power to remove the Secretary from the Constitution, which appear in the act establishing the Department of Foreign Affairs. An Assistant Secretary of the Treasury was created, and it was provided that he should take charge of the books and papers of the Department "whenever the Secretary shall be removed from office by the President of the United States." The Secretary of the Treasury being appointed by the President, and being considered as constitutionally removable by him, it appears never to have occurred to anyone in the Congress of 1789, or since until very recently, that he was other than an executive officer, the mere instrument of the Chief Magistrate in the execution of the laws, subject, like all other heads of Departments, to his supervision and control. No such idea as an officer of the Congress can be found in the Constitution or appears to have suggested itself to those who organized the Government. There are officers of each House the appointment of which is authorized by the Constitution, but all officers referred to in that instrument as coming within the appointing power of the President, whether established thereby or created by law, are "officers of the United States." No joint power of appointment is given to the two Houses of Congress, nor is there any accountability to them as one body; but as soon as any office is created by law, of whatever name or character, the appointment of the person or persons to fill it devolves by the Constitution upon the President, with the advice and consent of the Senate, unless it be an inferior office, and the appointment be vested by the law itself "in the President alone, in the courts of law, or in the heads of Departments."

But at the time of the organization of the Treasury Department an incident occurred which distinctly evinces the unanimous concurrence of the First Congress in the principle that the Treasury Department is wholly executive in its character and responsibilities. A motion was made to strike out the provision of the bill making it the duty of the Secretary "to digest and report plans for the improvement and management of the revenue and for the support of public credit," on the ground that it would give the executive department of the Government too much influence and power in Congress. The motion was not opposed on the ground that the Secretary was the officer of Congress and responsibile to that body, which would have been conclusive if admitted, but on other ground, which conceded his executive character throughout. The whole discussion evinces an unanimous concurrence in the principle that the Secretary of the Treasury is wholly an executive officer, and the struggle of the minority was to restrict his power as such. From that time down to the present the Secretary of the Treasury, the Treasurer, Register, Comptrollers, Auditors, and clerks who fill the offices of that Department have in the practice of the Government been considered and treated as on the same footing with corresponding grades of officers in all the other Executive Departments.

The custody of the public property, under such regulations as may be prescribed by legislative authority, has always been considered an appropriate function of the executive department in this and all other Governments. In accordance with this principle, every species of property belonging to the United States (excepting that which is in the use of the several coordinate departments of the Government as means to aid them in performing their appropriate functions) is in charge of officers appointed by the President, whether it be lands, or buildings, or merchandise, or provisions, or clothing, or arms and munitions of war. The superintendents and keepers of the whole are appointed by the President, responsible to him, and removable at his will.

Public money is but a species of public property. It can not be raised by taxation or customs, nor brought into the Treasury in any other way except by law; but whenever or howsoever obtained, its custody always has been and always must be, unless the Constitution be changed, intrusted to the executive department. No officer can be created by Congress for the purpose of taking charge of it whose appointment would not by the Constitution at once devolve on the President and who would not be responsible to him for the faithful performance of his duties. The legislative power may undoubtedly bind him and the President by any laws they may think proper to enact; they may prescribe in what place particular portions of the public property shall be kept and for what reason it shall be removed, as they may direct that supplies for the Army or Navy shall be kept in particular stores, and it will be the duty of the President to see that the law is faithfully executed; yet will the custody remain in the executive department of the Government. Were the Congress to assume, with or without a legislative act, the power of appointing officers, independently of the President, to take the charge and custody of the public property contained in the military and naval arsenals, magazines, and storehouses, it is believed that such an act would be regarded by all as a palpable usurpation of executive power, subversive of the form as well as the fundamental principles of our

Government. But where is the difference in principle whether the public property be in the form of arms, munitions of war, and supplies or in gold and silver or bank notes? None can be perceived; none is believed to exist. Congress can not, therefore, take out of the hands of the executive department the custody of the public property or money without an assumption of executive power and a subversion of the first principles of the Constitution.

The Congress of the United States have never passed an act imperatively directing that the public moneys shall be kept in any particular place or places. From the origin of the Government to the year 1816 the statute book was wholly silent on the subject. In 1789 a Treasurer was created, subordinate to the Secretary of the Treasury, and through him to the President. He was required to give bond safely to keep and faithfully to disburse the public moneys, without any direction as to the manner or places in which they should be kept. By reference to the practice of the Government it is found that from its first organization the Secretary of the Treasury, acting under the supervision of the President, designated the places in which the public moneys should be kept, and especially directed all transfers from place to place. This practice was continued, with the silent acquiescence of Congress, from 1789 down to 1816, and although many banks were selected and discharged, and although a portion of the moneys were first placed in the State banks, and then in the former Bank of the United States, and upon the dissolution of that were again transferred to the State banks, no legislation was thought necessary by Congress, and all the operations were originated and perfected by Executive authority. The Secretary of the Treasury, responsible to the President, and with his approbation, made contracts and arrangements in relation to the whole subject-matter, which was thus entirely committed to the direction of the President under his responsibilities to the American people and to those who were authorized to impeach and punish him for any breach of this important trust.

The act of 1816 establishing the Bank of the United States directed the deposits of public money to be made in that bank and its branches in places in which the said bank and branches thereof may be established, "unless the Secretary of the Treasury should otherwise order and direct," in which event he was required to give his reasons to Congress. This was but a continuation of his preexisting power as the head of an Executive Department to direct where the deposits should be made, with the superadded obligation of giving his reasons to Congress for making them elsewhere than in the Bank of the United States and its branches. It is not to be considered that this provision in any degree altered the relation between the Secretary of the Treasury and the President as the responsible head of the executive department, or released the latter from his constitutional obligation to "take care that the laws be faithfully executed." On the contrary, it increased his responsibilities by adding another to the long list of laws which it was his duty to carry into effect.

It would be an extraordinary result if because the person charged by law with a public duty is one of his Secretaries it were less the duty of the President to see that law faithfully executed than other laws enjoining duties upon subordinate officers or private citizens. If there be any difference, it would seem that the obligation is the stronger in relation to the former, because the neglect is in his presence and the remedy at hand.

It can not be doubted that it was the legal duty of the Secretary of the Treasury to order and direct the deposits of the public money to be made elsewhere than in the Bank of the United States *whenever sufficient reasons existed for making the change.* If in such a case he neglected or refused to act, he would neglect or refuse to execute the law. What would be the sworn duty of the President? Could he say that the Constitution did not bind him to see the law faithfully executed because it was one of his Secretaries and not himself upon whom the service was specially imposed? Might he not be asked whether there was any such limitation to his obligations prescribed in the Constitution? Whether he is not equally bound to take care that the laws be faithfully executed, whether they impose duties on the highest officer of State or the lowest subordinate in any of the Departments? Might he not be told that it was for the sole purpose of causing all executive officers, from the highest to the lowest, faithfully to perform the services required of them by law that the people of the United States have made him their Chief Magistrate and the Constitution has clothed him with the entire executive power of this Government? The principles implied in these questions appear too plain to need elucidation.

But here also we have a cotemporaneous construction of the act which shows that it was not understood as in any way changing the relations between the President and Secretary of the Treasury, or as placing the latter out of Executive control even in relation to the deposits of the public money. Nor on that point are we left to any equivocal testimony. The documents of the Treasury Department show that the Secretary of the Treasury did apply to the President and obtained his approbation and sanction to the original transfer of the public deposits to the present Bank of the United States, and did carry the measure into effect in obedience to his decision. They also show that transfers of the public deposits from the branches of the Bank of the United States to State banks at Chillicothe, Cincinnati, and Louisville, in 1819, were made with the approbation of the President and by his authority. They show that upon all important questions appertaining to his Department, whether they related to the public deposits or other matters, it was the constant practice of the Secretary of the Treasury to obtain for his acts the approval and sanction of the President. These acts and the principles on which they were founded were known to all the departments of the Government, to Congress and the country, and until very recently appear never to have been called in question.

Thus was it settled by the Constitution, the laws, and the whole practice of the Government that the entire executive power is vested in the President of the United States; that as incident to that power the right of appointing and removing those officers who are to aid him in the execution of the laws, with such restrictions only as the Constitution prescribes, is vested in the President; that the Secretary of the Treasury is one of those officers; that the custody of the public property and money is an Executive function which, in relation to the money, has always been exercised through the Secretary of the Treasury and his subordinates; that in the performance of these duties he is subject to the supervision and control of the President, and in all important measures having relation to them consults the Chief Magistrate and obtains his approval and sanction; that the law establishing the bank did not, as it could not, change the relation between the President and the Secretary—did not release the former from his obligation to see the law faithfully executed nor the latter from the President's supervision and control; that afterwards and before the Secretary did in fact consult and obtain the sanction of the President to transfers and removals of the public deposits, and that all departments of the Government, and the nation itself, approved or acquiesced in these acts and principles as in strict conformity with our Constitution and laws.

During the last year the approaching termination, according to the provisions of its charter and the solemn decision of the American people, of the Bank of the United States made it expedient, and its exposed abuses and corruptions made it, in my opinion, the duty of the Secretary of the Treasury, to place the moneys of the United States in other depositories. The Secretary did not concur in that opinion, and declined giving the necessary order and direction. So glaring were the abuses and corruptions of the bank, so evident its fixed purpose to persevere in them, and so palpable its design by its money and power to control the Government and change its character, that I deemed it the imperative duty of the Executive authority, by the exertion of every power confided to it by the Constitution and laws, to check its career and lessen its ability to do mischief, even in the painful alternative of dismissing the head of one of the Departments. At the time the removal was made other causes sufficient to justify it existed, but if they had not the Secretary would have been dismissed for this cause only.

His place I supplied by one whose opinions were well known to me, and whose frank expression of them in another situation and generous sacrifices of interest and feeling when unexpectedly called to the station he now occupies ought forever to have shielded his motives from suspicion and his character from reproach. In accordance with the views long before expressed by him he proceeded, with my sanction, to make arrangements for depositing the moneys of the United States in other safe institutions.

The resolution of the Senate as originally framed and as passed, if it refers to these acts, presupposes a right in that body to interfere with this exercise of Executive power. If the principle be once admitted, it is not difficult to perceive where it may end. If by a mere denunciation like this resolution the President should ever be induced to act in a matter of official duty contrary to the honest convictions of his own mind in compliance with the wishes of the Senate, the constitutional independence of the executive department would be as effectually destroyed and its power as effectually transferred to the Senate as if that end had been accomplished by an amendment of the Constitution. But if the Senate have a right to interfere with the Executive powers, they have also the right to make that interference effective, and if the assertion of the power implied in the resolution be silently acquiesced in we may reasonably apprehend that it will be followed at some future day by an attempt at actual enforcement. The Senate may refuse, except on the condition that he will surrender his opinions to theirs and obey their will, to perform their own constitutional functions, to pass the necessary laws, to sanction appropriations proposed by the House of Representatives, and to confirm proper nominations made by the President. It has already been maintained (and it is not conceivable that the resolution of the Senate can be based on any other principle) that the Secretary of the Treasury is the officer of Congress and independent of the President; that the President has no right to control him, and consequently none to remove him. With the same propriety and on similar grounds may the Secretary of State, the Secretaries of War and the Navy, and the Postmaster-General each in succession be declared independent of the President, the subordinates of Congress, and removable only with the concurrence of the Senate. Followed to its consequences, this principle will be found effectually to destroy one coordinate department of the Government, to concentrate in the hands of the Senate the whole executive power, and to leave the President as powerless as he would be useless—the shadow of authority after the substance had departed.

The time and the occasion which have called forth the resolution of the Senate seem to impose upon me an additional obligation not to pass it over in silence. Nearly forty-five years had the President exercised, without a question as to his rightful authority, those powers for the recent assumption of which he is now denounced. The vicissitudes of peace and war had attended our Government; violent parties, watchful to take advantage of any seeming usurpation on the part of the Executive, had distracted our councils; frequent removals, or forced resignations in every sense tantamount to removals, had been made of the Secretary and other officers of the Treasury, and yet in no one instance is it known that any man, whether patriot or partisan, had raised his voice against it as a violation of the Constitution. The expediency and justice of such changes in reference to public officers of all grades have frequently been the topic of discussion, but the constitutional right of the President to appoint, control, and remove the head of the Treasury as well as all other Departments seems to have been universally conceded. And what is the occasion upon which other principles have been first officially asserted? The Bank of the United States, a great moneyed monopoly, had attempted to obtain a renewal of its charter by controlling the elections of the people and the action of the Government. The use of its corporate funds and power in that attempt was fully disclosed, and it was made known to the President that the corporation was putting in train the same course of measures, with the view of making another vigorous effort, through an interference in the elections of the people, to control public opinion and force the Government to yield to its demands. This, with its corruption of the press, its violation of its charter, its exclusion of the Government directors from its proceedings, its neglect of duty and arrogant pretensions, made it, in the opinion of the President, incompatible with the public interest and the safety of our institutions that it should be longer employed as the fiscal agent of the Treasury. A Secretary of the Treasury appointed in the recess of the Senate, who had not been confirmed by that body, and whom the President might or might not at his pleasure nominate to them, refused to do what his superior in the executive department considered the most imperative of his duties, and became in fact, however innocent his motives, the protector of the bank. And on this occasion it is discovered for the first time that those who framed the Constitution misunderstood it; that the First Congress and all its successors have been under a delusion; that the practice of near forty-five years is but a continued usurpation; that the Secretary of the Treasury is not responsible to the President, and that to remove him is a violation of the Constitution and laws for which the President deserves to stand forever dishonored on the journals of the Senate.

There are also some other circumstances connected with the discussion and passage of the resolution to which I feel it to be not only my right, but my duty, to refer. It appears by the Journal of the Senate that among the twenty-six Senators who voted for the resolution on its final passage, and who had supported it in debate in its original form, were one of the Senators from the State of Maine, the two Senators from New Jersey, and one of the Senators from Ohio. It also appears by the same Journal and by the files of the Senate that the legislatures of these States had severally expressed their opinions in respect to the Executive proceedings drawn in question before the Senate.

The two branches of the legislature of the State of Maine on the 25th of January, 1834, passed a preamble and series of resolutions in the following words:

Whereas at an early period after the election of Andrew Jackson to the Presidency, in accordance with the sentiments which he had uniformly expressed, the attention of Congress was called to the constitutionality and expediency of the renewal of the charter of the United States Bank; and

Whereas the bank has transcended its chartered limits in the management of its business transactions, and has abandoned the object of its creation by engaging in political controversies, by wielding its power and influence to embarrass the Administration of the General Government, and by bringing insolvency and distress upon the commercial community; and

Whereas the public security from such an institution consists less in its present pecuniary capacity to discharge its liabilities than in the fidelity with which the trusts reposed in it have been executed; and

Whereas the abuse and misapplication of the powers conferred have destroyed the confidence of the public in the officers of the bank and demonstrated that such powers endanger the stability of republican institutions: Therefore,

Resolved, That in the removal of the public deposits from the Bank of the United States, as well as in the manner of their removal, we recognize in the Administration an adherence to constitutional rights and the performance of a public duty.

Resolved, That this legislature entertain the same opinion as heretofore expressed by preceding legislatures of this State, that the Bank of the United States ought not to be rechartered.

Resolved, That the Senators of this State in the Congress of the United States be instructed and the Representatives be requested to oppose the restoration of the deposits and the renewal of the charter of the United States Bank.

On the 11th of January, 1834, the house of assembly and council composing the legislature of the State of New Jersey passed a preamble and a series of resolutions in the following words:

Whereas the present crisis in our public affairs calls for a decided expression of the voice of the people of this State; and

Whereas we consider it the undoubted right of the legislatures of the several States to instruct those who represent their interests in the councils of the nation in all matters which intimately concern the public weal and may affect the happiness or well-being of the people: Therefore,

1. Be it resolved by the council and general assembly of this State, That while we acknowledge with feelings of devout gratitude our obligations to the Great Ruler of Nations for His mercies to us as a people that we have been preserved alike from foreign war, from the evils of internal commotions, and the machinations of designing and ambitious men who would prostrate the fair fabric of our Union, that we ought nevertheless to humble ourselves in His presence and implore His aid for the perpetuation of our republican institutions and for a continuance of that unexampled prosperity which our country has hitherto enjoyed.

2. Resolved, That we have undiminished confidence in the integrity and firmness of the venerable patriot who now holds the distinguished post of Chief Magistrate of this nation, and whose purity of purpose and elevated motives have so often received the unqualified approbation of a large majority of his fellow-citizens.

3. Resolved, That we view with agitation and alarm the existence of a great moneyed incorporation which threatens to embarrass the operations of the Government and by means of its unbounded influence upon the currency of the country to scatter distress and ruin throughout the community, and that we therefore solemnly believe the present Bank of the United States ought not to be rechartered.

4. Resolved, That our Senators in Congress be instructed and our members of the House of Representatives be requested to sustain, by their votes and influence, the course adopted by the Secretary of the Treasury, Mr. Taney, in relation to the Bank of the United States and the deposits of the Government moneys, believing as we do the course of the Secretary to have been constitutional, and that the public good required its adoption.

5. Resolved, That the governor be requested to forward a copy of the above resolutions to each of our Senators and Representatives from this State to the Congress of the United States.

On the 21st day of February last the legislature of the same State reiterated the opinions and instructions before given by joint resolutions in the following words:

Resolved by the council and general assembly of the State of New Jersey, That they do adhere to the resolutions passed by them on the 11th day of January last, relative to the President of the United States, the Bank of the United States, and the course of Mr. Taney in removing the Government deposits.

Resolved, That the legislature of New Jersey have not seen any reason to depart from such resolutions since the passage thereof, and it is their wish that they should receive from our Senators and Representatives of this State in the Congress of the United States that attention and obedience which are due to the opinion of a sovereign State openly expressed in its legislative capacity.

On the 2d of January, 1834, the senate and house of representatives composing the legislature of Ohio passed a preamble and resolutions in the following words:

Whereas there is reason to believe that the Bank of the United States will attempt to obtain a renewal of its charter at the present session of Congress; and

Whereas it is abundantly evident that said bank has exercised powers derogatory to the spirit of our free institutions and dangerous to the liberties of these United States; and

Whereas there is just reason to doubt the constitutional power of Congress to grant acts of incorporation for banking purposes out of the District of Columbia; and

Whereas we believe the proper disposal of the public lands to be of the utmost importance to the people of these United States, and that honor and good faith require their equitable distribution: Therefore,

Resolved by the general assembly of the State of Ohio, That we consider the removal of the public deposits from the Bank of the United States as required by the best interests of our country, and that a proper sense of public duty imperiously demanded that that institution should be no longer used as a depository of the public funds.

Resolved also, That we view with decided disapprobation the renewed attempts in Congress to secure the passage of the bill providing for the disposal of the public domain upon the principles proposed by Mr. Clay, inasmuch as we believe that such a law would be unequal in its operations and unjust in its results.

Resolved also, That we heartily approve of the principles set forth in the late veto message upon that subject; and

Resolved, That our Senators in Congress be instructed and our Representatives requested to use their influence to prevent the rechartering of the Bank of the United States, to sustain the Administration in its removal of the public deposits, and to oppose the passage of a land bill containing the principles adopted in the act upon that subject passed at the last session of Congress.

Resolved, That the governor be requested to transmit copies of the foregoing preamble and resolutions to each of our Senators and Representatives.

It is thus seen that four Senators have declared by their votes that the President, in the late Executive proceedings in relation to the revenue, had been guilty of the impeachable offense of "assuming upon himself authority and power not conferred by the Constitution and laws, but in derogation of both," whilst the legislatures of their respective States had deliberately approved those very proceedings as consistent with the Constitution and demanded by the public good. If these four votes had been given in accordance with the sentiments of the legislatures, as above expressed, there would have been but twenty-two votes out of forty-six for censuring the President, and the unprecedented record of his conviction could not have been placed upon the Journal of the Senate.

In thus referring to the resolutions and instructions of the State legislatures I disclaim and repudiate all authority or design to interfere with the responsibility due from members of the Senate to their own consciences, their constituents, and their country. The facts now stated belong to the history of these proceedings, and are important to the just development of the principles and interests involved in them as well as to the proper vindication of the executive department, and with that view, and that view only, are they here made the topic of remark.

The dangerous tendency of the doctrine which denies to the President the power of supervising, directing, and controlling the Secretary of the Treasury in like manner with the other executive officers would soon be manifest in practice were the doctrine to be established. The President is the direct representative of the American people, but the Secretaries are not. If the Secretary of the Treasury be independent of the President in the execution of the laws, then is there no direct responsibility to the people in that important branch of this Government to which is committed the care of the national finances. And it is in the power of the Bank of the United States, or any other corporation, body of men, or individuals, if a Secretary shall be found to accord with them in opinion or can be induced in practice to promote their views, to control through him the whole action of the Government (so far as it is exercised by his Department) in defiance of the Chief Magistrate elected by the people and responsible to them.

But the evil tendency of the particular doctrine adverted to, though sufficiently serious, would be as nothing in comparison with the pernicious consequences which would inevitably flow from the approbation and allowance by the people and the practice by the Senate of the unconstitutional power of arraigning and censuring the official conduct of the Executive in the manner recently pursued. Such proceedings are eminently calculated to unsettle the foundations of the Government, to disturb the harmonious action of its different departments, and to break down the checks and balances by which the wisdom of its framers sought to insure its stability and usefulness.

The honest differences of opinion which occasionally exist between the Senate and the President in regard to matters in which both are obliged to participate are sufficiently embarrassing; but if the course recently adopted by the Senate shall hereafter be frequently pursued, it is not only obvious that the harmony of the relations between the President and the Senate will be destroyed, but that other and graver effects will ultimately ensue. If the censures of the Senate be submitted to by the President, the confidence of the people in his ability and virtue and the character and usefulness of his Administration will soon be at an end, and the real power of the Government will fall into the hands of a body holding their offices for long terms, not elected by the people and not to them directly responsible. If, on the other hand, the illegal censures of the Senate should be resisted by the President, collisions and angry controversies might ensue, discreditable in their progress and in the end compelling the people to adopt the conclusion either that their Chief Magistrate was unworthy of their respect or that the Senate was chargeable with calumny and injustice. Either of these results would impair public confidence in the perfection of the system and lead to serious alterations of its framework or to the practical abandonment of some of its provisions.

The influence of such proceedings on the other departments of the Government, and more especially on the States, could not fail to be extensively pernicious. When the judges in the last resort of official misconduct themselves overleap the bounds of their authority as prescribed by the Constitution, what general disregard of its provisions might not their example be expected to produce? And who does not perceive that such contempt of the Federal Constitution by one of its most important departments would hold out the strongest temptations to resistance on the part of the State sovereignties whenever they shall suppose their just rights to have been invaded? Thus all the independent departments of the Government, and the States which compose our confederated Union, instead of attending to their appropriate duties and leaving those who may offend to be reclaimed or punished in the manner pointed out in the Constitution, would fall to mutual crimination and recrimination and give to the people confusion and anarchy instead of order and law, until at length some form of aristocratic power would be established on the ruins of the Constitution or the States be broken into separate communities.

Far be it from me to charge or to insinuate that the present Senate of the United States intend in the most distant way to encourage such a result. It is not of their motives or designs, but only of the tendency of their acts, that it is my duty to speak. It is, if possible, to make Senators themselves sensible of the danger which lurks under the precedent set in their resolution, and at any rate to perform my duty as the responsible head of one of the coequal departments of the Government, that I have been compelled to point out the consequences to which the discussion and passage of the resolution may lead if the tendency of the measure be not checked in its inception. It is due to the high trust with which I have been charged, to those who may be called to succeed me in it, to the representatives of the people whose constitutional prerogative has been unlawfully assumed, to the people and to the States, and to the Constitution they have established that I should not permit its provisions to be broken down by such an attack on the executive department without at least some effort "to preserve, protect, and defend" them. With this view, and for the reasons which have been stated, I do hereby *solemnly protest* against the aforementioned proceedings of the Senate as unauthorized by the Constitution, contrary to its spirit and to several of its express provisions, subversive of that distribution of the powers of government which it has ordained and established, destructive of the checks and safeguards by which those powers were intended on the one hand to be controlled and on the other to be protected, and calculated by their immediate and collateral effects, by their character and tendency, to concentrate in the hands of a body not directly amenable to the people a degree of influence and power dangerous to their liberties and fatal to the Constitution of their choice.

The resolution of the Senate contains an imputation upon my private as well as upon my public character, and as it must stand forever on their journals, I can not close this substitute for that defense which I have not been allowed to present in the ordinary form without remarking that I have lived in vain if it be necessary to enter into a formal vindication of my character and purposes from such an imputation. In vain do I bear upon my person enduring memorials of that contest in which

American liberty was purchased; in vain have I since periled property, fame, and life in defense of the rights and privileges so dearly bought; in vain am I now, without a personal aspiration or the hope of individual advantage, encountering responsibilities and dangers from which by mere inactivity in relation to a single point I might have been exempt, if any serious doubts can be entertained as to the purity of my purposes and motives. If I had been ambitious, I should have sought an alliance with that powerful institution which even now aspires to no divided empire. If I had been venal, I should have sold myself to its designs. Had I preferred personal comfort and official ease to the performance of my ardous duty, I should have ceased to molest it. In the history of conquerors and usurpers, never in the fire of youth nor in the vigor of manhood could I find an attraction to lure me from the path of duty, and now I shall scarcely find an inducement to commence their career of ambition when gray hairs and a decaying frame, instead of inviting to toil and battle, call me to the contemplation of other worlds, where conquerors cease to be honored and usurpers expiate their crimes. The only ambition I can feel is to acquit myself to Him to whom I must soon render an account of my stewardship, to serve my fellowmen, and live respected and honored in the history of my country. No; the ambition which leads me on is an anxious desire and a fixed determination to return to the people unimpaired the sacred trust they have confided to my charge; to heal the wounds of the Constitution and preserve it from further violation; to persuade my countrymen, so far as I may, that it is not in a splendid government supported by powerful monopolies and aristocratical establishments that they will find happiness or their liberties protection, but in a plain system, void of pomp, protecting all and granting favors to none, dispensing its blessings, like the dews of Heaven, unseen and unfelt save in the freshness and beauty they contribute to produce. It is such a government that the genius of our people requires; such an one only under which our States may remain for ages to come united, prosperous, and free. If the Almighty Being who has hitherto sustained and protected me will but vouchsafe to make my feeble powers instrumental to such a result, I shall anticipate with pleasure the place to be assigned me in the history of my country, and die contented with the belief that I have contributed in some small degree to increase the value and prolong the duration of American liberty.

To the end that the resolution of the Senate may not be hereafter drawn into precedent with the authority of silent acquiescence on the part of the executive department, and to the end also that my motives and views in the Executive proceedings denounced in that resolution may be known to my fellow-citizens, to the world, and to all posterity, I respectfully request that this message and protest may be entered at length on the journals of the Senate.

Andrew Jackson

Jackson's "Protest" fell on many deaf ears in the Senate, however, and that body refused to enter the document into its official journal. This, of course, infuriated Jackson and his supporters, and Senator Benton vowed on the Senate floor to have the Clay resolution expunged from the official Senate record. With the majority against him and the country in the throes of an economic panic, this appeared at the time an idle boast, but within three years time, Benton was able to make good his promise. Largely through his efforts, the legislatures of state after state repudiated their representatives' votes on this measure, and in the elections of 1834 and 1836, the people denounced Biddle and the Bank and most of the politicians who had supported them. Benton has recorded a vivid description of the actual expunging of the resolution from the Senate journal, and of the celebration of Jackson and his supporters afterwards:

> The passage of the resolution was announced from the chair. Mr. Benton rose, and said that nothing now remained but to execute the order of the Senate; which he moved be done forthwith. It was ordered accordingly. The Secretary thereupon produced the original manuscript journal of the Senate, and opening at the page which contained the condemnatory sentence of March 28th, 1834, proceeded in open Senate to draw a square of broad black lines around the sentence, and to write across its face in strong letters these words: "Expunged by order of the Senate, this 16th day of March, 1837."
>
> The whole scene was impressive; but no part of it so much so as to see the great leaders who, for seven long years had warred upon General Jackson, and a thousand times had pronounced him ruined, each rising in his place, with pain and reluctance, to confess themselves vanquished—to admit his power, and their weakness—and to exhale their griefs in unavailing reproaches, and impotent deprecations. It was a tribute to his invincibility which cast into the shade all the eulogiums of his friends. The gratification of General Jackson was extreme. He gave a grand dinner to the expungers (as they were called) and their wives; and being too weak to sit at the table, he only met the company, placed the "head expunger" in his chair, and withdrew to his sick chamber. That expurgation! It was the "crowning mercy" of his civil, as New Orleans had been of his military, life![73]

The opposition to Jackson and his strong and energetic concept of the presidency did not disappear with his victory, nor did his opponents abandon the field of battle. Calhoun, Webster and Clay continued to attack the Madison-Jackson theory of the removal power even after the Bank crisis had subsided. Soon after his first successful vote on the censure motion Clay introduced a series of resolutions designed to strip the President of his independent removal power.[74] The objective of the resolutions was to involve the Senate in the removal of all presidentially-appointed officials, except diplomats. The issue was not pushed with any real enthusiasm by Senator Clay, however, and it was buried under other business and largely forgotten by the end of the session. The next year Calhoun introduced a bill designed to substantially restrict the number of officials appointed by the President, and also to eliminate the President's independent removal power. It took the form of amending the Tenure of Office Act of 1821. Calhoun was warmly supported in this effort by his colleagues Webster and Clay, and both spoke out against the removal power in the debate on the floor of the Senate. Webster's speech was perhaps the most effective, because its reasoning and construction were very cautious and thoughtful.

He began by admitting what the Senate had been helplessly opposing the previous year, namely, that the decision at the conclusion of the debate in Congress in 1789 remained the controlling precedent up to that time, and it was no longer possible simply to argue a contrary interpretation of the decision made by Congress. Webster, a strict constructionist, indicated that the President's independent removal power was a settled point, "settled by construction, settled by precedent, settled by the practice of the government and settled by statute."[75] He quickly added that in considering the question "time and again within the last six years, I am very willing to say, that, in my deliberate judgment, the original decision was wrong."[76] He then struck at the heart of the matter. Since there was no specific assignment of the removal power to the President in the Constitution, Madison and others had argued that such power was implied or inherent in the general grant of executive power. Webster challenged this reasoning:

I think, therefore, Sir, that very great caution is to be used, and the ground well considered before we admit that the President derived any distinct and specific power from those general words which vest the executive authority in him. The Constitution itself does not rest satisfied with these general words. It immediately goes into particulars, and carefully enumerates the several authorities which the President shall possess. The very first of the enumerated powers is the command of the army and navy. This, most certainly, is an executive power. And why is it particularly set down and expressed, if any power was intended to be granted under the general words? This would pass, if any thing would pass, under those words. But enumeration, specification, particularization, was evidently the design of the framers of the Constitution, in this as in other parts of it. I do not, therefore, regard the declaration that the executive power shall be vested in a President as being any grant at all; any more than the declaration that the legislative power shall be vested in Congress constitutes, by itself, a grant of such power. In the one case, as in the other, I think the object was to describe and denominate the department, which should hold, respectively, the legislative and executive authority; very much as we see, in some of the state constitutions, that the several articles are headed with titles "legislative power," "executive power," "judicial power;" and this entitling of the articles with the name of the power has never been supposed, of itself, to confer any authority whatever. It amounts to no more than naming the departments.

If, then, the power of removal be admitted to be an executive power, still it must be sought for and found among the enumerated executive powers, or fairly implied from some one or more of them. It cannot be implied from the general words. The power of appointment was not left to be so implied; why, then, should the power of removal have been so left? They are both closely connected; one is indispensable to the other; why, then, was one carefully expressed, defined, and limited, and not one word said about the other?

Sir, I think the whole matter is sufficiently plain. Nothing is said in the Constitution about the power of removal, because it is not a separate and distinct power. It is part of the power of appointment, naturally going with it or necessarily resulting from it.

The power of placing one man in office necessarily implies the power of turning another out. If one must be Secretary of State, and another be appointed, the first goes out by the mere force of the appointment of the other, without any previous act of removal whatever. And this is the practice of the government, and has been, from the first. In all the removals which have been made, they have generally been effected simply by making other appointments. I cannot find a case to the contrary. There is no such thing as any distinct act of removal.[77]

Calhoun's proposed law that all appointed officials remain in office until the Senate ratified the explanation submitted by the President for their removal was finally defeated. Webster's arguments were eloquent, but did not succeed in moving his colleagues to repudiate, as he had, the determination made in 1789. Perhaps the most influential rebuttal came from outside the Senate from a fellow New Englander, Charles Francis Adams. Adams ridiculed Webster's warmed-over argument from 1789 (which had been defeated at that time), and pointed out that linking the removal power with the appointing power would not make both joint executive-senatorial enterprises. He argued that the Executive must go through three distinct stages in appointing an official—nominating, appointing, and commissioning. The Senate does not participate in all three stages, but has a veto power over only one of those steps—the appointment. This veto does not qualify the Senate to share equally in the rest of the procedure. By this reasoning both the appointive and removal powers are defined executive responsibilities, and the appointive power is only referred to specifically in the Constitution in order to qualify this one step of an otherwise executive process.[78]

Although the proposed change was not successful, this did not discourage Clay and the others from continuing to advocate a change in the law on this question. In 1836 an unsuccessful amendment to the Constitution was proposed which would give Congress the power to appoint the secretary of the treasury and other financial officers of the government. Five years later Clay introduced a constitutional amendment calling for the appointment and removal by Congress of the secretary of the treasury and the treasurer of the United States, but again he did not demonstrate sufficient interest in working for its passage. Several other unsuccessful attempts to take from the President his effective executive control over members of his cabinet were made; all of them failed and would continue to fail until after the Civil War when this problem suddenly erupted with a vengeance.

During the 1830s Jackson's opposition to the Bank of the United States and his removal of the government deposits along with the dismissal of his secretary of the treasury, William Duane, helped his determined opponents in the Senate—Webster, Clay and Calhoun—to create and eventually to strengthen an opposition party which was able to harass his successor, Martin Van Buren, and to win the presidential race in 1840. The central thrust of Whig opposition to Jacksonianism focused upon the independent power that the old Indian fighter had brought to the presidential office. As legislators and charter members of the Senate, all resented Jackson's manipulation of the executive branch of government and were opposed to or did not understand the new identity which he had irrevers placed upon the office. (Although Calhoun continued to oppose Jackson, he so abandoned the Whig "troika," and returned to the Democracy to support Va Buren.)

The Whig attack on presidential power did not succeed in its basic objective, to cripple the institutional power of the presidency which Jackson had expanded, but it did set the tone and arouse congressional animosity which would not quickly disappear. With several notable wartime exceptions the presidency would not again rise to such preeminence during the rest of the nineteenth century, and Congress would attempt, over and over again, to wrest from the executive branch, prerogatives which Jackson had jealously guarded and even enhanced.

The economic history of the United States since Jackson's time provides substantial evidence of the weakness of the Jacksonian solution to the Bank problem, but not necessarily to all aspects of the attack mounted by the President and his supporters against the Bank of the United States. In fact, the panic created by Biddle's counteroffensive against Jackson, where credit policies were severely tightened and loans and discounts contracted, partially bore out the Jacksonian charge of the power of the Bank as a threat to the national economy. However, Ralph Catterall and Bray Hammond, with careful scholarship, have discounted many of the sweeping charges of corruption and profit exploitation that punctuated the Jackson-Benton-Taney case against the Bank.[79] These two thorough historians have demonstrated the necessity for a central bank or some form of central banking system as a dynamic and regulative force in the national economy, an argument Jackson and his supporters discounted, and one which subsequent banking crises and resulting national banking reforms in both the nineteenth and twentieth centuries have made crystal clear.

The most potent and valid argument against Biddle and the Bank—the independence of the Bank from governmental control or regulation—was not effectively made by the Jacksonians or when made, was usually drowned in the rhetoric of a demagogic appeal. Perhaps this was because they wanted to destroy the Bank completely and they realized that Biddle was willing to negotiate reforms, and if pressed, to accept them as the price for keeping the Bank alive. The country has since learned through bitter experience the vital necessity for national control and regulation of the banking and monetary system. Without it the citizen and his savings, the businessman and his loans, are vulnerable to the irregularity of the market economy, to poor judgment, bad investment policy, corruption and error on a scattered and decentralized scale which can easily and rapidly spread from city to city, town to town, until it envelops the entire country. Without a central banking system to put out the local fires, dampen excessive speculation and protect sound banks from the contagion of panic, a decentralized system like the one Jackson envisaged has no defense against the quickly related collapse of its weakest members.

Perhaps of even more critical importance than these shortcomings was the lack of a stable national currency and the financial weakness of the national government

ich this diffusion of economic power and substance contributed. These
lems were evident in many ways during the next 25 years, but became most
cal during the course of the Civil War. The inability of the national government
raise the money and provide the resources to win the war led to a financial crisis
hich required the Jacksonian economic "reforms" to be partially reversed, with
ederal control established throughout a system of national banks in the National
Bank Act of 1863. This provided a stable and national currency and although it did
not create a national banking system to protect the credit and savings of all of its
participants, it did establish the principle of federal responsibility in the monetary
and banking system, and closed the harmful gap between the economy and the
national government.

Jackson was fundamentally right in his instinctive suspicion of and opposition
to the private control of a central or national bank, where the decision-makers were
not really responsible to the national welfare or the political state. He was wrong in
his notion that, as a solution, the state banks could take over the regulatory role of a
centralized banking system. His early frontier populist antagonism to higher
finance and the eastern commercial establishment betrayed him into a dangerous
and destructive campaign against the Bank, which proved costly in terms of the
public welfare and the long-range economic stability of the country.

But in his struggle with Duane, and later with Calhoun, Webster and Clay, over
the removal power (which came about because of the Bank situation), the President
was clearly acting within his constitutional powers. His emphatic and brilliant
defense of his actions provided later Presidents, who possessed less self-confidence
and courage than he, with striking insights and a magnificent example of a
legitimate defense of the prerogatives of the administrative head of the executive
branch of the government. The principle that the President possesses constitutional
authority to control, and if necessary, to remove members of his executive family
for administrative insubordination would be seriously challenged but never
conceded or abandoned by Jackson's successors in the White House.

NOTES

1. Quoted in Douglas Southall Freeman, *George Washington: Patriot and President* (New York, 1954), 98.
2. Max Farrand, ed., *The Records of the Federal Convention* (New Haven, Connecticut, 1911) II, 337.
3. Edward Corwin, *Court Over Constitution* (New York, 1950), 88.
4. Quoted in Richard F. Fenno, jr., *The President's Cabinet* (Cambridge, Massachusetts, 1959), 18.
5. Quoted in James Hart, *The American Presidency in Action* (New York, 1948), 111-12.
6. Hart, 111-12.
7. George H. Haynes, *The Senate of the United States* (New York, 1960) I, 54.
'. Quoted in Carl Russell Fish, *The Civil Service and the Patronage* (New York, 1963), 35.
F h, 35-36.
F 51.
' in had been in Washington, served as a cabinet member during Jefferson's two terms and in
dison administration, and probably yearned for a change of scene and a new role on the
ge, particularly if the mission could serve a significant goal for the new republic. But he

also was probably not adverse to retiring to private life after many years in the administrative and legislative branches of the government. At any rate, he indicated at the time that "he was well aware that my going to Russia will probably terminate in the appointment of another Secretary of the Treasury and in my returning to private life," but the prospect of such possibilities did not deter him. Quoted in Irving Brant, *James Madison: Commander in Chief* (Indianapolis, Indiana, 1961), 159.

12. Quoted in Haynes, II, 730.
13. Haynes, II, 731.
14. Haynes, II, 731.
15. Leonard D. White, *The Jeffersonians* (New York, 1959), 387.
16. The positions involved included district attorneys, collectors of the customs, naval officers and surveyors of the customs, navy agents, receivers of public money for lands, registers of the land offices, paymasters in the army, the apothecary general, the assistant apothecary general, and the commissary general of purchasers. Indian agents, postmasters, or any of the accounting or clerical officers and employees in Washington were not affected. (White, 387.)
17. Quoted in Joseph P. Harris, *The Advice and Consent of the Senate: A Study of the Confirmation of Appointments* (Berkeley, California, 1953), 52.
18. White, 129.
19. White, 390.
20. White, 390.
21. Quoted in M. Ostrogorski, "The Rise and Fall of the Nominating Caucus, Legislative and Congressional," in *The American Historical Review*, V, No. 2 (January 1900), 253.
22. The states referred to were Virginia, Ohio. Very similar proportions were noted in other states. Ostrogorski, "The Nominating Caucus," 272, footnote 2.
23. Ostrogorski, "The Nominating Caucus," 272-73. (Niles in *Niles' Register*.)
24. Quoted in Ostrogorski, 275.
25. Quoted in Robert V. Remini, *The Election of Andrew Jackson* (Philadelphia, Pennsylvania, 1963), 77.
26. Remini, 77.
27. Roy F. Nichols, *The Invention of the American Political Parties* (New York, 1967), 287-88.
28. Nichols, 288.
29. M. Ostrogorski, *Democracy and the Organization of Political Parties* (New York, 1902) II, 35.
30. Ostrogorski, *Democracy and the Organization of Political Parties*, II, 52-53.
31. Ostrogorski, *Democracy and the Organization of Political Parties*, II, 58.
32. Quoted in Marquis James, *The Life of Andrew Jackson* (Indianapolis, Indiana, 1938), Part II, 180.
33. James, 182-83.
34. James, 187.
35. Quoted in White, 307.
36. White, 391.
37. White, 320.
38. James, 182.
39. Carl Russell Fish, "Removal of Officials by the Presidents of the United States," *Annual Report of the American Historical Association, 1899* (Washington, D.C., 1900), I, 74.
40. Fish, *The Civil Service and the Patronage*, 125.
41. Fish, "*Removal of Officials*," 76, 78.
42. Joseph Gales, ed., *Debates and Proceedings in the Congress of the United States* (Washington, D.C., 1834) I, 385.
43. Charles C. Thach, jr., *The Creation of the Presidency, 1775-1789* (Baltimore, Maryland, 1922), 141.
44. Gales, I, 514-16.
45. Other members of the House of Representatives who had been delegates to the Convention were: Baldwin, Caroll, Clymer, Fitzsimmons, Gerry, Gilman and Sherman.
46. Members of the Senate who had been Convention delegates were: Langdon, Strong, Ellsworth, Johnson, Paterson, Robert Morris, Bassett, Read, Butler and Few. Subsequently, when New York was represented, King became the 11th Convention delegate to participate.
47. Gales, I, 387.
48. Gales, I, 473.
49. Gales, I, 474.
50. Quoted in Gales.
51. Quoted in *Myers* v. *United States*, 272 U.S. 138-39 (1926).
52. Edward S. Corwin, *The President's Removal Power Under the Constitution* (New York
53. Gales, I, 507.
54. Of the eight House Members who had been delegates to the Philadelphia Convent

236

Sherman and Gerry, voted against the measure, and Gerry was one of the delegates who refused to sign the Constitution.

55. Gales, I, 397.
56. Quoted in White, 388.
57. White, 389.
58. James D. Richardson, ed., *Messages and Papers of the Presidents* (New York, 1897) III, 1025.
59. John Spencer Bassett, ed., *Correspondence of Andrew Jackson* (Washington, D.C., 1931) V, 40.
60. Bassett, V, 40-41.
61. Bassett, V, 41; 43.
62. William J. Duane, *Narrative and Correspondence Concerning the Removal of Deposites (sic) and Occurrences Connected Therewith* (Philadelphia, Pennsylvania, 1838), 7.
63. Bassett, V, 139.
64. Bassett, V, 113.
65. Duane, Duane to Jackson, July 10, 1833, 39-40.
66. Duane, Duane to Jackson, July 22, 1833, 90.
67. Duane, 100.
68. Duane was concerned over personal attacks upon him that appeared in what he termed "semi-official newspapers" in Concord, Boston, Albany, New York, Trenton, and Cincinnati, and also about the quality of investigation which the President's representatives conducted concerning the ability of the state banks to accept the deposits and perform their required role.
69. Duane, 100.
70. Bassett, V, 203.
71. Calvin Colton, ed., *The Works of Henry Clay* (New York, 1904) VII, 576.
72. Colton, VIII, 45.
73. Thomas Hart Benton, *Thirty Years View; or, A History of the Working of the American Government for Thirty Years, From 1820 to 1850* (New York, 1854), 730-31.
74. 1. *Resolved*, that the Constitution of the United States does not vest in the President power to remove at his pleasure officers under the Government of the United States whose offices have been established by law.
2. *Resolved*, that in all cases of offices created by the law, the tenure of holding which is not prescribed by the Constitution, Congress is authorized by the Constitution to prescribe the tenure, terms, and conditions on which they are to be holden.
3. *Resolved*, that the Committee on the Judiciary be instructed to inquire into the expediency of providing by law that in all instances of appointment to office by the President, by and with the advice and consent of the Senate, other than diplomatic appointments, the power of removal shall be exercised only in concurrence with the Senate, and, when the Senate is not in session, that the President may suspend any such officer, communicating his reasons for the suspension to the Senate at its first succeeding session; and if the Senate concur with him the officer shall be restored to office.
4. *Resolved*, that the Committee on the Post Office and the Post Roads be instructed by law to inquire into the expediency of making provision by law for the appointment, by and with the advice and consent of the Senate, of all deputy postmasters whose annual emoluments exceed a prescribed amount. Quoted in Charles Morganston, *The Appointing and Removal Power of the President of the United States* (Washington, D.C., 1929), footnote 51-52.
75. Daniel Webster, *The Writings and Speeches of Daniel Webster* (Boston, 1903) VII, 185.
76. Webster, VII, 185.
77. Webster, VII, 188-89.
78. Charles Francis Adams, *Appeal to the Whigs*, a pamphlet (Boston, 1835), 59-60.
79. Ralph C. H. Catterall, *The Second Bank of the United States* (Chicago, 1903), and Bray Hammond, *Banks and Politics in America From the Revolution to the Civil War* (Princeton, New Jersey, 1957).

Bibliography

Adams, Charles Francis. *Appeal to the Whigs* (a pamphlet). Boston: n.p., 1835.

. *The Works of John Adams.* Vol. IV. Boston: Charles C. Little and James Brown, 1852

Adams, Henry Brooks, ed. *History of the United States of America During the Administration of James Madison.* Vol. I. New York: Charles Scribner's Sons, 1921.

Bassett, John Spencer, ed. *Correspondence of Andrew Jackson.* Vol. V. Washington, D.C.: Carnegie Institution of Washington, 1931.

Benton, Thomas Hart. *Thirty Years View; or, A History of the Working of the American Government For Thirty Years, From 1820 to 1850.* New York: D. Appleton and Company, 1854.

Binkley, Wilfred E. *Presidents and Congress.* Third Revised Edition. New York: Vintage Books, 1962.

Catterall, Ralph C. H. *The Second Bank of the United States.* Chicago: University of Chicago Press, 1903.

Colton, Calvin, ed. *The Works of Henry Clay.* Vols. VII, VIII. New York: G. P. Putnam's Sons, 1904.

Commager, Henry Steele, ed. *Documents of American History.* Fifth Edition. New York: Appleton-Century-Crofts, Inc., 1949.

Corwin, Edward S. *Court Over Constitution.* New York: Peter Smith, 1950.

. *The President: Office and Powers, 1787-1957.* Fourth Revised Edition. New York: New York University Press, 1957.

. *The President's Removal Power Under the Constitution.* New York: National Municipal League, 1927.

Duane, William J. *Narrative and Correspondence Concerning the Removal of Deposites (sic) and Occurrences Connected Therewith.* Philadelphia, Pennsylvania: n.p., 1838.

238

Farrand, Max, ed. *The Records of the Federal Convention.* Vols. II, IV. New Haven, Connecticut: Yale University Press, 1911.

Fenno, Richard F., jr. *The President's Cabinet.* Cambridge, Massachusetts: Harvard University Press, 1959.

Fish, Carl Russell. *The Civil Service and the Patronage.* New York: Russell and Russell, Inc., 1963.

"Removal of Officials by the Presidents of the United States." *Annual Report of the American Historical Association, 1899.* Vol. I. Washington, D.C.: U.S. Government Printing Office, 1900.

Gales, Joseph, ed. *Debates and Proceedings in the Congress of the United States.* Vol. I. Washington, D.C.: Gales and Seaton, 1834.

Hammond, Bray. *Banks and Politics in America, From the Revolution to the Civil War.* Princeton, New Jersey: Princeton University Press, 1957.

Harris, Joseph P. *The Advice and Consent of the Senate: A Study on the Confirmation of Appointments.* Berkeley, California: University of California Press, 1953.

Hart, James. *Tenure of Office Under the Constitution.* Baltimore, Maryland: The Johns Hopkins Press, 1930.

The American Presidency in Action, 1789. New York: The Macmillan Company, 1948.

Haynes, George H. *The Senate of the United States.* Vol. II. New York: Russell and Russell, 1960.

James, Marquis. *The Life of Andrew Jackson.* Part II. Indianapolis, Indiana: The Bobbs-Merrill Company, 1938.

Mason, Alpheus Thomas. *William Howard Taft: Chief Justice.* New York: Simon and Schuster, 1965.

Morganston, Charles. *The Appointing and Removal Power of the President of the United States.* Washington, D.C.: U.S. Government Printing Office, 1929.

Myers v. United States, 272 U.S. 136 (1926).

Nichols, Roy F. *The Invention of the American Political Parties.* New York: The Macmillan Company, 1967.

Ostrogorski, M. *Democracy and the Organization of Political Parties.* Vol. II. New York: The Macmillan Company, 1902.

"The Rise and Fall of the Nominating Caucus, Legislative and Congressional." *The American Historical Review.* Vol. V. No. 2 (January 1900).

Remini, Robert V. *The Election of Andrew Jackson.* Philadelphia, Pennsylvania: J. B. Lippincott Company, 1963.

Richardson, James D., ed. *Messages and Papers of the Presidents.* Vol. III. New York: Bureau of National Literature, 1897.

Stanwood, Edward. *A History of the Presidency.* Boston: Houghton Mifflin Company, 1898.

Webster, Daniel. *The Writings and Speeches of Daniel Webster.* Vol. VII. Boston: Little, Brown and Company, 1903.

White, Leonard D. *The Jacksonians.* New York: The Macmillan Company, 1954.

The Jeffersonians. New York: The Macmillan Company, 1959.

III. The President As Executive Leader

THE PRESIDENT
AS EXECUTIVE LEADER

George Washington Enforces the Law

Although the Constitution carefully enumerates the powers of the legislature, it rather vaguely states that the "executive power shall be vested in a President of the United States of America." In the broadest sense such executive power refers to everything the President does, including his specific responsibilities spelled out in Article II. When he acts in the capacity of Commander in Chief, when he assumes the role of national leader in the area of foreign relations, when he exercises the appointive power—these are all executive responsibilities. But when I refer to the President as Executive leader, I have a much narrower definition in mind. This definition limits the responsibilities of the President to that section of the Constitution which provides that "he shall take care that the laws be faithfully executed," and beyond that, to the functions which are *not* specifically referred to in the body of Article II, but which are implicit in the broadest sense of the term "executive power." This would include the interpretation of statutes as well as their enforcement, the responsibility for maintaining domestic peace, and the suppression of insurrection (dealt with in part elsewhere in the Constitution— Article IV, Section 4); the complex area of delegated powers; and above all the responsibility of the Chief Executive to respond sensitively to the social and public welfare problems of the nation. Such a wide range of activities encompasses a very essential part of the duties and responsibilities of the President of the United States, and clearly requires careful examination and analysis.

The President's power "to take care that the laws be carefully executed" has been affirmed, tested and reaffirmed often in the history of the republic. In the course of these developments, the right of the President to use all the force at his command that is necessary to carry out the mandates of Congress and the principles of the Constitution has not only been firmly established by the precedents set by two of our greatest Presidents, George Washington and Andrew Jackson, but strengthened by later applications based upon their strong examples.

The initial test of this power came in the first administration of George Washington. He was confronted with a serious problem when strong opposition to a national excise tax upon the production of whiskey arose in several parts of the country, particularly in the four westernmost counties of Pennsylvania. Outrages were committed against the government revenue collectors and a serious defiance of national law appeared to be in the offing. When apprised of the situation by members of his cabinet, Washington issued a proclamation in September 1792 on the recommendation of the secretary of the treasury, Alexander Hamilton, admonishing and exhorting the offenders to cease and desist from their obstruction of the laws of the land.

President George Washington
First Warning to the Pennsylvania Farmers
September 1792

Richardson, I, 116-17.

PROCLAMATION

Whereas certain violent and unwarrantable proceedings have lately taken place tending to obstruct the operation of the laws of the United States for raising a revenue upon spirits distilled within the same, enacted pursuant to express authority delegated in the Constitution of the United States, which proceedings are subversive of good order, contrary to the duty that every citizen owes to his country and to the laws, and of a nature dangerous to the very being of a government; and

Whereas such proceedings are the more unwarrantable by reason of the moderation which has been heretofore shown on the part of the Government and of the disposition which has been manifested by the Legislature (who alone have authority to suspend the operation of laws) to obviate causes of objection and to render the laws as acceptable as possible; and

Whereas it is the particular duty of the Executive "to take care that the laws be faithfully executed," and not only that duty but the permanent interests and happiness of the people require that every legal and necessary step should be pursued as well to prevent such violent and unwarrantable proceedings as to bring to justice the infractors of the laws and secure obedience thereto:

Now, therefore, I, George Washington, President of the United States, do by these presents most earnestly admonish and exhort all persons whom it may concern to refrain and desist from all unlawful combinations and proceedings whatsoever having the object or tending to obstruct the operation of the laws aforesaid, inasmuch as all lawful ways and means will be strictly put in execution for bringing to justice the infractors thereof and securing obedience thereto.

And I do moreover charge and require all courts, magistrates, and officers whom it may concern, according to the duties of their several offices, to exert the powers in them respectively vested by law for the purposes aforesaid, hereby also enjoining and requiring all persons whomsoever, as they tender the welfare of their country, the just and due authority of Government, and the preservation of the public peace, to be aiding and assisting therein according to law.

In testimony whereof I have caused the seal of the United States to be affixed to these presents, and signed the same with my hand.

Done this 15th of September, A. D. 1792, and of the Independence of the United States the seventeenth.

Geo. Washington

Both Washington and his advisors hoped that an official warning would be sufficient to restrain the western Pennsylvania farmers from any further resistance to the law. But from the very beginning the President was counselled by his secretary of the treasury that stronger measures might eventually be necessary. In drafting the proclamation Hamilton clearly perceived the value of the President's role in the situation. He argued that:

> The appearance of the President in the business will awaken the attention of a great number of persons . . . to the evil tendency of the conduct reprehended, who have not yet viewed it with due seriousness. And from the co-operation of these circumstances good may reasonably be expected. . . .[1]

But in the event that such was not the case, the secretary of the treasury was quite prepared to recommend more extensive action:

> My present clear conviction is, that it is indispensable, if competent evidence can be obtained, to exert the full force of the law against the offenders, with every circumstance that can manifest the determination of the government to enforce execution; and if the processes of the courts are resisted, *as is rather to be expected, to employ those means which in the last resort are put in the power of the Executive.*[2]

It is clear that Hamilton had objectives in mind that even went beyond the suppression of a threatened insurrection. He was anxious to assert unequivocally the supremacy of the national government when in conflict with local assertions of independence; his concern was to establish the role of the President in such situations, to dramatize and enhance the responsibility and initiative of the Chief Executive to utilize all of the instruments of power available to the national government (including military force) to enforce the law and to keep the peace. He suggested as much to the President when he added to his opinion that force would probably have to be used when the orderly processes of the courts were resisted:

> If this is not done, the spirit of disobedience will naturally extend, and the authority of the government will be prostrated. Moderation enough has been shown; it is time to assume a different tone. The well-disposed part of the community will begin to think the Executive wanting in decision and vigor. . . .[3]

The warning was effective for a time but unrest and dissatisfaction built up against the prosecution of earlier offenders in the courts, exacerbating strong resentments already existing. Washington issued a second proclamation on August 7, 1794, which put teeth into the earlier warning. This time he initiated the proper action to alert the militia of the various states and warned the rebellious citizens that the President would brook no further delay in their full compliance with the law. He promised them that full compliance would bring about a presidential pardon for past resistance, but that if it was not immediately forthcoming, he would resort to coercion.

Once again Alexander Hamilton was instrumental in urging this further warning and the action by the President. Very much on top of the situation,

Hamilton had become alarmed by reports of increasing acts of violence and bitter resentment on the part of large numbers of citizens of this area. Five days before the President's ultimatum, Hamilton recommended such action and suggested that 12,000 militia (9,000 on foot and 3,000 on horse) be assembled in order to implement the President's decision. Presumably this recommendation was at hand when the President met on August 2, 1794, with most of the high officials of his administration and of the State of Pennsylvania at the Morris House in Philadelphia. The Pennsylvania officials were opposed to the President's action at this time; the chief justice of the state supreme court, Thomas McKean, argued that "the judiciary power was equal to the task of quelling and punishing the riots, and that the employment of military force at this period would be as bad as anything that Rioters had done—equally unconstitutional and illegal."[4]

The chief justice was refuted by Hamilton, who countered that it was imperative that action be taken at this time. He had fully documented for the President the acts of insurrection which had already taken place, and he asserted in reply to another state official who quoted a western Pennsylvania judge's opinion that force would only promote further resistance, that this same judge had been identified as being part of the insurrection.[5] Apparently Hamilton's position prevailed, for the President acted upon his recommendation. The procedure which the secretary had outlined was followed to the letter. Acting under a law passed in 1792, the President was required to obtain a certification by an associate or district federal judge that the laws of the United States were being opposed "by combinations too powerful to be suppressed by the ordinary course of judicial proceedings or by the powers vested in the marshals by that act," and authorizing the President to call forth the militia "to cause the laws to be duly executed."[6]

President George Washington
Final Warning of a Resort to Force
August 7, 1794

Richardson, I, 150-52.

A PROCLAMATION

Whereas combinations to defeat the execution of the laws laying duties upon spirits distilled within the United States and upon stills have from the time of the commencement of those laws existed in some of the western parts of Pennsylvania; and

Whereas the said combinations, proceeding in a manner subversive equally of the just authority of government and of the rights of individuals, have hitherto effected their dangerous and criminal purpose by the influence of certain irregular meetings whose proceedings have tended to encourage and uphold the spirit of opposition by misrepresentations of the laws calculated to render them odious; by endeavors to deter those who might be so disposed from accepting offices under them through fear of public resentment and of injury to person and property, and to compel those who had accepted such offices by actual violence to surrender or forbear the execution of them; by circulating vindictive menaces against all those who should otherwise, directly or indirectly, aid in the execution of the said laws, or who, yielding to the dictates of conscience and to a sense of obligation, should themselves comply therewith; by actually injuring and destroying the property of persons who were understood to have so complied; by inflicting cruel and humiliating punishments upon private citizens for no other cause than that of appearing to be the friends of the laws; by intercepting the public officers on the highways, abusing, assaulting, and otherwise ill treating them; by going to their houses in the night, gaining admittance by force, taking away their papers, and committing other outrages, employing for these unwarrantable purposes the agency of armed banditti disguised in such manner as for the most part to escape discovery; and

Whereas the endeavors of the Legislature to obviate objections to the said laws by lowering the duties and by other alterations conducive to the convenience of those whom they immediately affect (though they have given satisfaction in other quarters), and the endeavors of the executive officers to conciliate a compliance with the laws by explanations, by forbearance, and even by particular accommodations founded on the suggestion of local considerations, have been disappointed of their effect by the machinations of persons whose industry to excite resistance has increased with every appearance of a disposition among the people to relax in their opposition and to acquiesce in the laws, insomuch that many persons in the said western parts of Pennsylvania have at length been hardy enough to perpetrate acts which I am advised amount to treason, being overt acts of levying war against the United States, the said persons having on the 16th and 17th July last past proceeded in arms (on the second day amounting to several hundreds) to the house of John Neville, inspector of the revenue for the fourth survey of the district of Pennsylvania; having repeatedly attacked the said house with the persons therein, wounding some of them; having seized David Lenox, marshal of the district of Pennsylvania, who previous thereto had been fired upon while in the execution of his duty by a party of armed men, detaining him for some time prisoner, till for the preservation of his life and the obtaining of his liberty he found it necessary to enter into stipulations to forbear the execution of certain official duties touching processes issuing out of a court of the United States; and having finally obliged the said inspector of the said revenue and the said marshal from considerations of personal safety to fly from that part of the country, in order, by a circuitous route, to proceed to the seat of Government, avowing as the motives of these outrageous proceedings an intention to prevent by force of arms the execution of the said laws, to oblige the said inspector of the revenue to renounce his said office, to withstand by open violence the lawful authority of the Government of the United States, and to compel thereby an alteration in the measures of the Legislature and a repeal of the laws aforesaid; and

Whereas by a law of the United States entitled "An act to provide for calling forth the militia to execute the laws of the Union, suppress insurrections, and repel invasions," it is enacted "that whenever the laws of the United States shall be opposed or the execution thereof obstructed in any State by combinations too powerful to be suppressed by the ordinary course of judicial proceedings or by the powers vested in the marshals by that act, the same being notified by an associate justice or the district judge, it shall be lawful for the President of the United States to call forth the militia of such State to suppress such combinations and to cause the laws to be duly executed. And if the militia of a State where such combinations may happen shall refuse or be insufficient to suppress the same, it shall be lawful for the President, if the Legislature of the United States shall not be in session, to call forth and employ such numbers of the militia of any other State or States most convenient thereto as may be necessary; and the use of the militia so to be called forth may be continued, if necessary, until the expiration of thirty days after the commencement of the ensuing session: *Provided always*, That whenever it may be necessary in the judgment of the President to use the military force hereby directed to be called forth, the President shall forthwith and previous thereto, by proclamation, command such insurgents to disperse and retire peaceably to their respective abodes within a limited time;" and

Whereas James Wilson, an associate justice, on the 4th instant, by writing under his hand, did from evidence which had been laid before him notify to me that "in the counties of Washington and Allegeny, in Pennsylvania, laws of the United States are opposed and the execution thereof obstructed by combinations too powerful to be suppressed by the ordinary course of judicial proceedings or by the powers vested in the marshal of that district;" and

Whereas it is in my judgment necessary under the circumstances of the case to take measures for calling forth the militia in order to suppress the combinations aforesaid, and to cause the laws to be duly executed; and I have accordingly determined so to do, feeling the deepest regret for the occasion, but withal the most solemn conviction that the essential interests of the Union demand it, that the very existence of Government and the fundamental principles of social order are materially involved in the issue, and that the patriotism and firmness of all good citizens are seriously called upon, as occasions may require, to aid in the effectual suppression of so fatal a spirit:

Wherefore, and in pursuance of the proviso above recited, I, George Washington, President of the United States, do hereby command all persons being insurgents as aforesaid, and all others whom it may concern, on or before the 1st day of September next to disperse and retire peaceably to their respective abodes. And I do moreover warn all persons whomsoever against aiding, abetting, or comforting the perpetrators of the aforesaid treasonable acts, and do require all officers and other citizens, according to their respective duties and the laws of the land, to exert their utmost endeavors to prevent and suppress such dangerous proceedings.

In testimony whereof I have caused the seal of the United States of America to be affixed to these presents, and signed the same with my hand.

Done at the city of Philadelphia, the 7th day of August, 1794, and of the Independence of the United States of America the nineteenth.

Geo. Washington

By the President:
Edm. Randolph

The Pennsylvania officials continued to protest the President's decision, the governor pleading that he did not want the national government to act before the judicial powers of the state had exhausted their efforts. But Hamilton charged into the fray once again, drafting a reply to their protests in the form of a letter to Governor Mifflin from the President and signed by the secretary of state. Hamilton's reply, as usual, went to the heart of the issue. He asserted that:

1. The State judicial authority, "after full and fair experiment, has proved incompetent to enforce obedience to, or to punish infractions of the laws. . . ."[7]

2. The people of the United States have established a government for the management of their general interests; they have instituted executive organs for administering that government; and their representatives have established rules by which these organs are to act. When their authority in that of their government is attacked, by lawless combinations of the citizens of a part of a State, they could never be expected to approve that the care of vindicating their authority, of enforcing their laws, should be transferred from the officers of their own government to those of a State, and this to wait the issue of a process so undeterminate in its duration as that which it is proposed to pursue. . . .[8]

Special commissioners were appointed by the President to go to the western counties and to explain to the rebels the folly and futility of further resistance to the national government. President Washington reported all of these events in his Sixth Annual Message to Congress. It should be noted that although the President had accepted Hamilton's advice and was preparing to use maximum force to achieve compliance to the law, he restrained any precipitate action on the government's part, reflecting "his earnest wish to avoid a resort to coercion."[9]

President George Washington
Sixth Annual Message
November 19, 1794

Richardson, I, 154-56.

During the session of the year 1790 it was expedient to exercise the legislative power granted by the Constitution of the United States "to lay and collect excises." In a majority of the States scarcely an objection was heard to this mode of taxation. In some, indeed, alarms were at first conceived, until they were banished by reason and patriotism. In the four western counties of Pennsylvania a prejudice, fostered and imbittered by the artifice of men who labored for an ascendency over the will of others by the guidance of their passions, produced symptoms of riot and violence. It is well known that Congress did not hesitate to examine the complaints which were presented, and to relieve them as far as justice dictated or general convenience would permit. But the impression which this moderation made on the discontented did not correspond with what it deserved. The arts of delusion were no longer confined to the efforts of designing individuals. The very forbearance to press prosecutions was misinterpreted into a fear of urging the execution of the laws, and associations of men began to denounce threats against the officers employed. From a belief that by a more formal concert their operation might be defeated, certain self-created societies assumed the tone of condemnation. Hence, while the greater part of Pennsylvania itself were conforming themselves to the acts of excise, a few counties were resolved to frustrate them. It was now perceived that every expectation from the tenderness which had been hitherto pursued was unavailing, and that further delay could only create an opinion of impotency or irresolution in the Government. Legal process was therefore delivered to the marshal against the rioters and delinquent distillers.

No sooner was he understood to be engaged in this duty than the vengeance of armed men was aimed at *his* person and the person and property of the inspector of the revenue. They fired upon the marshal, arrested him, and detained him for some time as a prisoner. He was obliged, by the jeopardy of his life, to renounce the service of other process on the west side of the Allegheny Mountain, and a deputation was afterwards sent to him to demand a surrender of that which he *had* served. A numerous body repeatedly attacked the house of the inspector, seized his papers of office, and finally destroyed by fire his buildings and whatsoever they contained. Both of these officers, from a just regard to their safety, fled to the seat of Government, it being avowed that the motives to such outrages were to compel the resignation of the inspector, to withstand by force of arms the authority of the United States, and thereby to extort a repeal of the laws of excise and an alteration in the conduct of Government.

Upon the testimony of these facts an associate justice of the Supreme Court of the United States notified to me that "in the counties of Washington and Allegheny, in Pennsylvania, laws of the United States were opposed, and the execution thereof obstructed, by combinations too powerful to be suppressed by the ordinary course of judicial proceedings or by the powers vested in the marshal of that district." On this call, momentous in the extreme, I sought and weighed what might best subdue the crisis. On the one hand the judiciary was pronounced to be stripped of its capacity to enforce the laws; crimes which reached the very existence of social order were perpetrated without control; the friends of Government were insulted, abused, and overawed into silence or an apparent acquiescence; and to yield to the treasonable fury of so small a portion of the United States would be to violate the fundamental principle of our Constitution, which enjoins that the will of the majority shall prevail. On the other, to array citizen against citizen, to publish the dishonor of such excesses, to encounter the expense and other embarrassments of so distant an expedition, were steps too delicate, too closely interwoven with many affecting considerations, to be lightly adopted. I postponed, therefore, the summoning the militia immediately into the field, but I required them to be held in readiness, that if my anxious endeavors to reclaim the deluded and to convince the malignant of their danger should be fruitless, military force might be prepared to act before the season should be too far advanced.

My proclamation of the 7th of August last was accordingly issued, and accompanied by the appointment of commissioners, who were charged to repair to the scene of insurrection. They were authorized to confer with any bodies of men or individuals. They were instructed to be candid and explicit in stating the sensations which had been excited in the Executive, and his earnest wish to avoid a resort to coercion; to represent, however, that, without submission, coercion *must* be the resort; but to invite them, at the same time, to return to the demeanor of faithful citizens, by such accommodations as lay within the sphere of Executive power. Pardon, too, was tendered to them by the Government of the United States and that of Pennsylvania, upon no other condition than a satisfactory assurance of obedience to the laws.

The commissioners appointed by the President (aided by two additional representatives appointed by the governor of Pennsylvania) proceeded to the western counties and met with a committee representing the disgruntled rebels. The meetings were reasonably amicable, but the President's commissioners noted that there was still substantial resistance within the group, particularly among those from Washington County. They reported back to the President:

> We regret that we have still much Reason to apprehend that the Authority of the Laws will not be *universally & perfectly* restored, without military Coercion.[10]

On the strength of this report made at the end of August, the mobilization of the militia continued. Secretary of State Edmund Jennings Randolph thanked the commissioners for their labors and remarked, ". . . let the opposition be what it will, you have at least amply prepared the public mind for the support of any measures, which may be necessary on the occasion."[11] The governors of four states responded to the call and 12,900 men were gradually mobilized from Virginia, Maryland, New Jersey and Pennsylvania. The President reviewed the troops himself, travelling to Carlisle, Williamsport, Maryland and Fort Cumberland, Maryland. He had already issued a final proclamation indicating that ". . . a force which, according to every reasonable expectation, is adequate to the exigency is already in motion to the scene of disaffection. . . ."[12]

President George Washington Calls Out the Militia
September 25, 1974

Richardson, I, 153-54.

A PROCLAMATION

Whereas from a hope that the combinations against the Constitution and laws of the United States in certain of the western counties of Pennsylvania would yield to time and reflection I thought it sufficient in the first instance rather to take measures for calling forth the militia than immediately to embody them, but the moment is now come when the overtures of forgiveness, with no other condition than a submission to law, have been only partially accepted; when every form of conciliation not inconsistent with the being of Government has been adopted without effect; when the well-disposed in those counties are unable by their influence and example to reclaim the wicked from their fury, and are compelled to associate in their own defense; when the proffered lenity has been perversely misinterpreted into an apprehension that the citizens will march with reluctance; when the opportunity of examining the serious consequences of a treasonable opposition has been employed in propagating principles of anarchy, endeavoring through emissaries to alienate the friends of order from its support, and inviting its enemies to perpetrate similar acts of insurrection; when it is manifest that violence would continue to be exercised upon every attempt to enforce the laws; when, therefore, Government is set at defiance, the contest being whether a small portion of the United States shall dictate to the whole Union, and, at the expense of those who desire peace, indulge a desperate ambition:

Now, therefore, I, George Washington, President of the United States, in obedience to that high and irresistible duty consigned to me by the Constitution "to take care that the laws be faithfully executed," deploring that the American name should be sullied by the outrages of citizens on their own Government, commiserating such as remain obstinate from delusion, but resolved, in perfect reliance on that gracious Providence which so signally displays its goodness towards this country, to reduce the refractory to a due subordination to the law, do hereby declare and make known that, with a satisfaction which can be equaled only by the merits of the militia summoned into service from the States of New Jersey, Pennsylvania, Maryland, and Virginia, I have received intelligence of their patriotic alacrity in obeying the call of the present, though painful, yet commanding necessity; that a force which, according to every reasonable expectation, is adequate to the exigency is already in motion to the scene of disaffection; that those who have confided or shall confide in the protection of Government shall meet full succor under the standard and from the arms of the United States; that those who, having offended against the laws, have since entitled themselves to indemnity will be treated with the most liberal good faith if they shall not have forfeited their claim by any subsequent conduct, and that instructions are given accordingly.

And I do moreover exhort all individuals, officers, and bodies of men to contemplate with abhorrence the measures leading directly or indirectly to those crimes which produce this resort to military coercion; to check in their respective spheres the efforts of misguided or designing men to substitute their misrepresentation in the place of truth and their discontents in the place of stable government, and to call to mind that, as the people of the United States have been permitted, under the Divine favor, in perfect freedom, after solemn deliberation, and in an enlightened age, to elect their own government, so will their gratitude for this inestimable blessing be best distinguished by firm exertions to maintain the Constitution and the laws.

And, lastly, I again warn all persons whomsoever and wheresoever not to abet, aid, or comfort the insurgents aforesaid, as they will answer the contrary at their peril; and I do also require all officers and other citizens, according to their several duties, as far as may be in their power, to bring under the cognizance of the laws all offenders in the premises.

In testimony whereof I have caused the seal of the United States of America to be affixed to these presents, and signed the same with my hand.

Done at the city of Philadelphia, the 25th day of September, 1794, and of the Independence of the United States of America the nineteenth.

Geo. Washington

By the President:
   Edm. Randolph

Washington reported to the Congress that in his judgment these firm steps by the government had been necessary and successful. He urged them to provide for organizing, arming, and disciplining the militia so that it would be available in similar situations to support the President in executing the laws.

President George Washington
Report to Congress on Successes of Operation
November 19, 1794

Richardson, I, 157-59.

As commander in chief of the militia when called into the actual service of the United States, I have visited the places of general rendezvous to obtain more exact information and to direct a plan for ulterior movements. Had there been room for a persuasion that the laws were secure from obstruction; that the civil magistrate was able to bring to justice such of the most culpable as have not embraced the proffered terms of amnesty, and may be deemed fit objects of example; that the friends to peace and good government were not in need of that aid and countenance which they ought always to receive, and, I trust, ever will receive, against the vicious and turbulent, I should have caught with avidity the opportunity of restoring the militia to their families and homes. But succeeding intelligence has tended to manifest the necessity of what has been done, it being now confessed by those who were not inclined to exaggerate the ill conduct of the insurgents that their malevolence was not pointed merely to a particular law, but that a spirit inimical to all order has actuated many of the offenders. If the state of things had afforded reason for the continuance of my presence with the army, it would not have been withholden. But every appearance assuring such an issue as will redound to the reputation and strength of the United States, I have judged it most proper to resume my duties at the seat of Government, leaving the chief command with the governor of Virginia.

Still, however, as it is probable that in a commotion like the present, whatsoever may be the pretense, the purposes of mischief and revenge may not be laid aside, the stationing of a small force for a certain period in the four western counties of Pennsylvania will be indispensable, whether we contemplate the situation of those who are connected with the execution of the laws or of others who may have exposed themselves by an honorable attachment to them. Thirty days from the commencement of this session being the legal limitation of the employment of the militia, Congress can not be too early occupied with this subject.

Among the discussions which may arise from this aspect of our affairs, and from the documents which will be submitted to Congress, it will not escape their observation that not only the inspector of the revenue, but other officers of the United States in Pennsylvania have, from their fidelity in the discharge of their functions, sustained material injuries to their property. The obligation and policy of idemnifying them are strong and obvious. It may also merit attention whether policy will not enlarge this provision to the retribution of other citizens who, though not under the ties of office, may have suffered damage by their generous exertions for upholding the Constitution and the laws. The amount, even if all the injured were included, would not be great, and on future emergencies the Government would be amply repaid by the influence of an example that he who incurs a loss in its defense shall find a recompense in its liberality.

While there is cause to lament that occurrences of this nature should have disgraced the name or interrupted the tranquillity of any part of our community, or should have diverted to a new application any portion of the public resources, there are not wanting real and substantial consolations for the misfortune. It has demonstrated that our prosperity rests on solid foundations, by furnishing an additional proof that my fellow-citizens understand the true principles of government and liberty; that they feel their inseparable union; that notwithstanding all the devices which have been used to sway them from their interest and duty, they are now as ready to maintain the authority of the laws against licentious invasions as they were to defend their rights against usurpation. It has been a spectacle displaying to the highest advantage the value of republican government to behold the most and the least wealthy of our citizens standing in the same ranks as private soldiers, preeminently distinguished by being the army of the Constitution—undeterred by a march of 300 miles over rugged mountains, by the approach of an inclement season, or by any other discouragement. Nor ought I to omit to acknowledge the efficacious and patriotic cooperation which I have experienced from the chief magistrates of the States to which my requisitions have been addressed.

To every description of citizens, indeed, let praise be given. But let them persevere in their affectionate vigilance over that precious depository of American happiness, the Constitution of the United States. Let them cherish it, too, for the sake of those who, from every clime, are daily seeking a dwelling in our land. And when in the calm moments of reflection they shall have retraced the origin and progress of the insurrection, let them determine whether it has not been fomented by combinations of men who, careless of consequences and disregarding the unerring truth that those who rouse can not always appease a civil convulsion, have disseminated, from an ignorance or perversion of facts, suspicions, jealousies, and accusations of the whole Government.

Having thus fulfilled the engagement which I took when I entered into office, "to the best of my ability to preserve, protect, and defend the Constitution of the United States," on you, gentlemen, and the people by whom you are deputed, I rely for support.

In the arrangements to which the possibility of a similar contingency will naturally draw your attention it ought not to be forgotten that the militia laws have exhibited such striking defects as could not have been supplied but by the zeal of our citizens. Besides the extraordinary expense and waste, which are not the least of the defects, every appeal to those laws is attended with a doubt on its success.

The devising and establishing of a well-regulated militia would be a genuine source of legislative honor and a perfect title to public gratitude. I therefore entertain a hope that the present session will not pass without carrying to its full energy the power of organizing, arming, and disciplining the militia, and thus providing, in the language of the Constitution, for calling them forth to execute the laws of the Union, suppress insurrections, and repel invasions.

In the face of this show of force, the resistance collapsed. The President obtained from Congress appropriations to support a garrison of 2,500 men in the western counties during the winter in order to discourage any recurrence of such lawless acts, but no further incidents developed. Washington was delighted with the effect of this decisive action and encouraged by its long-range implications:

> I hope, and believe, that the spirit of anarchy in the western counties of this State (to quell which the force of the Union was called for) is *entirely* subdued; and altho' to effect it, the community has been saddled with a considerable expence, yet I trust no money could have been more advantageously expended; both as its respects the internal peace and welfare of *this* country, and the impression it will make on *others*. The spirit with which the Militia turned out, in support of the Constitution, and the laws of our country, at the same time that it does them immortal honor, is the most conclusive refutation that could have been given to the assertions of Lord Sheffield, and the prediction of others of his cast, that without the protection of G. Britain, we should be unable to govern ourselves; and would soon be involved in anarchy and confusion. They will see that republicanism is not the phantom of a deluded imagination: on the contrary, that under no form of government, will laws be better supported, liberty and property better secured, or happiness be more effectually dispensed to mankind.[13]

The first President clearly understood that a government which cannot enforce its laws is no government at all, and he also realized that within the framework of our complex political system, with its deliberate distribution of power, it is the responsibility of the Executive to see to it that the laws are obeyed.

Of course there is another level on which this episode can be interpreted. This was a young country in the 1790s and its citizens, particularly those who lived on the western frontier, were inexperienced with the forms and substance of constitutional government; they felt remote from its influence and bewildered by the new procedures of its operation. They thought that they had a legitimate grievance and that they were not being listened to or fairly treated. They wished to assert their newly-won rights, and many of them gave little thought to the consequences or to the broader implications of their actions. An historian sympathetic to their situation concluded:

> The Whiskey Insurrection was one of the signposts that marked the cleavage amidst the people, particularly between the agrarians and the rising industrial and mercantile class. Probably the thinking members of both sides did not fail to note this. The anger of the dominant elements against the West showed the hollowness of their tirades in favor of Liberty—at least from the equalitarian standpoint—and laid them open to the accusation of having wanted independence so that they could rule without British interference. Confronted with such charges the Federalists, with the wisdom of the children of this world, ignored them and consistently stuck to their tale of treason, ingratitude, and injured innocence.
>
> . . . The Whiskey Insurrection was at last abortive, and the Jeffersonian revolution when it came was not as complete as the Democratic societies might have advocated in 1793. The westerner of the seventeen-nineties saw more or less clearly that it was the economy of the frontier individualist that was being undermined. With the limited vision incident to any decade he thought he had his back to the wall making his last stand against plutocratic individualism. As a matter of fact Armageddon, that mythical struggle that is always coming but never arrives, was as far in the future as ever. There was too much cheap land farther west to make it worth while to stand and fight to the bitter end.[14]

Andrew Jackson Stems the Tide of Revolt

The law under which Washington acted was amended in 1795 and again in 1807 to strengthen Thomas Jefferson's hand in policing the provisions of the unpopular Embargo Act. The amendment of 1807 broadened the powers of the President to call upon "part of the land or naval force of the United States," in addition to the militia, to aid in the enforcement of law and the suppression of domestic violence and insurrection. Jefferson even went beyond the specific language of the law in a proclamation issued the following year, in which he added to the militia and the armed or naval forces, "all officers having authority, civil or military, and all other persons, civil or military, who shall be found in the vicinity" to join in suppressing any violation of the law.[15]

When the problem arose again in the Jackson administration, an entirely new dimension had been added. In this instance a state, South Carolina, instead of a group of indignant farmers, challenged the authority of the national government to impose a tariff law. Since the enactment of the Tariff Act of 1820, individual districts in South Carolina had protested to the national government about its inequity. In 1825 the state legislature declared the tariff law of 1824 unconstitutional and reacted even more strenuously in 1828 and 1830. In 1832 the state legislature called into session a special state convention which declared the federal tariff laws of 1828 and 1832 null and void. The convention named a Committee of Twenty-One which drew up the famous "Ordinance of Nullification." That document not only proclaimed that the tariff laws in question were unconstitutional and thus not binding upon the citizens or officers of the State of South Carolina, but it further stipulated that no case which called into question the validity of the ordinance could be taken to the Supreme Court of the United States on appeal from a decision in a state court, that no copy of the record of such a case could be made, and that any person attempting to initiate such an appeal would be found in contempt of the court. Finally, the document asserted that the state would not submit to forceful imposition of the law, and indeed, if any steps in such a direction were taken, the state would consider itself separated from the Union and thereafter independent and sovereign.

Although these arguments appear to be extreme today, they had a very respectable foundation at that time, and their adherents could trace their genesis back to Thomas Jefferson and James Madison, who drafted the Kentucky and Virginia Resolutions respectively. These resolutions were provoked by the passage of the alien and sedition laws, statutes which certainly tampered with basic constitutional rights in the administration of John Adams. At any rate, both the reasoning and language of these resolutions were similar to the reasoning and language of the South Carolina Ordinance of Nullification, and were based upon the premise that the Constitution was a limited charter, entered into by independent and sovereign states:

> . . . and that whensoever the general government assumes undelegated powers, its acts were unauthoritative, void and of no force.[16]

Although this doctrine predominated in the South, it was not confined to any single region; the Hartford Convention of 1814, which brought together official delegates from Massachusetts, Connecticut and Rhode Island, adopted resolutions very similar to the Virginia measures passed 15 years earlier. A full year and a half before the South Carolina Ordinance was promulgated, the Vice President, John C. Calhoun, endorsed the principle of nullification in an address issued from his South Carolina plantation, Fort Hill. This was, however, after Calhoun had already broken with Jackson. Calhoun argued that:

> The great and leading principle is, that the General Government emanated from the people of the several States, forming distinct political communities, and acting in their separate and sovereign capacity, and not

from all of the people forming one aggregate political community; that the Constitution of the United States is, in fact, a compact, to which each State is a party, in the character already described; and that the several States, or parties, have a right to judge of its infractions; and in the case of a deliberate, palpable, and dangerous exercise of power not delegated, they have the right, in the last resort, to use the language of the Virginia Resolutions, "to interpose for arresting the progress of the evil, and for maintaining, within their respective limits, the authorities, rights, and liberties appertaining to them."[17]

Such a frontal assault upon the power of the national government was not accepted passively by Andrew Jackson. Weeks before the ordinance was promulgated, President Jackson had obtained as much accurate information as possible about the situation in South Carolina. He corresponded extensively with an old friend in Charleston (Joel Poinsett), who was loyal to the Union, and he informed Jackson as to current developments in the state. Jackson also sent George Breathitt, the brother of the governor of Kentucky, to Charleston, ostensibly as a post office agent, but with the real intent of cooperating with Poinsett and checking out his assessments of the temper of the people, the state of the federal government's military power, and, indeed, the loyalty of its representatives in the area. Long before Jackson acted, he was extremely well informed as to what kind of resistance he could expect, and of the nature of the support he could count on from South Carolinians loyal to the federal government. Jackson responded quickly after having received Poinsett's warning and instructed his secretary of war to alert the officers of the United States Army in command of the forts in Charleston Harbor to be prepared to repel an attempt by the secessionists to capture their installations by force.

Joel R. Poinsett
Letter to President Andrew Jackson
October 16, 1832

Bassett, IV, 481-83.

Dear Sir, you will have seen by the public papers, that the Union party throughout the state of So. Carolina have been beaten at the ballot box; and you must be prepared to hear very shortly of a State Convention and an act of Nullification. Our party met last night, the first time after our defeat, and past resolutions expressive of our firm determination to oppose nullification and to adhere to our allegiance to the United States. But allegiance implies protection and we rely upon the Government acting with vigor in our behalf. The impression on the minds of the Nullifiers undoubtedly is that no measures will be taken against them, and that they will be left to carry out their designs with impunity. If so we have nothing to do but witness the triumph of Mr. Calhoun. I have on every occasion told my fellow Citizens that the Executive of the United States would act decidedly and vigorously. What that action ought to be I have not the presumption to hint at; but it is right you should know, that it is believed the Nullifiers intend to proceed first by process of law agreably to an act to be passed. They will proceed by replevin, and I suppose if the Collector refuses (as he surely will do, for he is a firm determined man) they will either imprison him or break open the Custom Stores. If the government in addition to any other measures they may chuse to take, think proper to aid the Collector in resisting this illegal and unconstitutional act, Measures ought to be taken immediately. Col. Lindsay ought to be ordered to take up his residence in the Citadel. He is now on the Island. I do not know what number of men he has, but more could be sent, by sending full companies and withdrawing such as are deficient, so as not to excite distrust—two or three hundred muskets and a number of hand grenades ought to be in the Citadel with their corresponding ammunition. Indeed whether the Government is disposed to resist the replevin and protect its Stores or not, the precautions I propose ought to be taken.

We are not disposed to make any riotous or tumultous resistance; but we are ready to support the laws if legally called upon so to do at the hazard of our lives. I am sure I speak the sentiments of the party when I say so. Judging from the late conduct of these men we may have to defend ourselves against lawless violence, and we ought not to be left entirely defenceless, I mean without arms and ammunition. I am exceedingly anxious on this subject. The party in the city look to me for precautionary measures and I would not have them disappointed. All the officers ought to be men on whom you can rely and in whom we can place our confidence. Major Belton has, I believe, been sent away very properly. Mathias pay master ought not to be suffered to remain here taking the part he does agt. the government. Lining, Surgeon, ought to be removed. The custom house where the battle will be fought is crowded with Nullifiers, ought they not to be removed? I shall send Mr. McLane a list of them. The post office is filled with the Enemies of the government. I am advised even not to put a letter in the Post office of Charleston directed to you! Ought such things to be at such a crisis? If the executive should resolve to remove these officers I hope Col. Drayton or some leading Union men will be consulted as to their Successors.

On the issue of this contest between the federal government and a faction in this State depends the permanency of the Union and the future character of this nation. We feel therefore a deep interest in the measures which will be adopted by the Executive and an earnest desire to lend our aid to render them effectual.

   I am, dear Sir, respectfully Yours

President Andrew Jackson
Letter to Secretary of War Lewis Cass
October 29, 1832

Bassett, IV, 483.

   The Secretary at War will forthwith cause secrete and confidential orders to be Issued to the officers commanding the Forts in the harbour of charleston So

Carolina to be vigilant to prevent a surprise in the night or by day, against any attempt to seize and occupy the Fts. by any Set of people under whatever pretext the Forts may be approached. Warn them that the attempt will be made, and the officers commanding will be responsible for the defence of the Forts and garrisons, against all intrigue or assault, and they are to defend them to the last extremity—permitting no armed force to approach either by night or day. *The attempt will be made to surprise the Forts and garrisons* by the militia, and must be guarded against with *vestal vigilence* and any attempt by force repelled with prompt and examplary punishment.

President Andrew Jackson
Letter to George Breathitt
November 7, 1832

Mr. Breathitt during his visit to charleston on the business with which he is charged by the Treasury and Post office Departments, will collect all the information he can obtain from correct sources on the following points, 1st. What foundation there is for the statements he has seen that several officers employed in the revenue service are aiding the views of the party that have declared the Tariff laws inoperative and void within the limits of the state of South carolina. If they are well founded Mr. Breathitt will collect the evidence and bring it with him, specifying the names of all officers so engaged.

2d. What foundation there is for the report that the Post master of the city of charleston and his clerks or deputies are aiding the views of the same party, and that communications from the Government passing thro' that office at this time are subjected to examination before they reach their address. The evidence of this charge and the names of the persons implicated Mr. Breathitt will collect.

3d. Should it appear that there are any other officers holding commissions from the General Government, aiding or countenancing in any form the scheme of the Nullifiers to thwart the execution of the laws of the Union, Mr. Breathitt will make it his business to ascertain their names and the evidence of their misconduct in this respect. He will also by consultation with Col. Drayton and Mr. Poinsett and other discreet friends of the Union obtain all such information as may be useful to the Government to enable it to take timely steps towards the counteraction of the effort of the Nullifiers to render inoperative the laws of the Union:

November 7, 1832

Dear sir, The recent movements in So Carolina have awakened in my boosom the most painful sensations, and, altho nothing of serious and dangerous character may result from them, it becomes my duty to ascertain, as far as practicable, to what extremity the nullifyers intend to proceed, and to counteract, to the extent of authority vested in the executive and the high obligations incumbent upon him, such of their movements as tend to defeat the collection of revenue imposed by the united states, and thus render null and void the laws of congress on this subject. You will be able fully to comprehend the views of the Executive by the perusal of the instructions from the Secretary of the Treasury to the Collector of Charleston, which are herewith intrusted to your care for safe delivery, and the instructions herewith inclosed to you.

Having entire confidence in your fidelity and capacity, it is desired, in addition to your other instructions, that you make the enquiry how far the Civil Jurisdiction of South Carolina extends over the bay and harbour of charleston, and whether, before the date of the Federal constitution, that State had established courts of admiralty, and whether the State now has Courts of admiralty jurisdiction.

You will observe the real situation of Sulivans Island, and see whether it could be assailed and carried in its rear. You will also observe the situation of the armament of Castle Pinckny, and what Space of dry land surrounds the Forts.

You will collect all the information touching the subject intrusted to your inquiries that you can obtain, which may be serviceable to the government.

Perceiving, as you must, the highly delicate and confidential character of your business, it is not necessary to give you a caution as to your conduct.

Wishing you a pleasant journey and a speedy return I am

very respectfully your friend

President Andrew Jackson
Letter to Joel R. Poinsett
November 7, 1832

Bassett, IV, 485-86.

Dear Sir, This will be handed to you by my young friend George Breathitt Esqr., brother of the present Governor of Kentucky, in whom every confidence may be reposed. I beg leave to make him known to you as such.

Mr. Breathitt goes to your state and city as agent for the Post office Depart. He bears instructions from the secretary of the Treasury to the collector of Charleston, but we want him only known as agent of the Post office.

I wish him to see the Fts. and revenue cutters in your harbour and to visit Sulivans Island—This to be done merely as a stranger having curiosity to examine your capacity for defence and facilities for commerce, to your polite aid I recommend him for this object.

I have instructed him to obtain the real intentions of the nullifyers, whether they mean really to resort to force to prevent the collection of the revenue and to resist the due execution of the laws and if so, what proof exists to shew that the imputations against important individuals and officers of the government in being engaged in advising, aiding and abetting in this threatened Nullification and rebelous course are true.

It is desirable that the Executive should be in possession of all the evidence on these points, and I have referred Mr. Breathitt to you and Col. Drayton believing that you will afford *him* all the knowledge you possess.

Mr. Breathitt is charged with the enquiry what officers, if any, in the Customs or Post office Department belong to or have adhered to the Nullifyers and the character of Mr. Pruson Simpson, from whom I have recd. a long letter today, and all and every information of the views and measures of the nullifyers which they mean to adopt.

We have been looking for some information from some friend of the union in that quarter, but have hitherto been disappointed, but it appears a crisis is about to approach, when the government must act and that with energy. My own astonishment is that my fellow citizens of So. Carolina should be so far deluded, by the wild theory and sophistry of a few ambitious demagogues, as to place themselves in the attitude of rebellion against their government, and become the destroyers of their own prosperity and liberty. There appears in their whole proceedings nothing but madness and folly. If grievances do exist there are constitutional means to redress them. Patriots would seek those means only.

The duty of the Executive is a plain one, the laws will be executed and the union preserved by all the constitutional and legal means he is invested with and I rely with great confidence on the support of every honest patriot in So. Carolina who really loves his country and the prosperity and happiness we enjoy under our happy and peaceful republican government.

By the return of Mr. Breathitt I shall expect to hear from you.

with my sincere regards I am yr mo. obdt. sert.

Joel R. Poinsett
Letter to President Andrew Jackson
November 16, 1832

Bassett, IV, 486-88.

Dear Sir, I received your very welcome letter by the hands of Mr. Breathitt yesterday afternoon, and hasten to reply to it, as that gentleman appears desirous of returning to Washington as early as possible.

His desire to return by the way of Columbia will prevent his examining the precise state of the forts and revenue cutters in our harbour; but I have undertaken to do that for him, and will from personal inspection give you all the details you require. This duty shall be performed as soon as the North Eastern gale now blowing passes over. I hope to be able to send the report so as to anticipate Mr. Breathitt's arrival. With respect to the real intentions of the Nullifiers Mr. Breathitt may be able better to ascertain them by a short stay in Columbia during the session of their convention; but in the mean time I will tell you what we believe them to be.

The principal object of these unprincipled men has always appeared to me to be to embar[r]ass your administration and defeat your election; but they have led the people on so far under other pretexts that they must proceed. They are now somewhat divided. Mr. McDuffie will probably urge the convention to secede from the Union in the event of the government using any means to coerce the state. Many of their party will be opposed to such a measure. They are however so organised that if the leaders of the political club resolve upon this course it will be adopted. It is believed that Mr. Calhoun is against this measure and insists that the state may be in and out of the Union at the same time and that the government has no right to cause the laws to be executed in South Carolina. Both parties are anxious and indulge the hope, that the general government will commit some act of violence, which will enlist the sympathies of the bordering states: provided it be not their own they care not how soon blood is shed. It will be necessary therefore to proceed with great caution in counteracting their schemes. It is probable they will proceed by writ of replevin, served on the Collector. He will resist by refusing to give up the goods and I am at present of opinion that it will be better to allow them to commit that act of violence; namely breaking open the public stores, which will rouse the indignation of the people of the United States against them. The custom house ought then to be removed to one of the forts, which can be decided upon hereafter. This decision [sic] will be made with a view to repel any attack which in the wildness of their folly the Nullifiers might attempt.

With respect to the officers of government who are aiding and abetting the nullifying party, I am sorry to tell you, that there are many. The Post Office is entirely filled with them. The Post Master, His Deputy, his son, and all the clerks are active Agents of that party and clamourous Nullifiers. I have no evidence however of any letters or communications between the government and any individuals in Charleston being opened or stopped, and I must in candour state, that I very much doubt it, if I do not discredit it altogether. Such however is the common impression and I hesitate to act against the advice of my friends and to confide a letter on confidential business to the Charleston post office. I have reason to believe, that the merchants generally are not satisfied with the manner the business of the office is conducted by Mr. Bacot and I know that his dismissal will be acceptable to the friends of the Union in this City. He ought to be succeeded by an inhabitant of the State and a member of the union party.

In the Custom house there are many violent nullifiers, a list will be again furnished through Mr. Breathitt. The most active is I regret to say, Major Laval. He has proved extremely ungrateful to you and there is but one opinion among us of the urgent necessity of his removal. If you could offer him a Place in New Orleans, his entire removal would be useful to the cause of the Union.

The Officers of the army had been seduced by the attentions of the Nullifiers. Major Belton and Major Massias were very properly removed: but I was very much surprised to see Major Massias in Charleston during the last election in October. He ought to be removed so far from this city that he cannot return to it on such occasions. I would not be unjust to Major Heilman. I believe him to be an honorable man, and do not think he has been concerned in any party matters; but he is on very intimate terms with all those gentlemen, so much so that we are and would be afraid to open ourselves to him. If therefore you could send us an officer of the same rank, a Southern man if possible, we should greatly prefer it. I say Southern because prejudices have been excited against Northerners, and as it is considered a Southern question exclusively it might be politic to have it settled by Southern men. I should have preferred therefore on that account and on that account only that a Southern Navy Officer should have been sent here. I know Commodore Elliott and have a great personal regard and respect for him. I know of no one, who unites more firmness with consummate prudence than Elliott, but a Virginian who was true to the union would succeed better. If however Commodore Elliott does come no one will be more happy than myself to greet him and to aid him in the performance of his duties.

You desire to know something of the character of a Mr. Simpson from whom you have received a letter. He is a very good man, a friend of the union; but is considered by us as an extremely weak man. The letter in question was not written by him. I heard the history of it after it was sent. He had, he said known you in Nashville and he asked a respectable gentleman who stands very high in our union ranks to write you a letter for him, which he accordingly did and availed himself of the opportunity to relate what he believed and what is the general impression.

Mr. Breathitt has put some queries to me, which I will answer here. He wishes to know if the Civil Jurisdiction of So. Ca. extends over the bay and harbour of Charleston? It does. Sullivan's Island is attached to Christ Church parish the rest of the bay to St. Philips. Whether before the date of the federal constitution that state had established Courts of admiralty, and whether she now has any such Courts? The admiralty Court existed before the revolution and was continued until the adoption of the present federal constitution when it ceased altogether.

I mentioned to you in a former letter, that some arms and ammunition ought to be sent here. The union party require to be armed to repel lawless violence and I will endeavour to organise them for that purpose. Hand grenades and small rockets are excellent weapons in a street fight and I should like to have some of them. A few of the United States Rifles would be serviceable, say one hundred, and with one sent to me I would instruct the men in the use of that formidable arm. They must be furnished with bayonets. These arms can be kept in the United States forts and will only be called for for self protection and in defence of the laws. I wish some of our small vessels of war would look into this harbour. If they should require repairs so much the better. They can be done [here] as well as elsewhere and if they cost a few dollars more, it matters not to the govt.: the good such expenditures will do is very great. The discontent at no part of the revenue raised from among us being expended among our citizens is general and every opportunity ought to be seized of allaying this cause of discontent.

I hope you may be able to sooth the conflicting parties and to unite all the patriotic men in Congress in one effort to support the laws and to cooperate with you in your praiseworthy determination by every legal and constitutional means to preserve the union. You may rely upon the aid of all the brave and patriotic men, who compose our party in this city and state.

I am Dear Sir, respectfully and with great regard,

Joel R. Poinsett
Letter to President Andrew Jackson
November 24, 1832

Bassett, IV, 490-91.

Dear Sir, According to my engagement I have visited and thoroughly examined the forts in this harbour, and will now proceed to give you an account of their situation. This duty should have been executed earlier but the weather has been such as to render it difficult to cross the bay until within these two days.

Fort Moultrie is in a very dilapidated state, The South western wall is cracked in such a manner as to endanger its fall if great guns were fired from the parapet over it. That part of the fort could not however well be attacked, and the wharves Captn Eliason proposes throwing out, at the same time that they will protect the works from the action of the currents will furnish a flank fire along the Curtain sea ward, which is very much required. The rear about which you enquire particularly has a regular work, two bastions connected by a curtain and the flank fires are good, when this is picketed it will be strong enough to resist such forces as can be brought against it here. The whole work is surrounded by houses, which to give it fair play in case of attack must come down. There is besides a sand hill about a hundred yards from the fort, which has been thrown up by the eddying winds, and is high enough to command the fort and large enough to hold four pieces of field artillery. A few rifle men on this hill would make the men uncomfortable in the fort. There are no platforms yet on the land side, and the guns about 60 of large calibre are not mounted, indeed there are no carriages to mount them on. These could be made here of Cypress, a very durable wood that abounds with us. This fort would require 4 or 500 men and when put in order might defy all the Militia of the State.

At fort Johnson there are no works at all except a Martello tower, which being upon the land of the State ought to be pulled down for it commands the buildings belonging to the government. Both Fort Moultrie and Fort Johnson must be regarded as most important points for the defence of this harbour and ought to be preserved most carefully. At both positions Break Waters are required to secure the works from the action of the tides and currents and might be constructed by sinking hulks at the proper points. The most important work is the one projected by General Bernard and now in progress; but that would be inefficient without the forts on Sullivan's and James Islands. This work is just appearing above water and I think ought to be driven on as rapidly as may be for at a crisis like this the possession of such a position would render us very secure. I have conversed with Captn. Eliason on the subject and am induced to believe, that a small steam boat would facilitate his operations very considerably and prove in the end a great saveing of money. The small vessels now employed in the transportation of Stone in the harbour are frequently detained for days together by calms and high winds and a great many more men are necessarily employed upon them, than would be required to manage a

Steam boat towing properly constructed stone boats, which would discharge themselves.

Castle Pinckney is in fine order. The Armament Consists of 8-24 pounders 1-10 inch Mortar 2-12 pounders and 2-6 ditto. It is situated on a marshy Island a mile from the city and occupies the only spot of solid earth the Island contains. It could only be attacked in the rear by a flotilla in hog Island channel. By a reference to the survey of Major Bache, which is in the department you will see how it is exposed to such an attack. There are no works in the rear, as all the defences are Seaward and Captn. Saunders has placed two field pieces mounted on travelling carriages outside of the Castle, on the small esplanade in the rear of it. I should think some temporary work ought to be thrown up in the rear capable of mounting two heavy guns. In the present state of the works in this harbour Castle Pinckney is the only place where the custom house could be established with safety and upon consulting with Captn. Eliason I find that two buildings might be erected to serve for stores and accommodations for the revenue officers, which would materially strengthen the works. To protect the works from insult if not from danger there ought to be a small floating force in the harbour—one schooner or a sloop of war would be sufficient. Gun boats or smaller vessels are exposed, to be boarded and taken by a superior force of resolute men. You will perceive by a reference to the survey, that such a force would render it impracticable for an enemy to attack the either fort Moultrie or Castle Pickney—the Vessel of war ought to be furnished with an additional number of boats capable of bearing small cannon.

I am, Dear Sir, respectfully

I have submitted this letter to Col. Drayton. He approves of the suggestions it contains; but says, that it might be expedient to have two sloops of war in the harbour in the event of a simultaneous attack being made upon Castle Pinckney and fort Moultrie. In that case one sloop of war and one schooner is the force I would recommend, the latter being rather more manageable in passing in and out of our Harbour.

Joel R. Poinsett
Letter to President Andrew Jackson
November 29, 1832

Bassett, IV, 491-92.

Dear Sir, The deep interest I know you feel in the situation of this state induces me to write to you without hesitation or reserve as often as there is any thing of interest to communicate. The violent measures adopted by the nullifiers have roused the indignation of a great many of their opponents, but it cannot be disguised, that some of them have been intimidated by them. The party will meet on the second monday in December and we will use our best efforts to excite them to do their duty.

In any event I do not [*sic*] believe, nay I am sure, that they will remain firm in their allegiance to the United States, and I cannot but hope, that many of them will be induced to despise the threats of their Enemies and lend their active aid to crush this rebellion. For my own part no threats, no bills of pains and penalties nor definitions of treason to the state shall stop my course and I believe some brave men will go with me. We had rather die, than submit to the tyranny of such an oligarchy as J. C. Calhoun, James Hamilton, Robt. Y. Hayne and McDuffie and we implore our sister states and the federal govt. to rescue us from these lawless and reckless men.

I am more especially anxious about this because I am aware my friend Col. Drayton does not think with me. He is of opinion, that the United States in Congress will say to us, Let South Carolina go out of the union if she will go, and I am afraid believes this to be the best policy which Congress can follow. With great deference for his opinion I think him entirely wrong. If such a course should be adopted the union must be dissolved in all its parts and foreign and domestic wars necessarily ensue. Whereas if these bad men are put down by the strong arm, the union will be cemented by their conduct and by the vigour of the government, and you will earn the imperishable glory of having preserved this great confederacy from destruction. Remember too, that there are 16,000 Americans, your own Countrymen who call upon you to save them from tyranny and oppression. I will not comment upon the ordinance of the convention nor upon the Governor's message, nor the contemplated bills of pains and penalties. They speak for themselves. 16,000 freemen are proscribed and disfranchised by a few ambitious Demagogues. The Ordinances of Charles the tenth were not by half so destructive of personal liberty.

Many of my friends talk of emigrating and leaving these bad men to their fate. I, Sir, shall not do so. I will remain to lead the few brave men, who place confidence in me, and, if we are left unprotected, to sustain them by my example and my determined resistance to the Tyrants who seek to ruin this once glorious Republic. I have been appointed to go to North Carolina, to Virginia and urged even to go to Washington. But this is my post so long as it is surrounded with so much danger. I have strong hopes in the wisdom of Congress, in their patriotism and in your firmness and decision. I explained to you fully in my last sent under cover to the Secretary of the Treasury my views of what ought to be done by the union party and we will do it at all hazards whenever you say it is time to act. I wrote you under cover to Mr. Oliver of Baltimore respecting the forts. But as this is a circuitous route I will propose to you to write under cover to Mr. Mason of Georgetown either the General or his Son John Mason jr. as you may please to direct. If it be judged expedient to change the post master of this City, We would recommend Edward McCrady for that Office.

I am, Dear Sir, very respectfully

President Andrew Jackson
Notes Perhaps Intended for the Annual Message
November [1832?]

Bassett, IV, 493.

The attitude of So. Carolina having organised her volunteers with the avowed and declared intent of opposing the execution of the laws of the United States, keeping the [m] organised and continuing to drill and discipline them, with the declared views as expressed by the Govr. of the State in his addresses to them as well as by all the nullifying public Journals of that State that their services will soon be wanted to aid their fellow citizens of the State of Alabama, in resisting the authority of the United States in removing the intruders from the Creek nation and the public Lands and thereby exciting and encouraging rebellion and resistance to the laws of the United States has induced the Executive to bring this subject before Congress for their consideration and action, it appearing to him that the raising arming, and dicipline volunteers and keeping them organised and trained to resist the authority and execution of the laws of the Union, is such a crisis as the Sages who formed the constitution anticipated and intended to prohibit. It is therefore recommended to Congress that by proper enactments it may define what shall be considered by any State of these United States, "as keeping of troops or ships of war in time of peace, or entering into any agreement or compact with another State or Forign power"— and not only to define the offence, but the punishment. Nothing can be more injurious to the peace and harmony of society and more dangerous to the existing of the Union, than the late proceedings of So Carolina in keeping in time of peace, a standing army of well drilled volunteers, for the declared purpose of resisting the laws but aiding the lawless citizens of other States to resist the execution of the laws of the Union and ought to [be] prohibited.

President Andrew Jackson
Letter to Joel R. Poinsett
December 2, 1832

Bassett, IV, 493-94.

My D'r Sir, Your two letters of Novr. 24 and 25th last have been received, and I hasten to answer them.

I fully concur with you in your views of Nullification. It leads directly to civil war and bloodshed and deserves the execration of every friend of the country. Should the civil power with your aid as *a posse comitatus* prove not strong enough to carry into effect the laws of the Union, you have a right to call upon the

Government for aid and the Executive will yield it as far as he has been vested with the power by the constitution and the laws made in pursuance thereof.

The precautionary measures spoken of in your last letter have been in some degree anticipated. Five thousand stand of muskets with corresponding equipments have been ordered to Castle Pinckney; and a Sloop of war with a smaller armed vessel (the experiment) will reach Charleston harbor in due time. The commanding officer of Castle Pinckney will be instructed by the Secretary of War to deliver the arms and their equipment to your order, taking a receipt for them, and should the emergency arise he will furnish to your requisition such ordnance and ordnance stores as can be spared from the arsenals.

The Union must be preserved; and its laws duly executed, but by proper means. With calmness and firmness such as becomes those who are conscious of being right and are assured of the support of public opinion, we must perform our duties without suspecting that there are those around us desiring to tempt us into the wrong. We must act as the instruments of the law and if force is offered to us in that capacity then we shall repel it with the certainty, even should we fall as individuals, that the friends of liberty and union will still be strong enough to prostrate their enemies.

Your union men should act in concert: Their designation as unionists should teach them to be prepared for every emergency: and inspire them with the energy to overcome every impediment that may be thrown in the way of the laws of their constitution, whose cause is now not only their cause but that of free institutions throughout the world. They should recollect that perpetuity is stamped upon the constitution by the blood of our Fathers—by those who atchieved as well as those who improved our system of free Government. For this purpose was the principle of amendment inserted in the constitution which all have sworn to support and in violation of which no state or states have the right to secede, much less to dissolve the union. Nullification therefore means insurrection and war; and the other states have a right to put it down: and you also and all other peaccable citizens have a right to aid in the same patriotic object when summoned by the violated laws of the land. Should an emergency occur for the arms before the order of the Secretary of war to the commanding officer to deliver them to your order, shew this to him and he will yield a compliance

I am great haste yr. mo obdt. Servt.

President Andrew Jackson
Letter to Joel R. Poinsett
December 9, 1832

Bassett, IV, 497-98.

My D'r Sir, Your letters were this moment recd, from the hands of Col. Drayton, read and duly considered, and in haste I reply. The true spirit of patriotism that they breath fills me with pleasure. If the Union party unite with you, heart and hand in the text you have laid down, you will not only preserve the union, but save our native state, from that ruin and disgrace into which her treasonable leaders have attempted to plunge her. All the means in my power, I will employ to enable her own citizens, those faithful patriots, who cling to the Union to put it down.

The proclamation I have this day Issued, and which I inclose you, will give you my views, of the treasonable conduct of the convention and the Governors recommendation to the assembly—it is not merely rebellion, but the act of raising troops, positive treason, and I am assured by all the members of congress with whom I have conversed that I will be sustained by congress. If so, I will meet it at the threshold, and have the leaders arrested and arraigned for treason—I am only waiting to be furnished with the acts of your Legislature, to make a communication to Congress, ask the means necessary to carry my proclamation into compleat affect, and by an exemplary punishment of those leaders for treason so unprovoked, put down this rebellion, and strengthen our happy government both at home and abroad.

My former letter and the communication from the Dept. of War, will have informed you of the arms and equipments having been laid in Deposit subject to your requisition, to aid the civil authority in the due execution of the law, *whenever called on as the posse comitatus*, etc. etc.

The vain threats of resistance by those who have raised the standard of rebellion shew their madness and folly. You may assure those patriots who cling to their country, and this union, which alone secures our liberty, prosperity and happiness, that in forty days, I can have within the limits of So. Carolina fifty thousand men, and in forty days more another fifty thousand—However potant the threat of resistance with only a population of 250,000 whites and nearly that double in blacks with our ships in the port to aid in the execution of our laws?—The wickedness, madness and folly of the leaders and the delusion of their followers in the attempt to destroy themselves and our union has not its paralel in the history of the world. The Union will be preserved, The safety of the republic, the supreme law, which will be promptly obeyed by me.

I will be happy to hear from you often, thro' Col. Mason or his son, if you think the postoffice unsafe.

> I am with sincere respect
> yr. mo. obdt. servt.

Several weeks after the South Carolina Nullification Ordinance was issued, President Jackson responded with an executive proclamation that today remains one of the outstanding and more eloquent state papers in our history. The words are those of Jackson's secretary of state, Edward Livingston, but the force and clarity of the document are traceable to the President himself.

The President's proclamation made it crystal clear that the ordinance was based upon premises that could not be tolerated under a constitutional system of government. Jackson argued that the power to annul a law of the United States was "incompatible with the existence of the Union, contradicted expressly by the letter of the Constitution, unauthorized by its spirit, inconsistent with every principle upon which it was founded, and destructive of the great object for which it was formed." He also very bluntly warned the "fellow citizens of my native state" that he intended to mobilize the full power of the federal government under his constitutional authorization "to take care that the laws be faithfully executed," and to crush what he considered to be a treasonable action. He wanted to leave no doubt in their minds as to what kind of response they could expect to actions based upon their nullification doctrine.

President Andrew Jackson
Proclamation in Response to the South Carolina
Nullification Proclamation
December 10, 1832

Richardson, III, 1203-19.

PROCLAMATION

Whereas a convention assembled in the State of South Carolina have passed an ordinance by which they declare "that the several acts and parts of acts of the Congress of the United States purporting to be laws for the imposing of duties and imposts on the importation of foreign commodities, and now having actual operation and effect within the United States, and more especially" two acts for the same purposes passed on the 29th of May, 1828, and on the 14th of July, 1832, "are unauthorized by the Constitution of the United States, and violate the true meaning and intent thereof, and are null and void and no law," nor binding on the citizens of that State or its officers; and by the said ordinance it is further declared to be unlawful for any of the constituted authorities of the State or of the United States to enforce the payment of the duties imposed by the said acts within the same State, and that it is the duty of the legislature to pass such laws as may be necessary to give full effect to the said ordinance; and

Whereas by the said ordinance it is further ordained that in no case of law or equity decided in the courts of said State wherein shall be drawn in question the validity of the said ordinance, or of the acts of the legislature that may be passed to give it effect, or of the said laws of the United States, no appeal shall be allowed to the Supreme Court of the United States, nor shall any copy of the record be permitted or allowed for that purpose, and that any person attempting to take such appeal shall be punished as for contempt of court; and, finally, the said ordinance declares that the people of South Carolina will maintain the said ordinance at every hazard, and that they will consider the passage of any act by Congress abolishing or closing the ports of the said State or otherwise obstructing the free ingress or egress of vessels to and from the said ports, or any other act of the Federal Government to coerce the State, shut up her ports, destroy or harass her commerce, or to enforce the said acts otherwise than through the civil tribunals of the country, as inconsistent with the longer continuance of South Carolina in the Union, and that the people of the said State will thenceforth hold themselves obsolved from all further obligation to maintain or preserve their political connection with the people of the other States, and will forthwith proceed to organize a separate government and do all other acts and things which sovereign and independent states may of right do; and

Whereas the said ordinance prescribes to the people of South Carolina a course of conduct in direct violation of their duty as citizens of the United States, contrary to the laws of their country, subversive of its Constitution, and having for its object the destruction of the Union—that Union which, coeval with our political existence, led our fathers, without any other ties to unite them than those of patriotism and a common cause, through a sanguinary struggle to a glorious independence; that sacred Union, hitherto inviolate, which, perfected by our happy Constitution, has brought us, by the favor of Heaven, to a state of prosperity at home and high consideration abroad rarely, if ever, equaled in the history of nations:

To preserve this bond of our political existence from destruction, to maintain inviolate this state of national honor and prosperity, and to justify the confidence my fellow-citizens have reposed in me, I, Andrew Jackson, President of the United States, have thought proper to issue this my proclamation, stating my views of the Constitution and laws applicable to the measures adopted by the convention of South Carolina and to the reasons they have put forth to sustain them, declaring the course which duty will require me to pursue, and, appealing to the understanding and patriotism of the people, warn them of the consequences that must inevitably result from an observance of the dictates of the convention.

Strict duty would require of me nothing more than the exercise of those powers with which I am now or may hereafter be invested for preserving the peace of the Union and for the execution of the laws; but the imposing aspect which opposition has assumed in this case, by clothing itself with State authority, and the deep interest which the people of the United States must all feel in preventing a resort to stronger measures while there is a hope that anything will be yielded to reasoning and remonstrance, perhaps demand, and will certainly justify, a full exposition to South Carolina and the nation of the views I entertain of this important question, as well as a distinct enunciation of the course which my sense of duty will require me to pursue.

The ordinance is founded, not on the indefeasible right of resisting acts which are plainly unconstitutional and too oppressive to be endured, but on the strange position that any one State may not only declare an act of Congress void, but prohibit its execution; that they may do this consistently with the Constitution; that the true construction of that instrument permits a State to retain its place in the Union and yet be bound by no other of its laws than those it may choose to consider as constitutional. It is true, they add, that to justify this abrogation of a law it must be palpably contrary to the Constitution; but it is evident that to give the right of resisting laws of that description, coupled with the uncontrolled right to decide what laws deserve that character, is to give the power of resisting all laws; for as by the theory there is no appeal, the reasons alleged by the State, good or bad, must prevail. If it should be said that public opinion is a sufficient check against the abuse of this power, it may be asked why it is not deemed a sufficient guard against the passage of an unconstitutional act by Congress? There is, however, a restraint in this last case which makes the assumed power of a State more indefensible, and which does not exist in the other. There are two appeals from an unconstitutional act passed by Congress—one to the judiciary, the other to the people and the States. There is no appeal from the State decision in theory, and the practical illustration shows that the courts are closed against an application to review it, both judges and jurors being sworn to decide in its favor. But reasoning on this subject is superfluous when our social compact, in express terms, declares that the laws of the United States, its Constitution, and treaties made under it are the supreme law of the land, and, for greater caution, adds "that the judges in every State shall be bound thereby, anything in the constitution or laws of any State to the contrary notwithstanding." And it may be asserted without fear of refutation that no federative government could exist without a similar provision. Look for a moment to the consequence. If South Carolina considers the revenue laws unconstitutional and has a right to prevent their execution in the port of Charleston, there would be a clear constitutional objection to their collection in every other port; and no revenue could be collected anywhere, for all imposts must be equal. It is no answer to repeat that an unconstitutional law is no law so long as the question of its legality is to be decided by the State itself, for every law operating injuriously upon any local interest will be perhaps thought, and certainly represented, as unconstitutional, and, as has been shown, there is no appeal.

If this doctrine had been established at an earlier day, the Union would have been dissolved in its infancy. The excise law in Pennsylvania, the embargo and nonintercourse law in the Eastern States, the carriage tax in Virginia, were all deemed unconstitutional, and were more unequal in their operation than any of the laws now complained of; but, fortunately, none of those States discovered that they had the right now claimed by South Carolina. The war into which we were forced to support the dignity of the nation and the rights of our citizens might have ended in defeat and disgrace, instead of victory and honor, if the States who supposed it a ruinous and unconstitutional measure had thought they possessed the right of nullifying the act by which it was declared and denying supplies for its prosecution. Hardly and unequally as those measures bore upon several members of the Union, to the legislatures of none did this efficient and peaceable remedy, as it is called, suggest itself. The discovery of this important feature in our Constitution was reserved to the present day. To the statesmen of South Carolina belongs the invention, and upon the citizens of that State will unfortunately fall the evils of reducing it to practice.

If the doctrine of a State veto upon the laws of the Union carries with it internal evidence of its impracticable absurdity, our constitutional history will also afford abundant proof that it would have been repudiated with indignation had it been proposed to form a feature in our Government.

In our colonial state, although dependent on another power, we very early considered ourselves as connected by common interest with each other. Leagues were formed for common defense, and before the declaration of independence we were known in our aggregate character as *the United Colonies of America*. That decisive and important step was taken jointly. We declared ourselves a nation by a joint, not by several acts, and when the terms of our Confederation were reduced to form it was in that of a solemn league of several States, by which they agreed that they would collectively form one nation for the purpose of conducting some certain domestic concerns and all foreign relations. In the instrument forming that Union is found an article which declares that "every State shall abide by the determinations of Congress on all questions which by that Confederation should be submitted to them."

Under the Confederation, then, no State could legally annul a decision of the Congress or refuse to submit to its execution; but no provision was made to enforce these decisions. Congress made requisitions, but they were not complied with. The Government could not operate on individuals. They had no judiciary, no means of collecting revenue.

But the defects of the Confederation need not be detailed. Under its operation we could scarcely be called a nation. We had neither prosperity at home nor consideration abroad. This state of things could not be endured, and our present happy Constitution was formed, but formed in vain if this fatal doctrine prevails. It was formed for important objects that are announced in the preamble, made in the name and by the authority of the people of the United States, whose delegates framed and whose conventions approved it. The most important among these objects—that which is placed first in rank, on which all the others rest—is "*to form a more perfect union*." Now, is it possible that even if there were no express provision giving supremacy to the Constitution and laws of the United States over those of the States, can it be conceived that an instrument made for the purpose of "*forming a more perfect union*" than that of the Confederation could be so constructed by the assembled wisdom of our country as to substitute for that Confederation a form of government dependent for its existence on the local interest, the party spirit, of a State, or of a prevailing faction in a State? Every man of plain, unsophisticated understanding who hears the question will give such an answer as will preserve the Union. Metaphysical subtlety, in pursuit of an impracticable theory, could alone have devised one that is calculated to destroy it.

I consider, then, the power to annul a law of the United States, assumed by one State, *incompatible with the existence of the Union, contradicted expressly by the letter of the Constitution, unauthorized by its spirit, inconsistent with every principle on which it was founded, and destructive of the great object for which it was formed.*

After this general view of the leading principle, we must examine the particular application of it which is made in the ordinance.

The preamble rests its justification on these grounds: It assumes as a fact that the obnoxious laws, although they purport to be laws for raising revenue, were in reality intended for the protection of manufactures, which purpose it asserts to be unconstitutional; that the operation of these laws is unequal; that the amount raised by them is greater than is required by the wants of the Government; and, finally, that the proceeds are to be applied to objects unauthorized by the Constitution. These are the only causes alleged to justify an open opposition to the laws of the country and a threat of seceding from the Union if any attempt should be made to enforce them. The first virtually acknowledges that the law in question was passed under a power expressly given by the Constitution to lay and collect imposts; but its constitutionality is drawn in question from the *motives* of those who passed it. However apparent this purpose may be in the present case, nothing can be more dangerous than to admit the position that an unconstitutional purpose entertained by the members who assent to a law enacted under a constitutional power shall make that law void. For how is that purpose to be ascertained? Who is to make the scrutiny? How often may bad purposes be falsely imputed, in how many cases are they concealed by false professions, in how many is no declaration of motive made? Admit this doctrine, and you give to the States an uncontrolled right to decide, and every law may be annulled under this pretext. If, therefore, the absurd and dangerous doctrine should be admitted that a State may annul an unconstitutional law, or one that it deems such, it will not apply to the present case.

The next objection is that the laws in question operate unequally. This objection may be made with truth to every law that has been or can be passed. The wisdom of man never yet contrived a system of taxation that would operate with perfect equality. If the unequal operation of a law makes it unconstitutional, and if all laws of that description may be abrogated by any State for that cause, then, indeed, is the Federal Constitution unworthy of the slightest effort for its preservation. We have hitherto relied on it as the perpetual bond of our Union; we have received it as the work of the assembled wisdom of the nation; we have trusted to it as to the sheet anchor of our safety in the stormy times of conflict with a foreign or domestic foe; we have looked to it with sacred awe as the palladium of our liberties, and with all the solemnities of religion have pledged to each other our lives and fortunes here and our hopes of happiness hereafter in its defense and support. Were we mistaken, my countrymen, in attaching this importance to the Constitution of our country? Was our devotion paid to the wretched, inefficient, clumsy contrivance which this new doctrine would make it? Did we pledge ourselves to the support of an airy nothing—a bubble that must be blown away by the first breath of disaffection? Was this self-destroying, visionary theory the work of the profound statesmen, the exalted patriots, to whom the task of constitutional reform was intrusted? Did the name of Washington sanction, did the States deliberately ratify, such an anomaly in the history of fundamental legislation? No; we were not mistaken. The letter of this great instrument is free from this radical fault. Its language directly contradicts the imputation; its spirit, its evident intent, contradicts it. No; we did not err. Our Constitution does not contain the absurdity of giving power to make laws and another to resist them. The sages whose memory will always be reverenced have given us a practical and, as they hoped, a permanent constitutional compact. The Father of his Country did not affix his revered name to so palpable an absurdity. Nor did the States, when they severally ratified it, do so under the impression that a veto on the laws of the United States was reserved to them or that they could exercise it by implication. Search the debates in all their conventions, examine the speeches of the most zealous opposers of Federal authority, look at the amendments that were proposed; they are all silent—not a syllable uttered, not a vote given, not a motion made to correct the explicit supremacy given to the laws of the Union over those of the States, or to show that implication, as is now contended, could defeat it. No; we have not erred. The Constitution is still the object of our reverence, the bond of our Union, our defense in danger, the source of our prosperity in peace. It shall descend, as we have received it, uncorrupted by sophistical construction, to our posterity; and the sacrifices of local interest, of State prejudices, of personal animosities, that were made to bring it into existence, will again be patriotically offered for its support.

The two remaining objections made by the ordinance to these laws are that the sums intended to be raised by them are greater than are required and that the proceeds will be unconstitutionally employed.

The Constitution has given, expressly, to Congress the right of raising revenue and of determining the sum the public exigencies will require. The States have no control over the exercise of this right other than that which results from the power of changing the representatives who abuse it, and thus procure redress. Congress may undoubtedly abuse this discretionary power; but the same may be said of others with which they are vested. Yet the discretion must exist somewhere. The Constitution has given it to the representatives of all the people, checked by the representatives of the States and by the Executive power. The South Carolina construction gives it to the legislature or the convention of a single State, where neither the people of the different States, nor the States in their separate capacity, nor the Chief Magistrate elected by the people have any representation. Which is the most discreet disposition of the power? I do not ask you, fellow-citizens, which is the constitutional disposition; that instrument speaks a language not to be misunderstood. But if you were assembled in general convention, which would you think the safest depository of this discretionary power in the last resort? Would you add a clause giving it to each of the States, or would you sanction the wise provisions already made by your Constitution? If this should be the result of your deliberations when providing for the future, are you, can you, be ready to risk all that we hold dear, to establish, for a temporary and a local purpose, that which you must acknowledge to be destructive, and even absurd, as a general provision? Carry out the consequences of this right vested in the different States, and you must perceive that the crisis your conduct presents at this day would recur whenever any law of the United States displeased any of the States, and that we should soon cease to be a nation.

The ordinance, with the same knowledge of the future that characterizes a former objection, tells you that the proceeds of the tax will be unconstitutionally applied. If this could be ascertained with certainty, the objection would with more propriety be reserved for the law so applying the proceeds, but surely can not be urged against the laws levying the duty.

These are the allegations contained in the ordinance. Examine them seriously, my fellow-citizens; judge for yourselves. I appeal to you to determine whether they are so clear, so convincing, as to leave no doubt of their correctness; and even if you should come to this conclusion, how far they justify the reckless, destructive course which you are directed to pursue. Review these objections and the conclusions drawn from them once more. What are they? Every law, then, for raising revenue, according to the South Carolina ordinance, may be rightfully annulled, unless it be so framed as no law ever will or can be framed. Congress have a right to pass laws for raising revenue and each State have a right to oppose their execution—two rights directly opposed to each other; and yet is this absurdity supposed to be contained in an instrument drawn for the express purpose of avoiding collisions between the States and the General Government by an assembly of the most enlightened statesmen and purest patriots ever embodied for a similar purpose.

In vain have these sages declared that Congress shall have power to lay and collect taxes, duties, imposts, and excises; in vain have they provided that they shall have power to pass laws which shall be necessary and proper to carry those powers into execution, that those laws and that Constitution shall be the "supreme law of the land, and that the judges in every State shall be bound thereby, anything in the constitution or laws of any State to the contrary notwithstanding;" in vain have the people of the several States solemnly sanctioned these provisions, made them their paramount law, and individually sworn to support them whenever they were called on to execute any office. Vain provisions! ineffectual restrictions! vile profanation of oaths! miserable mockery of legislation! if a bare majority of the voters in any one State may, on a real or supposed knowledge of the intent with which a law has been passed, declare themselves free from its operation; say, here it gives too little, there, too much, and operates unequally; here it suffers articles to be free that ought to be taxed; there it taxes those that ought to be free; in this case the proceeds are intended to be applied to purposes which we do not approve; in that, the amount raised is more than is wanted. Congress, it is true, are invested by the Constitution with the right of deciding these questions according to their sound discretion. Congress is composed of the representatives of all the States and of all the people of all the States. But we, part of the people of one State, to whom the Constitution has given no power on the subject, from whom it has expressly taken it away; we, most of whom have sworn to support it—we now abrogate this law and swear, and force others to swear, that it shall not be obeyed; and we do this not because Congress have no right to pass such laws—this we do not allege—but because they have passed them with improper views. They are unconstitutional from the motives of those who passed them, which we can never with certainty know; from their unequal operation, although it is impossible, from the nature of things, that they should be equal; and from the disposition which we presume may be made of their proceeds, although that disposition has not been declared. This is the plain meaning of the ordinance in relation to laws which it abrogates for alleged unconstitutionality. But it does not stop there. It repeals in express terms an important part of the Constitution itself and of laws passed to give it effect, which have never been alleged to be unconstitutional.

The Constitution declares that the judicial powers of the United States extend to cases arising under the laws of the United States, and that such laws, the Constitution, and treaties shall be paramount to the State constitutions and laws. The judiciary act prescribes the mode by which the case may be brought before a court of the United States by appeal when a State tribunal shall decide against this provision of the Constitution. The ordinance declares there shall be no appeal— makes the State law paramount to the Constitution and laws of the United States, forces judges and jurors to swear that they will disregard their provisions, and even makes it penal in a suitor to attempt relief by appeal. It further declares that it shall not be lawful for the authorities of the United States or of that State to enforce the payment of duties imposed by the revenue laws within its limits.

Here is a law of the United States, not even pretended to be unconstitutional, repealed by the authority of a small majority of the voters of a single State. Here is a provision of the Constitution which is solemnly abrogated by the same authority.

On such expositions and reasonings the ordinance grounds not only an assertion of the right to annul the laws of which it complains, but to enforce it by a threat of seceding from the Union if any attempt is made to execute them.

This right to secede is deduced from the nature of the Constitution, which, they say, is a compact between sovereign States who have preserved their whole sovereignty and therefore are subject to no superior; that because they made the compact they can break it when in their opinion it has been departed from by the other States. Fallacious as this course of reasoning is, it enlists State pride and finds advocates in the honest prejudices of those who have not studied the nature of our Government sufficiently to see the radical error on which it rests.

The people of the United States formed the Constitution, acting through the State legislatures in making the compact, to meet and discuss its provisions, and acting in separate conventions when they ratified those provisions; but the terms used in its construction show it to be a Government in which the people of all the States, collectively, are represented. We are *one people* in the choice of President and Vice-President. Here the States have no other agency than to direct the mode in which the votes shall be given. The candidates having the majority of all the votes are chosen. The electors of a majority of States may have given their votes for one candidate, and yet another may be chosen. The people, then, and not the States, are represented in the executive branch.

In the House of Representatives there is this difference, that the people of one State do not, as in the case of President and Vice-President, all vote for the same officers. The people of all the States do not vote for all the members, each State electing only its own representatives. But this creates no material distinction. When chosen, they are all representatives of the United States, not representatives of the particular State from which they come. They are paid by the United States, not by the State; nor are they accountable to it for any act done in the performance of their legislative functions; and however they may in practice, as it is their duty to do, consult and prefer the interests of their particular constituents when they come in conflict with any other partial or local interest, yet it is their first and highest duty, as representatives of the United States, to promote the general good.

The Constitution of the United States, then, forms a *government*, not a league; and whether it be formed by compact between the States or in any other manner, its character is the same. It is a Government in which all the people are represented, which operates directly on the people individually, not upon the States; they retained all the power they did not grant. But each State, having expressly parted with so many powers as to constitute, jointly with the other States, a single nation, can not, from that period, possess any right to secede, because such secession does not break a league, but destroys the unity of a nation; and any injury to that unity is not only a breach which would result from the contravention of a compact, but it is an offense against the whole Union. To say that any State may at pleasure secede from the Union is to say that the United States are not a nation, because it would be a solecism to contend that any part of a nation might dissolve its connection with the other parts, to their injury or ruin, without committing any offense. Secession, like any other revolutionary act, may be morally justified by the extremity of oppression; but to call it a constitutional right is confounding the meaning of terms, and can only be done through gross error or to deceive those who are willing to assert a right, but would pause before they made a revolution or incur the penalties consequent on a failure.

Because the Union was formed by a compact, it is said the parties to the compact may, when they feel themselves aggrieved, depart from it; but it is precisely because it is a compact that they can not. A compact is an agreement or binding obligation. It may by its terms have a sanction or penalty for its breach, or it may not. If it contains no sanction, it may be broken with no other consequence than moral guilt; if it have a sanction, then the breach incurs the designated or implied penalty. A league between independent nations generally has no sanction other than a moral one; or if it should contain a penalty, as there is no common superior it can not be enforced. A government, on the contrary, always has a sanction, express or implied; and in our case it is both necessarily implied and expressly given. An attempt, by force of arms, to destroy a government is an offense, by whatever means the constitutional compact may have been formed; and such government has the right by the law of self-defense to pass acts for punishing the offender, unless that right is modified, restrained, or resumed by the constitutional act. In our system, although it is modified in the case of treason, yet authority is expressly given to pass all laws necessary to carry its powers into effect, and under this grant provision has been made for punishing acts which obstruct the due administration of the laws.

It would seem superfluous to add anything to show the nature of that union which connects us, but as erroneous opinions on this subject are the foundation of doctrines the most destructive to our peace, I must give some further development to my views on this subject. No one, fellow-citizens, has a higher reverence for the reserved rights of the States than the Magistrate who now addresses you. No one would make greater personal sacrifices or official exertions to defend them from violation; but equal care must be taken to prevent, on their part, an improper interference with or resumption of the rights they have vested in the nation. The line has not been so distinctly drawn as to avoid doubts in some cases of the exercise of power. Men of the best intentions and soundest views may differ in their construction of some parts of the Constitution; but there are others on which dispassionate reflection can leave no doubt. Of this nature appears to be the assumed right of secession. It rests, as we have seen, on the alleged undivided sovereignty of the States and on their having formed in this sovereign capacity a compact which is called the Constitution, from which, because they made it, they have the right to secede. Both of these positions are erroneous, and some of the arguments to prove them so have been anticipated.

The States severally have not retained their entire sovereignty. It has been shown that in becoming parts of a nation, not members of a league, they surrendered many of their essential parts of sovereignty. The right to make treaties, declare war, levy taxes, exercise exclusive judicial and legislative powers, were all of them functions of sovereign power. The States, then, for all these important purposes were no longer sovereign. The allegiance of their citizens was transferred, in the first instance, to the Government of the United States; they became American citizens and owed obedience to the Constitution of the United States and to laws made in conformity with the powers it vested in Congress. This last position has not been and can not be denied. How, then, can that State be said to be sovereign and independent whose citizens owe obedience to laws not made by it and whose magistrates are sworn to disregard those laws when they come in conflict with those passed by another? What shows conclusively that the States can not be said to have reserved an undivided sovereignty is that they expressly ceded the right to punish treason—not treason against their separate power, but treason against the United States. Treason is an offense against *sovereignty*, and sovereignty must reside with the power to punish it. But the reserved rights of the States are not less sacred because they have, for their common interest, made the General Government the depository of these powers. The unity of our political character (as has been shown for another purpose) commenced with its very existence. Under the royal Government we had no separate character; our opposition to its oppressions began as *united colonies*. We were the *United States* under the Confederation, and the name was perpetuated and the Union rendered more perfect by the Federal Constitution. In none of these stages did we consider ourselves in any other light than as forming one nation. Treaties and alliances were made in the name of all. Troops were raised for the joint defense. How, then, with all these proofs that under all changes of our position we had, for designated purposes and with defined powers, created national governments, how is it that the most perfect of those several modes of union should now be considered as a mere league that may be dissolved at pleasure? It is from an abuse of terms. Compact is used as synonymous with league, although the true term is not employed, but it would at once show the fallacy of the reasoning. It would not do to say that our Constitution was only a league, but it is labored to prove it a compact (which in one sense it is) and then to argue that as a league is a compact every compact between nations must of course be a league, and that from such an engagement every sovereign power has a right to recede. But it has been shown that in this sense the States are not sovereign, and that even if they were, and the national Constitution had been formed by compact, there would be no right in any one State to exonerate itself from its obligations.

So obvious are the reasons which forbid this secession that it is necessary only to allude to them. The Union was formed for the benefit of all. It was produced by mutual sacrifices of interests and opinions. Can those sacrifices be recalled? Can the States who magnanimously surrendered their title to the territories of the West recall the grant? Will the inhabitants of the inland States agree to pay the duties that may be imposed without their assent by those on the Atlantic or the Gulf for their own benefit? Shall there be a free port in one State and onerous duties in another? No one believes that any right exists in a single State to involve all the others in these and countless other evils contrary to engagements solemnly made. Everyone must see that the other States, in self-defense, must oppose it at all hazards.

These are the alternatives that are presented by the convention—a repeal of all the acts for raising revenue, leaving the Government without the means of support, or an acquiescence in the dissolution of our Union by the secession of one of its members. When the first was proposed, it was known that it could not be listened to for a moment. It was known, if force was applied to oppose the execution of the laws, that it must be repelled by force; that Congress could not, without involving itself in disgrace and the country in ruin, accede to the proposition; and yet if this is not done in a given day, or if any attempt is made to execute the laws, the State is by the ordinance declared to be out of the Union. The majority of a convention assembled for the purpose have dictated these terms, or rather this rejection of all terms, in the name of the people of South Carolina. It is true that the governor of the State speaks of the submission of their grievances to a convention of all the States, which, he says, they "sincerely and anxiously seek and desire." Yet this obvious and constitutional mode of obtaining the sense of the other States on the construction of the federal compact, and amending it if necessary, has never been attempted by those who have urged the State on to this destructive measure. The State might have proposed the call for a general convention to the other States, and Congress, if a sufficient number of them concurred, must have called it. But the first magistrate of South Carolina, when he expressed a hope that "on a review by Congress and the functionaries of the General Government of the merits of the controversy" such a convention will be accorded to them, must have known that neither Congress nor any functionary of the General Government has authority to call such a convention unless it be demanded by two-thirds of the States. This suggestion, then, is another instance of the reckless inattention to the provisions of the Constitution with which this crisis has been madly hurried on, or of the attempt to persuade the people that a constitutional remedy had been sought and refused. If the legislature of South Carolina "anxiously desire" a general convention to consider their complaints, why have they not made application for it in the way the Constitution points out? The assertion that they "earnestly seek" it is completely negatived by the omission.

This, then, is the position in which we stand: A small majority of the citizens of one State in the Union have elected delegates to a State convention; that convention has ordained that all the revenue laws of the United States must be repealed, or that they are no longer a member of the Union. The governor of that State has recommended to the legislature the raising of an army to carry the secession into effect, and that he may be empowered to give clearances to vessels in the name of the State. No act of violent opposition to the laws has yet been committed, but such a state of things is hourly apprehended. And it is the intent of this instrument to *proclaim*, not only that the duty imposed on me by the Constitution "to take care that the laws be faithfully executed" shall be performed to the extent of the powers already vested in me by law, or of such others as the wisdom of Congress shall devise and intrust to me for that purpose, but to warn the citizens of South Carolina who have been deluded into an opposition to the laws of the danger they will incur by obedience to the illegal and disorganizing ordinance of the convention; to exhort those who have refused to support it to persevere in their determination to uphold the Constitution and laws of their country; and to point out to all the perilous situation into which the good people of that State have been led, and that the course they are urged to pursue is one of ruin and disgrace to the very State whose rights they affect to support.

Fellow-citizens of my native State, let me not only admonish you, as the First Magistrate of our common country, not to incur the penalty of its laws, but use the influence that a father would over his children whom he saw rushing to certain ruin. In that paternal language, with that paternal feeling, let me tell you, my countrymen, that you are deluded by men who are either deceived themselves or wish to deceive you. Mark under what pretenses you have been led on to the brink of insurrection and treason on which you stand. First, a diminution of the value of your staple commodity, lowered by overproduction in other quarters, and the consequent diminution in the value of your lands were the sole effect of the tariff laws. The effect of those laws was confessedly injurious, but the evil was greatly exaggerated by the unfounded theory you were taught to believe—that its burthens were in proportion to your exports, not to your consumption of imported articles. Your pride was roused by the assertion that a submission to those laws was a state of vassalage and that resistance to them was equal in patriotic merit to the opposition our fathers offered to the oppressive laws of Great Britain. You were told that this opposition might be peaceably, might be constitutionally, made; that you might enjoy all the advantages of the Union and bear none of its burthens. Eloquent appeals to your passions, to your State pride, to your native courage, to your sense of real injury, were used to prepare you for the period when the mask which concealed the hideous features of *disunion* should be taken off. It fell, and you were made to look with complacency on objects which not long since you would have regarded with horror. Look back to the arts which have brought you to this state; look forward to the consequences to which it must inevitably lead! Look back to what was first told you as an inducement to enter into this dangerous course. The great political truth was repeated to you that you had the revolutionary right of resisting all laws that were palpably unconstitutional and intolerably oppressive. It was added that the right to nullify a law rested on the same principle, but that it was a peaceable remedy. This character which was given to it made you receive with too much confidence the assertions that were made of the unconstitutionality of the law and its oppressive effects. Mark, my fellow-citizens, that by the admission of your leaders the unconstitutionality must be *palpable*, or it will not justify either resistance or nullification. What is the meaning of the word *palpable* in the sense in which it is here used? That which is apparent to everyone; that which no man of ordinary intellect will fail to perceive. Is the unconstitutionality of these laws of that description? Let those among your leaders who once approved and advocated the principle of protective duties answer the question; and let them choose whether they will be considered as incapable then of perceiving that which must have been apparent to every man of common understanding, or as imposing upon your confidence and endeavoring to mislead you now. In either case they are unsafe guides in the perilous path they urge you to tread. Ponder well on this circumstance, and you will know how to appreciate the exaggerated language they address to you. They are not champions of liberty, emulating the fame of our Revolutionary fathers, nor are you an oppressed people, contending, as they repeat to you, against worse than colonial vassalage. You are free members of a flourishing and happy

Union. There is no settled design to oppress you. You have indeed felt the unequal operation of laws which may have been unwisely, not unconstitutionally, passed; but that inequality must necessarily be removed. At the very moment when you were madly urged on to the unfortunate course you have begun a change in public opinion had commenced. The nearly approaching payment of the public debt and the consequent necessity of a diminution of duties has already produced a considerable reduction, and that, too, on some articles of general consumption in your State. The importance of this change was underrated, and you were authoritatively told that no further alleviation of your burthens was to be expected at the very time when the condition of the country imperiously demanded such a modification of the duties as should reduce them to a just and equitable scale. But, as if apprehensive of the effect of this change in allaying your discontents, you were precipitated into the fearful state in which you now find yourselves.

I have urged you to look back to the means that were used to hurry you on to the position you have now assumed and forward to the consequences it will produce. Something more is necessary. Contemplate the condition of that country of which you still form an important part. Consider its Government, uniting in one bond of common interest and general protection so many different States, giving to all their inhabitants the proud title of *American citizen*, protecting their commerce, securing their literature and their arts, facilitating their intercommunication, defending their frontiers, and making their name respected in the remotest parts of the earth. Consider the extent of its territory, its increasing and happy population, its advance in arts which render life agreeable, and the sciences which elevate the mind! See education spreading the lights of religion, morality, and general information into every cottage in this wide extent of our Territories and States. Behold it as the asylum where the wretched and the oppressed find a refuge and support. Look on this picture of happiness and honor and say, *We too are citizens of America*. Carolina is one of these proud States; her arms have defended, her best blood has cemented, this happy Union. And then add, if you can, without horror and remorse, This happy Union we will dissolve; this picture of peace and prosperity we will deface; this free intercourse we will interrupt; these fertile fields we will deluge with blood; the protection of that glorious flag we renounce; the very name of Americans we discard. And for what, mistaken men? For what do you throw away these inestimable blessings? For what would you exchange your share in the advantages and honor of the Union? For the dream of a separate independence—a dream interrupted by bloody conflicts with your neighbors and a vile dependence on a foreign power. If your leaders could succeed in establishing a separation, what would be your situation? Are you united at home? Are you free from the apprehension of civil discord, with all its fearful consequences? Do our neighboring republics, every day suffering some new revolution or contending with some new insurrection, do they excite your envy? But the dictates of a high duty oblige me solemnly to announce that you can not succeed. The laws of the United States must be executed. I have no discretionary power on the subject; my duty is emphatically pronounced in the Constitution. Those who told you that you might peaceably prevent their execution deceived you; they could not have been deceived themselves. They know that a forcible opposition could alone prevent the execution of the laws, and they know that such opposition must be repelled. Their object is disunion. But be not deceived by names. Disunion by armed force is *treason*. Are you really ready to incur its guilt? If you are, on the heads of the instigators of the act be the dreadful consequences; on their heads be the dishonor, but on yours may fall the punishment. On your unhappy State will inevitably fall all the evils of the conflict you force upon the Government of your country. It can not accede to the mad project of disunion, of which you would be the first victims. Its First Magistrate can not, if he would, avoid the performance of his duty. The consequence must be fearful for you, distressing to your fellow-citizens here and to the friends of good government throughout the world. Its enemies have beheld our prosperity with a vexation they could not conceal; it was a standing refutation of their slavish doctrines, and they will point to our discord with the triumph of malignant joy. It is yet in your power to disappoint them. There is yet time to show that the descendants of the Pinckneys, the Sumpters, the Rutledges, and of the thousand other names which adorn the pages of your Revolutionary history will not abandon that Union to support which so many of them fought and bled and died. I adjure you, as you honor their memory, as you love the cause of freedom, to which they dedicated their lives, as you prize the peace of your country, the lives of its best citizens, and your own fair fame, to retrace your steps. Snatch from the archives of your State the disorganizing edict of its convention; bid its members to reassemble and promulgate the decided expressions of your will to remain in the path which alone can conduct you to safety, prosperity, and honor. Tell them that compared to disunion all other evils are light, because that brings with it an accumulation of all. Declare that you will never take the field unless the star-spangled banner of your country shall float over you; that you will not be stigmatized when dead, and dishonored and scorned while you live, as the authors of the first attack on the Constitution of your country. Its destroyers you can not be. You may disturb its peace, you may interrupt the course of its prosperity, you may cloud its reputation for stability; but its tranquillity will be restored, its prosperity will return, and the stain upon its national character will be transferred and remain an eternal blot on the memory of those who caused the disorder.

Fellow-citizens of the United States, the threat of unhallowed disunion, the names of those once respected by whom it is uttered, the array of military force to support it, denote the approach of a crisis in our affairs on which the continuance of our unexampled prosperity, our political existence, and perhaps that of all free governments may depend. The conjuncture demanded a free, a full, and explicit enunciation, not only of my intentions, but of my principles of action; and as the claim was asserted of a right by a State to annul the laws of the Union, and even to secede from it at pleasure, a frank exposition of my opinions in relation to the origin and form of our Government and the construction I give to the instrument by which it was created seemed to be proper. Having the fullest confidence in the justness of the legal and constitutional opinion of my duties which has been expressed, I rely with equal confidence on your undivided support in my determination to execute the laws, to preserve the Union by all constitutional means, to arrest, if possible, by moderate and firm measures the necessity of a recourse to force; and if it be the will of Heaven that the recurrence of its primeval curse on man for the shedding of a brother's blood should fall upon our land, that it be not called down by any offensive act on the part of the United States.

Fellow-citizens, the momentous case is before you. On your undivided support of your Government depends the decision of the great question it involves—whether your sacred Union will be preserved and the blessing it secures to us as one people shall be perpetuated. No one can doubt that the unanimity with which that decision will be expressed will be such as to inspire new confidence in republican institutions, and that the prudence, the wisdom, and the courage which it will bring to their defense will transmit them unimpaired and invigorated to our children.

May the Great Ruler of Nations grant that the signal blessings with which He has favored ours may not, by the madness of party or personal ambition, be disregarded and lost; and may His wise providence bring those who have produced this crisis to see the folly before they feel the misery of civil strife, and inspire a returning veneration for that Union which, if we may dare to penetrate His designs. He has chosen as the only means of attaining the high destinies to which we may reasonably aspire.

In testimony whereof I have caused the seal of the United States to be hereunto affixed, having signed the same with my hand.

Done at the city of Washington, this 10th day of December, A. D. 1832, and of the Independence of the United States the fifty-seventh.

Andrew Jackson

By the President:
   Edw. Livingston
    Secretary of State

Jackson did not rely upon words alone to dampen the fires of resistance in South Carolina. On the basis of the earlier reports from Poinsett and Breathitt, he had already made available to the Unionists (of which Poinsett was the leader) 5,000 stands of muskets—although they had only requested 200 or 300—and had transferred four companies of artillery and several cannons to Fort Moultrie outside of Charleston. In a letter to his new Vice President, Martin Van Buren, he outlined further plans to suppress the resistance.

President Andrew Jackson
Letter to Vice President Martin Van Buren
On South Carolina Crisis
January 13, 1833

Bassett, V, 2-4.

I beg of you not to be disturbed by any thing you hear from the alarmists at this place. many nullifiers are here under disguise, working hard to save calhoun and would disgrace their country and the Executive to do it. Be assured that I have and will act with all the forbearance [I possess] to do my duty, and extend that protection to our good citizens and the officers of our Government in the south who are charged with the execution of the laws; but it would destroy all confidence in our government, both at home and abroad, was I to sit with my arms folded and permit our good citizens in So. Carolina who are standing forth in aid of the laws to be imprisoned, fined, and perhaps hung, under the ordinance of South Carolina and the laws to carry it into effect, all which, are palbable [sic] violations of the constitution and subversive of every right of our citizens. Was this to be permitted the Government would loose the confidence of its citizens and it would induce disunion every where.

No my friend, the crisis must be now met with firmness, our citizens protected, and the modern doctrine of nullification and secession put down forever—for we have yet to learn, whether some of the eastern states may not secede or nullify, if the tariff is reduced. I have to look at both ends of the union to preserve it. I have only time to add, that So Carolina, has by her replevin, and other laws, closed our courts, and authorised the Governor to raise 12,000 men to keep them closed, giving all power to the sheriffs to use this army as the *posse comitatus*. I must appeal to congress to cloath our officers and marshall with the same power to aid them in executing the laws, and apprehending those who may commit treasonable acts. This call upon congress must be made as long before the 1rst. of Feby next as will give congress time to act before that day, or I would be chargeable with neglect of my duty, and as congress are in session, and as I have said in my message, which was before the So. C. ordinance reached me, if other powers were wanted I would appeal to congress, was I therefore to act without the aid of congress, or without communicating to it, I would be branded with the epithet, *tyrant*. from these remarks you will at once see the propriety of my course, and be prepared to see the communication I will make to congress on the 17th instant, which will leave congress ten days to act upon it before the 1rst of February after it is printed. The parties in So. C. are arming on both sides, and drilling in the night, and I expect soon to hear that a civil war of extermination has commenced. I will meet all things with deliberate firmness and forbearance, but wo, to those nullifiers who shed the first blood. The moment I am prepared with proof I will direct prosecutions for treason to be instituted against the leaders, and if they are surrounded with 12,000 bayonets our marshall shall be aided by 24,000 and arrest them in the midst thereof—nothing must be permitted to weaken our government at home or abroad.

Virginia except a few nullifiers and politicians, is true to the core; I could march from that state 40,000 men in forty days—nay, they are ready in N. C. in Tennessee, in all the western states, and from good old democratic Pennsylvania I have a tender of upwards of 50,000, and from the borders of So. C. in No. C. I have a tender of one entire Reggt. The union *shall be* preserved.

In haste yr friend

President Jackson obtained the desired authority from the Congress to press the militia into action when he deemed it necessary, and he thoroughly frightened some of the more important South Carolina leaders in Washington (such as Calhoun and Hayne) by letting it be known that he would press charges of treason against all of those involved in the insurrection if there was forcible resistance to the federal government. He is reputed to have told a departing South Carolina congressman:

"Tell . . . [the Nullifiers] from me that they can talk and write resolutions and print threats to their hearts' content. But if one drop of blood be shed there in defiance of the laws of the United States, I will hang the first man of them I can get my hands on to the first tree I can find." In [Senator] Benton's (an old friend and supporter of Jackson's) hearing, South Carolina's senior Senator expressed a doubt as to whether the President would go that far. "I tell you Hayne," the Missourian replied, "when Jackson begins to talk about hanging, they can begin to look for the ropes."[18]

In the face of such strong and resolute indications of action, South Carolina began to back down. Five days after the President delivered his special message to the Congress, the Nullification Ordinance was suspended. Both the nullifiers and the government acted with restraint in South Carolina and were able to avoid an open clash. Subsequently, the tariff was modified by Congress, and in time, the fevered opposition died down. President Jackson distinguished himself in this executive crisis by the strength and clarity of his actions, as well as by his rhetoric. He managed throughout to keep himself well-informed at all times, enabling him to anticipate both the moves and the temper of mind of the South Carolina nullifiers. He successfully communicated to the nullifiers his convictions and clearly indicated what the consequences of any precipitate action on their part would be. Finally, he backed up his words and threats with resolute actions on a scale sufficient to make it clear from the outset that their definace would not be tolerated, and that their plans could not possibly succeed.

Energy and Initiative in Creating
Broad Executive Power

Alexander Hamilton felt strongly about the role of the Executive in the maintenance of public order, and in the whiskey tax crisis he had pressured Washington vigorously for the immediate and definitive action that was taken. But the executive role of the President encompasses much more than this fighting responsibility, important as it may be, and Hamilton was extremely attentive to a number of different areas of presidential concern, many of which related directly to the executive initiative of the President. In fact there has probably never been a presidential advisor and/or cabinet member who was as instrumental in influencing presidential policy as Alexander Hamilton. Taney was extremely useful to Jackson; William Jennings Bryan necessary and at times helpful to the Wilson administration and Dean Acheson indispensable to Harry Truman; but never in the history of the office has there been anything comparable to the influence of Alexander Hamilton. His energy and initiative, his ability and knowledge were so dynamic and comprehensive that it would be impossible to evaluate the debt Washington and the American people owe to his prodigous efforts in the early days of the republic. Croly was not far off when he wrote that:

> During Washington's two administrations, the United States was governed practically by his ideas, if not by his will. . . .[19]

Hamilton's role was even more significant because his advice and contributions came at a time when there were no precedents to rely upon; consequently every action and policy was initiated *de nova*. The sinews of presidential power were being stretched and toughened for the first time, and the importance of the care and precision of their initial definition cannot be exaggerated. Washington relied heavily upon Hamilton's advice and his suggestions during this period, and although there were powerful countervailing pressures within his cabinet on most of the critical issues, it was Hamilton's counsel which usually prevailed. The American presidency owes much to the maturity of these decisions. From the beginning Hamilton urged, in fact demanded, a strong and assertive role for presidential leadership, and it was largely due to his influence upon our first President that the die was finally cast in this pattern.

Clinton Rossiter has written that "Hamilton has never been given a full and fair shake by most of the men who write American history. . . ."[20] Although he was "cast in only a supportive role in 1787 when the words of the constitution were strung together, [he] was cast in an epic role in 1791 when the words had to be translated into actions."[21]

Hamilton was as agressive in asserting the power of the national government as he was in defining the powers of the President. In fact the two powers were symbiotic. A weak President attempting to preside over a strong federal government would have been a disaster, but no more so than a powerful President trying to lead a weak central government. From the beginning, in his persuasive essays in the *Federalist*, Hamilton argued for the placement of energy and decisive power in the hands of a strong President presiding over a powerful central government, and it was essentially because his brilliant constitutional understanding embraced both of these concepts that our structures of national government and presidential power have been adequate or at least potentially adequate to the great tasks that lay before them. [Editor's Note: At the same time it is important to realize, as Henry Steele Commager has so wisely observed, that energy in the Executive is only as valuable as the prudence he possesses to use it constructively, and without prudence it can easily become destructive to the ends of a free society. *The New York Review of Books*, XX, No. 16 (October 18, 1973), 50-52.]

Hamilton's role in advising Washington to bear down heavily to stamp out the early whiskey rebellion challenge has already been described and his influence in persuading Washington to assert his role in the area of foreign affairs and presidential privilege will be described later. But critical to this use and implementation of presidential power in a broad range of activities was the resolution of the constitutional question of the power of the government to act and assume responsibilities in social, political and economic areas. Hamilton asserted this right of the government and designed many blueprints for action to be taken in a series of important state papers he drafted at the beginning of Washington's administration. None was more decisive in establishing the power of the government to act in the public interest than was Hamilton's advisory opinion submitted to Washington and directed towards convincing the President not to veto the bill establishing a national bank.

Of greater interest to this study than the substantive question of banks as an institution was the constitutional question which subsumed it. This did not directly involve presidential power, but rather addressed the problem of the right of the Congress to legislate in this area. It nevertheless belongs in a study of presidential power, because without first establishing the power of the government to act in this area, future Presidents would have been helpless to move decisively on many other critical levels of executive responsibility.

The constitutional question arose when Thomas Jefferson, secretary of state under Washington, and Attorney General Edmund Randolph advised the President to veto a bill establishing the Bank of the United States on constitutional grounds. The bill was passed by both houses of Congress and sent to the President on February 14, 1791. It had won approval in Congress largely on the strength of the arguments offered by Alexander Hamilton in a special report submitted to the Congress at its request. In the report Hamilton effectively mobilized the economic arguments in favor of creating such a quasi-national bank and refuted objections which has been raised against its establishment. He also outlined the organizational structure the Bank should take and prescribed its operating procedures. Long an advocate of such an institution, he was thoroughly familiar with banking procedures, having served as attorney and a director of the bank of New York.[22] Apparently his arguments were quite persuasive, for a proposal entirely acceptable to him was approved by 3-1 majority in the Senate and by nearly a 2-1 majority in the House.

Opposition to the plan for a Bank was not totally absent in the Congress, however. Led by James Madison, its opponents raised serious questions regarding its constitutionality. In the first of two speeches against the measure delivered on the floor of the House, Madison argued:

> In fine, if the power were in the Constitution, the immediate exercise of it cannot be essential; if not there, the exercise of it involves the guilt of usurpation, and establishes a precedent of interpretation, levelling all the barriers which limit the power of the General Government and protect those of the state Government. . . .
>
> It appeared on the whole, that he concluded, that the power exercised by the bill was condemned by the silence of the Constitution; was condemned by

the rule of interpretation arising out of the Constitution; was condemned by its tendency to destroy the main characteristic of the Constitution; was condemned by the expositions of the friends of the Constitution, whilst depending before the public; was condemned by the apparent intention of the parties which ratified the Constitution, was condemned by the explanatory amendments proposed by Congress themselves to the Constitution; and he hoped it would receive its final condemnation, by the vote of this House.[23]

Despite Madison's opposition, the measure was passed and went to the President for his consideration. He called first upon Jefferson and Randolph, and then went to Hamilton for advice on the subject. Having received Jefferson's and Randolph's negative opinions immediately, the President sent these objections along with the bill to Hamilton for his opinion with the proviso that "no copies of them be taken, as it is for my own satisfaction they have been called for."[24] The President was clearly disturbed by the question. Three of this closest advisors and fellow Virginians were warning him that the Constitution did not permit the incorporation of such a Bank. He turned to Hamilton as a final court of appeal, obviously upset at the prospect of vetoing such an important measure, a measure which had been vigorously supported by the Congress.

In his statement urging Washington to veto the Bank Act, Secretary of State Jefferson came quickly to the point. "The incorporation of a Bank, and the powers assumed by this bill, have not, in my opinion, been delegated to the United States by the Constitution."[25] He then went on to review both the specially enumerated powers and those that were general in nature as related to financial activity in order to demonstrate that there was nothing in the Constitution which provided for the operation of such a Bank. Jefferson was particularly critical of the argument which pertained to the general phrase "to make all laws *necessary* and proper for carrying into execution the enumerated powers." He argued that all such powers could be carried into execution without a Bank.

A Bank therefore is not necessary, and consequently not authorized by this phrase.

It has been urged that a Bank will give great facility or convenience in the collection of taxes. Suppose this were true: yet the Constitution allows only the means which are "*necessary*," not those which are merely convenient for effecting the enumerated powers. If such latitude of construction be allowed to this phrase as to give non-enumerated power, it will go to every one, for there is not one which ingenuity nor torture into a *convenience* in some instance or *other*, to *some one* or so long a list of enumerated powers. It would swallow up all the delegated powers, and reduce the whole to the one power, as before observed. Therefore it was that the Constitution restrained them to the *necessary* means, that is to say, to those means without which the grant of power would be nugatory.[26]

Hamilton had not introduced any constitutional arguments in his first report to the Congress but had directed his presentation to strictly economic questions.

After Jefferson's objections, however, he was forced to defend what he had heretofore assumed: that the Constitution recognized the inherent right of the government to perform those functions which properly advanced its interests. In asserting this basic principle of constitutional philosophy, Hamilton placed himself in polar opposition to the early Republican position outlined in Jefferson's and Madison's objections to the proposal—namely that the Constitution was essentially a barrier, an inhibiting force restricting the practices and policies of government from deviating from a clearly defined and limited concept of powers. The secretary of the treasury advocated a point of view diametrically opposed to this "strict constructionist" theory. Hamilton believed that the Constitution empowered the government to create any agency or to perform any function that was in its interests unless it was specifically prohibited. As Rossiter has put it, he searched "for ways to get things done rather than ways to keep things from being done."[27]

> If the Constitution were to be converted into a source of energy, it would have to be interpreted broadly, loosely, liberally. . . .[28]

The argument really hinged upon the "necessary and proper" clause of the Constitution. Jefferson's position was that the government could do nothing which was not either specifically granted as a power under the Constitution or was not *necessary* to carry out more of these enumerated powers. This position came to be known in modern times as strict constructionism. Hamilton, on the other hand, argued that a broad construction of the "necessary and proper" clause was indispensable to the effective and dynamic operation of government:

> It is essential to the being of the National government, that so erroneous a conception of the meaning of the word *necessary*, should be exploded.
>
> It is certain that neither the grammatical, nor popular sense of the term requires that construction. According to both, *necessary* often means no more than *needful, requisite, incidental, useful*, or *conducive to*. It is a common mode of expression to say, that it is *necessary* for the government or a person to do this or that thing, when nothing more is intended or understood, than that the interests of the government or person require, or will be promoted, by the doing of this or that thing. The imagination can be at no loss for exemplifications of the use of the word in this sense.
>
> And it is the true one in which it is to be understood as used in the Constitution. The whole turn of the clause containing it, indicates, that it was the intent of the convention, by that clause to give a liberal latitude to the specified powers. The expressions have peculiar comprehensiveness. They are—"to make *all laws*, necessary and proper for *carrying into execution* the foregoing powers & all *other powers* vested by the Constitution in the *government* of the United States, or in any *department* or *officer* thereof." To understand the word as the Secretary of State does, would be to depart from its obvious and popular sense, and to give it a *restrictive* operation; an idea never before entertained. It would be to give the same force as if the word *absolutely* or *indispensably* had been prefixed to it.[29]

The overwhelming force of Hamilton's arguments convinced the President not to veto the Bank measure, but rather to embrace the secretary of the treasury's concept of the extended power of government, as opposed to Jefferson and Madison's restricted views. The significance of this turning point cannot be exaggerated with regard to the future of the national government, as well as to the power of the presidency. Had Washington accepted Jefferson's advice at this point and vetoed the bank bill, a narrow and restricted interpretation of the power of the government to act in cases not specifically described in the language of the Constitution would have been almost inevitably established as a guiding principle of the American system of government. But Hamilton's position prevailed in this instance, as well as in other critical precedents in the formative years of the republic; we remain indebted to his early advisor to the President for the power, the strength and the scope of our political system.

As the creative genius of the first administration under the Constitution, Hamilton was as determined to pile up the precedents of a strong Presidency as he was to untie the hands of a strong Congress. In his political science, and thus in his constitutional law and theory, there was no contradiction between these two designs. A legislature was "strong" if it grappled with problems of economic growth and national security by interpreting its mandate loosely and enacting far-ranging laws. It displayed not strength but indecorum when it followed its natural bent and tried to do the job of the executive. The executive, in its turn, was "strong" if it called attention to problems and suggested remedies, made use of the discretionary powers granted by the legislature, and guarded against invasions of its own area of constitutional responsibility. The balance between legislature and executive was one that changed with changing circumstances, yet the latter was always intended, in Hamilton's opinion, to be "one up" in the mixed pattern of cooperation and contention ordained in the Constitution.[30]

Secretary of the Treasury Alexander Hamilton Opinion on the Constitutionality of an Act to Establish a Bank
February 23, 1791

Harold C. Syrett and Jacob E. Cooke, eds., *The Papers of Alexander Hamilton* (New York, 1965) VIII, 97-134.

The Secretary of the Treasury having perused with attention the papers containing the opinions of the Secretary of State and Attorney General concerning the constitutionality of the bill for establishing a National Bank proceeds according to the order of the President to submit the reasons which have induced him to entertain a different opinion.

It will naturally have been anticipated that, in performing this task he would feel uncommon solicitude. Personal considerations alone arising from the reflection that the measure originated with him would be sufficient to produce it: The sense which he has manifested of the great importance of such an institution to the successful administration of the department under his particular care; and an expectation of serious ill consequences to result from a failure of the measure, do not permit him to be without anxiety on public accounts. But the chief solicitude arises from a firm persuasion, that principles of construction like those espoused by the Secretary of State and the Attorney General would be fatal to the just & indispensible authority of the United States.

In entering upon the argument it ought to be premised, that the objections of the Secretary of State and Attorney General are founded on a general denial of the authority of the United States to erect corporations. The latter indeed expressly admits, that if there be any thing in the bill which is not warranted by the constitution, it is the clause of incorporation.

Now it appears to the Secretary of the Treasury, that this *general principle* is *inherent* in the very *definition* of *Government* and *essential* to every step of the progress to be made by that of the United States; namely—that every power vested in a Government is in its nature *sovereign*, and includes by *force* of the *term*, a right to employ all the *means* requisite, and fairly *applicable* to the attainment of the *ends* of such power; and which are not precluded by restrictions & exceptions specified in the constitution; or not immoral, or not contrary to the essential ends of political society.

This principle in its application to Government in general would be admitted as an axiom. And it will be incumbent upon those, who may incline to deny it, to *prove* a distinction; and to shew that a rule which in the general system of things is essential to the preservation of the social order is inapplicable to the United States.

The circumstances that the powers of sovereignty are in this country divided between the National and State Governments, does not afford the distinction required. It does not follow from this, that each of the portions of powers delegated to the one or to the other is not sovereign *with regard to its proper objects*. It will only *follow* from it, that each has sovereign power as to *certain things*, and not as to *other things*. To deny that the Government of the United States has sovereign power as to its declared purposes & trusts, because its power does not extend to all cases, would be equally to deny, that the State Governments have sovereign power in any case; because their power does not extend to every case. The tenth section of the first article of the constitution exhibits a long list of very important things which they may not do. And thus the United States would furnish the singular spectacle of a *political society* without *sovereignty*, or of a people *governed* without *government*.

If it would be necessary to bring proof to a proposition so clear as that which affirms that the powers of the federal government, *as to its objects*, are sovereign, there is a clause of its constitution which would be decisive. It is that which declares, that the constitution and the laws of the United States made in pursuance of it, and all treaties made or which shall be made under their authority shall be the supreme law of the land. The power which can create the *Supreme law* of the land, in any case, is doubtless sovereign *as to such case*.

This general & indisputable principle puts at once an end to the *abstract* question—Whether the United States have power to *erect a corporation?* that is to say, to give a *legal* or *artificial capacity* to one or more persons, distinct from the natural. For it is unquestionably incident to *sovereign power* to erect corporations, and consequently to *that* of the United States, in *relation to the objects* intrusted to the management of the government. The difference in this—where the authority of the government is general, it can create corporations in *all cases*; where it is confined to certain branches of legislation, it can create corporations only in those cases.

Here then as far as concerns the reasonings of the Secretary of State & the Attorney General, the affirmative of the constitutionality of the bill might be permitted to rest. It will occur to the President that the principle here advanced has been untouched by either of them.

For a more complete elucidation of the point nevertheless, the arguments which they have used against the power of the government to erect corporations, however foreign they are to the great & fundamental rule which has been stated, shall be particularly examined. And after shewing that they do not intend to impair its force, it shall also be shewn, that the power of incorporation incident to the government in certain cases, does fairly extend to the particular case which is the object of the bill.

The first of these arguments is, that the foundation of the constitution is laid on this ground "that all powers not delegated to the United States by the Constitution nor prohibited to it by the States are reserved to the States or to the people", whence it is meant to be inferred, that congress can in no case exercise any power not included in those enumerated in the constitution. And it is affirmed that the power of erecting a corporation is not included in any of the enumerated powers.

The main proposition here laid down, in its true signification is not to be questioned. It is nothing more than a consequence of this republican maxim, that all government is a delegation of power. But how much is delegated in each case, is a question of fact to be made out by fair reasoning & construction upon the particular provisions of the constitution—taking as guides the general principles & general ends of government.

It is not denied, that there are *implied*, as well as *express* powers, and that the former are as effectually delegated as the latter. And for the sake of accuracy it shall be mentioned, that there is another class of powers, which may be properly denominated *resulting* powers. It will not be doubted that if the United States should make a conquest of any of the territories of its neighbours, they would possess sovereign jurisdiction over the conquered territory. This would rather be a result from the whole mass of the powers of the government & from the nature of political society, than a consequence of either of the powers specially enumerated.

But be this as it may, it furnishes a striking illustration of the general doctrine contended for. It shews an extensive case, in which a power of erecting corporations is either implied in, or would result from some or all of the powers, vested in the National Government. The jurisdiction acquired over such conquered territory would certainly be competent to every species of legislation.

To return—It is conceded, that implied powers are to be considered as delegated equally with express ones.

Then it follows, that as a power of erecting a corporation may as well be *implied* as any other thing; it may as well be employed as an *instrument* or *mean* of carrying into execution any of the specified powers, as any other instrument or mean whatever. The only question must be, in this as in every other case, whether the mean to be employed, or in this instance the corporation to be erected, has a natural relation to any of the acknowledged objects or lawful ends of the government. Thus a corporation may not be erected by congress, for superintending the police of the city of Philadelphia because they are not authorised to *regulate* the *police* of that city; but one may be erected in relation to the collection of the taxes, or to the trade with foreign countries, or to the trade between the States, or with the Indian Tribes, because it is the province of the federal government to regulate those objects & because it is incident to a general *sovereign* or *legislative power* to *regulate* a thing, to employ all the means which relate to its regulation to the *best & greatest advantage*.

A strange fallacy seems to have crept into the manner of thinking & reasoning upon the subject. Imagination appears to have been unusually busy concerning it. An incorporation seems to have been regarded as some great, independent, substantive thing—as a political end of peculiar magnitude & moment; whereas it is truly to be considered as a *quality, capacity,* or *mean* to an end. Thus a mercantile company is formed with a certain capital for the purpose of carrying on a particular branch of business. Here the business to be prosecuted is the *end*; the association in order to form the requisite capital is the primary mean. Suppose that an incorporation were added to this; it would only be to add a new *quality* to that association; to give it an artificial capacity by which it would be enabled to prosecute the business with more safety & convenience.

That the importance of the power of incorporation has been exaggerated, leading to erroneous conclusions, will further appear from tracing it to its origin. The roman law is the source of it, according to which a *voluntary* association of individuals at *any time* or *for any purpose* was capable of producing it. In England, whence our notions of it are immediately borrowed, it forms a part of the executive authority, & the exercise of it has been often *delegated* by that authority. Whence therefore the ground of the supposition, that it lies beyond the reach of all those very important portions of sovereign power, legislative as well as executive, which belong to the government of the United States?

To this mode of reasoning respecting the right of employing all the means requisite to the execution of the specified powers of the Government, it is objected that none but *necessary* & proper means are to be employed, & the Secretary of State maintains, that no means are to be considered as *necessary*, but those without which the grant of the power would be *nugatory*. Nay so far does he go in his restrictive interpretation of the word, as even to make the case of *necessity* which shall warrant the constitutional exercise of the power to depend on *casual & temporary* circumstances, an idea which alone refutes the construction. The *expediency* of exercising a particular power, at a particular time, must indeed depend on *circumstances*; but the constitutional right of exercising it must be uniform & invariable—the same to day, as to morrow.

All the arguments therefore against the constitutionality of the bill derived from the accidental existence of certain State-banks: institutions which *happen* to exist to day, & for ought that concerns the government of the United States, may disappear to morrow, must not only be rejected as fallacious, but must be viewed as demonstrative, that there is a *radical* source of error in the reasoning.

It is essential to the being of the National government, that so erroneous a conception of the meaning of the word *necessary*, should be exploded.

It is certain, that neither the grammatical, nor popular sense of the term requires that construction. According to both, *necessary* often means no more than *needful, requisite, incidental, useful*, or *conducive to*. It is a common mode of expression to say, that it is *necessary* for a government or a person to do this or that thing, when nothing more is intended or understood, than that the interests of the government or person require, or will be promoted, by the doing of this or that thing. The imagination can be at no loss for exemplifications of the use of the word in this sense.

And it is the true one in which it is to be understood as used in the constitution. The whole turn of the clause containing it, indicates, that it was the intent of the convention, by that clause to give a liberal latitude to the exercise of the specified powers. The expressions have peculiar comprehensiveness. They are—"to make *all laws*, necessary & proper for *carrying into execution* the foregoing powers & all *other powers* vested by the constitution in the *government* of the United States, or in any *department* or *officer* thereof." To understand the word as the Secretary of State does, would be to depart from its obvious & popular sense, and to give it a *restrictive* operation; an idea never before entertained. It would be to give it the same force as if the word *absolutely* or *indispensibly* had been prefixed to it.

Such a construction would beget endless uncertainty & embarassment. The cases must be palpable & extreme in which it could be pronounced with certainty, that a measure was absolutely necessary, or one without which the exercise of a given power would be nugatory. There are few measures of any government, which would stand so severe a test. To insist upon it, would be to make the criterion of the exercise of any implied power a *case of extreme necessity*; which is rather a rule to justify the overleaping of the bounds of constitutional authority, than to govern the ordinary exercise of it.

It may be truly said of every government, as well as of that of the United States, that it has only a right, to pass such laws as are necessary & proper to accomplish the objects intrusted to it. For no government has a right to do *merely what it pleases*. Hence by a process of reasoning similar to that of the Secretary of State, it might be proved, that neither of the State governments has a right to incorporate a bank. It might be shewn, that all the public business of the State, could be performed without a bank, and inferring thence that it was unnecessary it might be argued that it could not be done, because it is against the rule which has been just mentioned. A like mode of reasoning would prove, that there was no power to incorporate the Inhabitants of a town, with a view to a more perfect police: For it is certain, that an incorporation may be dispensed with, though it is better to have one. It is to be remembered, that there is no *express* power in any State constitution to erect corporations.

The *degree* in which a measure is necessary, can never be a test of the *legal* right to adopt it. That must ever be a matter of opinion; and can only be a test of expediency. The *relation* between the *measure* and the *end*, between the *nature* of *the mean* employed towards the execution of a power and the object of that power, must be the criterion of constitutionality not the more or less of *necessity* or *utility*.

The practice of the government is against the rule of construction advocated by the Secretary of State. Of this the act concerning light houses, beacons, buoys & public piers, is a decisive example. This doubtless must be referred to the power of regulating trade, and is fairly relative to it. But it cannot be affirmed, that the exercise of that power, in this instance, was strictly necessary; or that the power itself would be *nugatory* without that of regulating establishments of this nature.

This restrictive interpretation of the word *necessary* is also contrary to this sound maxim of construction namely, that the powers contained in a constitution of government, especially those which concern the general administration of the affairs of a country, its finances, trade, defence etc. ought to be construed liberally, in advancement of the public good. This rule does not depend on the particular form of a government or on the particular demarkation of the boundaries of its powers, but on the nature and objects of government itself. The means by which national exigencies are to be provided for, national inconveniencies obviated, national prosperity promoted, are of such infinite variety, extent and complexity, that there must, of necessity, be great latitude of discretion in the selection & application of those means. Hence consequently, the necessity & propriety of exercising the authorities intrusted to a government on principles of liberal construction.

The Attorney General admits the *rule*, but takes a distinction between a State, and the federal constitution. The latter, he thinks, ought to be construed with greater strictness, because there is more danger of error in defining partial than general powers.

But the reason of the *rule* forbids such a distinction. This reason is—the variety & extent of public exigencies, a far greater proportion of which and of a far more critical kind, are objects of National than of State administration. The greater danger of error, as far as it is supposeable, may be a prudential reason for caution in practice, but it cannot be a rule of restrictive interpretation.

In regard to the clause of the constitution immediately under consideration, it is admitted by the Attorney General, that no *restrictive* effect can be ascribed to it. He defines the word necessary thus. "To be necessary is to be *incidental*, and may be denominated the natural means of executing a power."

But while, on the one hand, the construction of the Secretary of State is deemed inadmissible, it will not be contended on the other, that the clause in question gives any *new* or *independent* power. But it gives an explicit sanction to the doctrine of *implied* powers, and is equivalent to an admission of the proposition, that the government, *as to its specified powers* and *objects*, has plenary & sovereign authority, in some cases paramount to that of the States, in other coordinate with it. For such is the plain import of the declaration, that it may pass *all laws* necessary & proper to carry into execution those powers.

It is no valid objection to the doctrine to say, that it is calculated to extend the powers of the general government throughout the entire sphere of State legislation. The same thing has been said, and may be said with regard to every exercise of power by *implication* or *construction*. The moment the literal meaning is departed from, there is a chance of error and abuse. And yet an adherence to the letter of its powers would at once arrest the motions of the government. It is not only agreed, on all hands, that the exercise of constructive powers is indispensible, but every act which has been passed is more or less an exemplification of it. One has been already mentioned, that relating to light houses etc. That which declares the power of the President to remove officers at pleasure, acknowlidges the same truth in another, and a signal instance.

The truth is that difficulties on this point are inherent in the nature of the foederal constitution. They result inevitably from a division of the legislative power. The consequence of this division is, that there will be cases clearly within the power of the National Government; others clearly without its power; and a third class, which will leave room for controversy & difference of opinion, & concerning which a reasonable latitude of judgment must be allowed.

But the doctrine which is contended for is not chargeable with the consequence imputed to it. It does not affirm that the National government is sovereign in all respects, but that it is sovereign to a certain extent: that is, to the extent of the objects of its specified powers.

It leaves therefore a criterion of what is constitutional, and of what is not so. This criterion is the *end* to which the measure relates as a *mean*. If the end be clearly comprehended within any of the specified powers, & if the measure have an obvious relation to that end, and is not forbidden by any particular provision of the constitution—it may safely be deemed to come within the compass of the national authority. There is also this further criterion which may materially assist the decision. Does the proposed measure abridge a preexisting right of any State, or of any individual? If it does not, there is a strong presumption in favour of its constitutionality; & slighter relations to any declared object of the constitution may be permitted to turn the scale.

The general objections which are to be inferred from the reasonings of the Secretary of State and of the Attorney General to the doctrine which has been advanced, have been stated and it is hoped satisfactorily answered. Those of a more particular nature shall not be examined.

The Secretary of State introduces his opinion with an observation, that the proposed incorporation undertakes to create certain capacities properties or attributes which are *against* the laws of *alienage, descents, escheat* and *forfeiture, distribution* and *monopoly*, and to confer a power to make laws paramount to those of the States. And nothing says he, in another place, but a *necessity invincible by other means* can justify such a *prostration* of *laws* which constitute the pillars of our whole system of jurisprudence, and are the foundation laws of the State Governments.

If these are truly the foundation laws of the several states, then have most of them subverted their own foundations. For there is scarcely one of them which has not, since the establishment of its particular constitution made material alterations in some of those branches of its jurisprudence especially the law of descents. But it is not conceived how any thing can be called the fundamental law of a State Government which is not established in its constitution unalterable by the ordinary legislature. And with regard to the question of necessity it has been shewn, that this can only constitute a question of expediency, not of right.

To erect a corporation is to substitute a *legal* or *artificial* to a *natural* person, and where a number are concerned to give them *individuality*. To that legal or artificial person once created, the common law of every state of itself *annexes* all those incidents and attributes, which are represented as a prostration of the main pillars of their jurisprudence. It is certainly not accurate to say, that the erection of a corporation is *against* those different *heads* of the State laws; because it is rather to create a kind of person or entity, to which *they* are inapplicable, and to which the general rule of those laws assign a different regimen. The laws of alienage cannot apply to an artificial person, because it can have no country. Those of descent cannot apply to it, because it can have no heirs. Those of escheat are foreign from it for the same reason. Those of forfeiture, because it cannot commit a crime. Those of distribution, because, though it may be dissolved, it cannot die. As truly might it be said, that the exercise of the power of prescribing the rule by which foreigners shall be naturalised, is *against* the law of alienage; while it is in fact only to put them in a situation to cease to be the subject of that law. To do a thing which is *against* a law, is to do something which it forbids or which is a violation of it.

But if it were even to be admitted that the erection of a corporation is a direct alteration of the State laws in the enumerated particulars; it would do nothing towards proving, that the measure was unconstitutional. If the government of the United States can do no act, which amounts to an alteration of a State law, all its powers are nugatory. For almost every new law is an alteration, in some way or other of an old *law*, either *common*, or *statute*.

There are laws concerning bankruptcy in some states—some states have laws regulating the values of foreign coins. Congress are empowered to establish uniform laws concerning bankruptcy throughout the United States, and to regulate the values of foreign coins. The exercise of either of these powers by Congress necessarily involves an alteration of the laws of those states.

Again: Every person by the common law of each state may export his property to foreign countries, at pleasure. But Congress, in pursuance of the power of regulating trade, may prohibit the exportation of commodities: in doing which, they would alter the common law of each state in abridgement of individual rights.

It can therefore never be good reasoning to say—this or that act is unconstitutional, because it alters this or that law of a State. It must be shewn, that the act which makes the alteration is unconstitutional on other accounts, not *because* it makes the alteration.

There are two points in the suggestions of the Secretary of State which have been noted that are peculiarly incorrect. One is, that the proposed incorporation is against the laws of monopoly, because it stipulates an exclusive right of banking under the national authority. The other that it gives power to the institution to make laws paramount to those of the states.

But with regard to the first point, the bill neither prohibits any State from erecting as many banks as they please, nor any number of Individuals from associating to carry on the business: & consequently is free from the charge of establishing a monopoly: for monopoly implies a *legal impediment* to the carrying on of the trade by others than those to whom it is granted.

And with regard to the second point, there is still less foundation. The bye-laws of such an institution as a bank can operate only upon its own members; can only concern the disposition of its own property and must essentially resemble the rules of a private mercantile partnership. They are expressly not to be contrary to law; and law must here mean the law of a State as well as of the United States. There never can be a doubt, that a law of the corporation, if contrary to a law of a state, must be overruled as void; unless the law of the State is contrary to that of the United States; and then the question will not be between the law of the State and that of the corporation, but between the law of the State and that of the United States.

Another argument made use of by the Secretary of State, is, the rejection of a proposition by the convention to empower Congress to make corporations, either generally, or for some special purpose.

What was the precise nature or extent of this proposition, or what the reasons for refusing it, is not ascertained by any authentic document, or even by accurate recollection. As far as any such document exists, it specifies only canals. If this was the amount of it, it would at most only prove, that it was thought inexpedient to give a power to incorporate for the purpose of opening canals, for which purpose a special power would have been necessary; except with regard to the Western Territory, there being nothing in any part of the constitution respecting the regulation of canals. It must be confessed however, that very different accounts are given of the import of the proposition and of the motives for rejecting it. Some affirm that it was confined to the opening of canals and obstructions in rivers; others, that it embraced banks; and others, that it extended to the power of incorporating generally. Some again alledge, that it was disagreed to, because it was thought improper to vest in Congress a power of erecting corporations—others, because it was thought unnecessary to *specify* the power, and inexpedient to furnish an additional topic of objection to the constitution. In this state of the matter, no inference whatever can be drawn from it.

But whatever may have been the nature of the proposition or the reasons for rejecting it concludes nothing in respect to the real merits of the question. The Secretary of State will not deny, that whatever may have been the intention of the framers of a constitution, or of a law, that intention is to be sought for in the instrument itself, according to the usual & established rules of construction. Nothing is more common than for laws to *express* and *effect*, more or less than was intended. If then a power to erect a corporation, in any case, be deducible by fair inference from the whole or any part of the numerous provisions of the constitution of the United States, arguments drawn from extrinsic circumstances, regarding the intention of the convention, must be rejected.

Most of the arguments of the Secretary of State which have not been considered in the foregoing remarks, are of a nature rather to apply to the expediency than to the constitutionality of the bill. They will however be noticed in the discussions which will be necessary in reference to the particular heads of the powers of the government which are involved in the question.

Those of the Attorney General will now properly come under review.

His first observation is, that the power of incorporation is not *expressly* given to congress. This shall be conceded, but in *this sense* only, that it is not declared in *express terms* that congress may erect a *corporation*. But this cannot mean, that there are not certain *express* powers, which *necessarily* include it.

For instance, Congress have express power "to exercise exclusive legislation in all cases whatsoever, over such *district* (not exceeding ten miles square) as may by cession of particular states, & the acceptance of Congress become the seat of the government of the United states; and to exercise *like authority* over all places purchased by consent of the legislature of the State in which the same shall be for the erection of forts, arsenals, dock yards & other needful buildings."

Here then is express power to exercise *exclusive legislation in all cases whatsoever over certain places*; that is to do in respect to those places, all that any government whatever may do: For language does not afford a more complete designation of sovereign power, than in those comprehensive terms. It is in other words a power to pass all laws whatsoever, & consequently to pass laws for erecting corporations, as well as for any other purpose which is the proper object of law in a free government. Surely it can never be believed, that Congress with *exclusive power of legislation in all cases whatsoever*, cannot erect a corporation within the district which shall become the seat of government, for the better regulation of its police. And yet there is an unqualified denial of the power to erect corporations in every case on the part both of the Secretary of State and of the Attorney General. The former indeed speaks of that power in these emphatical terms, that it is *a right remaining exclusively with the states*.

As far then as there is an express power to do any *particular act of legislation*, there is an express one to erect corporations in the cases above described. But accurately speaking, no *particular power* is more than *implied* in a *general one*. Thus the power to lay a duty on a *gallon of rum*, is only a particular *implied* in the general power to lay and collect taxes, duties, imposts and excises. This serves to explain in what sense it may be said, that congress have not an express power to make corporations.

This may not be an improper place to take notice of an argument which was used in debate in the House of Representatives. It was there urged, that if the constitution intended to confer so important a power as that of erecting corporations, it would have been expressly mentioned. But the case which has been noticed is clearly one in which such a power exists, and yet without any specification or express grant of it, further than as every *particular implied* in a general power, can be said to be so granted.

But the argument itself is founded upon an exaggerated and erroneous conception of the nature of the power. It has been shewn, that it is not of so transcendent a kind as the reasoning supposes; and that viewed in a just light it is a mean which ought to have been left to *implication*, rather than an *end* which ought to have been *expressly* granted.

Having observed, that the power of erecting corporations is not expressly granted to Congress, the Attorney General proceeds thus. . . .

If it can be exercised by them, it must be
1. because the nature of the foederal government implies it.
2. because it is involved in some of the specified powers of legislation or

3. because it is necessary & proper to carry into execution some of the specified powers.

To be implied in the *nature of the foederal government*, says he, would beget a doctrine so indefinite, as to grasp every power.

This proposition it ought to be remarked is not precisely, or even substantially, that, which has been relied upon. The proposition relied upon is, that the *specified powers* of Congress are in their nature sovereign—that it is incident to sovereign power to erect corporations; & that therefore Congress have a right within the *sphere & in relation to the objects of their power, to erect corporations*.

It shall however be supposed, that the Attorney General would consider the two propositions in the same light, & that the objection made to the one, would be made to the other.

To this objection an answer has been already given. It is this; that the doctrine is stated with this express *qualification*, that the right to erect corporations does *only* extend to *cases & objects* within the *sphere* of the *specified powers* of the government. A general legislative authority implies a power to erect corporations *in all cases*—a particular legislative power implies authority to erect corporations, in relation to cases arising under that power only. Hence the affirming, that as an *incident* to sovereign power, congress may erect a corporation in relation to the *collection* of their taxes, is no more than to affirm that they may do whatever else they please; than the saying that they have a power to regulate trade would be to affirm that they have a power to regulate religion: or than the maintaining that they have sovereign power as to taxation, would be to maintain that they have sovereign power as to every thing else.

The Attorney General undertakes, in the next place, to shew, that the power of erecting corporations is not involved in any of the specified powers of legislation confided to the National government.

In order to this he has attempted an enumeration of the particulars which he supposes to be comprehended under the several heads of the *powers* to lay & collect taxes etc—to borrow money on the credit of the United States—to regulate commerce with foreign nations—between the states, and with the Indian Tribes—to dispose of and make all needful rules & regulations respecting the territory or other property belonging to the United States; the design of which enumeration is to shew *what is* included under those different heads of power, & *negatively*, that the power of erecting corporations is not included.

The truth of this inference or conclusion must depend on the accuracy of the enumeration. If it can be shewn that the enumeration is *defective*, the inference is destroyed. To do this will be attended with no difficulty.

The heads of the power to lay & collect taxes, he states to be

1. To ascertain the subject of taxation etc.
2. to declare the quantum of taxation etc.
3. to prescribe the *mode* of collection.
4. to ordain the manner of accounting for the taxes etc.

The defectiveness of this enumeration consists in the generality of the third division "*to prescribe the mode* of collection"; which is in itself an immence chapter.

It will be shewn hereafter, that, among a vast variety of particulars, it comprises the very power in question; namely to *erect corporations*.

The heads of the power to borrow money are stated to be

1. to stipulate the sum to be lent.
2. an interest or no interest to be paid.
3. the time & manner of repaying, unless the loan be placed on an irredeemable fund.

This enumeration is liable to a variety of objections. It omits, in the first place, the *pledging* or *mortgaging* of a fund for the security of the money lent, an usual and in most cases an essential ingredient.

The idea of a stipulation of *an interest or no interest* is too confined. It should rather have been said, to stipulate *the consideration* of the loan. Individuals often borrow upon considerations other than the payment of interest. So may government; and so they often find it necessary to do. Every one reCollects the lottery tickets & other douceurs often given in Great Britain, as collateral inducements to the lending of money to the Government.

There are also frequently collateral conditions, which the enumeration does not contemplate. Every contract which has been made for monies borrowed in Holland includes stipulations that the sum due shall be *free from taxes*, and from sequestration in time of war, and mortgages all the land & property of the United States for the reimbursement.

It is also known, that a lottery is a common expedient for borrowing money, which certainly does not fall under either of the enumerated heads.

The heads of the power to regulate commerce with foreign nations are stated to be

1. to prohibit them or their commodities from our ports.
2. to impose duties on *them* where none existed before, or to increase existing duties on them.
3. to subject *them* to any species of custom house regulation.
4. to grant *them* any exemptions or privileges which policy may suggest.

This enumeration is far more exceptionable than either of the former. It omits *every thing* that relates to the *citizens vessels* or *commodities* of the United States. The following palpable omissions occur at once.

1. Of the power to prohibit the exportation of commodities which not only exists at all times, but which in time of war it would be necessary to exercise, particularly with relation to naval and warlike stores.
2. Of the power to prescribe rules concerning the *characteristics & priviledges* of an american bottom—how she shall be navigated, as whether by citizens or foreigners, or by a proportion of each.
3. Of the power of regulating the manner of contracting with seamen, the police of ships on their voyages etc. of which the act for the government & regulation of seamen in the merchants service is a specimen.

That the three preceding articles are omissions, will not be doubted. There is a long list of items in addition, which admit of little, if any question; of which a few samples shall be given.

1. The granting of bounties to certain kinds of vessels, & certain species of

merchandise. Of this nature is the allowance on dried & pickled fish & salted provisions.

2. The prescribing of rules concerning the *inspection* of commodities to be exported. Though the states individually are competent to this regulation, yet there is no reason, in point of authority at least, why a general system might not be adopted by the United States.

3. The regulation of policies of insurance; of salvage upon goods found at sea, and the disposition of such goods.

4. The regulation of pilots.

5. The regulation of bills of exchange drawn by a merchant of *one state* upon a merchant of *another state*. This last rather belongs to the regulation of trade between the states, but is equally omitted in the specification under that head.

The last enumeration relates to the power "to dispose of & make *all needful rules and regulations* respecting the territory *or other property* belonging to the United States."

The heads of this power are said to be

1. to exert an ownership over the territory of the United States, which may be properly called the property of the United States, as in the Western Territory, and to *institute a government therein*: or

2. to exert an ownership over the other property of the United States.

This idea of exerting an ownership over the Territory or other property of the United States, is particularly indefinite and vague. It does not at all satisfy the conception of what must have been intended by a power, to make all needful *rules* and *regulations*; nor would there have been any use for a special clause which authorised nothing more. For the right of exerting an ownership is implied in the very definition of property.

It is admitted that in regard to the western territory some thing more is intended—even the institution of a government; that is the creation of a body politic, or corporation of the highest nature; one, which in its maturity, will be able itself to create other corporations. Why then does not the same clause authorise the erection of a corporation in respect to the regulation or disposal of any other of the property of the United States? This idea will be enlarged upon in another place.

Hence it appears, that the enumerations which have been attempted by the Attorney General are so imperfect, as to authorise no conclusion whatever. They therefore have no tendency to disprove, that each and every of the powers to which they relate, includes that of erecting corporations; which they certainly do, as the subsequent illustrations will more & more evince.

It is presumed to have been satisfactorily shewn in the course of the preceding observations

1. That the power of the government, *as to* the objects intrusted to its management, is in its nature sovereign.

2. That the right of erecting corporations is one, inherent in & inseparable from the idea of sovereign power.

3. That the position, that the government of the United States can exercise no power but such as is delegated to it by its constitution, does not militate against this principle.

4. That the word *necessary* in the general clause can have no *restrictive* operation, derogating from the force of this principle, indeed, that the degree in which a measure is, or is not necessary, cannot be a *test* of *constitutional* right, but of expediency only.

5. That the power to erect corporations is not to be considered, as an *independent & substantive* power but as an *incidental & auxiliary* one; and was therefore more properly left to implication, than expressly granted.

6. That the principle in question does not extend the power of the government beyond the prescribed limits, because it only affirms a power to *incorporate* for *purposes within the sphere of the specified powers.*

And lastly that the right to exercise such a power, in certain cases, is unequivocally granted in the post *positive & comprehensive* terms.

To all which it only remains to be added that such a power has actually been exercised in two very eminent instances: namely in the erection of two governments, One, northwest of the river Ohio, and the other south west—*the last, independent of any antecedent compact.*

And there results a full & complete demonstration, that the Secretary of State & Attorney General are mistaken, when they deny generally the power of the National government to erect corporations.

It shall now be endeavoured to be shewn that there is a power to erect one of the kind proposed by the bill. This will be done, by tracing a natural & obvious relation between the institution of a bank, and the objects of several of the enumerated powers of the government; and by shewing that, *politically* speaking, it is necessary to the effectual execution of one or more of those powers. In the course of this investigation, various instances will be stated, by way of illustration, of a right to erect corporations under those powers.

Some preliminary observations maybe proper.

The proposed bank is to consist of an association of persons for the purpose of creating a joint capital to be employed, chiefly and essentially, in loans. So far the object is not only lawful, but it is the mere exercise of a right, which the law allows to every individual. The bank of New York which is not incorporated, is an example of such an association. The bill proposes in addition, that the government shall become a joint proprietor in this undertaking, and that it shall permit the bills of the company payable on demand to be receivable in its revenues & stipulates that it shall not grant privileges similar to those which are to be allowed to this company, to any others. All this is incontrovertibly within the compass of the discretion of the government. The only question is, whether it has a right to incorporate this company, in order to enable it the more effectually to accomplish *ends*, which are in themselves lawful.

To establish such a right, it remains to shew the relation of such an institution to one or more of the specified powers of the government.

Accordingly it is affirmed, that it has a relation more or less direct to the power of collecting taxes; to that of borrowing money; to that of regulating trade between the states; and to those of raising, supporting & maintaining fleets & armies. To the two former, the relation may be said to be *immediate.*

And, in the last place, it will be argued, that it is, *clearly*, within the provision which authorises the making of all *needful* rules & *regulations* concerning the *property* of the United States, as the same has been practiced upon by the Government.

A Bank relates to the collection of taxes in two ways; *indirectly*, by increasing the quantity of circulating medium & quickening circulation, which facilitates the means of paying—*directly*, by creating a *convenient species* of *medium* in which they are to be paid.

To designate or appoint the money or *thing* in which taxes are to be paid, is not only a proper, but a necessary *exercise* of the power of collecting them. Accordingly congress in the law concerning the collection of the duties on imports & tonnage, have provided that they shall be payable in gold & silver. But while it was an indispensible part of the work to say in what they should be paid, the choice of the specific thing was mere matter of discretion. The payment might have been required in the commodities themselves. Taxes in kind, however ill judged, are not without precedents, even in the United States. Or it might have been in the paper money of the several states; or in the bills of the bank of North America, New York and Massachusetts, all or either of them: or it might have been in bills issued under the authority of the United States.

No part of this can, it is presumed, be disputed. The appointment, then, of the *money* or *thing*, in which the taxes are to be paid, is an incident to the power of collection. And among the expedients which may be adopted, is that of bills issued under the authority of the United States.

Now the manner of issuing these bills is again matter of discretion. The government might, doubtless, proceed in the following manner. It might provide, that they should be issued under the direction of certain officers, payable on demand; and in order to support their credit & give them a ready circulation, it might, besides giving them a currency in its taxes, set apart out of any monies in its Treasury, a given sum and appropriate it under the direction of those officers as a fund for answering the bills as presented for payment.

The constitutionality of all this would not admit of a question. And yet it would amount to the institution of a bank, with a view to the more convenient collection of taxes. For the simplest and most precise idea of a bank, is, a deposit of coin or other property, as a fund for *circulating* a *credit* upon it, which is to answer the purpose of money. That such an arrangement would be equivalent to the establishment of a bank would become obvious, if the place where the fund to be set apart was kept should be made a receptacle of the monies of all other persons who should incline to deposit them there for safe keeping; and would become still more so, if the Officers charged with the direction of the fund were authorised to make discounts at the usual rate of interest, upon good security. To deny the power of the government to add these ingredients to the plan, would be to refine away all government.

This process serves to exemplify the natural & direct relation which may subsist between the institution of a bank and the collection of taxes. It is true that the species of bank which has been designated, does not include the idea of incorporation. But the argument intended to be founded upon it, is this: that the institution comprehended in the idea of a bank being one immediately relative to the collection of taxes, *in regard to the appointment* of *the money or thing* in which they are to be paid; the sovereign power of providing for the collection of taxes necessarily includes the right of granting a corporate capacity to such an institution, as a requisite to its greater security, utility and more convenient management.

A further process will still more clearly illustrate the point. Suppose, when the species of bank which has been described was about to be instituted, it were to be urged, that in order to secure to it a due degree of confidence the fund ought not only to be set apart & appropriated generally, but ought to be specifically vested in the officers who were to have the direction of it, and in their *successors* in office, to the end that it might acquire the character of *private property* incapable of being resumed without a violation of the sanctions by which the rights of property are protected & occasioning more serious & general alarm, the apprehension of which might operate as a check upon the government—such a proposition might be opposed by arguments against the expediency of it or the solidity of the reason assigned for it, but it is not conceivable what could be urged against its constitutionality.

And yet such a disposition of the thing would amount to the erection of a corporation. For the true definition of a corporation seems to be this. It is a *legal* person, or a person created by act of law, consisting of one or more natural persons authorised to hold property or a franchise in succession in a legal as contradistinguished from a natural capacity.

Let the illustration proceed a step further. Suppose a bank of the nature which has been described with or without incorporation, had been instituted, & that experience had evinced as it probably would, that being wholly under public direction it possessed not the confidence requisite to the credit of its bills—Suppose also that by some of those adverse conjunctures which occasionally attend nations, there had been a very great drain of the specie of the country, so as not only to cause general distress for want of an adequate medium of circulation, but to produce, in consequence of that circumstance, considerable defalcations in the public revenues—suppose also, that there was no bank instituted in any State—in such a posture of things, would it not be most manifest that the incorporation of a bank, like that proposed by the bill, would be a measure immediately relative to the *effectual collection* of the taxes and completely within the province of the sovereign power of providing by all laws necessary & proper for that collection?

If it be said, that such a state of things would render that necessary & therefore constitutional, which is not so now—the answer to this, and a solid one it doubtless is, must still be, that which has been already stated—Circumstances may affect the expediency of the measure, but they can neither add to, nor diminish its constitutionality.

A Bank has a direct relation to the power of borrowing money, because it is an usual and in sudden emergencies an essential instrument in the obtaining of loans to Government.

A nation is threatened with a war. Large sums are wanted, on a sudden, to make the requisite preparations. Taxes are laid for the purpose, but it requires time to obtain the benefit of them. Anticipation is indispensible. If there be a bank, the supply can, at once be had; if there be none loans from Individuals must be sought. The progress of these is often too slow for the exigency: in some situations they are not practicable at all. Frequently when they are, it is of great consequence to be able to anticipate the product of them by advances from a bank.

The essentiality of such an institution as an instrument of loans is exemplified at this very moment. An Indian expedition is to be prosecuted. The only fund out of which the money can arise consistently with the public engagements, is a tax which will only begin to be collected in July next. The preparations, however, are instantly to be made. The money must therefore be borrowed. And of whom could it be borrowed; if there were no public banks?

It happens, that there are institutions of this kind, but if there were none, it would be indispensible to create one.

Let it then be supposed, that the necessity existed, (as but for a casualty would be the case) that proposals were made for obtaining a loan; that a number of individuals came forward and said, we are willing to accommodate the government with this money; with what we have in hand and the credit we can raise upon it we doubt not of being able to furnish the sum required: but in order to this, it is indispensible, that we should be incorporated as a bank. This is essential towards putting it in our power to do what is desired and we are obliged on that account to make it the *consideration* or condition of the loan.

Can it be believed, that a compliance with this proposition would be unconstitutional? Does not this alone evince the contrary? It is a necessary part of a power to borrow to be able to stipulate the consideration or conditions of a loan. It is evident, as has been remarked elsewhere, that this is not confined to the mere stipulation of a sum of money by way of interest—why may it not be deemed to extend, where a government is the contracting party, to the stipulation of a *franchise*? If it may, & it is not perceived why it may not, then the grant of a corporate capacity may be stipulated as a consideration of the loan? There seems to be nothing unfit, or foreign from the nature of the thing in giving individuality or a corporate capacity to a number of persons who are willing to lend a sum of money to the government, the better to enable them to do it, and make them an ordinary instrument of loans in future emergencies of the state.

But the more general view of the subject is still more satisfactory. The legislative power of borrowing money, & of making all laws necessary & proper for carrying into execution that power, seems obviously competent to the appointment of the *organ* through which the abilities and wills of individuals may be most efficaciously exerted, for the accommodation of the government by loans.

The Attorney General opposes to this reasoning, the following observation. "To borrow money presupposes the accumulation of a fund to be lent, and is secondary to the creation of an ability to lend." This is plausible in theory, but it is not true in fact. In a great number of cases, a previous accumulation of a fund equal to the whole sum required, does not exist. And nothing more can be actually presupposed, than that there exist resources, which put into activity to the greatest advantage by the nature of the operation with the government, will be equal to the effect desired to be produced. All the provisions and operations of government must be presumed to contemplate things as they *really* are.

The institution of a bank has also a natural relation to the regulation of trade between the States: in so far as it is conducive to the creation of a convenient medium of *exchange* between them, and to the keeping up a full circulation by preventing the frequent displacement of the metals in reciprocal remittances. Money is the very hinge on which commerce turns. And this does not mean merely gold & silver, many other things have served the purpose with different degrees of utility. Paper has been extensively employed.

It cannot therefore be admitted with the Attorney General, that the regulation of trade between the States, as it concerns the medium of circulation & exchange ought to be considered as confined to coin. It is even supposeable in argument, that the whole, or the greatest part of the coin of the country, might be carried out of it.

The Secretary of State objects to the relation here insisted upon, by the following mode of reasoning—"To erect a bank, says he, & to regulate commerce, are very different acts. He who erects a bank, creates a subject of commerce, so does he, who makes a bushel of wheat, or digs a dollar out of the mines. Yet neither of these persons regulates commerce thereby. To make a thing which may be bought & sold is not to *prescribe* regulations for *buying & selling*: thus making the regulation of commerce to consist in prescribing rules for *buying & selling*."

This indeed is a species of regulation of trade; but is one which falls more aptly within the province of the local jurisdictions than within that of the general government, whose care must be presumed to have been intended to be directed to those general political arrangements concerning trade on which its aggregate interests depend, rather than to the details of buying and selling.

Accordingly such only are the regulations to be found in the laws of the United States; whose objects are to give encouragement to the entreprise of our own merchants, and to advance our navigation and manufactures.

And it is in reference to these general relations of commerce, that an establishment which furnishes facilities to circulation and a convenient medium of exchange & alienation, is to be regarded as a regulation of trade.

The Secretary of State further argues, that if this was a regulation of commerce, it would be void, *as extending as much to the internal commerce of every state as to its external*. But what regulation of commerce does not extend to the internal commerce of every state? What are all the duties upon imported articles amounting to prohibitions, but so many bounties upon domestic manufactures affecting the interests of different classes of citizens in different ways? What are all the provisions in the coasting act, which relate to the trade between district and district of the same State? In short what regulation of trade between the States, but must affect the internal trade of each State? What can operate upon the whole but must extend to every part!

The relation of a bank to the execution of the powers, that concern the common defence, has been anticipated. It has been noted, that at this very moment the aid of such an institution is essential to the measures to be pursued for the protection of our frontier.

It now remains to shew, that the incorporation of a bank is within the operation of the provision which authorises Congress to make all needful rules & regulations concerning the property of the United States. But it is previously necessary to advert to a distinction which has been taken by the Attorney General.

He admits, that the word *property* may signify personal property however acquired. And yet asserts, that it cannot signify money arising from the sources of revenue pointed out in the constitution; because, says he, "the disposal & regulation of money is the final cause for raising it by taxes."

But it would be more accurate to say, that the *object* to which money is intended to be applied is the *final cause* for raising it, than that the disposal and regulation of it is *such*. The support of Government; the support of troops for the common defence; the payment of the public debt, are the true *final causes* for raising money. The disposition & regulation of it when raised, are the steps by which it is applied to the *ends* for which it was raised, not the ends themselves. Hence therefore the money to be raised by taxes as well as any other personal property, must be supposed to come within the meaning as they certainly do within the letter of the authority, to make all needful rules & regulations concerning the property of the United States.

A case will make this plainer: suppose the public debt discharged, and the funds now pledged for it liberated. In some instances it would be found expedient to repeal the taxes, in others, the repeal might injure our own industry, our agriculture and manufactures. In these cases they would of course be retained. Here then would be monies arising from the authorised sources of revenue which would not fall within the rule by which the Attorney General endeavours to except them from other personal property, & from the operation of the clause in question.

The monies being in the coffers of the government, what is to hinder such a disposition to be made of them as is contemplated in the bill or what an incorporation of the parties concerned under the clause which has been cited.

It is admitted that with regard to the Western territory they give a power to erect a corporation—that is to institute a government. And by what rule of construction can it be maintained, that the same words in a constitution of government will not have the same effect when applied to one species of property, as to another, as far as the subject is capable of it? or that a legislative power to make all needful rules & regulations, or to pass all laws necessary & proper concerning the public property which is admitted to authorise an incorporation in one case will not authorise it in another? will justify the institution of a government over the western territory & will not justify the incorporation of a bank, for the more useful management of the money of the nation? If it will do the last, as well as the first, then under this provision alone the bill is constitutional, because it contemplates that the United States shall be joint proprietors of the stock of the bank.

There is an observation of the secretary of state to this effect, which may require notice in this place. Congress, says he, are not to lay taxes *ad libitum for any purpose they please*, but only to pay the debts, or provide for the *welfare* of the Union. Certainly no inference can be drawn from this against the power of applying their money for the institution of a bank. It is true, that they cannot without breach of trust, lay taxes for any other purpose than the general welfare but so neither can any other government. The welfare of the community is the only legitimate end for which money can be raised on the community. Congress can be considered as under only one restriction, which does not apply to other governments—They cannot rightfully apply the money they raise to any purpose *merely* or purely local. But with this exception they have as large a discretion in relation to the *application* of money as any legislature whatever. The constitutional *test* of a right application must always be whether it be for a purpose of *general* or *local* nature. If the former, there can be no want of constitutional power. The quality of the object, as how far it will really promote or not the welfare of the union, must be matter of conscientious discretion. And the arguments for or against a measure in this light, must be arguments concerning expediency or inexpediency, not constitutional right. Whatever relates to the general order of the finances, to the general interests of trade etc. being general objects are constitutional ones for *the application* of *money*.

A Bank then whose bills are to circulate in all the revenues of the country, is *evidently* a general object, and for that very reason a constitutional one as far as regards the appropriation of money to it. Whether it will really be a beneficial one, or not, is worthy of careful examination, but is no more a constitutional point, in the particular referred to; than the question whether the western lands shall be sold for twenty or thirty cents [per] acre.

A hope is entertained, that it has by this time been made to appear, to the satisfaction of the President, that a bank has a natural relation to the power of collecting taxes; to that of borrowing money; to that of regulating trade; to that of providing for the common defence: and that as the bill under consideration contemplates the government in the light of a joint proprietor of the stock of the bank, it brings the case within the provision of the clause of the constitution which immediately respects the property of the United States.

Under a conviction that such a relation subsists, the Secretary of the Treasury, with all deference conceives, that it will result as a necessary consequence from the position, that all the specified powers of the government are sovereign as to the proper objects; that the incorporation of a bank is a constitutional measure, and that the objections taken to the bill, in this respect, are ill founded.

But from an earnest desire to give the utmost possible satisfaction to the mind of the President, on so delicate and important a subject, the Secretary of the Treasury will ask his indulgence while he gives some additional illustrations of cases in which a power of erecting corporations may be exercised, under some of those heads of the specified powers of the Government, which are alledged to include the right of incorporating a bank.

1. It does not appear susceptible of a doubt, that if Congress had thought proper to provide in the collection law, that the bonds to be given for the duties should be given to the collector of each district in the name of the collector of the district A. or B. as the case might require, to enure to him & his successors in office, in trust for the United States, that it would have been consistent with the constitution to make such an arrangement. And yet this it is conceived would amount to an incorporation.

2. It is not an unusual expedient of taxation to farm particular branches of revenue, that is to mortgage or sell the product of them for certain definite sums, leaving the collection to the parties to whom they are mortgaged or sold. There are even examples of this in the United States. Suppose that there was any particular branch of revenue which it was manifestly expedient to place on this footing, & there were a number of persons willing to engage with the Government, upon condition, that they should be incorporated & the funds vested in them, as well for

their greater safety as for the more convenient recovery & management of the taxes. It is supposeable, that there could be any constitutional obstacle to the measure? It is presumed that there could be none. It is certainly a mode of collection which it would be in the discretion of the Government to adopt; though the circumstances must be very extraordinary, that would induce the Secretary to think it expedient.

3. Suppose a new & unexplored branch of trade should present itself with some foreign country. Suppose it was manifest, that, to undertake it with advantage, required an union of the capitals of a number of individuals; & that those individuals would not be disposed to embark without an incorporation, as well to obviate that consequence of a private partnership, which makes every individual liable in his whole estate for the debts of the company to their utmost extent, as for the more convenient management of the business—what reason can there be to doubt, that the national government would have a constitutional right to institute and incorporate such a company? None.

They possess a general authority to regulate trade with foreign countries. This is a mean which has been practiced to that end by all the principal commercial nations; who have trading companies to this day which have subsisted for centuries. Why may not the United States *constitutionally* employ the means *usual* in other countries for attaining the ends entrusted to them?

A power to make all needful rules & regulations concerning territory has been construed to mean a power to erect a government. A power to *regulate* trade is a power to make all needful rules & regulations concerning trade. Why may it not then include that of erecting a trading company as well as in the other case to erect a Government?

It is remarkable, that the State Conventions who have proposed amendments in relation to this point, have most, if not all of them, expressed themselves nearly thus—"Congress shall not grant monopolies, nor *erect any company* with exclusive advantages of commerce;" thus at the same time expressing their sense, that the power to erect trading companies or corporations, was inherent in Congress, & objecting to it no further, than as to the grant of *exclusive* priviledges.

The Secretary entertains all the doubts which prevail concerning the utility of such companies; but he cannot fashion to his own mind a reason to induce a doubt, that there is a constitutional authority in the United States to establish them. If such a reason were demanded, none could be given unless it were this—that congress cannot erect a corporation; which would be no better than to say they cannot do it, because they cannot do it: first presuming an inability, without reason, & then assigning that *inability* as the cause of itself.

Illustrations of this kind might be multiplied without end. They shall however be pursued no further.

There is a sort of evidence on this point, arising from an aggregate view of the constitution, which is of no inconsiderable weight. The very general power of laying & collecting taxes & appropriating their proceeds—that of borrowing money indefinitely—that of coining money & regulating foreign coins—that of making all needful rules and regulations respecting the property of the United States—these powers combined, as well as the reason & nature of the thing speak strongly this language: That it is the manifest design and scope of the constitution to vest in congress all the powers requisite to the effectual administration of the finances of the United States. As far as concerns this object, there appears to be no parsimony of power.

To suppose then, that the government is precluded from the employment of so usual as well as so important an instrument for the administration of its finances as that of a bank, is to suppose, what does not coincide with the general tenor & complexion of the constitution, and what is not agreeable to impressions that any mere spectator would entertain concerning it. Little less than a prohibitory clause can destroy the strong presumptions which result from the general aspect of the government. Nothing but demonstration should exclude the idea, that the power exists.

In all questions of this nature the practice of mankind ought to have great weight against the theories of Individuals.

The fact, for instance, that all the principal commercial nations have made use of trading corporations or companies for the purposes of *external commerce*, is a satisfactory proof, that the Establishment of them is an incident to the regulation of that commerce.

This other fact, that banks are an usual engine in the administration of national finances, & an ordinary & the most effectual instrument of loans & one which in this country has been found essential, pleads strongly against the supposition, that a government clothed with most of the most important prerogatives of sovereignty in relation to the revenues, its debts, its credit, its defence, its trade, its intercourse with foreign nations—is forbidden to make use of that instrument as an appendage to its own authority.

It has been stated as an auxiliary test of constitutional authority, to try, whether it abridges any preexisting right of any state, or any Individual. The proposed incorporation will stand the most severe examination on this point. Each state may still erect as many banks as it pleases; every individual may still carry on the banking business to any extent he pleases.

Another criterion may be this, whether the institution or thing has a more direct relation as to its uses, to the objects of the reserved powers of the State Governments, than to those of the powers delegated by the United States. This rule indeed is less precise than the former, but it may still serve as some guide. Surely a bank has more reference to the objects entrusted to the national government, than to those, left to the care of the State Governments. The common defence is decisive in this comparison.

It is presumed, that nothing of consequence in the observations of the Secretary of State and Attorney General has been left unnoticed.

There are indeed a variety of observations of the Secretary of State designed to shew that the utilities ascribed to a bank in relation to the collection of taxes and to trade, could be obtained without it, to analyse which would prolong the discussion beyond all bounds. It shall be forborne for two reasons—first because the report concerning the Bank may speak for itself in this respect; and secondly, because all those observations are grounded on the erroneous idea, that the *quantum* of necessity or utility is the test of a constitutional exercise of power.

One or two remarks only shall be made: one is that he has taken no notice of a very essential advantage to trade in general which is mentioned in the report, as peculiar to the existence of a bank circulation equal, in the public estimation to

314

Gold & silver. It is this, that it renders it unnecessary to *lock* up the money of the country to accumulate for months successively in order to the periodical payment of interest. The other is this; that his arguments to shew that treasury orders & bills of exchange from the course of trade will prevent any considerable displacement of the metals, are founded on a partial view of the subject. A case will prove this: The sums collected in a state may be small in comparison with the debt due to it. The balance of its trade, direct & circuitous, with the seat of government may be even or nearly so. Here then without bank bills, which in that state answer the purpose of coin, there must be a displacement of the coin, in proportion to the difference between the sum collected in the State and that to be paid in it. With bank bills no such displacement would take place, or, as far as it did, it would be gradual & insensible. In many other ways also, would there be at least a temporary & inconvenient displacement of the coin, even where the course of trade would eventually return it to its proper channels.

The difference of the two situations in point of convenience to the Treasury can only be appreciated by one, who experiences the embarassments of making provision for the payment of the interest on a stock continually changing place in thirteen different places.

One thing which has been omitted just occurs, although it is not very material to the main argument. The Secretary of State affirms, that the bill only contemplates a re-payment, not a loan to the government. But here he is, certainly mistaken. It is true, the government invests in the stock of the bank a sum equal to that which it receives on loan. But let it be remembered, that it does not, therefore, cease to be a proprietor of the stock; which would be the case, if the money received back were in the nature of a repayment. It remains a proprietor still, & will share in the profit, or loss, or the institution, according as the dividend is more or less than the interest it is to pay on the sum borrowed. Hence that sum is manifestly, and, in the strictest sense, a loan.

NOTES

1. Hamilton to Washington, September 9, 1792, in Henry Cabot Lodge, ed., *The Works of Alexander Hamilton* (New York, 1904) VI, 344.
2. Lodge, VI, 356. (My emphasis.)
3. Lodge, VI, 341. Richard Kohn has recently pointed out that the cabinet was divided on Hamilton's "hard line," Attorney General Edmund Randolph strongly opposing military action at the time. He was backed up by such key Federalists as Rufus King and John Jay, both of whom counseled against taking precipitate action. In the face of these opinions, Washington wavered and delayed acting until two years later, when his efforts to conciliate the matter were rejected. See Richard H. Kohn, "The Washington Administration's Decision to Crush the Whiskey Rebellion," *Journal of American History*, LIX, No. 3 (December 1972), 567-84.
4. Leland D. Baldwin, *Whiskey Rebels* (Pittsburgh, Pennsylvania, 1968), 183-84. This is an interesting account of the situation which emphasizes the rebels' situation and attitudes.
5. Baldwin, 184.
6. Lodge, VI, 392.
7 Lodge, VI, 403.

8. Lodge, VI, 404-05.
9. Richardson, I, 156.
10. Baldwin, 198.
11. Baldwin, 200.
12. See following document.
13. John C. Fitzpatrick, ed., *The Writings of George Washington* (Washington, D.C., 1940) XXXIV, 98-99.
14. Baldwin, 270-71.
15. Edward S. Corwin, *The President: Office and Powers, 1787-1957* (New York, 1957), 132.
16. Henry Steele Commager, ed., *Documents of American History*, 5th ed. (New York, 1949) I, 178.
17. Charles Sellers, *Andrew Jackson, Nullification and the States-Rights Tradition* (Chicago, 1963), 44.
18. Marquis James, *The Life of Andrew Jackson*, part II, *Portrait of a President* (Indianapolis, Indiana, 1938), 306.
19. Herbert Croly, *The Promise of American Life* (New York, 1965), 38-39.
20. Clinton Rossiter, *Alexander Hamilton and the Constitution* (New York, 1964), 4.
21. Rossiter, 25.
22. See introductory note of Hamilton's "Report on the Bank," in Harold C. Syrett and Jacob E. Cooke, eds., *The Papers of Alexander Hamilton* (New York, 1963) VII, 241 and 244.
23. Quoted in Rossiter, 78.
24. Syrett and Cooke, VIII, 50.
25. H. A. Washington, ed., *The Writings of Thomas Jefferson* (Washington, D.C., 1854) VII, 556.
26. Washington, VII, 558.
27. Rossiter, 189.
28. Rossiter, 190.
29. Syrett and Cooke, VIII, 102-03.
30. Rossiter, 208-09.

Bibliography

Baldwin, Leland D. *Whiskey Rebels: The Story of the Frontier Uprising.* Pittsburgh, Pennsylvania: University of Pittsburgh Press, 1968.

Bassett, John Spencer, ed. *Correspondence of Andrew Jackson.* Vols. IV, V. Washington, D.C.: Carnegie Institution of Washington, 1931.

Commager, Henry Steele, ed. *Documents of American History.* 2 vols. Fifth Edition. New York: Appleton-Century-Crofts, Inc., 1949.

Corwin, Edward S. *The President: Office and Powers, 1787-1957.* Fourth Revised Edition. New York: New York University Press, 1957.

Croly, Herbert. *The Promise of American Life.* Cambridge, Massachusetts: The Belknap Press of Harvard University, 1965.

Findley, William, ed. *History of the Insurrection in the Four Western Counties of Pennsylvania.* Proceedings of the Executive of the United States Respecting the Insurgents. Philadelphia, Pennsylvania: Samuel Harrison Smith, 1796.

Fitzpatrick, John C., ed. *The Writings of George Washington.* 39 vols. Washington, D.C.: U.S. Government Printing Office, 1940.

Freeman, Douglas Southall. *George Washington.* Vol. VI, *Patriot and President.* New York: Charles Scribner's Sons, 1954.

James, Marquis. *The Life of Andrew Jackson.* Indianapolis, Indiana: The Bobbs-Merrill Company, 1938.

Kohn, Richard H. "The Washington Administration's Decision to Crush the Whiskey Rebellion." *Journal of American History.* LIX, No. 3 (December 1972), 567-84.

Lodge, Henry Cabot, ed. *The Works of Alexander Hamilton.* New York: G. P. Putnam's Sons, 1904.

Rich, Bennett M. *The Presidents and Civil Disorder.* Washington, D.C.: The Brookings Institution, 1941.

Richardson, James D., ed. *Messages and Papers of the Presidents.* Vol. I. New York: Bureau of National Literature, 1897.

Rossiter, Clinton. *Alexander Hamilton and the Constitution*. New York: Harcourt, Brace and World, Inc., 1964.

Sellers, Charles. *Andrew Jackson, Nullification and the States-Rights Tradition*. Chicago: Rand McNally Company, 1963.

IV. The President's Legislative Role

THE PRESIDENT'S
LEGISLATIVE ROLE

Presidential Initiative

The President's role in the legislative process was not given special consideration at the Constitutional Convention, nor was there significant opposition voiced to the proposed legislative functions the Executive would assume. Some concern however was directed to the negative or veto power assigned to the President, a power with which he could defeat or delay legislation passed by both houses of the Congress. It was more or less assumed from the beginning that the President would have some form of veto power over legislation, but there was debate regarding the precise character and limits of such a veto.

But the Founding Fathers also wrote into the Constitution another clause which empowered the President "from time to time to give to the Congress information of the State of the Union, and recommend to their Consideration measures as he shall judge necessary and expedient." No debate whatsoever was conducted over this provision, for as Alexander Hamilton put it in Federalist No. 77: "No objection has been made to this class of authorities; nor could they possibly admit of any." The early Presidents took this injunction seriously, but they tended to limit its functional role to delivering a formal address or State of the Union Message during each year of their tenure. Part of this address was taken up with a report to the Congress and the nation which assessed the national condition—hence its title—State of the Union Message. These reports tended to be somewhat unctuous and self-serving; "self-congratulatory" as Arthur Schlesinger, jr. has characterized them. They were delivered personally to the Congress by Washington and Adams, but Jefferson broke with this tradition and established the long continued precedent of transmitting the message in writing.

In their messages Presidents invoked the praise of the almighty, counted the nation's blessings, remarked upon the plentiful harvest, and pointed with pride to the progress the country had made since the last such report. But from the beginning, most Chief Executives also cast their eyes upon the future and outlined, albeit usually in fairly general language, objectives which they recommended to the Congress to consider. In his First Annual Message, Washington urged:

—a well considered plan for the national defense;
—the development of the manufacture of military supplies to make our
   military forces independent of other nations;
—protection for inhabitants of frontier areas from hostile Indian tribes;

—a special fund to be created and designated to defray expenses of those engaged in foreign affairs;

—a uniform rule of naturalization of citizens;

—uniformity in weights and measures as well as a uniform currency;

—due attention to the post office and post roads;

—encouragement of agriculture, commerce and manufacturing, as well as the introduction of new inventions from abroad to aid in such development, with the hope of facilitating our own skill and genius in producing them at home;

—the promotion of science and literature;

—support of institutions of higher learning and/or the establishment of a national university.[1]

In some instances, documents with more specific details followed these very general proposals, and as time went on the messages increased in length but not necessarily in importance. Washington's first State of the Union Message encompassed only 15 brief paragraphs, covering two and one-half pages, while Andrew Jackson's last message took up 83 more lengthy paragraphs spread out over 24 pages. The early messages tended to emphasize major continuing problems in the nation's developing history. In the beginning, the question of national security was paramount, and the protection of American ships on the high seas and foreign relations were also stressed. The situation of the Indians continued to be a serious problem for some time, as did the state of the national debt and credit, and the development of agriculture and domestic industry.

But one of the most critical questions which most of the early Presidents addressed themselves to in their State of the Union Messages was the complex problem of internal improvements and the development of the American continent. These included such a wide spectrum of activities as exploring the unchartered areas of the continent, mapping the uninhabited regions, charting the coastal seas and harbors, building roads, turnpikes and canals, encouraging industrial and fine arts, supporting literature and science, inducing creative inventions and establishing a national university.

None of the early Presidents doubted either the wisdom or the necessity of national initiative and support for such constructive purposes, but despite Washington's *imprimatur*, the three other Virginians who occupied the early presidency had reservations about the constitutional power of the Congress to mandate most of these enterprises and appropriate funds for them. Jefferson rather diffidently suggested:

I suppose an amendment to the Constitution, by consent of the States necessary, because the objects now recommended are not among those enumerated in the Constitution, and to which it permits the public moneys to be applied.[2]

But John Quincy Adams was not deterred by such a narrow construction of the Constitution, even if it was endorsed by such illustrious "birthright" Republicans. He went much further than any of his predecessors in utilizing the State of the Union Message to advocate the creative use of the power of the national government to initiate and support such undertakings, and he ridiculed the notion that the existing provisions of the Constitution were not adequate to support such activities:

> The Constitution under which you are assembled is a charter of limited powers. After full and solemn deliberation upon all or any of the objects which, urged by an irresistible sense of my own duty, I have recommended to your attention should you come to the conclusion that, however desirable in themselves, the enactment of laws for effecting them would transcend the powers committed to you by that venerable instrument which we are all bound to support, let no consideration induce you to assume the exercise of powers not granted to you by the people. But if the power to exercise exclusive legislation in any cases whatsoever over the District of Columbia; if the power to lay and collect taxes, duties, imposts, and excises, to pay the debts and provide for the common defense and general welfare of the United States; if the power to regulate commerce with foreign nations and among the several states and with the Indian tribes, to fix the standard of weights and measures, to establish post offices and post-roads, to declare war, to raise and support armies, to provide and maintain a navy, to dispose of and make all needful rules and regulations respecting the territory or other property belonging to the United States, and to make all laws which shall be necessary and proper for carrying these powers into execution—if these powers and others enumerated in the Constitution may be effectually brought into action by laws promoting the improvement of agriculture, commerce, and manufactures, the cultivation and encouragement of the elegant arts, the advancement of literature, and the progress of the sciences, ornamental and profound, to refrain from exercising them for the benefit of the people themselves would be to hide in the earth the talent committed to our charge—would be treachery to the most sacred of trusts.[3]

Despite the serious reservations expressed by various members of his official family, Adams was determined to pursue his objectives in his first State of the Union Message. As he indicated in his diary, if he delayed presenting these proposals until a later message, there was always the possibility that fate would prevent such an event. So he decided that "the perilous experiment be made. Let me make it with full deliberation, and be prepared for the consequences."[4]

President John Quincy Adams
Diary Account of Cabinet Discussions
Of his First State of the Union Message
November 25-26, 1825

Charles Francis Adams, ed., *Memoirs of John Quincy Adams: Comprising Portions of His Diary* (Philadelphia, Pennsylvania, 1875) VII, 60-63.

25th.

Clay, S. S.; Rush, S. T.; Barbour, S. W.; Southard, S. N.; Cabinet meeting from one till near five. [Participants: Henry Clay, Secretary of State; Richard Rush, Secretary of the Treasury; James Barbour, Secretary of War; Samuel K. Southard, Secretary of the Navy; and of course President Adams.—Ed.] I read over again by paragraphs the draft of a message but Governor Barbour expressed the wish that the whole of the concluding part, respecting internal improvements, should be suppressed. Mr. Clay coincided in this opinion partially; was for discarding the University, and perhaps some other objects, but for retaining great part of the other things proposed. Mr. Clay was for recommending nothing which, from its unpopularity, would be unlikely to succeed; Governor Barbour, nothing so popular that it may be carried without recommendation. Clay good-humoredly remarked this alternate stripping off from my draft; and I told them I was like the man with his two wives—one plucking out his black hairs, and the other the white, till none were left. However, we adjourned till two o'clock to-morrow to discuss the question thoroughly.

26th.

Clay, S. S.; Rush, S. T.; Barbour, S. W.; Southard, S. N.; The adjourned Cabinet meeting followed immediately after the departure of the Indians. The first question was upon the whole of the concluding division of the message as projected.

Mr. Rush desired that the whole of it might be read again. I read it. Governor Barbour then withdrew his objection to it as a whole; but he and Mr. Clay persisted in objections to many detached parts of it. Mr. Clay wished to have the recommendations of a National University and of a new Executive Department struck out; almost everything relating to the Patent Office; and the final enumeration of all the purposes of internal improvements for which I asserted that Congress have powers. I agreed to give up all that relates to the Patent Office; and upon discussion most of the particular objections were abandoned. The University, Mr. Clay said, was entirely hopeless, and he thought there was something in the constitutional objection to it; for it did not rest upon the same principle as internal improvements, or the bank. I concurred entirely in the opinion that no projects absolutely impracticable ought to be recommended; but I would look to a practicability of a longer range than a simple session of Congress. General Washington had recommended the Military Academy more than ten years before it was obtained. The plant may come late, though the seed should be sown early. And I had not recommended a University—I had only referred to Washington's recommendations, and observed they had not been carried into effect.

The new Executive Department, Mr. Clay said, was of most urgent necessity. No one knew it better than he. Yet he was sure there would not be twenty votes for it in the House. He did not believe there would be five.

I said it was not very material to me whether I should present these views in the first or the last message I should send to Congress. They would not suit any other; but in one of them I should feel it my indispensable duty to suggest them. There is this consideration for offering them now—that of the future I can never be sure. I may be not destined to send another message.

Mr. Rush very earnestly urged the communication at this time. And Clay said he was anxious that almost the whole of what I had written should go. He himself was fully convinced that Congress had the powers; but he had no doubt that if they did not exercise them there would be a dissolution of the Union by the mountains.

The result of all was, that Barbour very reluctantly withdrew his objection to the whole topic; that Clay approved of the general principles, but scrupled great part of the details; Rush approved nearly the whole; and Southard said scarcely anything. Thus situated, the perilous experiment must be made. Let me make it with full deliberation, and be prepared for the consequences.

Henry Clay's political judgment proved to be more realistic than Adams' idealism and courage. The proposals, individually and collectively, were largely ignored, and when noticed, were ridiculed. Adams had to be content with morsels when he wanted the whole loaf; the passage of congressional appropriations for the repair of the Cumberland Road, several grants for stock in small canal companies and action on a few worthwhile projects like the Delaware breakwater were small rewards for Adams' zeal.

But the man from Braintree was almost a century ahead of his time, and his message established an inspiring model to which later Presidents would aspire. Adams lacked the political insight and skills to create the public environment and political support for such enlightened objectives. As a result he must be judged something of a failure in office for not having been able to gather support for his policies in the Congress. But he must be admired and respected for his great vision and integrity, as well as for being the first President to demonstrate the real scope and creative possibilities of the constitutional provision to "recommend to their consideration measures as he shall judge necessary and expedient."

President John Quincy Adams
First State of the Union Message
December 6, 1825

Richardson, II, 877-82.

Upon this first occasion of addressing the Legislature of the Union, with which I have been honored, in presenting to their view the execution so far as it has been effected of the measures sanctioned by them for promoting the internal improvement of our country, I can not close the communication without recommending to their calm and persevering consideration the general principle in a more enlarged extent. The great object of the institution of civil government is the improvement of the condition of those who are parties to the social compact, and no government, in whatever form constituted, can accomplish the lawful ends of its institution but in proportion as it improves the condition of those over whom it is established. Roads and canals, by multiplying and facilitating the communications and intercourse between distant regions and multitudes of men, are among the most important means of improvement. But moral, political, intellectual improvement are duties assigned by the Author of Our Existence to social no less than to individual man. For the fulfillment of those duties governments are invested with power, and to the attainment of the end—the progressive improvement of the condition of the governed—the exercise of delegated powers is a duty as sacred and indispensable as the usurpation of powers not granted is criminal and odious. Among the first, perhaps the very first, instrument for the improvement of the condition of men is knowledge, and to the acquisition of much of the knowledge adapted to the wants, the comforts, and enjoyments of human life public institutions and seminaries of learning are essential. So convinced of this was the first of my predecessors in this office, now first in the memory, as, living, he was first in the hearts, of our countrymen, that once and again in his addresses to the Congresses with whom he cooperated in the public service he earnestly recommended the establishment of seminaries of learning, to prepare for all the emergencies of peace and war—a national university and a military academy. With respect to the latter, had he lived to the present day, in turning his eyes to the institution at West Point he would have enjoyed the gratification of his most earnest wishes; but in surveying the city which has been honored with his name he would have seen the spot of earth which he had destined and bequeathed to the use and benefit of his country as the site for an university still bare and barren.

In assuming her station among the civilized nations of the earth it would seem that our country had contracted the engagement to contribute her share of mind, of labor, and of expense to the improvement of those parts of knowledge which lie beyond the reach of individual acquisition, and particularly to geographical and astronomical science. Looking back to the history only of the half century since the declaration of our independence, and observing the generous emulation with which the Governments of France, Great Britain, and Russia have devoted the genius, the intelligence, the treasures of their respective nations to the common improvement of the species in these branches of science, is it not incumbent upon us to inquire whether we are not bound by obligations of a high and honorable character to contribute our portion of energy and exertion to the common stock? The voyages of discovery prosecuted in the course of that time at the expense of those nations have not only redounded to their glory, but to the improvement of human knowledge. We have been partakers of that improvement and owe for it a sacred debt, not only of gratitude, but of equal or proportional exertion in the same common cause. Of the cost of these undertakings, if the mere expenditures of outfit, equipment, and completion of the expeditions were to be considered the only charges, it would be unworthy of a great and generous nation to take a second thought. One hundred expeditions of circumnavigation like those of Cook and La Pérouse would not burden the exchequer of the nation fitting them out so much as the ways and means of defraying a single campaign in war. But if we take into the account the lives of those benefactors of mankind of which their services in the cause of their species were the purchase, how shall the cost of those heroic enterprises be estimated, and what compensation can be made to them or to their countries for them? Is it not by bearing them in affectionate remembrance? Is it not still more by imitating their example—by enabling countrymen of our own to pursue the same career and to hazard their lives in the same cause?

In inviting the attention of Congress to the subject of internal improvements upon a view thus enlarged it is not my design to recommend the equipment of an expedition for circumnavigating the globe for purposes of scientific research and inquiry. We have objects of useful investigation nearer home, and to which our cares may be more beneficially applied. The interior of our own territories has yet been very imperfectly explored. Our coasts along many degrees of latitude upon the shores of the Pacific Ocean, though much frequented by our spirited commercial navigators, have been barely visited by our public ships. The River of the West, first fully discovered and navigated by a countryman of our own, still bears the name of the ship in which he ascended its waters, and claims the protection of our armed national flag at its mouth. With the establishment of a military post there or at some other point of that coast, recommended by my predecessor and already matured in the deliberations of the last Congress, I would suggest the expediency of connecting the equipment of a public ship for the exploration of the whole northwest coast of this continent.

The establishment of an uniform standard of weights and measures was one of the specific objects contemplated in the formation of our Constitution, and to fix that standard was one of the powers delegated by express terms in that instrument to Congress. The Governments of Great Britain and France have scarcely ceased to be occupied with inquiries and speculations on the same subject since the existence of our Constitution, and with them it has expanded into profound, laborious, and expensive researches into the figure of the earth and the comparative length of the pendulum vibrating seconds in various latitudes from the equator to the pole. These researches have resulted in the composition and publication of several works highly interesting to the cause of science. The experiments are yet in the process of performance. Some of them have recently been made on our own shores, within the walls of one of our own colleges, and partly by one of our own fellow-citizens. It would be honorable to our country if the sequel of the same experiments should be countenanced by the patronage of our Government, as they have hitherto been by those of France and Britain.

Connected with the establishment of an university, or separate from it, might be undertaken the erection of an astronomical observatory, with provision for the support of an astronomer, to be in constant attendance of observation upon the phenomena of the heavens, and for the periodical publication of his observations. It is with no feeling of pride as an American that the remark may be made that on the comparatively small territorial surface of Europe there are existing upward of 130 of these light-houses of the skies, while throughout the whole American hemisphere there is not one. If we reflect a moment upon the discoveries which in the last four centuries have been made in the physical constitution of the universe by the means of these buildings and of observers stationed in them, shall we doubt of their usefulness to every nation? And while scarcely a year passes over our heads without bringing some new astronomical discovery to light, which we must fain receive at second hand from Europe, are we not cutting ourselves off from the means of returning light for light while we have neither observatory nor observer upon our half of the globe and the earth revolves in perpetual darkness to our unsearching eyes?

. . . The spirit of improvement is abroad upon the earth. It stimulates the hearts and sharpens the faculties not of our fellow-citizens alone, but of the nations of Europe and of their rulers. While dwelling with pleasing satisfaction upon the superior excellence of our political institutions, let us not be unmindful that liberty is power; that the nation blessed with the largest portion of liberty must in proportion to its numbers be the most powerful nation upon earth, and that the tenure of power by man is, in the moral purposes of his Creator, upon condition that it shall be exercised to ends of beneficence, to improve the condition of himself and his fellowmen. While foreign nations less blessed with that freedom which is power than ourselves are advancing with gigantic strides in the career of public improvement, were we to slumber in indolence or fold up our arms and proclaim to the world that we are palsied by the will of our constituents, would it not be to cast away the bounties of Providence and doom ourselves to perpetual inferiority? In the course of the year now drawing to its close we have beheld, under the auspices and at the expense of one State of this Union, a new university unfolding its portals to the sons of science and holding up the torch of human improvement to eyes that seek the light. We have seen under the persevering and enlightened enterprise of another State the waters of our Western lakes mingle with those of the ocean. If undertakings like these have been accomplished in the compass of a few years by the authority of single members of our Confederation, can we, the representative authorities of the whole Union, fall behind our fellow-servants in the exercise of the trust committed to us for the benefit of our common sovereign by the accomplishment of works important to the whole and to which neither the authority nor the resources of any one State can be adequate?

The Veto Power

Early Experience

The notion of permitting the Chief Executive to have a veto power over the work of the legislature was not a unique idea to emerge from the Convention in Philadelphia in the summer of 1787. The royal governors of the crown colonies possessed such a veto, and the British monarch could constitutionally negate any act of Parliament, although such a veto had not been used after Queen Anne's death. Naturally then, there was great antipathy among the colonists to this delegated authority of the King's appointed representatives, and terrific resistance to their executive power and control throughout colonial America. By 1787, however, something of a "backlash" had developed in response to an overdose of legislative ascendency in the new states, and in Philadelphia, the New York and Massachusetts models, with their strong and relatively independent executives, were influential in convincing the delegates to provide the President of the new government with a limited legislative veto, among other things.

Surprisingly little resistance to the veto power was expressed during the debates, the major disputes involving the key questions of whether this negative power should be absolute or qualified, and if limited, what should be the exact number of votes required in Congress to override it? It was also suggested that the President share the veto power with some other group or individuals, as the governors did in New York and Massachusetts, but it was generally acknowledged from the beginning that the Executive needed some potent weapon to defend his position from legislative attack. No one at that time, however, anticipated the presidential veto's full potential as an instrument of legislative and even political influence. It was generally considered a necessary and useful check upon the potentially arbitrary power of the legislature.

Under the constitutional provisions for the veto power,[5] the President possesses five different options. First of all, if he approves of the bill that comes before him, he can simply sign it and it becomes a law. If he disapproves, he can veto it and return it to the Congress with his objections. If he neither officially approves or disapproves and does not sign the bill while Congress is still in session, the bill becomes a law after ten days. If Congress is not in session and the President receives the bill less than ten official days before Congress recesses, then he can "pocket veto" it by refusing to sign it, which under these conditions carries the full effect of a regular veto. Finally, the President can sign the bill and make it a law, but in addition register a protest to Congress, asserting his personal disagreement with the statute, despite his refusal to block its passage into law.

There have been Presidents who have taken liberal advantage of the veto power to block many bills passed by the Congress, and there have been others (John Adams, Thomas Jefferson, John Quincy Adams, Martin Van Buren, William H.

Harrison, Zachary Taylor, Millard T. Fillmore and James Garfield) who have not used it at all. Washington was the first President to veto a measure, giving as his reason that the bill as it was drawn was in conflict with the Constitution. It involved a proposal for changing the existing system of representation in the House of Representatives, and Washington quite rightly called attention to aspects of the bill which he thought violated the principle of representation established in Article I, Section 2 of the Constitution.

Because the first veto was based upon constitutional objections, many believed thereafter that this was the only basis a President could advance for rejecting a bill passed by the Congress. Five years later Washington disabused them of this by rejecting another piece of legislation for practical policy objections rather than constitutional reasons. Congress had wanted to reduce the already minuscule army, but Washington, as a military man with greater experience than any member of Congress and with a thorough knowledge of what was needed to protect the frontier, refused to go along with the reduction and vetoed the bill. In neither this case nor the first did Congress overturn the veto by the necessary two-thirds vote; thus, in these first uses of the presidential veto, the legislation was rejected and the legislature overpowered.

Despite Washington's use of the veto in a case which did not raise a constitutional issue, several of his successors persisted in maintaining that that was its only legitimate use. Neither Adams nor Jefferson vetoed a single bill, and Madison advanced only constitutional grounds for his six vetoes. Even when the veto was used it was usually done reluctantly, for it appeared to upset the fragile relationship existing between the Executive and Congress.

Andrew Jackson Taps the Political Potential of the Veto Power

It was Andrew Jackson who first sensed the real power of the presidential veto and used its power with more dramatic effect than perhaps any other President in the nineteenth century. He certainly broke the tradition of presidential reluctance to use this weapon as a last resort; he also transformed it from a modest form of constitutional review and theoretical check against legislative tyranny, into an effective instrument of presidential power and influence.

Early in his first term Jackson decided to utilize the veto power to prevent what he considered to be improper raids upon the national Treasury to secure money for purely local internal improvements such as roads and canals. He indicated in his First Annual Message to the Congress that he was determined to make every effort to retire the national debt, and looked forward to the day when any annual surplus could be distributed to the states and ear-marked for truly national improvements. But such an objective could be blocked by continued drains upon the Treasury for local projects, and "Old Hickory" was determined to assert his leadership to put a stop to it. On top of this Jackson had an unerring "instinct for the jugular," and the idea of getting the jump on Congress and taking the fight to the other branch of government apparently appealed to him strongly.

The result of this decision was his veto of a bill designed to underwrite the construction of a turnpike from Maysville to Lexington, Kentucky. His secretary of state and personal political advisor, Martin Van Buren, was heartily in accord with the decision and had, in fact, not only encouraged the President to move in this direction, but had actually suggested the particular measure which Jackson had decided to veto. Van Buren had long been an opponent of Treasury-financed local improvements, and he was delighted at the opportunity of enlisting such a powerful ally in discouraging their continuation.

But Jackson's plan to veto the Maysville Turnpike Bill reached the ears of some of his western supporters who were determined to see the measure pass. One of them, Congressman Richard "Tecumsah" Johnson, stormed into the executive mansion to confront Jackson and find out his intentions in this matter. Van Buren, who was with the President at the time, reported on what transpired.

Secretary of State Martin Van Buren
Description of Interview between
Representative Richard M. Johnson
And President Andrew Jackson on
The Maysville Road Bill Veto
1830

John C. Fitzpatrick, ed., *The Autobiography of Martin Van Buren*, Annual Report of the American Historical Association, 1920, (Washington, D.C., 1920) II, 323-24.

Col. [Richard M.] Johnson, of Kentucky, was induced by Western members, who had been alarmed by floating rumors, to sound the President and if he found that there existed danger of such a result to remonstrate with him, in their names and his own, against a *veto*. At the moment of his appearance the President and myself were engaged in an examination of the exposé of the state of the Treasury to which I have referred, and alone. After a delay natural to a man possessed as the Colonel was of much real delicacy of feeling and having an awkward commission in hand, he said that he had called at the instance of many friends to have some conversation with the General upon a very delicate subject and was deterred from entering upon it by an apprehension that he might give offense. He was kindly told to dismiss such fears, and assured that as the President reposed unqualified confidence in his friendship, he could say nothing on any public matter that would give offense. He then spoke of the rumors in circulation, of the feelings of the General's Western friends in regard to the subject of them, of his apprehensions of the uses that Mr. Clay would make of a *veto*, and encouraged by the General's apparent interest, and warmed by his own, he extended his open hand and exclaimed "General! If this hand were an anvil on which the sledge hammer of the smith was decending and a fly were to light upon it in time to receive the blow he would not crush it more effectually than you will crush your friends in Kentucky if you veto that Bill!" Gen. Jackson evidently excited by the bold figure and energetic manner of Col. Johnson, rose from his seat and advanced towards the latter, who also quitted his chair, and the following questions and answers succeeded very rapidly: "Sir, have you looked at the condition of the Treasury—at the amount of money that it contains—at the appropriations already made by Congress—at the amount of other unavoidable claims upon it?"—"No! General, I have not! But there has always been money enough to satisfy appropriations and I do not doubt there will be now!"—"Well, I have, and this is the result," (repeating the substance of the Treasury exhibit,) "and you see there is no money to be expended as my friends desire. Now, I stand committed before the Country to pay off the National Debt, at the earliest practicable moment; this pledge I am determined to redeem, and I cannot do this if I consent to encrease it without necessity. Are you willing—are my friends willing to lay taxes to pay for internal improvements?—for be assured I will not borrow a cent except in cases of absolute necessity!"—"No!" replied the Colonel, "that would be worse than a *veto!* "

Van Buren was convinced that Johnson would pass the word to his friends that the President was intent upon vetoing the bill, and feared that that would create certain problems which might upset Jackson and his well-laid plans. Van Buren, who had been nicknamed "the little magician" and also "the red fox of Kinderhook" by some of his colleagues, surmised that if the bill's supporters were certain of the President's veto, they might change it or modify it to such an extent that it would have been difficult if not impossible for Jackson to exercise the veto. To prevent this from happening, Van Buren hastily got hold of Johnson and convinced him that the President had not yet made up his mind on the matter and would carefully consider all of the arguments for and against the bill before taking any action.

The "little magician's" strategy apparently worked, probably because many supporters of the bill could not believe that the President would actually oppose a measure which so many of his friends wanted to see passed. The political "pork barrel" so familiar today in Congress apparently existed in that earlier period too. Representatives from Pennsylvania, for example, supported projects from Kentucky because they in turn expected, and received, the support of Kentucky members for projects in Pennsylvania. It appeared to many that Jackson would go along with the bill because it was believed that he wanted to please his constituents and share the public largess. Little did they know of his real character or views; they were dumbfounded when he vetoed the Maysville Bill. Jackson did want the government to serve the interests of the people to a greater extent than it had been doing, but he did not advocate serving the interests of some at the expense of others.

Jackson's and Van Buren's motives in applying the veto to the Maysville Bill appear to be extremely complex. There were first of all the constitutional objections. Jackson considered himself an old Jeffersonian Republican, and he inherited much of the Jefferson and Madison doctrine of strict interpretation of the Constitution. Jefferson, Madison and Monroe had all opposed the use of federal funds for national improvements because they thought that the Constitution did not specifically name the power to make such grants; on the other hand, they strongly advocated making such grants if a constitutional amendment could be passed authorizing such action.

Jackson and Van Buren agreed with this reasoning to a certain extent, but one gets the impression that it was not central to their real objections. Van Buren had previously argued on several occasions, and in this instance, convinced Jackson, that an appropriation for an internal improvement project to be constructed in certain states could render a real injustice to other states whose revenues were being appropriated for this purpose. In addition there was the difficult problem of distinguishing what was national from what was purely local, because a project constructed in only one state could serve basically national interests. They insisted that more definite criteria be used in defining such terms as "national" and "local" before such a justification could be made.

Furthermore, Jackson and Van Buren were strongly opposed to the pursuit of any such projects before the national debt was wiped out. At such a time, they argued, a constitutional amendment could be drafted which would eliminate the objections of the "birthright" Republicans and could also attempt to define more precisely the nature of national and local projects. They also insisted upon one further and very interesting addition to such a constitutional amendment, that was, to restrict the exercise of such power so as to protect fully the sovereignty and interests of the individual states. Their own preference in this respect would be to handle this matter through proportional disbursements of surplus revenue to the states.

The President drafted a rough memorandum of what he wanted to say in the veto message and gave it to Secretary Van Buren to rework. The transformation from the original document prepared by Jackson into the skillful message drafted by Van Buren was almost total. Yet, the two agreed on essentials, and Van Buren's legal background and experience were effectively put to work on the President's behalf. The two documents are included, for a comparative study and analysis of them is rewarding and instructive particularly in order to grasp how important and useful presidential advisors can be. Jackson probably made better use of able advisors and assistants than did any President up to the modern period.

President Andrew Jackson
Notes for the Maysville Road Veto Message
May [19-26?], 1830

Bassett, V, 137-39.

The Maysville road bill—Considered 1rst its Constitutionality. The objects intended by the confederation of states in framing the Constitution and the people who ratified it, were to give to Congress the power of Legislation over all exterior and interior national matters reserving to the states exclusively the sovereign power of regulating on all their local concerns. The grants are specific. To regulate our foreign relation for defence, for the regulation of commerce, and to establish not make, post roads. Can this Bill be considered to come within any of these grants—no. The sages who formed the constitution viewed it as a government of experiment and granted all powers thought necessary for national purposes, never expecting that congress would attempt to Legislate and appropriate money only where the powers granted gave them jurisdiction over the subject, and certainly it will not be contended where congress have no juris[diction] over the subject that it can appropriate money to that object. The framers of the constitution viewing it a Government of experiment on which it might be discovered that powers not granted, might be necessary for the prosperity and safety of the country provided for its amendment, and therefore it was presumed that Congress would never exercise doubtful powers, but where doubts existed a call would be made on the people to grant the power necessary. There are no powers granted by the constitution, to authorise the United States, to become a member of corporation created by the states, where is the grant in constitution, for the united states, to become a member of corporations created by the states. It is corrupting and must destroy the purity of our govt. It must lead to consolidation and the destruction of state rights. The Govt. of the United States owning half the capital in each state corporation will wield the state elections by corrupting and destroying the morales of your people. This will be more injurious and destructive to the morals and Liberty of the people than the U. States Bank so much and so justly complained of. This is not a power granted to Congress, and of course is an infringment upon the reserved powers of states, and at once destroys that harmony that by the framers of the constitution was intended to exist between the two govts. and which has for years destroyed the harmony of the union, and might have been avoided by submitting an amendment of the constitution, for this purpose, to the people. These considerations induced me to recommend the speedy payment of the public debt, and as soon as that was paid, to distribute the surplus revenue amongnst the states, as the most just fair and Federal distribution of it, and by which flagitious Legislation arising from combinations if you will vote with me I will vote with you so disgraceful to our country, would be prevented. This power is no where to be found in the constitution—adopt this system and where would you stop, where draw the distinction, would not every incorporated body by they states have equal claims upon your membership and on your bounty, and I repeat where could you stop—would the people suffer themselves to be taxed for such purposes—would not such a power be too dangerous to your liberties, what would it result in, in this, that the united states by becoming stockholders, in every petty state corporation, to the amount of half the stock, would wield its power in your elections and all the interior concerns of the state, this would lead to consolidation and that would destroy the liberty of your country.

I can no where find in our early Legislation under the Federal constitution, where the power by congress was assumed to appropriate money to objects where the constitution had not given jurisdiction over the subject, or where the object was not clearly national. Whereever the general Government have jurisdiction over the subject, and can appropriate money for its improvement, the power follows and is incidental, to pass all laws to protect and preserve it, and punish all persons who violates its regulations, nay to exercise exclusive jurisdiction over it. With this view of the subject and the powers exercised by congress to tax the people for local objects of improvements of a state, what power cannot congress exercise over and within a state and what jealousy will not arise from the partial legislation, by combinations in congress will not follow. We have seen this spirit prevail, and there can be no doubt it will increase in future. Believing as I do that the constitutional powers of Congress in Legislation under the granted powers of the constitution are entirely national, all local matters being reserved as appropriate objects of the states, I recommended in my message, the speedy payment of the public debt, and then an appropriation of the surplus revenue amonghst the states for internal improvement etc etc. This I then and still do believe is the only just fair and Federal mode in which our surpluss revenue could be applied leaving to the states their constitutional rights to regulate all their interior concerns and the General Government all its national.

The expediency. The voice of the people from main to Louisiana during the last canvass for the Presidency has answered this in the negative—they have cried aloud for reform, retrenchment for the public expenditures, and economy in the expenditures of the Government—they expect the public debt to be speedily paid, not increased by appropriations for local not national concerns, by subscribing to and becoming partners to brokers, corporations and insolvant Banks. What is the fact during the present congress, up to the 1rst of May the appropriations have exceeded the whole expenditures of the year 1829 by [blank] and the bills reported to the House if acted upon and passed will far exceed by many millions the amount available in the Treasury for the year 1830—is it not then inexpedient and unjust at this time if the constitutional power existed to exaust your Treasury on local improvements and create the necessity of resorting to a system of direct taxes, to cover the arre[ar]ages, or to loans, to redeem the national pledge in these subscriptions and appropriations.

President Andrew Jackson
Veto Message on the Maysville Road Bill
May 27, 1830

Richardson, III, 1046-56.

To the House of Representatives   Gentlemen: I have maturely considered the bill proposing to authorize "a subscription of stock in the Maysville, Washington, Paris, and Lexington Turnpike Road Company," and now return the same to the House of Representatives, in which it originated, with my objections to its passage.

Sincerely friendly to the improvement of our country by means of roads and canals, I regret that any difference of opinion in the mode of contributing to it should exist between us; and if in stating this difference I go beyond what the occasion may be deemed to call for, I hope to find an apology in the great importance of the subject, an unfeigned respect for the high source from which this branch of it has emanated, and an anxious wish to be correctly understood by my constituents in the discharge of all my duties. Diversity of sentiment among public functionaries actuated by the same general motives, on the character and tendency of particular measures, is an incident common to all Governments, and the more to be expected in one which, like ours, owes its existence to the freedom of opinion, and must be upheld by the same influence. Controlled as we thus are by a higher tribunal, before which our respective acts will be canvassed with the indulgence due to the imperfections of our nature, and with that intelligence and unbiased judgment which are the true correctives of error, all that our responsibility demands is that the public good should be the measure of our views, dictating alike their frank expression and honest maintenance.

In the message which was presented to Congress at the opening of its present session I endeavored to exhibit briefly my views upon the important and highly interesting subject to which our attention is now to be directed. I was desirous of presenting to the representatives of the several States in Congress assembled the inquiry whether some mode could not be devised which would reconcile the diversity of opinion concerning the powers of this Government over the subject of internal improvement, and the manner in which these powers, if conferred by the Constitution, ought to be exercised. The act which I am called upon to consider has, therefore, been passed with a knowledge of my views on this question, as these are expressed in the message referred to. In that document the following suggestions will be found:

> After the extinction of the public debt it is not probable that any adjustment of the tariff upon principles satisfactory to the people of the Union will until a remote period, if ever, leave the Government without a considerable surplus in the Treasury beyond what may be required for its current service. As, then, the period approaches when the application of the revenue to the payment of debt will cease, the disposition of the surplus will present a subject for the serious deliberation of Congress; and it may be fortunate for the country that it is yet to be decided. Considered in connection with the difficulties which have heretofore attended appropriations for purposes of internal improvement, and with those which this experience tells us will certainly arise whenever power over such subjects may be exercised by the General Government, it is hoped that it may lead to the adoption of some plan which will reconcile the diversified interests of the States and strengthen the bonds which unite them. Every member of the Union, in peace and in war, will be benefited by the improvement of inland navigation and the construction of highways in the several States. Let us, then, endeavor to attain this benefit in a mode which will be satisfactory to all. That hitherto adopted has by many of our fellow-citizens been deprecated as an infraction of the Constitution, while by others it has been viewed as inexpedient. All feel that it has been employed at the expense of harmony in the legislative councils.

And adverting to the constitutional power of Congress to make what I considered a proper disposition of the surplus revenue, I subjoined the following remarks:

To avoid these evils it appears to me that the most safe, just, and federal disposition which could be made of the surplus revenue would be its apportionment among the several States according to their ratio of representation, and should this measure not be found warranted by the Constitution that it would be expedient to propose to the States an amendment authorizing it.

The constitutional power of the Federal Government to construct or promote works of internal improvement presents itself in two points of view—the first as bearing upon the sovereignty of the States within whose limits their execution is contemplated, if jurisdiction of the territory which they may occupy be claimed as necessary to their preservation and use; the second as asserting the simple right to appropriate money from the National Treasury in aid of such works when undertaken by State authority, surrendering the claim of jurisdiction. In the first view the question of power is an open one, and can be decided without the embarrassments attending the other, arising from the practice of the Government. Although frequently and strenuously attempted, the power to this extent has never been exercised by the Government in a single instance. It does not, in my opinion, possess it; and no bill, therefore, which admits it can receive my official sanction.

But in the other view of the power the question is differently situated. The ground taken at an early period of the Government was "that whenever money has been raised by the general authority and is to be applied to a particular measure, a question arises whether the particular measure be within the enumerated authorities vested in Congress. If it be, the money requisite for it may be applied to it; if not, no such application can be made." The document in which this principle was first advanced is of deservedly high authority, and should be held in grateful remembrance for its immediate agency in rescuing the country from much existing abuse and for its conservative effect upon some of the most valuable principles of the Constitution. The symmetry and purity of the Government would doubtless have been better preserved if this restriction of the power of appropriation could have been maintained without weakening its ability to fulfill the general objects of its institution, an effect so likely to attend its admission, notwithstanding its apparent fitness, that every subsequent Administration of the Government, embracing a period of thirty out of the forty-two years of its existence, has adopted a more enlarged construction of the power. It is not my purpose to detain you by a minute recital of the acts which sustain this assertion, but it is proper that I should notice some of the most prominent in order that the reflections which they suggest to my mind may be better understood.

In the Administration of Mr. Jefferson we have two examples of the exercise of the right of appropriation, which in the considerations that led to their adoption and in their effects upon the public mind have had a greater agency in marking the character of the power than any subsequent events. I allude to the payment of $15,000,000 for the purchase of Louisiana and to the original appropriation for the construction of the Cumberland road, the latter act deriving much weight from the acquiescence and approbation of three of the most powerful of the original members of the Confederacy, expressed through their respective legislatures. Although the circumstances of the latter case may be such as to deprive so much of it as relates to the actual construction of the road of the force of an obligatory exposition of the Constitution, it must, nevertheless, be admitted that so far as the mere appropriation of money is concerned they present the principle in its most imposing aspect. No less than twenty-three different laws have been passed, through all the forms of the Constitution, appropriating upward of $2,500,000 out of the National Treasury in support of that improvement, with the approbation of every President of the United States, including my predecessor since its commencement.

Independently of the sanction given to the appropriations for the Cumberland and other roads and objects under this power, the Administration of Mr. Madison was characterized by an act which furnished the strongest evidence of his opinion of its extent. A bill was passed through both Houses of Congress and presented for his approval, "setting apart and pledging certain funds for constructing roads and canals and improving the navigation of water courses, in order to facilitate, promote, and give security to internal commerce among the several States and to render more easy and less expensive the means and provisions for the common defense." Regarding the bill as asserting a power in the Federal Government to construct roads and canals within the limits of the States in which they were made, he objected to its passage on the ground of its unconstitutionality, declaring that the assent of the respective States in the mode provided by the bill could not confer the power in question; that the only cases in which the consent and cession of particular States can extend the power of Congress are those specified and provided for in the Constitution, and superadding to these avowals his opinion that "a restriction of the power 'to provide for the common defense and general welfare' to cases which are to be provided for by the expenditure of money would still leave within the legislative power of Congress all the great and most important measures of Government, money being the ordinary and necessary means of carrying them into execution." I have not been able to consider these declarations in any other point of view than as a concession that the right of appropriation is not limited by the power to carry into effect the measure for which the money is asked, as was formerly contended.

The views of Mr. Monroe upon this subject were not left to inference. During his Administration a bill was passed through both Houses of Congress conferring the jurisdiction and prescribing the mode by which the Federal Government should exercise it in the case of the Cumberland road. He returned it with objections to its passage, and in assigning them took occasion to say that in the early stages of the Government he had inclined to the construction that it had no right to expend money except in the performance of acts authorized by the other specific grants of power, according to a strict construction of them, but that on further reflection and observation his mind had undergone a change; that his opinion then was "that Congress have an unlimited power to raise money, and that in its appropriation they have a discretionary power, restricted only by the duty to appropriate it to purposes of common defense, and of general not local, national, not State, benefit;" and this was avowed to be the governing principle through the residue of his Administration. The views of the last Administration are of such recent date as to render a particular reference to them unnecessary. It is well known that the appropriating power, to the utmost extent which had been claimed for it, in relation to internal improvements was fully recognized and exercised by it.

This brief reference to known facts will be sufficient to show the difficulty, if not impracticability of bringing back the operations of the Government to the construction of the Constitution set up in 1798, assuming that to be its true reading in relation to the power under consideration, thus giving an admonitory proof of the force of implication and the necessity of guarding the Constitution with sleepless vigilance against the authority of precedents which have not the sanction of its most plainly defined powers; for although it is the duty of all to look to that sacred instrument instead of the statute book, to repudiate at all times encroachments upon its spirit, which are too apt to be effected by the conjuncture of peculiar and facilitating circumstances, it is not less true that the public good and the nature of our political institutions require that individual differences should yield to a well-settled acquiescence of the people and confederated authorities in particular constructions of the Constitution on doubtful points. Not to concede this much to the spirit of our institutions would impair their stability and defeat the objects of the Constitution itself.

The bill before me does not call for a more definite opinion upon the particular circumstances which will warrant appropriations of money by Congress to aid works of internal improvement, for although the extension of the power to apply money beyond that of carrying into effect the object for which it is appropriated has, as we have seen, been long claimed and exercised by the Federal Government, yet such grants have always been professedly under the control of the general principle that the works which might be thus aided should be "of a general, not local, national, not State," character. A disregard of this distinction would of necessity lead to the subversion of the federal system. That even this is an unsafe one, arbitrary in its nature, and liable, consequently, to great abuses, is too obvious to require the confirmation of experience. It is, however, sufficiently definite and imperative to my mind to forbid my approbation of any bill having the character of the one under consideration. I have given to its provisions all the reflection demanded by a just regard for the interests of those of our fellow-citizens who have desired its passage, and by the respect which is due to a coordinate branch of the Government, but I am not able to view it in any other light than as a measure of purely local character; or, if it can be considered national, that no further distinction between the appropriate duties of the General and State Governments need be attempted, for there can be no local interest that may not with equal propriety be denominated national. It has no connection with any established system of improvements; is exclusively within the limits of a State, starting at a point on the Ohio River and running out 60 miles to an interior town, and even as far as the State is interested conferring partial instead of general advantages.

Considering the magnitude and importance of the power, and the embarrassments to which, from the very nature of the thing, its exercise must necessarily be subjected, the real friends of internal improvement ought not to be willing to confide it to accident and chance. What is properly *national* in its character or otherwise is an inquiry which is often extremely difficult of solution. The appropriations of one year for an object which is considered national may be rendered nugatory by the refusal of a succeeding Congress to continue the work on the ground that it is local. No aid can be derived from the intervention of corporations. The question regards the character of the work, not that of those by whom it is to be accomplished. Notwithstanding the union of the Government with the corporation by whose immediate agency any work of internal improvement is carried on, the inquiry will still remain, Is it national and conducive to the benefit of the whole, or local and operating only to the advantage of a portion of the Union?

But although I might not feel it to be my official duty to interpose the Executive veto to the passage of a bill appropriating money for the construction of such works as are authorized by the States and are national in their character, I do not wish to be understood as expressing an opinion that it is expedient at this time for the General Government to embark in a system of this kind; and anxious that my constituents should be possessed of my views on this as well as on all other subjects which they have committed to my discretion, I shall state them frankly and briefly. Besides many minor considerations, there are two prominent views of the subject which have made a deep impression upon my mind, which, I think, are well entitled to your serious attention, and will, I hope, be maturely weighed by the people.

From the official communication submitted to you it appears that if no adverse and unforeseen contingency happens in our foreign relations and no unusual diversion be made of the funds set apart for the payment of the national debt we may look with confidence to its entire extinguishment in the short period of four years. The extent to which this pleasing anticipation is dependent upon the policy which may be pursued in relation to measures of the character of the one now under consideration must be obvious to all, and equally so that the events of the present session are well calculated to awaken public solicitude upon the subject. By the statement from the Treasury Department and those from the clerks of the Senate and House of Representatives, herewith submitted, it appears that the bills which have passed into laws, and those which in all probability will pass before the adjournment of Congress, anticipate appropriations which, with the ordinary expenditures for the support of Government, will exceed considerably the amount in the Treasury for the year 1830. Thus, whilst we are diminishing the revenue by a reduction of the duties on tea, coffee, and cocoa the appropriations for internal improvement are increasing beyond the available means of the Treasury. And if to this calculation be added the amounts contained in bills which are pending before the two Houses, it may be safely affirmed that $10,000,000 would not make up the excess over the Treasury receipts, unless the payment of the national debt be postponed and the means now pledged to that object applied to those enumerated in these bills. Without a well-regulated system of internal improvement this exhausting mode of appropriation is not likely to be avoided, and the plain consequence must be either a continuance of the national debt or a resort to additional taxes.

Although many of the States, with a laudable zeal and under the influence of an enlightened policy, are successfully applying their separate efforts to works of this character, the desire to enlist the aid of the General Government in the construction of such as from their nature ought to devolve upon it, and to which the means of the individual States are inadequate, is both rational and patriotic, and if that desire is not gratified now it does not follow that it never will be. The general intelligence and public spirit of the American people furnish a sure guaranty that at the proper time this policy will be made to prevail under circumstances more auspicious to its successful prosecution than those which now exist. But great as this object undoubtedly is, it is not the only one which demands the fostering care of the Government. The preservation and success of the republican principle rest with us. To elevate its character and extend its influence rank among our most important duties, and the best means to accomplish this desirable end are those which will rivet the attachment of our citizens to the Government of their choice by the comparative lightness of their public burthens and by the attraction which the superior success of its operations will present to the admiration and respect of the world. Through the favor of an overruling and indulgent Providence our country is blessed with general prosperity and our citizens exempted from the pressure of taxation, which other less favored portions of the human family are obliged to bear; yet it is true that many of the taxes collected from our citizens through the medium of imposts have for a considerable period been onerous. In many particulars these taxes have borne severely upon the laboring and less prosperous classes of the community, being imposed on the necessaries of life, and this, too, in cases where the burthen was not relieved by the consciousness that it would ultimately contribute to make us independent of foreign nations for articles of prime necessity by the encouragement of their growth and manufacture at home. They have been cheerfully borne because they were thought to be necessary to the support of Government and the payment of the debts unavoidably incurred in the acquisition and maintenance of our national rights and liberties. But have we a right to calculate on the same cheerful acquiescence when it is known that the necessity for their continuance would cease were it not for irregular, improvident, and unequal appropriations of the public funds? Will not the people demand, as they have a right to do, such a prudent system of expenditure as will pay the debts of the Union and authorize the reduction of every tax to as low a point as the wise observance of the necessity to protect that portion of our manufactures and labor whose prosperity is essential to our national safety and independence will allow? When the national debt is paid, the duties upon those articles which we do not raise may be repealed with safety, and still leave, I trust, without oppression to any section of the country, an accumulating surplus fund, which may be beneficially applied to some well-digested system of improvement.

Under this view the question as to the manner in which the Federal Government can or ought to embark in the construction of roads and canals, and the extent to which it may impose burthens on the people for these purposes, may be presented on its own merits, free of all disguise and of every embarrassment, except such as may arise from the Constitution itself. Assuming these suggestions to be correct, will not our constituents require the observance of a course by which they can be effected? Ought they not to require it? With the best disposition to aid, as far as I can conscientiously, in furtherance of works of internal improvement, my opinion is that the soundest views of national policy at this time point to such a course. Besides the avoidance of an evil influence upon the local concerns of the country, how solid is the advantage which the Government will reap from it in the elevation of its character! How gratifying the effect of presenting to the world the sublime spectacle of a Republic or more than 12,000,000 happy people, in the fifty-fourth year of her existence, after having passed through two protracted wars—the one for the acquisition and the other for the maintenance of liberty—free from debt and with all her immense resources unfettered! What a salutary influence would not such an exhibition exercise upon the cause of liberal principles and free government throughout the world! Would we not ourselves find in its effect an additional guaranty that our political institutions will be transmitted to the most remote posterity without decay? A course of policy destined to witness events like these can not be benefited by a legislation which tolerates a scramble for appropriations that have no relation to any general system of improvement, and whose good effects must of necessity be very limited. In the best view of these appropriations, the abuses to which they lead far exceed the good which they are capable of promoting. They may be resorted to as artful expedients to shift upon the Government the losses of unsuccessful private speculation, and thus, by ministering to personal ambition and self-aggrandizement, tend to sap the foundations of public virtue and taint the administration of the Government with a demoralizing influence.

In the other view of the subject, and the only remaining one which it is my intention to present at this time, is involved the expediency of embarking in a system of internal improvement without a previous amendment of the Constitution explaining and defining the precise powers of the Federal Government over it. Assuming the right to appropriate money to aid in the construction of national works to be warranted by the cotemporaneous and continued exposition of the Constitution, its insufficiency for the successful prosecution of them must be admitted by all candid minds. If we look to usage to define the extent of the right, that will be found so variant and embracing so much that has been overruled as to involve the whole subject in great uncertainty and to render the execution of our respective duties in relation to it replete with difficulty and embarrassment. It is in regard to such works and the acquisition of additional territory that the practice obtained its first footing. In most, if not all, other disputed questions of appropriation the construction of the Constitution may be regarded as unsettled if the right to apply money in the enumerated cases is placed on the ground of usage.

This subject has been one of much, and, I may add, painful, reflection to me. It has bearings that are well calculated to exert a powerful influence upon our hitherto prosperous system of government, and which, on some accounts, may even excite despondency in the breast of an American citizen. I will not detain you with professions of zeal in the cause of internal improvements. If to be their friend is a virtue which deserves commendation, our country is blessed with an abundance of it, for I do not suppose there is an intelligent citizen who does not wish to see them flourish. But though all are their friends, but few, I trust, are unmindful of the means by which they should be promoted; none certainly are so degenerate as to desire their success at the cost of that sacred instrument with the preservation of which is indissolubly bound our country's hopes. If different impressions are entertained in any quarter; if it is expected that the people of this country, reckless of their constitutional obligations, will prefer their local interest to the principles of the Union, such expectations will in the end be disappointed or if it be not so, then indeed has the world but little to hope from the example of free government. When an honest observance of constitutional compacts can not be obtained from communities like ours, it need not be anticipated elsewhere, and the cause in which there has been so much martyrdom, and from which so much was expected by the friends of liberty, may be abandoned, and the degrading truth that man if unfit for self-government admitted. And this will be the case if *expediency* be made a rule of construction in interpreting the Constitution. Power in no government could desire a better shield for the insidious advance which it is ever ready to make upon the checks that are designed to restrain its action.

But I do not entertain such gloomy apprehensions. If it be the wise of the people that the construction of roads and canals should be conducted by the Federal Government, it is not only highly expedient, but indispensably necessary, that a previous amendment of the Constitution delegating the necessary power and defining and restricting its exercise with reference to the sovereignty of the States, should be made. Without it nothing extensively useful can be effected. The right to exercise as much jurisdiction as is necessary to preserve the works and to raise funds by the collection of tolls to keep them in repair can not be dispensed with. The Cumberland road should be an instructive admonition of the consequences of acting without this right. Year after year contests are witnessed, growing out of efforts to obtain the necessary appropriations for completing and repairing this useful work. Whilst one Congress may claim and exercise the power, a succeeding one may deny it; and this fluctuation of opinion must be unavoidably fatal to any scheme which from its extent would promote the interests and elevate the character of the country. The experience of the past has shown that the opinion of Congress is subject to such fluctuations.

If it be the desire of the people that the agency of the Federal Government should be confined to the appropriation of money in aid of such undertakings, in virtue of State authorities, then the occasion, the manner, and the extent of the appropriations should be made the subject of constitutional regulation. This is the more necessary in order that they may be equitable among the several States, promote harmony between different sections of the Union and their representatives, preserve other parts of the Constitution from being undermined by the exercise of doubtful powers or the too great extension of those which are not so, and protect the whole subject against the deleterious influence of combinations to carry by concert measures which, considered by themselves, might meet but little countenance.

That a constitutional adjustment of this power upon equitable principles is in the highest degree desirable can scarcely be doubted, nor can it fail to be promoted by every sincere friend to the success of our political institutions. In no government are appeals to the source of power in cases of real doubt more suitable than in ours. No good motive can be assigned for the exercise of power by the constituted authorities, while those for whose benefit it is to be exercised have not conferred it and may not be willing to confer it. It would seem to me that an honest application of the conceded powers of the General Government to the advancement of the common weal present a sufficient scope to satisfy a reasonable ambition. The difficulty and supposed impracticability of obtaining an amendment of the Constitution in this respect is, I firmly believe, in a great degree unfounded. The time has never yet been when the patriotism and intelligence of the American people were not fully equal to the greatest exigency, and it never will when the subject calling forth their interposition is plainly presented to them. To do so with the questions involved in this bill, and to urge them to an early, zealous, and full consideration of their deep importance, is, in my estimation, among the highest of our duties.

A supposed connection between appropriations for internal improvement and the system of protecting duties, growing out of the anxieties of those more immediately interested in their success, has given rise to suggestions which it is proper I should notice on this occasion. My opinions on these subjects have never been concealed from those who had a right to know them. Those which I have entertained on the latter have frequently placed me in opposition to individuals as well as communities whose claims upon my friendship and gratitude are of the strongest character, but I trust there has been nothing in my public life which has exposed me to the suspicion of being thought capable of sacrificing my views of duty to private considerations, however strong they may have been or deep the regrets which they are capable of exciting.

As long as the encouragement of domestic manufactures is directed to national ends it shall receive from me a temperate but steady support. There is no necessary connection between it and the system of appropriations. On the contrary, it appears to me that the supposition of their dependence upon each other is calculated to excite the prejudices of the public against both. The former is sustained on the grounds of its consistency with the letter and spirit of the Constitution, of its origin being traced to the assent of all the parties to the original compact, and of its having the support and approbation of a majority of the people, on which account it is at least entitled to a fair experiment. The suggestions to which I have alluded refer to a forced continuance of the national debt by means of large appropriations as a substitute for the security which the system derives from the principles on which it has hitherto been sustained. Such a course would certainly indicate either an unreasonable distrust of the people or a consciousness that the system does not possess sufficient soundness for its support if left to their voluntary choice and its own merits. Those who suppose that any policy thus founded can be long upheld in this country have looked upon its history with eyes very different from mine. This policy, like every other, must abide the will of the people, who will not be likely to allow any device, however specious, to conceal its character and tendency.

In presenting these opinions I have spoken with the freedom and candor which I thought the occasion for their expression called for, and now respectfully return the bill which has been under consideration for your further deliberation and judgment.

Admittedly such arguments found a friendly reception among southern and other Republican defenders of states' rights, but the veto message also skillfully directed its appeal to the mass of people who felt apprehensive about the high level of the national debt. The argument that the country should not undertake any further financial burdens until the present debt was eliminated fell upon the receptive ears of many taxpayers. Van Buren argued that the "powerful combination known as the Internal Improvement party was broken asunder and finally annihilated," but it also appears that potential enemies of the administration were given a preview of the kind of leadership they could expect from General Jackson.[6]

It would seem that Andrew Jackson's sure instinct for power dictated an early and dramatic action at the beginning of his administration in order to assert his own authority and to demonstrate that the presidency was a position of leadership as well as a vehicle for administering the will of the legislature. However, the President, under the Constitution, was given a voice in the legislative process, and Jackson (with Van Buren's approval) was anxious to assert this policymaking role and to put both the Congress and the country on warning that the age and feeble health of the old general would in no way restrict his vigorous pursuit of what he considered were the responsibilities of the President of the United States. Formal constitutional arguments were offered in the veto message, but the intent was political and the objective was the assertion of Jackson's policies—a sign which marked the beginning of a new and dynamic chapter in the growth of presidential power.

There were other indications that Jackson and Van Buren had significant political objectives in mind when considering the Maysville veto. Henry Clay, the architect of the American System, a program which combined the policy of a high protective tariff with encouraging the development of domestic industry and national internal improvements, was probably the principal target of their strategy. Although "Harry of the West" was not a member of Congress at that time and had retired to his plantation in Kentucky, he was by all odds the most likely opponent to run against Jackson in the election of 1832. Van Buren was almost certainly referring to Clay's American System program when he bragged of having "annihilated" the Internal Improvement party by the veto, because internal improvements were an integral element of Clay's nationalistic program. Here was an opportunity to pull the rug from under the opposition before it even took the field of battle.

Clay apparently thought differently. Having lost the southwestern states to the general when he headed up Adams' campaign in 1828, he felt the Maysville veto would weaken Jackson's support in that area in the next election, and allow him (Clay) to recover sufficient strength to win the presidency in 1832. Jackson, on the contrary, consolidated his southern support by his veto, strongly reflecting a states' rights philosophy, and later won back most of the West by his attack on the Bank of the United States and his other dramatic veto of the Clay supported measure to seek the premature rechartering of the Bank.

In that instance, Jackson had again demonstrated his mastery of the "new politics" in the second quarter of the nineteenth century. In his successful bid for the presidency in 1828, Jackson and his supporters were able to attract many of the new voters who had been recently brought into the electoral system. They were responsive to demands for the elimination of the elitism which had characterized government and politics of the earlier period. Although a strong case could be made for the value of internal improvements as they affected the interests of these new participants in the democratic process, particularly those in the West, the appeal to the pocketbook, while stressing the need for economy in national expenditures and savings in taxes, apparently had an even stronger attraction for them.

The Bank veto reflected the same partialities. A good case could be made for the necessity of a central bank and its monetary controls in an expanding economy, but the more demagogic appeal to class and economic antagonism of the veto message argument against the Bank of the United States inspired even greater support.

Jackson understood his people and their politics and he was able to create a political environment which was supportive of his policy objectives. An indication that he was more interested in such policies and political advantages than in theoretical constitutional questions was apparent when several days after the Maysville veto he approved bills which appropriated $150,000 for surveys and for an extension of the Cumberland Road.[7] But in the deeper sense Andrew Jackson understood that the American political system required strong presidential leadership, not only in military and foreign affairs or in the maintenance of law and order in national crises, but also in the continuing affairs of government and in the process of developing national domestic policies. His assertion of power in the legislative area by use of the veto further enhanced the presidential office and provided yet another model from which later twentieth century Presidents could learn and derive precedents.

But the veto power is a limited and somewhat negative instrument of leadership when considered in the very broad spectrum of legislative policymaking. It normally operates more as a negative psychological and persuasive factor than a creative source of direction and energy towards developing positive legislative objectives. For the earliest and perhaps most illuminating example of leadership in this level we will have to turn back to the administration of Thomas Jefferson.

Presidential Leadership

Although the State of the Union Message and the presidential veto related the functions of the Chief Executive in significant ways to the legislative process, in truth the Founding Fathers did not conceive of nor provide for a *major role* for the President in this critical governing area. It is true that the early state constitutional experiences modified somewhat their anti-executive attitudes, but not to the extent that they were ready to place the President and his influence directly within the functional operating sphere of the legislature. They were very much aware of Montesquieu's warnings of the resultant tyranny when legislative and executive power were united, and although Madison explained in Federalist No. 47 that this maxim should not be interpreted literally, and certainly did not mean that one branch should not have even "partial agency" or "control" over the other, in Federalist No. 51 he emphasized the principle that the Constitution provided both the members of the legislative and executive branches with the "means" and "personal motives to resist the encroachments of the other."

As the Congress and the country began to divide very sharply on the critical issues of the day, the experience of the 1790s indicates that the Republicans had been relatively ineffective in mobilizing their maximum legislative strength and leadership and directing it towards common political objectives. They were fortunate in possessing several brilliant legislative leaders, but the turnover of both senators and congressmen was rapid, and during the decade before 1800 the anti-Federalists, as the Republicans were first called, were unsuccessful in breaching Federalist control of both the Congress and the presidency, although in the earlier sessions they had outnumbered the Federalists.

They had found their rallying point in the early years of the Washington administration in their opposition to Alexander Hamilton's strong legislative influence, particularly in the House of Representatives, and in their general opposition to the Federalist aristocracy. After Madison left the House they floundered for some time without strong leadership, failing to produce a program of cohesive, positive effort of their own. Commenting on the situation, Madison wrote:

> The influence of the Ex[ecutive] on events, the use made of them, and the public confidence in the P[resident] are an overmatch for all the efforts Republicanism can make. The party of that sentiment in the Senate is completely wrecked; and in the H[ouse] of Rep[resentative]s in a much worse condition than in the earlier period of the session.[8]

Even when during the Fourth Congress such able legislative leaders as Albert Gallatin of Pennsylvania and William B. Giles of Virginia arrived on the scene, the Republicans continued to drift and to remain unproductive. Federalist critics were even harsher than Madison had been. Chauncey Goodrich complained:

> 'Tis true the disorganizers have now the power to bring forward their systems of reform, and they dare not—it would create a responsibility which above all things they fear; we think the leaders were never more discontented with their lot than at present.[9]

The dismal showing in the Congress may have aided the Republican cause in the long run, however; for as the party without power they hungered for the chance to wield it. Finally under Jefferson's leadership as Vice President and presiding officer of the Senate, the Republicans rallied their energy and resources into building a political organization outside of Congress on a state to state basis which triumphed in the election of 1800, capturing not only the new executive mansion, but also clear majorities in both houses of Congress. Once in power, Jefferson was anxious not to repeat the Republicans' lackluster history of the 1790s, and set forth in his inaugural basic objectives which would require legislative implementation.

As President, Jefferson was determined to restore the American experiment in democracy to what he considered to be its initial and true course. He was intent upon eliminating the contradictory developments which he felt had been grafted upon the system by the Federalists. Resolved to recover simplicity and frugality in government, he sought to eliminate burdensome taxes, reduce expenditures for both the army and the navy, plan carefully for the systematic elimination of the national debt, repeal the Judiciary Act of 1801 which had improperly inflated the court system with political appointees, and to restore the liberal naturalization law written by James Madison.[10] He incorporated these proposals into his first State of the Union Message which he communicated in writing to the new Congress, and the Republican majorities in both houses responded by passing legislation to accomplish these objectives.

In reviewing these accomplishments, Senator DeWitt Clinton from New York wrote: "Our friends here are as well united as can be expected from so strong and so varied a majority."[11] Jefferson was quite satisfied at the end of the session and commented that Congress had "carried into execution steadily almost all the propositions submitted to them in my message at the opening of the session."[12]

This was an excellent beginning, but at the next session of Congress problems began to emerge which suggested stormier seas ahead. The Republican members were by no means a homogeneous group of individuals, sharing a common set of principles and interests. They had been brought together initially by their opposition to Hamilton and his supporters and later by their growing dissatisfaction with the Federalists in power. Coming into the mere shell of the future city of Washington, D.C. at the turn of the century, they had to undergo hardships and inconveniences experienced by no governing body of national leaders in any capital city in the world. Washington was practically a prairie settlement and James Sterling Young argues very tellingly that the unique and limiting social environment in which the members of Congress were forced to exist had significant impact upon their political habits and attitudes, tending in time to exacerbate divisions and encourage a kind of anarchy rather than to build a unified and disciplined legislative party.[13]

Various descriptions reveal something of the setting of Washington at the turn of the century:

> The Federal city is in reality neither a town nor a village; it may be compared to a country seat where state sportsmen may run horses and fight cocks: kill time under cover and shoot Public service flying. . . . There sits the President . . . like a pelican in the wilderness, or a sparrow upon a housetop.[14]

Another referred to it as "this city which so many are willing to come to and all are willing to leave"; it was depicted as "a vast construction site 'bearing the marks of partial labor and general desertion.'"[15] The countryside seemed incapable of ever housing the capital city of the nation:

> Two unfinished white citadels towered above the terrain from the hilltops on opposite shores of a dismal swamp, more like ruins amid the fallen fragments of their own stone than new and rising edifices. Where monuments had been planned, brush piles moldered, and rubbish heaps accumulated. Where majestic avenues were to sweep, swaths of tree stumps stood, rough quarried stones marking the intersections. Where houses were to be, barren hillocks, stripped of vegetation, rose like desert islands amid a sea of bogs and marshes.
>
> Cows grazed on future plazas and bullfrogs chorused on the mall. Wildlife overran the premises.[16]

Nearly all of the senators and congressmen in early nineteenth century Washington lived in boarding houses where they spent literally all of their time when not at work conducting legislative business in the Capitol. In time these congressional messes (as the boarding houses were referred to) became small sub-communities, almost subcultures, where legislators nurtured friends and loyalties frequently as strong or stronger than party ties. The messes were grouped around the capital, but were physically separated from the administrative offices and living abodes of officials and clerks grouped around the executive mansion. These arrangements not only accentuated the division between the executive and legislative branches, but also made social contact between the various subgroups awkward and infrequent.

The political community which developed in this atmosphere was anything but unified. The period spent in Washington by members of Congress was relatively brief and the turnover extremely high (41.5 percent biennially). And although the living arrangements were conducive to the development of close ties among some of those sharing the same mess, the general living and social arrangements also tended to exacerbate many regional, social and economic differences and conflicts which existed among members of the same party.

As social intimacy bared the depth of their behavioral differences, tolerance among men from different regions strained to the breaking point. Political coexistence with the South and the frontier states was hard enough for New Englanders to accept. Social coexistence was insufferable with slaveholders "accustomed to speak in the tone of masters" and with frontiersmen having "a license of tongue incident to a wild and uncultivated state of society. With men of such states of mind and temperament," a Massachusetts delegate protested, "men educated in . . . New England . . . could have little pleasure in intercourse, less in controversy, and of course no sympathy." Close scrutiny of their New England neighbors in power could convince southerners, in their turn, that there was "not one [who] possesses the slightest tie of common interest, common feeling with us," planters and gentlemen cast among men "who raised 'beef and pork, and butter and cheese, and potatoes and cabbages'" and carried on "a paltry trade in potash and codfish." Cultural antipathies, crowded barracks, poor rations, and separation from families left at home combined to make tempers wear thin as the winters wore on, leading to sporadic eruptions of violence. In a sudden affray at the table in Miss Shield's boardinghouse, Randolph, "pouring out a glass of wine, dashed it in Alston's face. Alston sent a decanter at his head in return, and these and similar missiles continued to fly to and fro, until there was much destruction of glassware." The chamber of the Capitol itself witnessed more than one scuffle, and, though it was not yet the custom for legislators to arm themselves when legislating, pistols at twenty paces cracked more than once in the woods outside the Capitol.[17]

Jefferson was very much aware of this situation and quite early realized the serious and destructive impact this would have upon the quality and success of his administration. In the previous century he had leaned towards a clear separation of the executive from the legislative functions and after being elected Vice President in 1796, he indicated how he expected executive officials to respect this principle:

> As to duty, the constitution will allow me only as a member of a legislative body; and it's principle is, that of a separation of legislative, executive & judiciary functions, except in cases specified. If this principle be not expressed in direct terms, yet it is clearly the spirit of the constitution, & it ought to be so commented & acted on by every friend of true government.[18]

Confronted with the realities of presidential power, however, the problem appeared somewhat different to him. As early as the winter of 1802-03 he complained to DeWitt Clinton about the lack of political sophistication of his legislative allies:

> our leading friends are not yet sufficiently aware of the necessity of accomodation & mutual sacrifice of opinion for conducting a numerous assembly, where the opposition too is drilled to act in a phlanx on every question.[19]

The President attempted to convince strong figures like Caesar A. Rodney to stay in the Congress and assume party leadership, pleading rather desperately:

> I had looked to you as one of those calculated to give cohesion to our *rope of sand.* You now see the composition of our public bodies, and how essential system and plan are for conducting our affairs wisely with so bitter a party in opposition to us.... Talents in our public councils are at all times important; but perhaps there never was a moment when the loss of any would be more injurious than at the present.[20]

Rodney heeded the President's entreaties, but both were disappointed when the Delaware Republican was defeated when he ran for reelection.

Jefferson exerted great initiative and extraordinary skill in asserting as much legislative leadership as was necessary and indeed possible. He quickly realized the disadvantages of the lack of cohesion of his party in Congress and tried to exert sufficient influence to give it direction—his direction—with respect to the critical policies of his administration. But there was some resistance and accompanying problems involved in such delicate manuevering, and Jefferson did not always succeed. In the first place, by inviting both Madison and Gallatin into his cabinet, he had removed from the floor of the House the Republicans' two most effective legislative leaders.[21] This led to considerable difficulties because Jefferson had great trouble locating suitable replacements, and even when he did, his power vis à vis the party in both houses was not so absolute that he could impose his personally selected leader upon either body.

When his first chosen leader in the House, the experienced and able Virginian, William Branch Giles, left that body in 1802 and did not return (although he eventually went on to the Senate and served in a similar capacity there), Jefferson was forced to accept John Randolph as Giles' successor. Randolph, through his life-long friendship with the Speaker of the House, Nathaniel Macon, was named chairman of the important Ways and Means Committee, and in this capacity was grudgingly recognized as the party leader in that body. The President tried very hard to work with Randolph and to rely upon him to represent the administration's interests in the House, but the relationship was never entirely successful. Randolph's personality was one of the obstacles but there was also the ambiguity inherent in the role of the leader.[22] Was the leader simply the President's man in the legislature, or was his fundamental responsibility to his colleagues in the House, his own conscience or his personal constituency? These would have been formidable problems irrespective of who was involved, but in Randolph's case they proved to be disastrous.

By 1806 Randolph had broken openly with the administration on critical policy questions and Jefferson was forced to recruit another "leader." Randolph had never succeeded in really leading his colleagues in the House, and his personal relations with his fellow congressmen were in such disarray, he had created so much personal bitterness, that when he began to attack Jefferson and Madison, it did not prove too difficult to isolate him and eventually to deprive him of his committee chairmanship, along with all semblance of leadership in the House. This was not a battle which the President had sought or welcomed, but when the unity and direction of the Republican party were jeopardized by Randolph's public demeanor, Jefferson accepted the challenge and crushed his opponent.

During this period Jefferson continued his attempt to recruit able Republicans to assume party leadership in the House, although he was quite satisfied with Giles' performance in the Senate. The President succeeded in persuading a New England congressman, Barnabas Bidwell, to run for reelection and to take the leadership role. In his appeal to Bidwell to run again, the President pleaded along familiar lines:

> there never was a time when the services of those who possess talents, integrity, firmness and sound judgment, were more wanted in Congress. Some one of that description is particularly wanted to take the lead in the H. of R., to consider the business of the nation as his own business, to take it up as if he were singly charged with it, and carry it through.[23]

In the same letter, Jefferson went on to define his concept of what the role of a party leader or at least an administration spokesman in the Congress entailed. It is a rare and revealing statement of the President's function in the legislative process and it is worthy of careful examination in relation to the growth of presidential power.

President Thomas Jefferson
Letter to Representative Barnabas Bidwell
July 5, 1806

Andrew A. Lipscomb and Albert E. Bergh, eds., *The Writings of Thomas Jefferson* (Washington, D.C., 1904) XI, 115-17.

I do not mean that any gentleman, relinquishing his own judgment, should implicitly support all the measures of the administration; but that, where he does not disapprove of them, he should not suffer them to go off in sleep, but bring them to the attention of the House, and give them a fair chance. Where he disapproves, he will of course leave them to be brought forward by those who concur in the sentiment. Shall I explain my idea by an example? The classification of the militia was communicated to General Varnum and yourself merely as a proposition, which, if you approved, it was trusted you would support. I knew, indeed, that General Varnum was opposed to anything which might break up the present organization of the militia: but when so modified as to avoid this, I thought he might, perhaps, be reconciled to it. As soon as I found it did not coincide with your sentiments, I could not wish you to support it; but using the same freedom of opinion, I procured it to be brought forward elsewhere. It failed there, also, and for a time, perhaps, may not prevail; but a militia can never be used for distant service on any other plan; and Bonaparte will conquer the world, if they do not learn his secret of composing armies of young men only, whose enthusiasm and health enable them to surmount all obstacles. When a gentleman, through zeal for the public service, undertakes to do the public business, we know that we shall hear the cant of backstairs' councillors. But we never heard this while the declaimer was himself a backstairs' man, as he calls it, but in the confidence and views of the administration, as may more properly and respectfully be said. But if the members are to know nothing but what is important enough to be put into a public message, and indifferent enough to be made known to all the world; if the Executive is to keep all other information to himself, and the House to plunge on in the dark, it becomes a government of chance and not of design. The imputation was one of those artifices used to despoil an adversary of his most effectual arms; and men of mind will place themselves above a gabble of this order. The last session of Congress was indeed an uneasy one for a time; but as soon as the members penetrated into the views of those who were taking a new course, they rallied in as solid a phalanx as I have ever seen act together. Indeed I have never seen a House of better dispositions. . . . Perhaps I am not entitled to speak with so much frankness; but it proceeds from no motive which has not a right to your forgiveness. Opportunities of candid explanation are so seldom afforded me, that I must not lose them when they occur.

In an equally candid reply, Representative Bidwell assured the President that he would run for reelection, that he would have his cooperation in the House, and that he would endeavor to do what he could to advance the administration's interests. But he hastened to add that the existing power structure of the House would present formidable obstacles to his achieving much success in such an undertaking:

I am constrained to say, you appear to expect more from my exertions as a member of the House of Representatives, than it will be in my power to perform. The cant of back-stairs influence has no terrors; but there are obstacles in my way. In every legislature, the introduction, progress and conclusion of business depend much upon committees; and, in the House of Representatives of the U.S., more than in any other legislative body within my knowledge, the business referred to Committees, and reported on by them, is, by usage and common consent, controlled by their chairman. As the Speaker, according to the standing rules of the House, has the appointment of Committees, he has it in his power to place whom he pleases in the foreground, and whom he pleases in the background, and thus, in some measure, affect their agency in the transactions of the House. From the connections and attachments of the present Speaker, I have, at least no reason to expect to be very favourably considered in the distribution of committee business. This circumstance, with others, of more importance, which I will forbear to mention, but of which I am deeply sensible, will prevent my acting a very conspicuous part. So far, however, as industry and moderate abilities may be relied on, I shall feel it a duty to be attentive to the business of the House; and having had satisfaction of a cordial concurrence with the principles and measures of the Executive Administration, generally, it will be my happiness to give them the feeble aid of my support, both in and out of the House.[24]

This frank exchange does much to illuminate this very significant problem. Bidwell was pointing out to Jefferson that, even with his blessing, there were forces at work in the House which could substantially impede whatever impact his efforts might have; and he implied that those forces might be beyond the reach and influence of the President. Unquestionably there was some truth to this, and the administration had labored under such restrictions for several years, having been forced to accept Randolph as leader because he had been appointed to his important committee chairmanship by the elected Speaker of the House.

What Bidwell apparently did not realize was that these obstacles had not been critical enough to the administration's interest in the past for Jefferson to move seriously against them. The legislative objectives and routine business of his administration had not been seriously enough challenged by the Speaker or his appointed leader to warrant an all-out battle. But when Randolph broke with the administration openly and brazenly and opposed Jefferson's effort to obtain a suspension on the importation of British goods until His Majesty's Government changed its policies with regard to neutral trade and impressment, the President responded by crushing the eccentric Virginian politically, isolating him from some of his supporters and ultimately bringing about the removal of both he and the Speaker from their positions of power in the House of Representatives.

This time Jefferson decided to go outside of the House to recruit a strong leader; he wrote to a veteran Republican, Wilson Cary Nicholas from Virginia, who had previously served with distinction in the Senate. He urged Nicholas to climb into his armor and return to the struggle:

Never did the calls of patriotism more loudly assail you than at this moment. After excepting the Federalists, who will be 27., and the little band of schismatics, who will be 3. or 4. (all tongue), the residue of the H of R is as well disposed a body of men as I ever saw collected. But there is no one whose talents and standing, taken together, have weight enough to give him the lead. The consequence is, that there is no one who will undertake to do the public business, and it remains undone. Were you here, the whole would rally around you in an instant, and willingly cooperate in whatever is for the public good. Nor would it require you to undertake the drudgery in the House. There are enough able and willing to do that. A rallying point is all that is wanting. Let me beseech you then to offer yourself. You never will have it so much in your power again to render such eminent service.[25]

What emerged from this artful statecraft was that up until the twilight of Thomas Jefferson's second term, when the backlash caused by his embargo policy and all of its resultant hardships triggered a major defeat for his administration, the first Republican President was able to retain the leadership of his party while in power to a much greater extent than any other President in the nineteenth century. Of course this required constant and vigilant attention on his part. I have already alluded to certain factors which tended to promote division and disorganization among the Republicans in Congress: the lack of a systematic party ideology which could embrace all Republicans, and the social arrangements under which legislators and administrators lived and worked. In addition, the remoteness of Washington and its isolation from the constant pressures of well-informed special interests in the country gave the Congress something of a protective curtain which it certainly does not have today. One must add to these the almost universal American view of power as evil, and the distrust of executive power and influence within the legislature as an even greater evil. The cumulative effect of these countervailing forces made the task of exerting strong and effective party leadership within the legislature an increasingly difficult problem.

It is to Jefferson's credit that he not only solved this problem, but that in its solution he initiated the idea of presidential legislative leadership without any assistance or precedents established by either of his predecessors. Although Alexander Hamilton breached this inhibition towards presidential initiative long before Jefferson, neither Washington nor John Adams ever seriously considered interfering in the business or the organization of the legislature. How then did Jefferson accomplish this remarkable feat?

First of all the character of Thomas Jefferson should be considered as a factor. His towering intellect, his democratic principles, his inspiring idealism and his agreeable personality quickly elevated him to a role of leadership among his fellow Republicans who respected him without regard to regional, social or even economic prejudices. He enjoyed the confidence of his colleagues to a much greater extent that almost any national leader who comes to mind, with the exception of General Washington. Of course he had impassioned enemies of a partisan nature, but within his own party, which maintained a dominant majority in both houses of the legislature throughout his two terms in office, Jefferson retained the admiration, the respect and even the devotion of the vast number of Republicans. The pitiful challenge and quick collapse of Randolph's stature in the House was one indication of the strength of Jefferson's standing among his fellow Republicans.

In addition to this remarkable asset of leadership, Jefferson also possessed a strong political instinct and a sure sense of power. His writings reveal his ideals and his deep convictions, but his actions clearly demonstrate his superior art of statecraft. There was a happy wedding of these two aspects of his personality in the office of the presidency, for he was able to reinforce one with the other. He had no aversion to counting on his friends and admirers for political support, and he turned many a political supporter into a friend or an admirer by exposing him to his warm hospitality and gracious social charm.

In fact Jefferson drew no hard and fast distinction, as many other Presidents have done, between his social and political life. As President he devoted his full time to the public service, and although his frequent social gatherings were normally devoid of purely political discussion, the conversation ranging widely from the arts to agriculture, from history to philosophy, science and literature, much of the *raison d'etre* for these gatherings was the business of government, if only for the President to acquaint himself better with political figures whom he would eventually have to deal with and perhaps count on for support, Jefferson was candid enough to admit this:

> I cultivate personal intercourse with the members of the legislature that we may know one another and have opportunities of little explanations of circumstances, which, not understood might produce jealousies and suspicions injurious to the public interest, which is best promoted by harmony and mutual confidence among its functionaries. I depend much on the members for the local information necessary on local matters, as well as for the means of getting at public sentiment.[26]

Of course this was stated in the course of private correspondence, but if it had been more generally understood and practiced by some of Jefferson's successors, they might not have been so slow to respond to public needs and attitudes, and certainly not so ineffectual in persuading the Congress to follow their lead. The essence of successful politics is being sensitive and responsive to the problems and dilemnas of others, and at the same time effective in establishing rapport and trust among those whose support you need. Jefferson scored brilliantly in both respects, and as a result, particularly in the legislative area, he was one of the most successful and effective Presidents in our history.

There is no question that his role as the political leader of his party was enhanced tremendously by his charm and social grace as a host in the executive mansion. Merrill Peterson has graphically depicted the scene of Jefferson's frequent and enjoyable private dinner parties at the White House, which was an oasis of good taste, pleasant company and excellent food and wine in a wasteland that could rarely boast of the presence of any of these refinements:

> Every other day or so he sent a batch of billets to the Capitol. Guests were invited for 3:30 p.m., the hour Congress usually rose. Down Pennsylvania Avenue they came, to the great white house barren of landscape and (until late in Jefferson's presidency) surrounded by a crude post and rail fence. Servant or private secretary met them at the door and ushered them into a reception room, where the President joined the party and conversed for perhaps half an hour before dinner. Pell-mell was the rule of the house; the

guests accordingly, found what place they could at the table. The dining room, needless to say, was not the resplendent state dining room of the present-day White House. Jefferson had furnished the smaller dining room with an oval table, which he considered more democratic than the rectangular table used by his predecessors. There was neither head nor foot. Green canvas, instead of a bothersome Brussels carpet, covered the floor. Clergymen remarked that no blessing was ever offered. To facilitate the service Jefferson introduced some of his own contrivances, for example, a set of circular shelves on a revolving door that quickly dispatched dishes between kitchen and dining room with the minimum traffic, and dumb waiters sometimes sat beside the guests at the table. The food was abundant and good, a combination of French and Virginia cookery, and if hardly of gourmet quality a treat in this "land of hog, hominey and hoecake." Manassah Culter of Massachusetts described the menu of a dinner he rated below par for the President's table: "Rice soup, round of beef, turkey, mutton, ham, loin of veal, cutlets of mutton or veal, fried eggs, fried beef, a pie called macaroni. . . . Ice cream very good, crust wholly dried, crumbled into thin flakes; a dish somewhat like pudding— inside white as milk or curd, very porous and light, covered with cream sauce—very fine. Many other jimcracks, a great variety of fruit, plenty of wines, and good. . . ."[27] Ice cream was a delicacy, though Jefferson served it in all seasons by virtue of his ice house, filled every winter with two-inch thick cakes of ice cut from a pond below the house. As for the wines, they gave a truly Epicurean finish to the dinners. There were many kinds, all sent to Jefferson by consuls and friends in a dozen ports. No healths or toasts were ever drunk. "You drink as you please and converse at your ease." The ladies, when ladies were present, retired to another room; tea and coffee were served; games of cards, the usual evening diversion in other houses, were never played, general conversation taking its place. The guests were gone by eight o'clock.[28]

But the excellent cuisine was only preliminary to the *piece de resistance*:

Part of the enjoyment was the President's talk. Everyone expected him to take the lead, and he usually did, tactfully drawing out even the most retiring guests in conversation that encompassed the table. He made it a rule to avoid political talk lest it cause any uneasiness to his guests. Politeness, he once lectured his grandson and namesake, is "artificial good humor," the sacrifice of one's own little preferences and conveniences to the gratification of others. "Good humor and politeness never introduce into mixed society a question on which they forsee there will be a difference of opinion." At any other table than Jefferson's conversation on such a rule was almost sure to be insipid. But he could discourse on so many subjects, from travels in France to the natural history of parrots, there was never a void. Benjamin Latrobe rated a dinner at the President's House "an elegant mental treat." "Literature, wit, a little business, with a great deal of miscellaneous remarks on agriculture and building, filled every minute." John Quincy Adams, who came into Congress from Massachusetts in 1803, had long ago severed his youthful attachment to the Virginian, yet could still be enchanted by his talk. "You never can be an hour in this man's company without something of the marvelous."[29]

President Jefferson did not limit himself, however, to the skillful employment of his developed social graces in pursuing his policy objectives in the legislature. I have already noted his unrelenting efforts to secure loyal and able leadership in the House, but he went even further by utilizing the talents of his experienced cabinet members in communicating with and persuading members of both houses to support administration measures, and even permitting them to draft legislative committee reports and to attend committee meetings. Jefferson and his cabinet also frequently, but covertly, drafted legislation and amendments to bills and transmitted them to congressmen and senators upon their request and without such queries. Secretary of the Treasury Gallatin, an old hand at the legislative process who was on very friendly terms with individuals like Speaker Macon, Randolph, Nicholas and others, used his home like Jefferson as a gathering place for Republican legislators and worked closely with them in pressing the administration's business. With regard to two bills before the Congress, one to alter the form of government in Michigan and the other to give the governor and judges authority to decide all land claims in the territory, he reported to Jefferson:

> I found it necessary to interfere by speaking to members of the Senate, and succeeded in having the government bill postponed *sine die*, and the general principles of the land bill rejected.[30]

On another occasion the secretary wrote to Senator John Breckinridge of Kentucky, a close friend of the President's who had introduced the Jefferson-ghosted Kentucky Resolutions in the state legislature in 1798:

> I send in the shape of a bill, the substance of what the President seems to think necessary in order to authorize him to occupy and temporarily govern Louisiana. Will you consult with your friends and decide whether the authority be necessary, and if so, what form should be given it.[31]

Jefferson took great pains to invoke secrecy with respect to his communications with members of Congress. After having sent the same Senator Breckinridge a draft of a constitution for the newly acquired Louisiana territory, he implored the senator not to reveal its origin and in fact to return the original to him after he had copied it:

> In communicating it to you I must do it in confidence that you will never let any person know that I have put pen to paper on the subject and if you think the inclosed can be of any aid to you you will take the trouble to copy it and return me the original. I am this particular, because you know with what bloody teeth and fangs the federalists will attack any sentiment or principle known to come from me.[32]

Another time the recipient of a bill which the President had drafted was instructed:

Be so good as to copy the within and burn this original, as he is very unwilling to meddle personally with the details of the preceedings of the legislature.[33]

The President did not ignore the press in the development of his executive leadership in legislative matters. During Jefferson's two term Republican regime in the White House, the number of newspapers favorable to the majority party grew steadily. At the beginning of Jefferson's first term the Federalist press largely dominated the country, outnumbering Republican newspapers by a ratio of greater than 3 to 1; but by the end of his second term there were as many Republican newspapers being published as there were Federalist publications.

In one significant development, however, the Republicans had the jump on the opposition right from the start. Jefferson had encouraged a Republican editor in Philadelphia, Samuel Harrison Smith, to move over to Washington with the transfer of the national government and establish a national newspaper. Smith took the advice and risked everything by relocating in Washington before the results of the election in 1800 were known, but when the result was an overwhelming Republican victory, he profited from his daring and quickly became the major source of Republican news and opinion throughout the country.

Jefferson and other members of his administration utilized Smith's *National Intelligencer* for conveying the views of the administration, not only to its supporters in Congress, but to other Republican newspapers throughout the country and ultimately to their Republican readers who made up the party. Jefferson of course never actually wrote for the paper under his own name, but he did advise and consult with its editor, provide him with material he had prepared, and the editor was awarded generously with government printing contracts. At least one member of his official family, Gallatin, also submitted material to the paper. But its strongest contribution came through its very adequate news coverage (it carried a good part of the congressional debates) and its strongly pro-Republican editorial policy. Cunningham argues that "The *National Intelligencer* as a party organ of nationwide influence gave the Republican party an important advantage over the Federalists, who, even though they were supported by a powerful press, did not have a paper of such national stature and influence."[34]

The Republicans' use of the party caucus as an instrument of enforcing administration policy is a controversial subject, and insufficient evidence exists either for the extensive claims made of its continued influence, or the complete rejection of such claims on the basis of the lack of evidence relating to the caucus itself. We do know that there were formal caucus meetings held every four years by members of the party in Congress for the selection of presidential and vice presidential candidates. In all probability at least informal elements of this caucus met from time to time during the interim periods to shore up support for critical measures before the Congress. Whether or not such meetings were considered regular sessions of the party caucus is not known, nor is their frequency or the number in attendance. Certainly there is no substantial evidence, as has been alleged, that the President himself attended such meetings, nor that they functioned regularly. The major source of the obviously inflated description of their power and influence comes from members of the opposition party, who in bitterness and frustration over the success of the Jeffersonian Republicans, may well have conjured up a powerful chimera cut of bits and pieces of evidence which do not add up to such a formidable creature. What remains true, however, is the evidence of considerable agreement within the party on critical policy issues, which may have resulted from some form of meetings among party members from time to time.[35]

Once in office the Jeffersonian Republicans discovered that the earlier distinctions they had debated so brilliantly from the relatively free and irresponsible position of the party out of Executive office looked greatly different to them when confronted with real problems of presidential power. They had maintained, for example, that there was a significant difference between the powers of the Executive in the area of foreign policy as opposed to dealing with domestic problems; in the former case they asserted that it was the President who had primary responsibility, while in the latter situation it was the Congress and indeed the states. This delineation proved to be almost meaningless in practice, because foreign policy objectives have to be implemented domestically, or they may be jeopardized. The Executive can no more ignore this crucial domestic responsibility than he can the initiation of the policy in the first place, if it is a legitimate response to a real problem.[36]

If such a nice logical distinction broke down in practice, so did the theoretical division between the executive and legislative branches of the government. Jefferson once in office discovered that he could not appreciate—nor understand when out of power—that if an administration is going to act effectively and accomplish substantial goals, the President must assume a significant degree of legislative leadership and exploit every resource at his command to achieve the desired ends.

The tragedy of Jefferson's brilliant period of legislative leadership is that although he learned this lesson early enough to chart a successful course during the first seven years of his administration, he utterly failed to communicate this insight to his successors and to generations who came after him, many of whom profited from his ideological principles but were ignorant of his extraordinary performance in *realpolitick*. Ironically it was not really until the following century that historians were able to piece together the record of his political and legislative triumphs, a record that for curious reasons was not publicly revealed at the time. When it finally was documented, it clearly pointed up the contradictions between Jefferson's ideological principles and his skillful demonstration of statecraft while in office. But the latter was not only in conflict with Jefferson's ideology; it also challenged the prevailing value judgments with respect to uses of power. A curiously self-deceptive aspect of his personality allowed Jefferson to shroud his political activities and triumphs in silence, never publicly passing on to future Americans the deep insights into the nature of politics, particularly presidential politics and the legislative process, which he acquired through his experience in the White House.

In all fairness, however, it should be noted that one of the factors which contributed substantially to Jefferson's remarkable effectiveness in the legislative area was the fact that the policy objectives he sought for most of his two terms in office were not very controversial and could not have been expected to be bitterly

360

opposed by those generally in agreement with his overall political views. The elimination of internal federal taxes, the systematic retirement of the national debt, the curtailment of military and defense expenditures, the enlargement of the territorial boundaries of the country, and the practice of frugality in government were not exactly the types of issues which could be expected to stir up bitter opposition on the part of political representatives who were drawn together and elected by and large on the basis of their support for such objectives.

When Jefferson and his administration were finally forced to introduce and persist in a policy which not only irritated the general public, but imposed severe hardships on considerable numbers of persons—the ill fated Embargo Act—the President was abandoned by his former legislative supporters who were persuaded more by the threat to their political survival than the rational persuasion of a leader whom they both liked and admired. A discussion of these circumstances will be left to a later chapter on the limits of presidential power.

NOTES

1. Extrapolated from Washington's First Annual Message. Fred Israel, ed., *The State of the Union Messages of the Presidents: 1790-1966* (New York, 1966) I, 2-4.
2. Israel, I, 88.
3. Israel, I, 248.
4. Charles Francis Adams, ed., *Memoirs of John Quincy Adams: Comprising Portions of His Diary* (Philadelphia, Pennsylvania, 1875) VII, 63.
5. Article I, Section 7, of the Constitution prescribes the legislative veto power of the President of the United States:
      Every Bill which shall have passed the House of Representatives and the Senate shall, before it becomes a Law, be presented to the President of the United States; if he approves, he shall sign it, but if not he shall return it, with his Objections to that House in which it shall have originated, who shall enter the Objections at large on their Journal, and proceed to reconsider it. If after such Reconsideration two thirds of that House shall agree to pass the Bill, it shall be sent, together with the Objections, to the other House, by which it shall likewise be reconsidered, and if approved by two thirds of that House, it shall become a Law. But in all such Cases the Votes of both Houses shall be determined by Yeas and Nays, and the Names of the persons voting for and against the Bill shall be entered on the Journal of each House respectively. If any bill shall not be returned by the President within ten Days (Sundays excepted) after it shall have been presented to him, the Same shall be a Law, in like Manner as if he had signed it, unless the Congress by their Adjournment prevent its Return, in which Case it shall not be a Law.
      Every Order, Resolution, or Vote to which the Concurrence of the Senate and House of Representatives may be necessary (except on a question of Adjournment) shall be presented to the President of the United States; and before the Same shall take Effect, shall be approved by him, or being disapproved by him, shall be repassed by two-thirds of the Senate and House of Representatives, according to the Rules and Limitations prescribed in the Case of a Bill.
6. John C. Fitzpatrick, ed., *The Autobiography of Martin Van Buren* (Washington, D.C., 1920), 327.
7. Carlton Jackson, *Presidential Vetoes: 1792-1945* (Athens, Georgia, 1967), 15.
8. Quoted in Ralph Volney Harlow, *The History of Legislative Methods in the Period Before 1825* (New Haven, Connecticut, 1927), 154-55.
9. Harlow, 160.
10. Extrapolated from Jefferson's First Annual Message. Israel, I, 58-64.
11. Quoted in Noble E. Cunningham, *The Jefferson Republicans in Power: Party Operation* (Chapel Hill, North Carolina, 1963), 74.
12. Cunningham, 74.

13. James Sterling Young, *The Washington Community: 1800-1828* (New York, 1966). This is a brilliant book which presents a rare combination of historical depth and political analysis of men in power. The author corrects some exaggerations which appear in the famous Chapter X of Ralph Volney Harlow's study of legislative methods in the Jeffersonian era (see above), and it is severely critical of Harlow and the more recent historians he has influenced. His attack upon Harlow's treatment of the influence of the alleged party caucus is perhaps justified, but the acid tone and sweep of the criticism fail to credit Harlow with opening up a more accurate and even more balanced analysis of Jefferson's role vis à vis the Congress than any other scholar who described this period before him. Apparently Young was not familiar with Noble F. Cunningham's *The Jeffersonian Republicans in Power* (see above) which goes a long way towards clarifying and correcting whatever ambiguity and distortion exists in Harlow's early study.

14. Quoted in Young, 41-42.

15. Young, 41.

16. Young, 42.

17. Young, 93-94.

18. Harlow, 165.

19. Quoted in Harlow, 170.

20. Quoted in Cunningham, 76. (My emphasis—note Jefferson's brilliant metaphor for Congress.)

21. This is not to be interpreted literally since Madison had resigned from Congress at the end of the fourth session.

22. ". . . it is questionable whether the term 'leader' accurately denotes the relationship of these men to their fellow party members on the Hill. 'Spokesman' for the President would appear to better describe the legislative role of men whose position was legitimated by seniority or by election of their colleagues. . . ." Young, 164.

23. Jefferson to Barnabas Bidwell, July 5, 1806. Andrew A. Lipscomb and Albert E. Bergh, eds., *The Writings of Thomas Jefferson* (Washington, D.C., 1904) XI, 115.

24. Quoted in Cunningham, 90-91.

25. Cunningham, 91-92.

26. Cunningham, 95-96.

27. The cost of maintaining such a bountiful table was considerable. The price of food alone ran to $6500 annually, while Jefferson's wine bill his first year in office was $2400 to stock his cellar. All of these expenses came out of his salary of $25,000.

28. Merrill D. Peterson, *Thomas Jefferson and the New Nation* (New York, 1970), 725-26.

29. Peterson, 727.

30. Quoted in Harlow, 182.

31. Cunningham, 98.

32. Cunningham, 97.

33. Cunningham, 97. An excellent doctoral dissertation written by one of Professor Cunningham's graduate students came to my attention too late to include in this section. It provides a detailed examination of Jefferson's leadership in Congress indicating that three-fourths of the legislation passed during his two terms in office originated in the executive branch. See Everett Lee Long, *Jefferson and Congress: A Study of the Jeffersonian Legislative System, 1801-1809* (Ann Arbor, Michigan: University Microfilms, 1968).

34. Cunningham, 267.

35. For further discussions see Harlow, 183-93; Young, 125-26; and Cunningham, 99-100.

36. See section seven for discussion of the limits of presidential power in the embargo case.

Bibliography

Adams, Charles Francis, ed. *Memoirs of John Quincy Adams: Comprising Portions of His Diary.* Vol. VII. Philadelphia, Pennsylvania: J. B. Lippincott and Company, 1875.

Bassett, John Spencer, ed. *Correspondence of Andrew Jackson.* Vol. V. Washington, D.C.: Carnegie Institution of Washington, 1931.

Cunningham, Noble E., jr. *The Jeffersonian Republicans: The Formation of Party Organization, 1789-1801.* Chapel Hill, North Carolina: University of North Carolina Press, 1963.

        The Jeffersonian Republicans in Power: Party Operations. Chapel Hill, North Carolina: University of North Carolina Press, 1963.

Fitzpatrick, John C., ed. *The Autobiography of Martin Van Buren.* Annual Report of the American Historical Association, 1920. Vol. II. Washington, D.C.: U.S. Government Printing Office, 1920.

Harlow, Ralph Volney. *The History of Legislative Methods in the Period Before 1825.* New Haven, Connecticut: Yale University Press, 1927.

Israel, Fred, ed. *The State of the Union Messages of the Presidents: 1790-1966.* Vol. I. New York: Chelsea House/McGraw-Hill, 1966.

Jackson, Carlton. *Presidential Vetoes: 1792-1945.* Athens, Georgia: University of Georgia Press, 1967.

Lipscomb, Andrew A., and Bergh, Albert E., eds. *The Writings of Thomas Jefferson.* Vol. XI. Washington, D.C.: The Thomas Jefferson Memorial Association, 1904.

Long, Everett Lee. *Jefferson and Congress: A Study of the Jeffersonian Legislative System, 1801-1809.* Ann Arbor, Michigan: University Microfilms, 1968.

Malone, Dumas. *Jefferson the President.* Boston: Little, Brown and Company, 1970.

Mason, Edward Campbell. *The Veto Power.* Boston: Ginn and Co., 1891.

Peterson, Merrill D. *Thomas Jefferson and the New Nation.* New York: Oxford University Press, 1970.

Richardson, James D., ed. *Messages and Papers of the Presidents.* Vols. II, III. New York: Bureau of National Literature, 1897.

U.S. Congress. House. Committee on the Judiciary. *The Pocket Veto.* Hearings before Subcommittee No. 5, 92d Cong., 1st sess., April 7, 1971. Washington, D.C.: U.S. Government Printing Office, 1971.

U.S. Congress. *Presidential Vetoes.* List of bills vetoed and action taken thereon by the Senate and the House of Representatives from the 1st through the 86th Cong., 1798 to 1961. Senate Library. Washington, D.C.: U.S. Government Printing Office, 1961.

Young, James Sterling. *The Washington Community: 1800-1828.* New York: Columbia University Press, 1966.